MAPPINGS

Critical Views

In the same series

The New Museology
edited by Peter Vergo

Renaissance Bodies
edited by Lucy Gent and Nigel Llewellyn

Modernism in Design
edited by Paul Greenhalgh

Interpreting Contemporary Art
edited by Stephen Bann and William Allen

The Portrait in Photography
edited by Graham Clarke

Utopias and the Millennium
edited by Krishan Kumar and Stephen Bann

The Cultures of Collecting
edited by John Elsner and Roger Cardinal

Boundaries in China
edited by John Hay

Frankenstein, Creation and Monstrosity
edited by Stephen Bann

A New Philosophy of history
edited by Frank Ankersmit and Hans Kellner

Parisian Fields
edited by Michael Sheringham

Sculpture and Its Reproductions
edited by Anthony Hughes and Erich Ranfft

Voyages and Visions
Towards a Cultural History of Travel
edited by Jaś Elsner and Joan-Pau Rubiés

MAPPINGS

Edited by
Denis Cosgrove

REAKTION BOOKS

Published by Reaktion Books Ltd
11 Rathbone Place, London W1P 1DE, UK

Armand Mattelart's essay, 'Mapping Modernity:
Utopia and Communications Networks', has been translated
from French by Anne-Marie Glasheen.

*The publication of this book is supported by
the Cultural Service of the French Embassy in London.*

institut français

First published 1999

Copyright © Reaktion Books Ltd 1999

Index compiled by Orly Derzie

Designed by Humphrey Stone
Printed and bound in Great Britain by Biddles Ltd,
Guildford and King's Lynn

British Library Cataloguing in Publication Data:
Mappings. – (Critical views)
1. Culture
I. Cosgrove, Denis E.
306

ISBN 1 86189 021 4

Contents

Notes on the Editor and Contributors   vii

Introduction: Mapping Meaning   *Denis Cosgrove*   1

1 Mapping in the Mind: The Earth from Ancient Alexandria
   Christian Jacob   24

2 Mapping Eden: Cartographies of the Earthly Paradise
   Alessandro Scafi   50

3 Terrestrial Globalism: Mapping the Globe in Early Modern
   Europe   *Jerry Brotton*   71

4 Mapping Places: Chorography and Vision in the Renaissance
   Lucia Nuti   90

5 Mapping, the Body and Desire: Christopher Packe's
   Chorography of Kent   *Michael Charlesworth*   109

6 Dark with Excess of Bright: Mapping the Coastlines of
   Knowledge   *Paul Carter*   125

7 Mapping Tropical Waters: British Views and Visions of
   Rio de Janeiro   *Luciana de Lima Martins*   148

8 Mapping Modernity: Utopia and Communications Networks
   Armand Mattelart   169

9 The Uses of Cartographic Literacy: Mapping, Survey
   and Citizenship in Twentieth-Century Britain   *David Matless*   193

10 The Agency of Mapping: Speculation, Critique and Invention
   James Corner   213

11 Mapping and the Expanded Field of Contemporary Art
   Wystan Curnow   253

References   269

Bibliography   301

Photographic Acknowledgements   304

Index   305

Notes on the Editor and Contributors

DENIS COSGROVE is Professor of Human Geography at Royal Holloway, University of London. He is known for his writings on landscape and the visual tradition in geography, which include *Social Formation and Symbolic Landscape* (1984, rev. 1998); *The Iconography of Landscape* (1987, with Stephen Daniels); and *The Palladian Landscape* (1993). He has written numerous papers on the image of the globe in Western culture; his book *Apollo's Eye: A Genealogy of the Globe in the West* is due to be published in 2000.

CHRISTIAN JACOB is Researcher at the Centre National de la Recherche Scientifique, Paris. His main field is the history of cartography, ancient geography and Alexandrian scholarship. Among his published works are *Géographie et ethnographie en Grèce ancienne* (1990); *L'empire des cartes: approche théorique des cartes à travers l'histoire* (1992, English translation forthcoming 1999); and M. Baratin and C. Jacob, eds, *Le pouvoir des bibliothèques: la mémoire des livres en occident* (1996).

ALESSANDRO SCAFI graduated at the University of Rome 'La Sapienza' in 1989 with a thesis on Filarete's ideal city; he later studied the relationship between the Italian and Magyar Renaissances, publishing various articles on the subject. A Francis Yates Fellow at the Warburg Institute and holder of various scholarships of the British Academy and the Accademia Nazionale dei Lincei, he has been working on utopian concepts in the early modern era. He is currently completing his doctorate at the Warburg Institute on the notion of the Earthly Paradise from the Patristic era to the fifteenth century, and writing a book on Paradise on maps.

JERRY BROTTON is a lecturer in the Department of English, Royal Holloway, University of London. He is the author of *Trading Territories: Mapping the Early Modern World* (Reaktion, 1997).

LUCIA NUTI is Professor of Urban History and History of Architecture at the Dipartimento di Storia delle Arti, Università di Pisa. Her publications include *Pisa: progetto e città* (1986); 'The Perspective Plan in the Sixteenth Century: The Invention of Representational Language' (1994); and *Ritratti di città: visione e memoria tra medioevo e settecento* (1996).

MICHAEL CHARLESWORTH is Assistant Professor in Art History at the University of Texas at Austin, where he teaches nineteenth-century European art and photography. He is the author of *The English Garden: Literary Sources and Documents* (1993).

PAUL CARTER was educated at Oxford and has lived in Australia since 1981. His interest in the conceptual and epistemological bases of colonialism is expressed in *The Lie of the Land* (1996) and *Living in a New Country* (1992). Other publications document his performative use of historial materials.

LUCIANA DE LIMA MARTINS is a researcher at Royal Holloway, University of London, focusing on British images of Brazilian landscapes, 1800–1850. She has recently completed her PhD thesis at the Federal University of Rio de Janeiro, UFRJ.

ARMAND MATTELART is Professor of Information and Communication Sciences at the University of Paris VIII. He has authored or co-authored nearly 30 books on culture, politics, the mass media and communications theory and history, including *The Invention of Communication* (1996); *Mapping World Communication: War, Progress, Culture* (1994); and, with Michèle Mattelart, *Rethinking Media Theory: Signposts and New Directions* (1992); *The Carnival of Images: Brazilian Television Fiction* (1990); and *Theories of Communication* (1998).

DAVID MATLESS is Lecturer in Geography at the University of Nottingham. He is the author of *Landscape and Englishness* (1998), co-editor of *The Place of Music* (1998) and co-author of *Writing the Rural* (1994).

JAMES CORNER is Associate Professor of Landscape Architecture at the Graduate School of Fine Arts at the University of Pennsylvania. He is a registered landscape architect and practises in Philadelphia. He is author, with Alex S. MacLean, of *Taking Measures Across the American Landscape* (1996) and editor of *Recovering Landscape: Essays in Contemporary Landscape* (forthcoming, 1999).

WYSTAN CURNOW is Associate Professor of English at the University of Auckland.

Introduction: Mapping Meaning

DENIS COSGROVE

> Trying to remember how they ever came to this place, both speak of passage as by a kind of flight, all since Tenerife, and the Mountain slowly recessional, having pass'd like a sailor's hasty dream between Watches, as if, out of a sea holding scant color, blue more in name than in fact, the unreadable Map-scape of Africa had unaccountably emerg'd, as viewed from a certain height above the pale Waves, – tilted into the Light, as a geometer's Globe might be pick'd up and tilted for a look at this new Hemisphere, this haunted and other half of ev'rything known, where spirit powers run free among the green abysses and sudden mountain crests, – Cape Town's fortifications, sent crystalline by the Swiftness, rushing by from a low yet dangerous altitude as the Astronomers go swooping above the shipping in the Bays, topmen pointing in amazement, every detail, including the Invisible, set precisely, present in all its violent chastity.
>
> Thomas Pynchon, *Mason & Dixon*, p. 58

This passage from Thomas Pynchon's novel about the partnership between the two Enlightenment surveyors who, having observed the transit of Venus at Cape Town, went on to survey America's best-known state line, captures much of the imaginative scope and projective power of mapping. That a century later Mason and Dixon's astronomically surveyed Pennsylvanian border became the shatterbelt of America's most destructive war says as much about the social efficacy and disruptions of mapping. The essays written for this collection also deal with imagination and projection, efficacy and disruption; with processes of mapping rather than with maps as finished objects. Each author has selected a moment in the long evolution of Western spatiality in order to explore some of the contexts and contingencies which have helped shape acts of visualizing, conceptualizing, recording, representing and creating spaces graphically – in short, acts of *mapping*.

As a graphic register of correspondence between two spaces, whose explicit outcome is a space of representation, mapping is a deceptively simple activity. To map is in one way or another to take the measure of a world, and more than merely take it, to figure the measure so taken in such a way that it may be communicated between people, places or times. The measure of mapping is not restricted to the mathematical; it may equally be spiritual, political or moral. By the same token, the mapping's record is not confined to the archival; it includes the remembered, the imagined, the contemplated. The world figured through mapping may thus be material or immaterial, actual or desired, whole or part, in various ways experienced, remembered or projected. In scale, mapping may trace a line or delimit and limn a territory of any length or size, from the whole of creation to its tiniest fragments; notions of shape and area are themselves in some respects a product of mapping processes. Acts of mapping are creative, sometimes anxious, moments in coming to knowledge of the world, and the map is both the spatial embodiment of knowledge and a stimulus to further cognitive engagements. In the contemporary world, with its seemingly limitless capacities for producing, reproducing and transmitting graphic images, the map is a ubiquitous feature of daily life: the route map at the bus stop or subway station, the weather map on television, the location map in the travel brochure, the iconic map of the commercial advertisement. Maps are thus intensely familiar, naturalized, but not natural, objects working within a modern society of high if uneven cartographic literacy. They are also troubling. Their apparent stability and their aesthetics of closure and finality dissolve with but a little reflection into recognition of their partiality and provisionality, their embodiment of intention, their imaginative and creative capacities, their mythical qualities, their appeal to reverie, their ability to record and stimulate anxiety, their silences and their powers of deception. At the same time their spaces of representation can appear liberating, their dimensionality freeing the reader from both the controlling linearity of narrative description and the confining perspective of photographic or painted images.

Recognition of the complexities and uncertainties of mapping is no startling insight. For those engaged professionally or technically in making and using maps – for example cartographers, surveyors, geographers and planners – the ambiguities of mapping's claims have long been widely recognized: whether as problems to be overcome in a drive towards ever-increasing naturalism – representational accuracy, formal clarity and ease of use – or as intellectual and aesthetic opportunities and as stimuli to careful and critical interpretation. But the instrumental use of maps in daily life can obscure the epistemological and interpretative challenges that mapping presents. Thus, both for professionals and for many whose acquaintance with mapping and maps is more casual, the social authority acquired within modern culture through mapping's historical naturalization, has resulted recently in a startling explosion of academic, artistic and cultural interest in 'cartography' as an object of critical attention. The fact of this renewed interest is easily demonstrated: in the 1980s the University of Chicago Press began publishing a multi-volume *History of Cartography*, a project of decades, jointly edited by David Woodward, a world-renowned authority on the technical history of maps and mapping, and the late Brian Harley, an equally celebrated scholar, whose theoretical and critical reflections on the broader cultural and historical contexts of cartography have influenced thought well beyond his own discipline of geography.[1] The explicit intention of their project was to open the field of cartographic study far beyond a technical and internalist history of what had conventionally passed for a 'map', at least in the West: that is, an objective scientific representation of the earth's surface or a delimited territory upon it, or thematically of the spatial pattern of selected phenomena. In 1992, the five-hundredth anniversary of Columbus's first voyage stimulated a substantial scholarly re-evaluation of the relations between early modern mapping and colonialism, extending the scope of international conferences in the history of cartography held since then in Washington and Lisbon. Individual scholars have explored the status of mapping as a signifying process across historical time. Christian Jacob describes the changing paradigm of cartographic criticism as a shift from the 'transparent' view of the map as a neutral, informative transfer of external information into the simplified classificatory frame of the map space, conducted with the intention of achieving 'an ideal correspondence of the world and its image', to an 'opaque' view of the map which takes account of the selections, omissions, additions and inescapable contextual influences which shape the outcome of such transfers.[2] Mapping is a process which involves both a 'complex architecture of signs' (graphic elements with internal forms and logics capable of theoretical disconnection from any geographical reference) and a 'visual architecture' through which the worlds they construct are selected, translated, organized and shaped. Beyond such projects within the formally designated history of cartography as the *History of Cartography* and Jacobs's *Empire des cartes*,[3] fashionable fascination with the map within the humanities and cultural studies is widespread; the 'cartographic trope' is seemingly ubiquitous in intellectual enquiry. Conferences such as the international meeting on *Paper Landscapes* held in London in 1997 attract large and well-informed participants from historical, literary and cultural studies to explore the centrality of the map as both a material object and as metaphor within early modern culture, following the critical path signalled by the literature critics John Gillies and Richard Helgerson.[4] A number of very successful literary works in recent years have taken mapping as their principal theme, including Dava Sobel's *Longitude* and Umberto Eco's *The Island of the Day Before* which in different ways consider the seventeenth-century challenge of fixing the longitude at sea, and Pynchon's *Mason & Dixon*, quoted above. And mapping's significance within the contemporary visual arts was given the imprimatur of an 1994 exhibition organized by MoMA's Curator of Painting and Sculpture in New York, Robert Storr, which displayed the work of some 30 contemporary artists who deploy the ideas, practice and material products of mapping within their work.[5]

The reasons for this contemporary revisioning and rethinking of maps and mapping are not difficult to detect. For a politically, economically, technically and culturally globalizing world in which visual images have an unprecedented communicative significance, much is at stake in matters of space and its formal, graphic representation. The dissolution of an imperial, 'eurocentric' geopolitics and the end of the Cold War have not only reconfigured the political map of the globe, adding considerably to the kaleidoscope of colours and the tangle of lines used to demarcate the world's recognized states, but rendered enormously more visible the individual differences between regions formerly subordinated to simple East–West and North–South global divisions; differences most clearly revealed by representing them cartographically. Economic change, driven by technical advances in information processing and communication and by new and highly flexible financial and industrial production systems, has reworked the experience and meanings of space. These have tended to render boundaries of all kinds permeable, not only those demarcating the territorial limits of state sovereignty. Indeed, the concept and practice of precise and permanent separation, of spatial 'fixing', inherent in boundary definition and conventional mapping (whose *sine qua non* is the bounding frame) represent an urge towards classification, order, control and purification. These are today regarded as defining features of a 'modern' mentality whose historical life has been relatively brief, whose goals have always been compromised (as in the case of Paul Carter's coastal lines which connect as they separate), and whose cultural hegemony is today far from secure. In the opinion of many observers, it is the spatialities of connectivity, networked linkage, marginality and liminality, and the transgression of linear boundaries and hermetic categories – spatial 'flow' – which mark experience in the late twentieth-century world.[6] Such spatialities render obsolete conventional geographic and topographic mapping practices while stimulating new forms of cartographic representation, not only to express the liberating qualities of new spatial structures but also the altered divisions and hierarchies they generate. Gilles Deleuze and Félix Guattari's reference to the rhyzome as a metaphor for half-submerged, non-hierarchical, open and unplanned spatial connection is a signal example. Culturally, at every scale, connections between phenomena formerly considered distinct and relatively fixed, rooted in space or holding to stable patterns of distribution and identity, have been shown to be contingent and unstable: for example the connections between between workplace and community, ethnicity and nationality, diet or religious practice and identity. An implicit claim of mapping has conventionally been to represent spatial stability, at times to act as a tool in achieving it. In a world of radically unstable spaces and structures, it is unsurprising that the idea of mapping should require rethinking.

Reasons for this rethinking are also to be found in the changing techniques of seeing and of making and reproducing graphic images. Powered flight in the first part of the twentieth century, as the social theorist Patrick Geddes and other modernist visionaries foresaw, has forced a revisioning of a cartographic imagination inherited in large measure from the military and political spatialities of nineteenth-century states. Initially, of course, flying was confined in experience to a relatively small and privileged number of people. But aerial photography and the movie camera disseminated the new visions of space made available by flight to very large numbers. Over the past four decades – and not only for people in the richer countries of the world – the direct experience of seeing the earth's surface from ten thousand metres above it, passing 'as a map', through the perspex of an aircraft window, has become an astonishingly familiar one. During the same years, satellite photographs and remote-sensed images of the earth, produced at selected scale and with breathtaking clarity of resolution, have effectively replaced conventionally surveyed maps as the most practical way of accurately representing the earth's surface and its physical geography. Both these shifts inevitably place in question the apparent stability and authority of conventional mapping with its selectivity, its colours, codes, signs and aesthetic conventions. Official state topographic map series, for example, generally produced by military or at least state personnel, and marked with the crests and symbols of state authority, have conventionally claimed to stand 'for the country'. Between 1:50,000 and 1:150,000, their scale is comparable to that at which the ground appears when seen from the normal cruising altitude of a passenger jet. But the differences in appearance between the two views of land place in question the authority of the knowledge represented by the map, stimulating critical reflection on the context and contents of the topographic map.

A third strand of the revolution in spatial representation during the past three decades is information technology, which permits spatially referenced data to be generated, manipulated and illustrated with a speed, accuracy and facility quite unimaginable within the memory of even relatively youthful people. For example, it is already technically simple to print out an Ordnance Survey or USGS topographic sheet whose scale and coverage are tailored to individual needs, centring the map according to consumer choice rather than covering the arbitrary area predetermined by the division of sheets in a given series. Such a service, becoming available in map stores and bookshops, has the capacity to alter quite radically the spatiality of those who use and work with such maps. On the screen, the continuous manipulation and transformation of spatial coordinates and the data they reference, for example by postal coding systems, produces a kind of kinetic cartography.

The naturalism of satellite and computer-generated images of the earth and spatial distributions (while itself as misleading as that of conventional maps) has destabilized the conventional architecture, meanings and significance of mapping and of maps, helping to expose to scrutiny the 'authored' nature of the latter. While such changes enormously enhance the social and political significance of spatial representations, they have the effect of rendering conventional mapping techniques such as visual triangulation, levelling and framing, and stylistic conventions of colour coding and signs, of historical rather than contemporary technical interest, thereby opening them to the critical scrutiny of the humanities and social sciences. The sophistication of modern remote-survey techniques and the new spatial images they have generated have also stimulated artists to rework the long historical connections between art and cartography.[7] Art mappings have moved far beyond such early engagements as Nancy Graves's 1970s enhancing of the limited tonal range of NASA's Lunar Orbiter satellite's encoded moon maps by retouching them in gouache and ink colours. Artists today exploit the technical power of computers to construct art objects out of spatially referenced data that can be manipulated across the screen. Mapping has become an installation art.

Academically, mapping has attracted attention also for reasons connected to more profound ontological and epistemological questions about the nature, fabrication, communication and authentification of knowledge of the external world. A widely acknowledged 'spatial turn' across arts and sciences corresponds to post-structuralist agnosticism about both naturalistic and universal explanations and about single-voiced historical narratives, and to the concomitant recognition that position and context are centrally and inescapably implicated in all constructions of knowledge. 'Cognitive mapping' means much more today than was conceived by its 1960s investigators, who took for granted the existence of an objectively mappable and mapped space against which their 'mental maps' could be compared.[8] Not only is all mapping 'cognitive' in the broadest sense, inescapably bound within discursive frameworks that are historically and culturally specific, but all mapping involves sets of choices, omissions, uncertainties and intentions – authorship – at once critical to, yet obscured within, its final product, the map itself. Paul Carter gives a striking example in his discussion of the 'coastline', that elemental separating line between land and sea and at first sight the most fundamental and obvious boundary on any small-scale map. Not only are all coasts in fact zones rather than lines – the unstable space between high and low water in tidal zones, for example – which the cartographer has to 'fix' according to criteria which are inevitably arbitrary, but their linearity is mapped by determining a finite set of points which are then joined by a sweep of the cartographer's hand to create a coast-*line*. That sweep of the hand is governed as much by corporeal dexterity as by visual acuity and mimetic imperative. Draughtsmanship in mapping, as Luciana Martins shows here, is a complicated and learned process whose practice involves as many acts of forgetting as of observing and remembering. And, as Lucia Nuti's essay explores, the choice of mapping perspectives – vertical, horizontal, oblique – is a historical matter of shifting visual cultures which differently control not only the framed space of representation, but also the spatiality of the viewer, in position, scope and distanciation.

The critical attention that mapping and maps have thus attracted in the past decades has rendered any writing of 'the history of cartography' a vastly problematic task. From the early studies of Jomard and von Humboldt,[9] who sought through facsimile reproduction and critical philology to bring to scholarly attention the role that maps had played in Europe's progressive 'discovery' of the globe and organization of its varied spaces, to the critical collections of historical maps by scholars and archivists such as A. E. Nordenskiöld and R. Almagià,[10] a history of cartography was constructed over the course of the nineteenth and early twentieth centuries, governed by Enlightenment beliefs in disinterested observation, scientific calculation and objective representation as markers of universal rationality and progress. Mapping was figured as a form of literacy, a sign of civilization; it was thus restricted to a fairly closely defined form of knowledge collation and archiving. Mapping histories, while sensitive to the more or less distinctive non-European cartographic traditions of Islamic, Chinese and other non-European peoples, treated the latter according to criteria established in Europe rather than embracing the distinctive conceptual foundations upon which distinct mapping practices may be constructed, thus ignoring for example the fact that in Tibetan mapping the user 'is travelling not only through the areas and the places depicted but also through the related levels of signs, reality and abstraction, through logical steps, through cultural fields'.[11] 'Accurate' cartography was figured as a rationalist European science, rooted in pre-Socratic Greek astronomy and Alexandrian and Roman imperial administration, and synthesized by first-century Alexandrian scholars, most specifically Claudius Ptolemy. This cartographic tradition, 'rediscovered' by Latin Europe, after a regrettable medieval lapse into mythical mapping, was regarded as one element within a Burckhardtian Renaissance humanist project, which supposedly seized the 'torch' of ancient science from the faltering hands of Byzantium and Islam at the fortunate historical moment when Iberian navigators were introducing new spaces to a globalizing European *episteme*.[12] Thenceforth, with progressive technical and graphic accuracy, the shapes and surfaces of the earth's continents and oceans and, at more detailed scales, its regions and resources, have been brought within the orbit of a cartographic science which systematically ridded itself of its early and disabling associations with religious belief, with myth and with imaginative art.

Constructing an historical sequence of Western *maps* – world maps, maps of a specific country, region or town that service a now globalized cartographic literacy – can act as a persuasive illustration of this narrative of increasing accuracy, especially when its reading is governed by a teleological naturalism which assumes that the contemporary map is the truest representation of actual spatial form and patterns, an assumption supported by the apparent objectivity of mechanically generated representations such as photographs or remote-sensed images. It is a relatively uncomplicated and intellectually fascinating task to disclose the technical means by which the mimetic gains in cartographic representation have been secured, for example through the late sixteenth-century invention of triangulation, or the eighteenth-century solution of the problem of fixing the longitude at sea by means of the chronometer. It is equally possible, and engaging, to trace a history of style and convention in maps, revealing how map-makers have copied, drawn upon and transformed the work of their predecessors in graphical representation. But such histories of products and techniques can serve to obscure two other sets of questions which bear heavily on any history of mapping. The first is the complex accretion of cultural engagements with the world that surround and underpin the authoring of a map, that is, treating the map as a determined cultural outcome. The second is the insertion of the map, once produced, into various circuits of use, exchange and meaning: that is, the map as an element of material culture. It is attention to these sets of questions which is implied by the term *mapping*. Any map may thus be regarded as a hinge around which pivot whole systems of meaning, both prior and subsequent to its technical and mechanical production. Here, I outline briefly some of the questions that histories of mapping rather than of maps are obliged to confront; they are the questions variously addressed in each of the essays that make up this volume.

MAPPING MEANING INTO THE MAP

As an attempt to secure and convey spatial knowledge graphically, mapping may be regarded as a distinct epistemology, but one whose specific practices are historically and culturally variable. Among the consistent or *a priori* features of mapping are scale, framing, selection and coding. Scale is fundamental. James Corner in this collection, reminds us of the number of commentators who have used the idea of a map at the same scale as the territory it represents as the launch pad for speculation on questions of representation and reality. Enlarging or reducing the space generated and occupied by phenomena alters their form, their significance, their relations of meaning with other phenomena. Scale selection and manipulation is thus a powerfully imaginative and generative act which at once records and sets in train chains of meaning and association in an active process of knowing. Christian Jacob points to the origins of Greek mapping in speculative cosmology, an attempt to expose and explore the hidden rules and structures of physical creation by reducing them to the scale of a single, manageable representation: initially textual, later, with the aid of geometry, graphic. As an aid to philosophical speculation, scale played a different role from the one it would play in the production of topographical maps for artillery purposes. Michael Charlesworth's study of Christopher Packe's early eighteenth-century

chorography of Kent reveals a process in which choice of scale clarifies
relations among selected phenomena and reveals patterns and harmonies
invisible without such scalar manipulation.

Framing is as fundamental as scale: the preposition peri-, present in the
earliest forms of Greek geographical mapping – the *periplus*, or descriptive circuit of the known earth – has the dual meaning of 'surrounding' or
'containing' and also of 'overall'. Areal inclusion was initially achieved
through a linear progression which in the Greek context of navigating the
Aegean archipelago implied a distanciated and coastal perspective, quite
different from the conceptual containment of the survey lines of a triangulation. This serves to remind us that in mapping, as in picturing, the
frame can connect to quite distinct epistemologies in fulfilling its fundamental topological functions, not only of separating inside from outside,
but also of producing and organizing unity and totality within the space
so contained. As Jacob claims in the context of ancient Hellenistic map-
makers: 'one of the underlying dynamics of the Alexandrian culture is its
attractive and magnetic power: collecting all the books ever written by the
Greek world as well as by the Barbarians'. Framing is a territorializing,
even imperializing, process, the map inescapably a classificatory device.
Thus, as Alessandro Scafi points out, mapping a place such as Paradise
which acts as both a boundary and a centre creates almost insoluble epistemological contradictions. And self-conscious acts of frame-breaking,
such as that seen on the Ptolemaic world map printed in Ulm in 1482
where Scandinavia and Thule extend beyond the northernmost latitude
of the framed oecumene, are uncanny, signalling epistemological as much
as aesthetic anxiety. Failure fully to frame a land mass, or of mapped territory fully to occupy the map's bounding lines, as in seventeenth-century
maps of Van Diemen's Land, speak of failures of vision and knowledge,
of the uncertainty implied by the *peripateia* – the meandering, linear
progress whose trace may disappear into trackless space. 'Blank' spaces
within the frame also generate and reflect aesthetic and epistemological
anxiety; they are thus the favoured space of cartouches, scales, keys and
other technical, textual or decorative devices which thereby become active
elements within the mapping process. Scale and framing of course come
together in projection, that necessity within geographic and topographic
mapping to translate the globe's three-dimensional, curving surface onto
a two-dimensional plane through the agency of graticule. The abstract
lines of graticule and grid, whether left visible on the map or erased in its
final appearance, act both to secure a consistent semiotic connection
between sign and signified (map and territory), and to contain, distribute

and coordinate the internal signs and spaces of representation. Occupation of the abstract space they mutually produce is a matter of selection and coding.

The map differentiates itself from the territory precisely through acts of selection: in James Corner's terms, creating a field through processes of 'de-territorializing' and 're-territorializing'. Conventionally – and in practical terms quite usefully – a distinction is often made between geographical and topographic maps which purport to represent areas in correspondence with their appearance to the eye, and thematic maps which highlight the spatial features of a selected topic: population, climatic patterns, religious affiliation, highway systems or tourist attractions, for example, often consciously staging the conditions for the emergence of new or previously unobserved realities. In fact, of course, all maps are thematic: selecting and highlighting specific phenomena, consciously removing others, ignoring yet more and rendering some choices incapable of adoption by virtue of prior decisions about scale and frame. Such choices and the presences and absences they create are profoundly significant both in the making and the meaning of maps. Considerable attention has been given in recent years to the power–knowledge relations involved in mapping's selectivities: to the social and environmental exclusions involved in European colonial mapping, for instance, whose claims to objective knowledge practised a double denial of their selectivity, first of their often considerable dependence upon information supplied by non-European inhabitants of the territories mapped, and second of the physical and social landscapes as occupied and understood by those inhabitants themselves.[13] But selection is aesthetic and moral as much as it is oppressive and exclusionary, aspects of the mapping procedure which have attracted less critical attention. Thus Luciana Martins points to the selectivity of visualizing and mapping in relation to the fickleness of memory within a practice which conjoined practical navigational and commercial interest, learned techniques of visual record-taking and personal experience, across extended times and places. Selection in mapping generates its own anxieties, many of them circulating around questions of the status of the knowledge presented on the map. In ancient Alexandria as in eighteenth-century Paris or nineteenth-century Greenwich, securing the rules of selection at the centre where the map is constructed involved issues of accuracy, truthfulness, significance and the moral integrity of those conveying necessarily fragmentary information from the periphery, in the extended chain of knowledge making and recording which constituted the mapping process. The map's pretence to stable, uniform and smoothly mobile knowledge depends upon inherently unstable, uneven, fragmentary, specifically positioned and haphazardly transferred information.

That information is also translated through the complex semiotic systems of cartographic representation, which uniquely combine geometry (in projection, measure, scale, gridding and plotting) and graphic images (mimetic and conventional signs, colour coding and calligraphy) with numerical and alphabetic inscriptions and texts. All the resources of visualization and graphic communication are combined in mapping; the map is perhaps the most sophisticated form yet devised for recording, generating and transmitting knowledge. This is dramatically apparent in the maps of Paradise discussed by Alessandro Scafi, which seek to actualize graphically a place that could only be plotted by imaginative vision. Having no empirical referent, the signs used in such maps as those illustrating Dante's Hell seem more than usually realist, in the sense of being recognisable features: rocks, caves, castles and gateways taken from experienced space;[14] the use of conventional cartographic signs as mapping devices on such images would impose a double distanciation. Mapping experienced, as opposed to imagined, spaces requires a semiotics which connects represented space to an idea of the real. As Lucia Nuti makes clear in relation to urban mapping, the system adopted is historically and culturally determined. Thus the preference among Italian mappers for the orthographic perspective and the 'bird's eye' view which revealed the city as a unitary space, its contents such as house roofs and water bodies coloured according to the visual appearances of the external world, as opposed to the Flemish preference for the distance profile etched against a horizon, signals quite distinct visual cultures and their associated spatial languages. Ideals of social life and order and a projective planning imperative are as implicated in the Italian visual cultures as techniques of perspective and painterly convention. Panoramic mapping, which emerges from the convergence of these traditions, underpins Le Play's and Geddes's originating modernist visions of a planned civil society. More intriguing perhaps, is the emphasis placed by Geddes's followers on citizens' active participation in the panoramic mapping process, in the regional survey movement discussed here by David Matless. The possibilities for coding survey information through various signs and symbols placed within the representational spaces of the map, are theoretically unlimited, constrained only by the imagination of the map-maker and the practicalities of legibility and comprehension.

As Nuti's example indicates, the epistemological bases of mapping cannot be divorced from their cultural historical realization. In this respect it is possible to identify and group mapping styles and schools historically and geographically and to relate these to much broader cultural contexts and genealogies. In so doing, the practices of mapping offer a point of convergence for studies of the history and geography of art and science, design and technology. The central role that mapping practices have played in shaping and figuring Western modernity as a global encounter, their significance in collecting, collating, producing and mobilizing knowledge, make them a vital entry point into an appreciation of changing mentalities. Thus the sophisticated techniques of copper engraving and the elegance of line and lettering apparent on Italian sixteenth-century printed geographical maps from the workshops of Bertelli, Fortini and Camocchio, for example, coupled with their relative tardiness in recording the latest maritime discoveries, by comparison with less aesthetically refined Spanish and Portuguese productions, testify both to the closeness with which mapping was connected in Italy to a sophisticated market in the commercial reproduction of art engravings and to Italy's growing marginality in the political economy of European knowledge at this time. And not only do the design, colouring and lettering of many seventeenth-century Dutch and French maps make it appropriate to refer to them as 'Baroque' and relate them to aesthetic choices and styles in architecture, painting and illustration, but the very complexity and exhausting mass of intricately wrought and interlocking detail of their content unconsciously map too a mentality pivoting on the cusp of an overextended encyclopaedism, threatening to collapse into incoherence under the sheer mass of information they sought to synthesize, ever more ruthlessly elaborated in search of complex allegorical meanings and emblematic moral significance. Set against the simple frames, sparse styling, Roman lettering and uncluttered content of maps from a century later, these seventeenth-century works seem to be pleading for a new, 'rational' framework within which their promiscuous excesses of representation might be disciplined and controlled. Such a teleological reading, however, while indicating the capacity of mapping to connect with other practices in making and representing knowledge, serves to alert us also to the dangers of too great a reliance on stylistic analysis of the finished map at the expense of contextual re-engagement with the specific cultural practices of mapping from which it emerges.

MAPPING MEANING OUT OF THE MAP

Mapping begets further mappings. This is true not only in the sense that all maps are based on prior records – field observations, notes and sketches, terrestrial and maritime surveys, statistical collections, imaginative doodles, contemplative icons, preparatory studies – and are very often multi-authored productions, but also in the sense that a map, like any text or image, once completed and produced, escapes the contexts of its production and enters into new circuits of culture. Initial entry may be controlled to a greater or lesser degree, to be sure, as in the case of mapping for military officers or diplomats. Many of those historical maps that remain intact do so because they were celebratory icons such as the map cycles painted on the walls of palace galleries, the globes that graced the studios and halls of monarchs and the presentational atlases that ministered to the self-esteem of princes, generals and corporations, or objects of spiritual or moral contemplation such as the *mappaemundi* displayed in medieval cathedrals and the cosmological schemas on Hindu prayer wheels, or as legal documents to be conserved in archives, such as those accompanying peace treaties, marking the sale and purchase of real estate, planting a colony or planning a garrison, town or city. Fewer maps intended or used for practical purposes of navigation or location-finding remain, and still fewer of those sketched for immediate practical ends such as navigation, battle or field research, which are exhausted in the execution of their purpose. This distorted legacy tends to underemphasize the partial, open and contingent qualities of the map object in favour of its closures, certainties and aesthetics. Contemporary scholarship seeks often to reverse that tendency by seeking out the instabilities of meaning in the finished map, its openness to interpretation and its stimulus to further elaborations of spatial meaning. Thus Jerry Brotton's re-examination of one of the more intriguing questions in the history of cartography why terrestrial globes suddenly appeared almost *de novo* over a period of less than three decades as a popular item of material culture in early sixteenth-century Europe, seeks clues in their use rather than in the techniques and practices of their production. The diplomatic imperatives consequent upon Magellan's circumnavigation offer his answer: the application in an eastern hemisphere of the papal division of global space made on a flat map at Tordesillas in 1493 was possible only with the use of the new cartographic instrument of a spherical globe. Coincidentally, the same events, in relativizing the cardinal directions of east and west, helped finally to remove Paradise from European world maps. Once produced and used in such high diplomatic circumstances, the globe could be incorporated into the long tradition of regarding the sphere as a symbol of divinely authorized imperial status, enabling the rival claims of European potentates to universal empire to be simultaneously territorialized and symbolized.

The map as material object participates in wider discourses, or *mappings*, which generate sophisticated metaphorical meanings well beyond the confines of kingly symbolism and territorial imperialism. One example is the play of meanings between map and human body which so excited thinkers in the early seventeenth century. John Donne's frequent analogies between planispheres or colonial maps and the bodies of his female lovers has been widely commented upon, its implications of colonialist desire and appropriation an obvious target for critical attention.[15] Jonathan Sawday's examination of the parallels in Donne's time between geographical discovery and medical autopsy as discourses of personal vision that worked through similar representational processes of map-making and reading suggest that the poet was elaborating a widely recognized trope.[16] Further, the appearance of maps and globes among the most common features of seventeenth-century devices and emblems indicates mapping's widespread significance in popular culture, playing a role far beyond its function of recording and transmitting purely spatial information. Moral mapping used cartographic images as imaginative and devotional devices, a stimulus to self-reflection. It is thus that the map appears so commonly as a carefully crafted and displayed item within Dutch domestic paintings, for example in Vermeer's interiors. This moral or emblematic significance and use of maps continues into the twentieth century. David Matless's discussion of the regional survey movement in interwar Britain emphasizes mapping as a mode of harmonizing citizen, community and place in the visionary construction of a modern society. Connecting the mapping language of straight line, viewpoint, panorama, survey and vision to ecology and psychoanalysis, C. C. Fagg, Geoffrey Hutchings and Hilaire Belloc rework a long-standing mapping discourse which engenders moral and metaphysical connections between interior and exterior worlds. The physical, specifically sexual, human body mediates these worlds in the writings of both John Donne and the regional surveyors.

Another form of mapping is the creative probing, the tactical reworking, the imaginative projection of a surface. Here, mapping becomes the two-dimensional 'staging' of actuality or desire, and it has a long genealogy. 'Perspective' has a temporal as well as spatial meaning – looking forward, the sense of prospect. Thus the map excites imagination and graphs desire, its projection is the foundation for and stimulus to projects. Mapping Paradise or Hell can have no function other than to guide the viewers' faith and direct their conduct towards life after death. All utopias require mapping, their social order depends upon and generates a spatial order which reorganizes and improves upon existing models. The dominant tradition in orthogonal urban mapping since the earliest experiments by Alberti and Leonardo da Vinci to chart Rome or Imola, through the fortress plans of Vauban discussed by Armand Mattelart, to the garden cities proposed by Geddes's disciples, has been concerned with projects to secure the city as a single socio-territorial order, be it in the interests of ruler, military commander or democratic citizenry. Leon Battista Alberti's 1420s reworking of Vitruvius' architectural text (which itself grew out of Augustus' replanning of Imperial Rome) stimulated a stream of utopian urban designs from the hands of Renaissance architects: Filarete, Serlio, Scamozzi.[17] Enlightenment statistical mapping of urban poverty, crime or other social pathology was driven by the same implicitly totalizing impulse to visualize and authorize a new order, reaching a kind of apotheosis in the comprehensive planning strategies of the mid-twentieth century,[18] vast mapping exercises which both generated and depended upon volumes of spatially organized statistical data, charts and coloured images. These were paper landscapes of bewildering complexity which sought to envision and determine comprehensive social and spatial structures for entire metropolitan regions over decades into the future. Even the French Situationists' subversion of this totalizing cartography by means of a fragmentary and arbitrary mapping strategy owed its radical significance to the projective authority of mapping, its goal much more than simply to record the disconnected and personal nature of urban experience. The *dérive* was intended to project alternative ways of inhabiting the city through the imaginative power of the personal mapping act. Such a strategy highlights the oppositional opportunities offered by mapping as well as its repressive capacities. The same cartographic documents which in the eyes of colonists have so often secured the legality of their appropriation of aboriginal lands today act alongside quite distinct mappings such as rock markings and memory lines to secure land claims in a post-colonial era.[19]

MAPPING ESSAYS

In preparing the individual essays in this collection, the authors were asked to consider their subject matter in the light of revisioned conceptions of mapping. They might question what mapping has meant in the past and how its meanings have altered; how mappings have served to project, order and arrange as well as to represent physical, social and imaginative worlds; how mapping practices have shaped modern seeing and knowing; how contemporary changes in experiencing the world alter the meanings and practice of mapping; how mappings inaugurate as well as trace a poetics of space. While acknowledging the breadth of meaning and the metaphorical reach of 'map' and 'mapping' in current writing and encouraging contributors to embrace these in their own thinking, the intention was to focus the essays around actual graphic representations of spatial patterns which may fall under a broad category of maps. Thus, for example, while a circuit diagram, a tattooed torso or the topos of the heavenly Jerusalem could all fall within their remit, the textual narrative of a journey or a purely abstract, non-referential image of line and colour would not.

The essays are sequenced according to very broad historical and thematic criteria. Historically, they pinpoint 'moments' long recognized as significant in the genealogy of mapping in the West, but neither constructing an evolutionary narrative of mapping history nor pretending comprehensive coverage of such moments; indeed only the first pair fall outside the period of 'modern' mapping, and each essay makes forward reference to modernity. Greek mapping in Antiquity exercises a fascination because of its close connections with the Greek philosophical project of distinguishing rational thought and explanation from myth and poetic narrative. No corpus of maps survives from ancient Greece and Rome, only textual records of mapping practices, from which such scholars as Christian Jacob seek to reconstruct the cartographic concerns of Antiquity. From the medieval West, by contrast, we have been left in cosmographic diagrams and *imagini mundi* a variety of images long recognized as maps, but restricted evidence of the actual mapping practices through which these were conceived, made and used. As Alessandro Scafi reveals, they are best understood as exegetical and visionary rather than as secular and pragmatic exercises.

The profound connections between mapping and modernity were forged in the early fifteenth century with the coincidence over a mere five decades of a Latin translation of Ptolemy's *Geographia* which offered systematic methods of projection and graticule construction, and single-point perspective as a geometrical technique for manipulating two-dimensional representational space, and the development of moveable type, which allowed the rapid and cheap reproduction of graphic images, their circulation, scholarly comparison, revision and updating. That these conceptual and technical mapping tools converged over the succeeding centuries with oceanic navigation and commercial contacts between Western Europe and transatlantic regions and with the internal reorganization of European territorialities through nation-state construction,

commercialization of agriculture and urbanization, has served to give
mapping practices a powerful significance in representing and projecting
a distinctively modern mentality. Many of the debates that have circulated
around mapping and modernity are already apparent in the first century
of the new cartography, and are explored by Jerry Brotton and Lucia Nuti.
Thus circumnavigation produced a decisive moment in cartography as the technical and conceptual implications of representing a spherical earth
became immediate and material. The consequences of this achievement
in opening a seemingly unlimited volume of new geographic, climatic,
botanic, zoological and ethnographic materials to Western consciousness
challenged and eventually defeated cosmography, a form of mapping as
universal synthesis whose roots lay in the medieval encyclopaedia.[20] Such
problems of spatial representation were not confined to the global or geographical scale, they appeared also at the regional or chorographic scale
of Ptolemy's influential mapping hierarchy. Chorography's complex synthesis of scientific measurement and geometrical survey on the one hand
and painterly and artistic skill on the other offered the opportunities and
pleasures of mapping locally circumscribed land and life as a microcosm
of a greater order.

Consciousness of the issue of scale in conceptualizing and representing
space and its contents is by no means a product of modernity: Democritus
and Lucretius already theorized the atom as the tiniest scale at which
matter is realized, while medieval *mappaemundi* sought to map a cosmos
whose intelligible if not sensible space extended to the eternity of a
supercelestial realm. Modernity is distinguished by its concern with the
human eye's physical capacity to register and to visualize materiality at
every scale. The telescope and the microscope are the iconic instruments
of scientific revolution; to them we might add those instruments for topographic survey such as the sextant and the alidade. Each becomes a mapping instrument through the agency of those draughting tools by which
visual knowledge is pictured on the two dimensional surface: the pencil,
the compass and the set square. In early modern texts, these items are
the iconic accompaniments of philosophy, geography and architecture,
signifying respectively the disciplines of understanding, exploring and
creating space. Conscientious instrumentation of scientific kowledge, to
which mapping made an important contribution, was a significant feature of the Enlightenment from the seventeenth century, not only securing
knowledge but ensuring its accurate representation, as Michael Charlesworth reveals in the case of Christopher Packe's survey of Kent. While
Packe may have articulated his project in terms of natural theology, the

techniques he helped develop would be used for the increasingly secular ends of applied science in subsequent years, as both the techniques and products of mapping underwrote schemes of social and environmental improvement.

Two small images by William Blake from the late eighteenth century might serve as emblems of modern mapping's dual regard. In one, a patriarchal divinity reaches out of the circle, compass in hand to map the hidden order of creation; in the second it is Isaac Newton, paradigm of scientific reason, whose compass maps the human project. Appeals to intelligible spatial order have tended to lose the warrant of divine authority, forced in the past two centuries to negotiate perceptible patterns whose own truth claims are open to contestation and revision, thus requiring evidential support, such as that provided by 'scientific' mapping. Both Paul Carter's and Luciana Martins's essays subject the mapping practices of Enlightenment navigators to close scrutiny, exposing the limitations of their claims to scientific vision, archiving and recording. The mapping moments discussed by Armand Mattelart and David Matless bear witness to the survival in an era of empirical mapping of visionary desires to coordinate the incidental, discontinuous and contingent nature of perceptible space with more conceptual, and universal, patterns and morphologies. Finally, James Corner and Wystan Curnow consider mapping today, at a moment when faith in the possibilities of both disinterested, empirical mapping and universal projective mapping is shaky, and when mapping and imaginative art are reinvigorating their long-standing mutual connections. Their essays seek to move beyond the impasse into which theoretical discussions of mapping which are couched in oppositional terms of the real and the represented inevitably lead. The most challenging mappings today are found in the creative and imaginative work of artists, architects and designers, neither seeking absolute empirical warranty for their maps nor claiming for them any metaphysical revelation. Mapping in a flexible era has become a creative and critical intervention within broader discourses of space and the ways that it may be inhabited. Mapping is freed from the problems of factual legitimacy and authority with which a centric and rationalist model of absolute space has until recently burdened it.

Beyond their broad chronological arrangement, individual essays adopt a distinctive perspective on mapping. Comparing Alexandrian mapping in the classical past with the eighteenth-century D'Anville, Jacob reveals how that centric, rationalist and archival model of mapping which replaced its initial ontological purposes within Greek practice pressured the cartographer at the (rational) centre towards philological procedures and moral interrogations of mapping sources, designed to authenticate the data returned from a (potentially irrational) periphery. Alessandro Scafi's study of mapping Christian Paradise raises similar questions of rendering the unseen visible while fixing the boundaries of myth, but in a different context: that of a place which was on earth but not of earth, an unseen space for whose existence textual evidence alone was available and whose terrestrial location – which the mapping exercise was designed to determine – was a geographical paradox: simultaneously boundary and centre. The point where East meets West on a spherical earth, an apposite location perhaps for Eden, becomes in 1522 a matter of vital significance in the temporal relations between states. This is the theme of Jerry Brotton's essay which, in addition to examining the appearance of the terrestrial globe as a favoured mode of mapping earth space, points to Magellan's circumnavigation as a critical moment in the emergence of globalism as a 'spatiality' within modern consciousness.

Evolution of a global spatiality with its implications of boundlessness, uninterrupted movement and communication works dialectically across the evolution of modern consciousness with a discourse of localism, rootedness and bounded territoriality. Both Lucia Nuti and Michael Charlesworth broach the role of chorography in mapping such a sensibility. Nuti traces the fortunes of two sets of technical issues raised in such mapping: the first deriving from Ptolemy's distinction between *geographical* mapping – fundamentally a mathematical exercise which privileged theoretical knowledge over sensory experience – and *chorographic* mapping which places emphasis on the recognizable qualities of the visual image, including its colours, symbols and codes. The second paired techniques for positioning the 'mapping eye' in relation to the spaces represented. For city views, Nuti distinguishes between the Italian tradition of capturing the community as a totality, relating this to the humanist desire to figure the Renaissance city as a reincarnation of the ancient Greek *polis*, as a single social and spatial order, and the Northern, specifically Flemish, tradition of the profile. As Nuti points out, the story of their resolution in the bird's eye views of the later sixteenth century represents the beginnings of a search for global knowledge of a town or region which would eventually yield modernist social-scientific urban mappings. En route to these, natural theology makes its own contribution to the epistemological connection that mapping seeks between the global and the local. Charlesworth's study of Christopher Packe's mapping of the English county of Kent from the vantage point of Canterbury cathedral

tower shows how the limited and parochial autocelebration which constituted seventeenth-century chorography could be raised rhetorically to
global significance by connecting it with natural theology, whereby the
topographic and spatial perfection which Packe's complex semiology figures is at once macrocosm of the anatomized body and microcosm of the
greater physical creation.

The instrumentation with which Packe sought to bring his art to
greater perfection was the foundation of modern mapping's scientific
claims. The story is a familar one, of the invention of the chronometer for
accurate longitude-fixing at sea, of national academies and scientific societies competing through well-funded navigational expeditions to plot the
world's oceans and continents, together with their flora, fauna and peoples, onto the global chart: Bougainville's and Cooke's voyages are only
the most frequently cited. In focusing on mappings of the harbour at Rio
de Janeiro by British navigators trained 'to keep their eyes and ears open'
and to privilege drawing over written accounts because of the immediacy
of their record, Luciana Martins not only reveals the complexity of
connections between scientific mapping and the nexus of geostrategic,
imperial and commercial interests, but also the commerce of images and
the processes of seeing, recording, remembering and forgetting through
which distant places were mapped into European knowledge systems.
The issues of mobile knowledge, truth and authentification which extend
from ancient Alexandria to nineteenth-century Greenwich, as imperial
archiving centres sought accurately to map peripheries, are shown to
stretch far beyond the moral status of the individual informants; they are
structured into the cognitive and visual histories of those informants so
profoundly that even 'on the spot' mappings are also inescapably hybrid
products of other places and times. Paul Carter reinforces this recognition of the limitations of Enlightenment mapping's proclaimed transparency in transposing the objects of pure vision onto the chart.

For French St Simonians as for British Geddesians, mapping's capacity
to penetrate the incidental superficiality and contingency of the local and
immediately visible landscape and reveal larger intent in its structure and
pattern was both a social and an intellectual imperative. For the former it
was the *network*, a cartesian arrangement of points and connectivities
which constituted a territory. Technology materialized the network,
allowing information to pass ever more freely and speedily, equalizing
access and offering the promise of democratic social order and human
liberty. Armand Mattelart traces the imaginative appeal and the democratic limitations of this belief in the power of communications to map a

utopia across the space–time of idealized networks, from the semaphore telegraphy of revolutionary France, through electric cables, the telephone, satellites and the internet. British faith in the power of mapping to sustain and enhance civic cohesion appears, characteristically, more pragmatic and pedestrian, and also eccentric, even bizarre, as David Matless shows in an examination of the extraordinary amalgam of beliefs and theories with which a group of British social idealists surrounded regional survey in the interwar years. Supposedly controlling the unruly libido of young people, Geddesians drew upon Freudian theory to promote through survey and mapping a balanced citizen, liberated too from the potentially homogenizing effects of mass culture in modern society. From the perspective of the youthful mapper, atop a vantage point or at the Archimedian distance point offered by flight, the regional surveyors sought grounding, attachment and informed citizenship.

Two final essays address mappings today, drawing upon the freedom allowed by mapping's separation from narrowly scientific duties of survey, record and plan. James Corner reviews mapping's generative capacities to stage spatial arrangements in the context of contemporary space–time experience and understanding. He emphasizes the creative, even playful, process of discovering and engendering through mapping new connections and relationships among disparate elements. Where network enthusiasts and regional surveyors mapped to disclose and impose order, Corner maps to create fields for projects. Drawing on design practice, he offers four thematic ways of realizing mapping's projective capacities: 'drift', where mapping acknowledges open-ended even goal-less, movement across space; 'layering', which superimposes spatial elements and experiences, less exposing than intervening imaginatively in their interconnections; 'game-board', which recognizes and enables the actions of contesting agents across a design space; and 'rhizome', realizing graphically the metaphor of non-centric, organic spatiality. Curnow further opens mappings' imaginative capacities by tracing the ways in which conceptual artists since the late 1960s have used them to explore specifically artistic questions. What are the relations between site and artwork? How can mapping art enhance and record the performative aspects of relations with space? What are the implications of seeing the earthly globe from space? How can mappings contribute to the post-colonial disruption of taken-for-granted geographic and ethnographic assumptions? Above all, Curnow claims, it has been performance and installation artists, breaking with Western art's painterly conventions, who have most successfully exposed the limitations of mapping's visualist assumptions. Corner and

Curnow offer mappings of mapping at the Millennium, mappings in which the spatial and technical *a priori* of conventional practices examined in the preceding chapters no longer hold.

Mapping in the Mind: The Earth from Ancient Alexandria

CHRISTIAN JACOB

– Ce n'est pas le géographe qui va faire le compte des villes, des fleuves, des montagnes, des mers, des océans et des déserts. Le géographe est trop important pour flâner. Il ne quitte pas son bureau. Mais il y reçoit les explorateurs. Il les interroge, et il prend en note leurs souvenirs. Et si les souvenirs de l'un d'entre eux lui paraissent intéressants, le géographe fait faire une enquête sur la moralité de l'explorateur.
– Pourquoi ça?
– Parce qu'un explorateur qui mentirait entraînerait des catastrophes dans les livres de géographie. Et aussi un explorateur qui boirait trop.
– Pourquoi ça? fit le petit prince.
– Parce que les ivrognes voient double. Alors le géographe noterait deux montagnes là où il n'y en a qu'une seule.

Antoine de Saint-Exupéry, *Le petit prince*, ch. 15

How is it possible, and, indeed, why is it necessary, to depict and to make visible something invisible, something that does not exist as such in front of the human eyes until an analogical rendering has been achieved?[1]

Here, I focus on the small-scale mapping project of large areas, indeed the whole world, and investigate some of its technical, logistic and scientific components as well as some of its intellectual and social dimensions. I am concerned with the intellectual process that leads from gathering partial and empirical field data to assembling these within a single general frame and thus producing a new object, the map of the 'inhabited world'. Such questioning is probably the best way to understand what a map is, to interrogate its power and its social function. One could also interrogate the map's claim to represent the world in a way that challenges the concept of mimesis itself. Beyond its technical aspects and its cultural contexts, the history of small-scale cartography deals with this challenge: giving a material reality to something that human senses cannot grasp and providing this graphical device with a symbolic power, a social (and political) authority and an intellectual (or spiritual) efficiency. Any map is an interface – pragmatic, cognitive, metaphysical – between its users and the world that surrounds them. Those who look at it and who share the scientific, semiological keys to its understanding are assumed to concur that they look at something beyond the drawing itself. As an optical as well as an intellectual prosthesis, maps allow human senses and the human mind to achieve a new level of reality. Maps are impossible without such a shared belief about the materiality and the reality of the world they display, about the claim of the drawing to stand as a substitute for this world, more accessible to study than the reality itself. Even if such a map is criticized, corrected and completed, its power as a representation is never denied.

Cartographic history should not be confined within the frame of the history of sciences and of geographical knowledge *stricto sensu*. It encompasses many other components of a culture: its conception of the world, physical and metaphysical, its cognitive categories that bring knowledge and truth within reach of the human mind, the social construction and sharing of such knowledge about the world. Cultural context is a key to variation in the history of cartography. Chinese, Indian, Native American, Islamic and early European cartographies, beyond the apparent similarities of their maps as graphic artifacts, reflect deeply different intellectual and visual universes.

A precise and culturally specific investigation is perhaps the best way to contribute to a general understanding of the many implications and indeed the peculiarity of the mapping project itself.[2] My topic is a particular step in the development of ancient Greek cartography. I underline both its cultural specificity and its contribution to a broader reflection on the nature and the power of maps in general.

INVISIBLE MAPS, CARTOGRAPHIC DISCOURSES

In fact, we have lost most of the ancient small-scale maps.[3] I do not include Byzantine and early Renaissance Ptolemaic plates as specimens of ancient Greek cartography *stricto sensu*.[4] The *Tabula Peutingeriana* is an obvious exception, but it belongs to the class of Roman itinerary maps, and is a thirteenth- or fourteenth-century reproduction of a late Imperial Roman original. What we do possess, however, is a corpus of ancient texts and a set of statements about small-scale maps. Such sources provide the historian with indirect, diversely focused traces of the use and the impact of maps in the ancient world. They allow us to draw precise limits around the visual, intellectual and pragmatic area occupied by maps in this society.[5] Any mapping culture should itself be mapped, as a topography of interacting and sometimes overlapping intellectual zones, and the result of such a research, in ancient Greece, clearly suggests the very limited functions and diffusion of maps in this society.

Travelling, exploring, seafaring, war-making, ruling and founding remote colonies did not necessarily imply the use of maps. There is not a single ancient Greek source that depicts someone using maps in a practical situation.[6] Such a fact has two implications. First, 'geographical knowledge'[7] did not depend on maps, but on other media, such as travel reports, sea journeys and periegeses, descriptions of a particular country. Geography relied on words and discourses, on human memory. Second, maps had other functions: the way they were drawn, the information they encompassed, the way they were diffused, simply did not allow practical and field uses.

Literary testimonies about map-making may be read spatially, in concentric circles. Closest to the map itself are texts by cartographers or by geographers who had a technical interest in cartography. The second circle includes authors who occasionally depicted someone using a map. In the third circle are writers using maps to generate and organize a geographical description. Such texts stand in place of the map and had a far greater efficacy in shaping the mental horizon of their listeners or their readers. The information produced by maps was diffused through verbal descriptions, not through maps themselves. Consequently, one should be aware that categories such as vision, audition, memory and imagination do not escape the variations of culture and of history, and that in a precise cultural surrounding, listening to a geographical description could create for the listener mental forms as vivid and efficient as a world map.[8]

I shall focus on the first circle, where Greek cartographers and geographers wrote about maps and map-making. Strabo (*b. c.* 63 BC; *d.* AD 21–5), as a witness and a compiler of the Hellenistic cartographic tradition, is a major source for the historian of Greek science. The seventeen books of his *Geography* provide us with an ambiguous picture.[9] On the one hand, Strabo was familiar with maps, at least with a certain kind of small-scale map, and he discussed them at length, even reproducing some instructions about how to draw them. He also titled his work 'Geography' and as such followed the example of the cartographer Eratosthenes. On the other hand, most of this *Geography* is a literary description of the world, not a map, and this description relies on traditional patterns: catalogues of place names, terrestrial or maritime itineraries. Strabo's text thus belongs the third circle, even beyond – a literary geography that did not rely at all on map-making but on the compilation of a library.

When Strabo comments on map-making, he wants us to believe that he is familiar with the construction of maps, and he involves himself in polemical debates with the predecessors whose treatises and maps he read and used. Such a paradoxical situation – no maps in his *Geography*, but a technical discussion about maps in the first two books of the treatise – should be considered as a relevant sign. In the ancient Greek world, map-making could have implied a different balance between writing and drawing. It was perhaps a process in which debating, commenting, criticizing and correcting previous maps, translating into arguments and descriptions what could be fixed on the diagram, were equally aspects of map-making. We have to investigate the complex meaning of the Greek verb *graphein* – drawing, writing, depicting – a polysemy inherent in the term 'geo-graphy'.

GREEK MAPPING CULTURE: AN HISTORICAL OUTLINE

A preliminary question suggests itself: is it possible to write the history of an object such as the map? Are we certain that the presence of maps at successive periods warrants the intellectual cohesiveness of their history, even within the framework of the same culture? Maps were drawn and used in various intellectual contexts, and such variants determine the true meaning of these drawings. Herein lies the positive counterpart of the loss of actual Greek maps: we rediscover them through discourses, through the concepts and words of the Greeks themselves.

In the second half of the third century BC, when Eratosthenes, head librarian in the Ptolemies' palace in Alexandria, committed himself to rectifying the small-scale maps he probably found in the collection, Greek cartography had existed for more than three centuries.[10] Extant testimonies, although rare and elliptical, give us a clear enough picture of the early development of ancient Greek maps. Map-making did not start from practical needs, from empirical surveys or from a technical and professional tradition among Ionian tradesmen and sailors. The first Greek map was a part of a broader intellectual project: description of the cosmos or, more precisely, accounting for its genesis, from the 'boundless' element of its origin to the appearance of humankind on earth. Anaximander of Miletus, pupil of Thales, was one of those sixth-century learned and wise men, private persons and citizens in their small autonomous political communities, who decided to write their own views about the 'nature' of the world, as an alternative to the mythico-poetical tales of Homer and Hesiod.[11] Anaximander used technical metaphors, geometrical shapes, astronomical observations and calculations in order to understand and to render comprehensible for his listeners the natural phenomena and the order of the world. The map was a by-product of Anaximander's treatise *On Nature*. It probably looked like a geometrical drawing of a flat disk surface of the inhabited earth (the *oecumene*), displaying the rough shapes of the Mediterranean Sea while the outer limit was perfectly circular, surrounded by the river Okeanos. Such a drawing was abstract and indeed unsuited to practical use. It could have encompassed, in a very stylized way, some information about the areas explored by Greek colonization since the eighth-century BC – the Black Sea area, Italy and Sicily, the eastern Mediterranean shore.[12] But it is striking to note that the map did not create geographical knowledge from the ground. Anaximander drew his map at a stage when Homer's *Odyssey* and the various accounts of the Argonauts' saga, poetry, oral and possibly (but not attested) written nautical directions, had already conveyed a geographical knowledge, in lists of place- and tribe-names, orientations and itineraries.

Greek geography thus leads from a shared knowledge about more or less mythical places and tribes, from a general cosmological frame (structured by the sun's progression in the sky, and its variation, in summer and in winter) to this first visual model, elaborated by a thinker in search of the hidden rules, order and components of the natural world, beyond the traditional language of myth and poetry. As a result, this first map made possible a new way of conceiving and discussing the inhabited earth, and provided its users with a tool to organize the nomenclature of places and tribes, to gather knowledge about them, to order this information independently from any actual itinerary or travel, as a continuous mapped surface of places.

In the second half of the sixth century BC, Hecataeus of Miletus wrote a *Periegesis* (or 'Circuit of the Earth'), apparently attempting, as far as we can tell from the available fragments,[13] an inventory of places, countries, rivers, mountains and tribes, according to a circuit around the Mediterranean Sea. It is debatable whether he drew a new map or simply modified and completed Anaximander's. But his *Periegesis* was a text, gathering information from various sources: personal travels, information drawn from sailors and tradesmen, saga and poetry. Such an inventory of place- and tribe-names would have been impossible without the frame of a map: it helped to organize the distribution of names according to a methodical and abstract movement around the Mediterranean Sea. Herodotus, in the second half of the fifth century BC, is another witness to the use of maps to organize literary descriptions of space. He sought to translate the visual patterns into various geometrical metaphors, but we know that he did not draw a map himself.

During the sixth and fifth centuries BC, one can see the origins of both a distinction and interaction between map and discourse. The map helped to gather, organize and unify a heterogeneous knowledge about places and tribes, but its purpose was also more abstract and theoretical. Like the metaphor or the geometrical figure, illustrating the sphere of the universe, the map gave a material and visual reality to an invisible reality. It was an *a priori* and abstract device; it imposed a shape, borders and patterns of symmetry on the inhabited earth, whose Mediterranean shores only were known to the Greeks. If such maps sometimes interacted with and influenced geographical descriptions, all indications are that their development followed a path of its own beyond the mainstream current of Greek geography. Map-making in the Greek classical and Hellenistic world was practised by a tiny number of individuals, scholars interested in philosophy, mathematics, astronomy and geometry. During the fourth century BC, map-makers were found in philosophical schools at Athens: in Plato's Academy, Eudoxus was engaged in various mathematical and astronomical researches, and it seems he drew a map in connection with his treatise 'Circuit of the Earth'. In Aristotle's Lyceum, a world map was displayed on the wall of the 'lower portico'.[14] Aristotle himself used maps, as the *Meteorologics* treatise testifies. And his pupil and fellow researcher Dicaearchus committed himself to drawing a map, providing it with a new geometrical frame and probably using new topographical data available from Alexander's Asiatic campaigns.

Pre-Hellenistic Greek cartography displays some consistent characteristics. It dealt with small-scale maps only. We have not the slightest idea about their visual design, but since Anaximander, maps were always linked to written treatises, although they were not necessarily included in the papyrus roll. They were independent plates and we know that one of them, at least, was engraved on a bronze plate. The rarity of available data about maps in the Greek classical world followed from the fact that the political, commercial and military situation of Greek cities did not make necessary either the practical use of such small-scale drawings, nor of large-scale maps. On the contrary, map-making was an activity linked to philosophy and the sciences. There was no social or political control over map-making, upon its diffusion and its use. Nobody fixed norms or criteria regarding maps: each map-maker was absolutely free to propose his own views about the shape of the world, his own calculations of its size, his own geometrical frame, his own selection of places. Control over maps rose from the cartographers themselves, as they began to gather the work of their forerunners and to develop their own research from it.

Nor did the ancient technology of book-making (manuscript papyrus book-rolls) permit a wide-scale diffusion of these drawings, or their precise and exact reproduction. Even had such a technology existed, it is difficult to imagine who could have been the intended audience. Cartography was a part of the mathematical sciences, not of daily life. Descriptive geography and ethnography followed their own parallel paths, mainly among historical writers. There was no Greek cartographic school comparable to the Hippocratic school of medicine, for example, with its organization, its methodological and deontological rules, or to the philosophical schools, organized around the writings of their founders.

MAP-MAKING AND POWER IN PTOLEMAIC ALEXANDRIA

Did the shift from Athens to Alexandria, from the classical Greek city to the Hellenistic kingdoms, change this situation and create new functions for small-scale maps?

To answer this question, we need to evoke the new historical background. First, a vast volume of new field data was gathered during Alexander's expedition in Asia: road measurements, geographical and ethnographical observations, diaries, samples and such like. Second, the Ptolemaic rule in Egypt was a model example of the new Greek kingdoms created *ex novo* in the former satrapies of the Persian Empire. Greeks had to rule over large territories, over native populations, where each new kingdom was competing for prestige with its neighbours and to protect or to extend its borders. Last, the Ptolemaic dynasty created official institutions devoted to science and scholarship: the Museum and its Library.

Importing to the new Egyptian kingdom the model of the Aristotelian school in Athens, Ptolemy I Lagos changed the size as well as the functions of this institution. Royal sponsorship of culture, sciences and literature helped the new monarchy to establish its pre-eminence among the other kingdoms. Alexandria became an attractive place for scholars, poets and scientists, who found in the king's palace the greatest library of the ancient world and thus access to the whole Greek literary heritage. One of the underlying dynamics of Alexandrian culture is its magnetic power of attraction: collecting all the texts ever written in the Greek world as well as by the Barbarians, attracting individuals from across the Hellenized world. Producing a map of the earth was a logical development in this new capital city, itself a microcosm of the greater world beyond.

Curiously, the mapping project did not appear immediately. We have to wait until c. 245 BC, when Eratosthenes of Cyrene left the philosophical schools in Athens to become head librarian at Alexandria. He was given this prestigious appointment by Ptolemy III Euergetes, thanks to his reputation as a mathematician and Platonic philosopher. His new position allowed Eratosthenes to undertake various scholarly works – literary and grammatical studies, historical chronology – but he also committed himself to scientific research: mathematics and geometry, geodesy, geography.

At first glance the extant sources about Eratosthenes' map do not link it explicitly to a political project, to the ruling symbolism of the Greek dynasty. Eratosthenes' map belonged to the same tradition as Anaximander's, Eudoxus' and Dicaearchus' maps: it was an abstract and geometrical construction, deeply rooted in scientific studies rather than a practical device. Eratosthenes' cartographic activity did not include drawing large-scale maps of the Egyptian frontiers, of the Delta, of the Nile valley, of the Greek settlements such as those in the Fayum area. And Eratosthenes was not the head cartographer of the Land Survey Offices of the Ptolemies' administration. Cartography, as practised within the Museum, was not a tool for warriors, tax-collectors, merchants or ambassadors.

The Alexandrian map, however, cannot be divorced from the exercise of power. As a symbolic instrument, it superseded the actual limits of Ptolemaic rule and provided it with a universal dimension. If Alexandria realized Alexander's dream and became a microcosm in which the whole of the Greek and Barbarian culture was condensed, the map could illustrate the pretensions of the dynasty to rule over the whole world through symbolic mediations. The map, like the thousands of papyrus rolls archived in the Library, condensed the whole earth into the king's palace itself. Eratosthenes may have given the inhabited earth the shape of a chlamys – the Macedonian military cloak.[15] The chlamys was a consistent symbol of royal power in Greco-Egyptian iconography. The chlamys was also the shape of the city of Alexandria itself. The architect and city planner Deinokrates, who was appointed by Alexander the Great, was probably responsible for this design. If Eratosthenes chose to give the earth the shape of the city, the political symbolism was obvious: there was an analogical link between Alexandria and the earth, the microcosm and the macrocosm.

On a more general level, mapping the whole earth could be considered as a process of intellectual control. Through their geometry and their language, the Greeks took hold of the earth, its countries and tribes, and organized them according to their own categories. Thus they acquired intellectual mastery of this space: its most remote parts were absorbed within a single homogeneous mathematical space, according to a single geometrical order. In an act of power, through lines, shapes, place names and mathematical positions, the map-maker appropriated the earth and imposed his own view of its order, through the territorial, political and cultural divisions in which he organized it.

The Alexandrian map also foregrounded another feature. The map-maker, the recipients of the map, the intellectual and political circles that commissioned the map, all appropriated a local knowledge and empirical data about remote places and countries. These were gathered from the periphery of the world to its centre, the Ptolemies' palace in Alexandria. The power inherent in the map lies in conveying a knowledge beyond the sum of the many bits of information it encompasses. Local data are given new meaning, are integrated into a set of relationships that brings forth new information about them, in an interplay between the centre and the periphery, empirical data and geometrical construction, to which I now turn.

MAPPING THE WORLD FROM WITHIN A LIBRARY

The two first books of Strabo's *Geography* are one of the principal ancient Greek sources for the conceptual and scientific frame of cartography. Our entry point into this discussion is a statement about a whole picture of the earth. Before starting the chorographical description of the earth, Strabo reminds his readers about his own travels through the Mediterranean world, far more extensive than those of all other geographers. These travels delimit an area of direct geographical knowledge: outside it, Strabo had to rely on oral or written sources; he had to 'trust' other travellers. This insistence on travels should not be overestimated: it is a topos whose origin should be sought in Herodotus' *Histories*.[16] The personal look at a country, at tribes, at historical events and characters ('autopsy') is the most valuable epistemological criterion in ancient historiography. But geography challenges this traditional conception of knowledge. To what extent does autopsy help the geographer or the map-maker in his project to represent the whole earth?

Strabo himself was aware of this paradox, and he added the following refinement, whereby the autopsy of travellers is relativized:[17]

However, the greater part of our material both they and I receive by hearsay (*akoé*) and then form our ideas of shape and size and also other characteristics, qualitative and quantitative, precisely as the mind forms its ideas from sense impressions – for our senses report the shape, color, and size of an apple, and also its smell, feel, and flavor; and from all this the mind forms the concept of apple. So, too, even in the case of large figures, while the senses perceive only the parts, the mind forms a concept of the whole from what the senses have perceived. And men who are eager to learn (*philomatheîs*) proceed in just that way: they trust as organs of sense those who have seen or wandered over any region, no matter what, some in this and some in that part of the earth, and they form in one diagram their mental image of the whole inhabited world.

This statement echoes a shared topic in Hellenistic philosophy: what is the 'criterion' of knowledge? And how does one reach the concept of an object, from and through the various and partial testimonies of senses? If the concept of apple results from the gathering of the heterogeneous data of perception and from their intellectual synthesis, the concept of earth itself also results from the addition and transformation of partial data. Strabo describes a twofold process: first, the mental assembly of partial data to produce a whole picture; second, the shift from empirical and visual data to the mental diagram. Such processes divide the tasks between two categories of actors. First, travellers who have a direct but limited knowledge of a country. These act as the sense organs moving at the periphery of the world and bringing experience back to the centre. Second, the geographer, who remains at the centre and reorganizes partial and empirical visions into a coherent mental diagram. The key points of Strabo's description are the hierarchical organization of knowledge and the conception of *akoé* (hearsay) as a medium of communication of visual data, as a 'tele-visual device'.

The central position of the map-maker, collecting information from travelling sources about the most various parts of the world, is a variant in a more general Alexandrian process. This 'imperial' culture displayed a strong centripetal dynamic. The Alexandrian Library gathered all the books ever written in both the Greek and Barbarian worlds and from this totality scholars produced new intellectual projects such as bio-biblio-graphical catalogues, organizing the corpus of poets, of dramatists and prose-writers, and building up encyclopedic collections of words, quotations and facts.[18] Alexandria is a perfect example of what Bruno Latour calls 'les centres de calculs' ('centres of calculation'), those places where local and partial information, samples or extracts are collected and processed in order to produce a more general level of knowledge and synthetic devices such as maps, diagrams, tables of measures or statistics.[19]

Another key element in Strabo's description is his model of the trans-mission of field observations, from the traveller to the cartographer through the *akoé*, that is through discourse. *Akoé* encompasses both oral and written testimonies, 'hearsay' as well read texts.[20] Such a fact has several consequences. Writing and then reading a travel report does not prevent the transmission of the data gathered by the traveller's senses. This proficiency of the *logos* as a medium for local knowledge implies that to verify its reliability one cannot use empirical checks, but is forced to interrogate the *logos* itself, according to internal criteria of cohesiveness and credibility. Another indirect way to check the *logos* is to examine carefully the credibility of its author.

The diagram of the inhabited earth is like the concept of an apple: a result of the synthetic activity of the mind, gathering data from the senses. Such a philosophical statement about the production of conceptual knowledge could be read as an account not only of Strabo's own practice as a geographer but also of Eratosthenes' map-making activity within the Alexandrian Library. That Eratosthenes perfectly matched such a motionless, disembodied cartographer, exploring the world through the written reports found in the Library, is emphasized by Strabo when he discusses the polemic between Eratosthenes and Hipparchus about the dimensions of India. Eratosthenes considered his own theory was 'fully attested by those who were in these places, since he read many reports that his Library had in abundance, this library whose importance Hipparchus himself evokes'.[21]

We cannot reconstruct the holdings of the geographical section in the Alexandrian Library, but it is beyond doubt that there were geographical texts, travel reports and probably a few maps as well. They were perhaps registered in the 'Tables' (*pinakes*) of Callimachus, the standard reference-work of Alexandrian librarianship, but we do not know if geography had a section of its own.[22]

The Alexandrian Library acted as an archive for recent documents. Among them, the surveys of the so-called 'bematists', those land-surveyors and distance-measurers who accompanied Alexander's army during its expedition through Asia, in the Persian Empire and its eastern allies (331–323 BC).[23] Surveyors such as Baiton, Diognetos, Philonides, Amyntas, Archelaos are only names today, known from a few rare fragments quoted by Pliny or Eratosthenes. It is beyond doubt that the bematists brought back to the Greek world a huge amount of field data, place names, distances, but also various descriptions of landscape, fauna and flora. The Seleucid kings, who ruled over the inner tracks of Asia after Alexander's death, probably gathered similar materials. Nearchus, as the commander of Alexander's navy, sailed from the mouth of the Indus to that of the Tigris, along the shore of the Indian Ocean, and wrote a

Periplus describing his sea-journey. Seleucid ambassadors or governors in eastern Asia, such as Deimachos, Patrokles and Megasthenes, were the main Hellenistic sources for the ethnography and geography of India. Another geographical text used by Eratosthenes was the treatise *On the Ocean* by the physician Pytheas of Massalia (*fl.* end of the fourth century BC), who sailed along the Atlantic shore of Europe as far as the mysterious island of Thule and was the major pre-Roman source about far western and northern lands.

The Ptolemies also ordered commercial and military expeditions into the interior of Africa (under such men as Philon, Dalion, Aristocreon, Bion, Basilis and Simonides Minor), while Timosthenes, the commander of their navy, was asked by Ptolemy II Philadelphus to survey the Mediterranean Sea, to describe and register its harbours and the notable points of its shores. The result was the treatise *On Harbours*, in ten books, which included measurements, orientations, lists of place names and quotations from previous geographical treatises. Such fieldwork was certainly available to Eratosthenes in the Alexandrian Library. A later geographer, Marcianus of Heraclea, accused Eratosthenes of plagiarizing Timosthenes' treatise word for word.[24]

These various travel reports fit rather well with Strabo's description of the genesis of the cartographic image. A striking fact is that the Ptolemies, looking for crucial geographical information (for military, political and commercial purposes), did not ask for maps but for written reports, land and sea itineraries. Transforming these field data into a map would not have answered the pragmatic needs of the Ptolemies. Eratosthenes' map and geographical treatise encompassed the information in part, while modifying its form, content and scope, a modification which prompts an enquiry into this Alexandrian concept of the map itself. What was a map? What was its purpose? To answer this, I broaden the scope of enquiry to encompass mapping in the early modern world.

THE 'CARTOGRAPHIE DE CABINET' PARADIGM

Within the Alexandrian Library, in order to build up a whole picture of the world, one had to move slowly along a course of mediations and analogical operations, from empirical data to the final intellectual scheme. Claudius Ptolemy (*fl.* second century AD), Al-Idrisi at the court of Roger II of Sicily in Palermo (*fl.* twelfth century),[25] and Jean-Baptiste Bourguignon d'Anville (1697–1782)[26] are other examples of what may be regarded as a major paradigm in the history of cartography.

Beyond their specific historical context, all these map-makers shared a basic common position: all were 'motionless minds', processing the scattered data provided by travellers, geographers, ambassadors and former map-makers. Drawing a new map – of the whole earth or of a part of it – demanded some basic conditions: first, being settled in a place where a large amount of information was available, such as a royal court, a library and a commercial crossroads; second, a precise working method. Geographers had to read and interpret texts, to extract and classify bits of information, to order them, to translate them according to a common unity of measure. The basic operations were selecting data, cross-checking them, coordinating them and then translating them into orientations and distances in order to project them into the graphic space of the map itself. Such a conception of map-making was an extended pratice of geometry.

Jean-Baptiste d'Anville is one of the best documented examples of such a 'cartographie de cabinet'. This French *érudit* was trained in the Classics and historical geography. His historical maps and dissertations provided him with an intellectual background as well as a corpus of sources, measurements and place names for his mapping projects. As a 'géographe du roi', he produced an impressive amount of treatises and maps of individual countries as well as of the whole earth. In his work, there was a continuity from the regional maps to the maps of continents and to the *mappaemundi* themselves. His world map was first published in 1761 and was a landmark in Enlightenment cartography. It was updated in 1772 and 1777, after Bougainville and Cook's navigations.

D'Anville could be considered as an heir of the Alexandrian geographers: he used identical methods. One of the differences, however, was the larger range of evidence available. D'Anville had many strata of geographical knowledge at his disposal: Greco-Roman sources, medieval and Renaissance sources, Arab sources, as well as modern reports. As a 'géographe du roi', he was at the very centre of a unique network of correspondents, ambassadors and merchants: each of them, through written reports or oral statements, from their own experience or from indirect field testimonies, were as many substitutes and delegates of the cartographer himself, who never travelled in order to draw his maps.

D'Anville's first task was to draw regional maps, and then to recombine these partial drawings in small-scale maps: he was interested in the detail of topographical data and his main concern was, so to speak, filling in the blank spaces enclosed within the outline of the mapped regions. Map-making remained an abstract synthesizing operation, the last step in a complex process relying on scholarship and the philological treatment of evidence. The key word in d'Anville's practice was 'criticism', that is internal criticism of sources. Comparing data, resolving inconsistencies, finding modern equivalents for ancient place names, translating textual and descriptive information into locations, distances and orientations were some of these operations. For d'Anville, ancient measurements were an inescapable source of topographical information for the modern map-maker and were expected to provide the same exactness as the rare modern astronomically established positions. As a matter of fact, Roman itineraries, in the areas familiar to the Romans, appeared as very exact. For this reason, it was essential to find out the modern equivalents of ancient measurement units: 'Pied Romain et Pied Grec, Palme majeur et mineur, Coudée, Orgye, Mille Romain, Mille Grec, Stades de différentes longueurs, Schène Égyptien, Parasangue Persane, Li chinois etc.'.[27] Such a set of equivalences allowed the modern map-maker to use a wide range of heterogeneous data and to provide historical geography with an instrumental function for modern geography. The final map, resulting from this assembling and combining process, produced a visual cohesiveness which concealed all the calculations, translations and critical adjustments that made it possible.

Luckily enough, we still possess d'Anville's draft notes, his *Papiers géographiques*.[28] These archives allow us to observe the map-maker at work. They are a series of small sheets and fragments of papers, covered with manuscript notes. We find pieces of topographical information gathered from oral testimonies, modern travel reports and ancient sources: place names and their variants, distances, descriptions of a road, quotations from books, quotations from ancient sources, astronomical observations fixing the position of a city, comparisons of ancient sections of itineraries, sketch drawings offering a first visualization of these data, draft versions of dissertations. The accumulation, comparison and addition of such partial data are by themselves heuristic tools: they allow the painstaking construction of local configurations that will be assembled on the map. The *Papiers* display the rough material collected in order to draw maps of Turkey, Greece, Hungary, Africa, Egypt and others. D'Anville cross-checks these data, adds up local measurements, looks for the convergence of sources. This is an infinite process, and new data are added even after the map has been drawn. D'Anville stores this new information in order to correct or to confirm his map. The map of a given country, such as d'Anville's famous *Carte d'Italie* (1743),[29] results from the assembling of local data, from this transformation of written information into a distribution of locations according to a common scale. In such a process, geometry is the principal tool: it allows the transformation into segments of straight lines and the alignment of points of what was formerly a succession of stopping-places along an itinerary. Further, it helps to interconnect all these segments in a network of places: their relative positions shifted according to an absolute location system.

From Eratosthenes to d'Anville and beyond, geographers faced the same challenge: they knew the way to calculate longitude and latitude. But practical calculations were rare. Several reasons explain this situation. Technically, calculating a longitude position implied a precise measure of the time at which an astronomical phenomenon, such as a solar or a lunar eclipse, was visible in different places located on the same parallel. The theoretical principle had been known since the Greeks, but it was definitely applied only during the eighteenth century, thanks to the manufacturing of precise clockwork.[30] Second, logistic factors: launching systematic field surveys and measurement campaigns implied an institutional frame, economic means, instruments and a trained staff, as well as the possibility to develop international cooperation or to travel freely and systematically through the areas to be mapped. Without such a systematic process, map-makers had to deal with scarce astronomical observations that provided their maps with few positions. The greatest part of topographical data, however, was provided by itinerary and travel reports, while the map relied mainly on geometry.

The production of a world map always implies a centripetal dynamic, collecting data from the periphery at a centre, and translating empirical and field data into a network of measured distances, defining mathematical positions easily handled and combined within the geometrical frame of the map. One of the dynamics in the history of small-scale maps has been the progressive control of the data to be collected, their format, their reliability. Eratosthenes,[31] Ptolemy, al-Idrisi and d'Anville did not have such direct control. Their mapping projects relied on the corpus of currently available evidence, without the possibility of enlarging it through field survey and systematic geodetical campaigns.

These geographers used the map to give a cohesiveness to whatever heterogeneous data they were able to collect. They faced the same difficulty: how to process and organize tiny bits of geographical knowledge, such as place names, tribe-names, distances expressed according to various standards (days of travel, of navigation, indigenous measures), orientations, former maps, descriptions. The map gave a spatial and temporal cohesiveness and homogeneity to data, sometimes pertaining to different historical periods.[32] The way this information was established, collected and translated into cartographic forms became hidden under the drawing itself, but could be archived in the treatise of the geographer or among his draft papers. D'Anville's notes help us to imagine what might have been Eratosthenes' methods in the Alexandrian Library – although we should remember the specific practical difficulties of working with papyrus rolls, without indexes, page numbers or other devices for a quick retrieval of data.

FUNCTION OF THE MAP

From Eratosthenes to d'Anville, one observes the permanence of a model of map-making, relying on the mediation of various sources and their progressive synthesis through critical operations. We should not, however, underestimate the differences between these cartographers. D'Anville worked at a time when cartography had already a well-established tradition, when a new cartographic project could rely on the many existing maps it had to correct and improve. The difference, however, lies also in the function and efficiency of the maps thus produced. The 'missing link' between Eratosthenes' world map and d'Anville's maps is the new cartographic paradigm developed by another map-maker from ancient Alexandria, Claudius Ptolemy.

Ptolemy's second-century-AD *Geographia* had other purposes than Eratosthenes' work. The treatise provided any new map-maker with the theoretical principles and the technical material necessary to draw regional maps or even a *mappamundi*. His tables listed around eight thousand geographical positions (longitude and latitude). As far as we can judge, Ptolemy's *Geographia* did not have real echoes during the Roman Empire. The text, however, was transmitted through the Arab world and in the Byzantine libraries, and from there, at the end of the fourteenth century, it made its way to the West where it was studied by Italian humanists and European geographers and printers. The nature and the internal organization of Ptolemy's work explained its fortune. Even when they corrected its locations or updated the geographical place names or added new ones and deleted outdated ones, Arab and European geographers still worked within the conceptual frame defined by Ptolemy: the map, regional as well as geographical, was ruled by a graticule, either orthogonal or with the meridians convergent towards the pole. There was coherence and continuity between regional and geographical grids, since they were drawn according to a general partition of the terrestrial globe by regular meridian and parallel lines. An arbitrary decision fixed the primary meridian in relation to which longitude would be calculated.[33] Such a device allowed infinite ways to frame and distribute Ptolemy's eight thousand positions into large-scale or small-scale maps, without ever losing their position or the relationship of the part to the whole.

On such grids, individual places could be plotted as dots, and a line drawn through them in order to reveal the shape of a coastline, the track of a river or a mountain chain. The basic element in Ptolemy's *Geographia*, however, is not the line but the point, fixed by a set of two geometrical coordinates. But this point is the last step in the processing of data collected from travel reports or from written descriptions. Most of these longitude and latitude positions were not established through astronomical observations, but were drawn from heterogeneous sources, from texts and previous maps. It should be stressed that the precise figures lined up in Polemy's tables are themselves products of mapping, the result of a shift from the relative position of places to their absolute positions, once a grid of numbered parallels and meridians has been drawn in cartographic space.

The regional maps in Ptolemy's *Geographia* are the ultimate encoding and archiving device for bits of geographical information. Such a system articulates various levels and forms of knowledge. Thanks to the coordinate system, places remained unchanged across several frames, producing special intellectual effects, whether appearing in a chorographic map frame, a geographic map frame or within a written catalogue where each entry was given its longitude and latitude and to which was added further information (climatic, historical etc.). These catalogues could be ruled by geographical order or alphabetical order without losing their efficiency.

Understanding Eratosthenes' work within its own categories is more difficult, since we do not have his map and his treatise. From Strabo's quotations and paraphrases, however, we could try to draw a few general inferences about the purpose of Eratosthenes' map.

A first key feature is its abstract nature and purpose. Abstraction is the key word in the process that leads from the empirical vision to the mental schematization, since the map-maker deconstructs the periplus, the land itinerary, the exploration report, in order to extract alignments of places, segments of added distances, orientations, and descriptive data (climate, landscape etc.) and help to determine the location. If Ptolemy's regional maps were a catalogue of positions, Eratosthenes' world map was perhaps more like a relational database: a device wherein a given place was meaningful and relevant only as an element within a system of relations. Ptolemy was interested in the inventory of the world and no limits restricted the continuous addition of new locations. This was to happen during the European Renaissance. Eratosthenes was interested in the structure rather than the inventory. His map relied on a set of notable points, each defining its unique meridian and parallel. These lines were not organized into a systematic grid, and the aim of the map was not to locate points, but to organize a space of *summetria* (commensurability), wherein measured intervals (*diastèmata*) would build up a frame of non-regular perpendicular lines. Other places could subsequently be located on one of the parallels or meridians thus defined. Since the map was an orthogonal space, it was possible to add new places, to draw new parallel or perpendicular lines, in order to fix the limits of the inhabited world and to measure its greater length and width. Eratosthenes' purpose was thus to build a structure of abstract geometrical lines and shapes which did not represent anything real in the geographical space but made visible mathematical relationships within the orthogonal frame of the map.

The map was ruled by the geometry of Euclid's *Elements*, written in Alexandria at the beginning of the third century BC. It established a set of mathematical correspondences between places that were not interrelated. Such an underlying network of parallel and perpendicular lines allowed the reorganization of empirical data extracted from travel reports and previous geographical descriptions. Thus it allowed new kinds of journeys – analogical and syllogistical ones. A given measured distance between the latitudes of two places could be exported from the western extremity of the map to the eastern one. It remained the same distance and defined two parallel lines, which could themselves be used as starting points for new calculations. It was thus possible to travel through the inhabited world in an abstract and geometrical way, thanks to this network of lines creating non-empirical relationships between remote places.

Eratosthenes' map was thus a computing device. It allowed the mathematical cohesiveness of the step-by-step construction of the picture of the world to be checked by the progressive discovery of new topographical data. It was also a tool, allowing choice between various accounts about the same place. Maps could reveal the absurdity of an incorrect location provided by an imprecise textual source by making immediately visible what such a location implied in terms of landscape, fauna and flora, through analogy with other places on the same parallel. One might say that such a map was a regulated system where any local addition, any local modification should be coherent with the whole structure and had repercussions on it. Such cartographic thinking was ruled by the syllogism.

Eratosthenes' map was not the ultimate result of the geographical work, as in Ptolemy's project. It was the tool of this work, making visible, step by step, the critical decisions made by the geographer, his choices, his calculations. As such, the map was a communication tool between geographers. There was a complex link between the written treatise and the map (drawn on a sheet of the papyrus roll, perhaps, or a separate tablet). When such a treatise was read, the map offered a background for the discussion, made it possible to check and to correct mistakes. The astronomer Hipparchus and the geographer Strabo used Eratosthenes' map in such a way, as a device for making visible the inferences and conclusions of its maker, the cohesiveness of the sources he chose, the way he used them.

MAP-MAKING AS A TRADITION: BETWEEN RHETORICS AND PHILOLOGY

Strabo's text about the 'cartographic mind' as well as the nature and purpose of Eratosthenes' map pinpoints another key feature. Map-making is no longer possible as a project from the ground, the demiurgic attempt to draw the world as in Anaximander's first map. Between sixth-century Ionia and third-century Alexandria, the map has lost its ontological power. Map-making takes place within a tradition and a particular time frame. First, because the map synthesizes data extracted from previous texts. Second, because map-making is dependent on history, on conquests, on new explorations. Alexander's campaign unveiled the inner and eastern parts of Asia for the Greeks. Polybius and Strabo expressed their conviction that Roman conquests helped to uncover new areas, new tribes. Geographers could map only the part of the world known at their own time. Their work was a step in an ongoing process and they were aware that their successors would bring new improvements, corrections and complements to their map or description. Third, because since Eratosthenes, drawing a new map was possible only if one relied on a previously existing one: map-making was conceived and practised as a complex set of operations and implied a critical work on previous maps – rectification, addition of new data and deletion of incorrect or outdated data.

Such a process calls to mind what happened in Alexandrian philology. The Alexandrian Library played an important part in Eratosthenes' cartographic project and method, not only because he found within its holdings a wide range of sources, but also because these texts and maps displayed ambiguous or incorrect information, discrepancies, outdated features that demanded rectification (*diorthôsis*). In the same way, librarians such as Zenodotus and, after Eratosthenes, Aristophanes of Byzantium and Aristarchus of Samothrace decided they could not keep unchanged the different versions of the same literary texts (such as Homer's *Iliad* and *Odyssey*), but, instead, chose to process them through the various operations of philology in order to reduce the plurality and the discrepancies of material books into a single and coherent text – rectification here again was the main step.[34]

Strabo, Polybius and Ptolemy followed the model of the cartographic work determined by Eratosthenes. The process was the same for the mapmaker as for the author of a geographical description. First, one had to choose, as a starting point, the work of a forerunner, who provided a general reference frame as well as a corpus of data. This author should be as recent as possible – his geographical information should not be outdated and, more important, he should have already done a critical recension of the sources.[35] Second, this author should display some specific qualities: much of his information is to be correct, and the new geographer may simply repeat it; but he has omitted some points, and new explorations have been made since his work. The new geographer had to fill these gaps. Last, this forerunner made mistakes, errors also to be corrected.[36]

Such criteria define the reference source that a new geographer should use and at the same time the nature of his personal contribution to the progress of geography: perpetuating a corpus of knowledge, completing gaps, correcting errors. Such criteria also help to select the additional sources one will use to correct and update the existing map. They give a good insight into the textual dynamics of ancient geography. A map or a geographical description synthesizes and supersedes previous maps, previous descriptions. It collects and combines in a new device the information checked and deemed trustworthy after the rectification of sources. This process alters the status of information: from individual statements about countries, places and tribes, to objective and granted facts. The map and the description could be considered as the condensed and the mobile library of Greek geographical knowledge.

Source selection is the most crucial step. One should select authors who are reliable and responsible at most for errors, never for lies. This distinction is essential in the tradition of Hellenistic geography.[37] Error is to be an unintentional mistake, and as such may be corrected without harsh polemics. On the contrary, the lie is a deliberate perversion of the truth. A statement might be wrong, but a lie pinpoints the man himself as unreliable. One could never henceforth trust him or any of his statements: some might be true, but this does not matter. Such an author lacks all credibility and should be ignored. One should not even criticize him and thus help to transmit his tales.[38]

We can scarcely overestimate the importance of such a rule in the geographical discussions of Polybius or Strabo. Being deceived by a liar is
their common obsession and also the main point on which they reproach
their forerunners. Liars introduce fiction and myth, marvels and wonders
within the field of geography. The love of incredible stories belongs to
another sphere than the sphere of knowledge. The problem, however, is
that liars are to be found in a particular category of characters: travellers
and tradesmen, coming back from remote countries.[39] 'Anybody giving
an account of his own travels is a boaster,' wrote Strabo.[40] Such a precon-
ception had dramatic consequences upon the Greco-Roman reception of
geographical innovations.

In order to understand what is at stake, we should recall the epistemological model of Alexandrian cartography as described by Strabo. At the
periphery, travellers observe, measure, discover. At the centre is the mind
of the map-maker, who listens to these reports or reads them. Truth and
reliability are the key issues since the location and sometimes the reality of
a place rely on written sources. Two geographical areas focused the
fiercest polemics: the island of Thule, at the northern extremity of the
inhabited world, and India, at its eastern extremity. They were both representative of the most remote areas of the earth, its confines. New reports
and new evidence were becoming available about these areas, rendering
necessary the rectification of old maps. For the historian Polybius, it
should be remembered that writers about the ends of earth write only
myths.[41] Thule offers the best case study. This island in the Northern
Ocean was mentioned and described enigmatically by its discoverer,
Pytheas of Massalia (c. 325 BC). Nobody else in the ancient world had ever
seen this island. Its existence or its imaginary nature, that is, its position
on a geographical map, relied entirely on the credibility of Pytheas, on the
critical decision to accept or reject his testimony. Eratosthenes accepted it,
and the 'parallel of Thule' is the northern limit of the inhabited earth on
his map. Polybius and then Strabo denied Pytheas' credibility: he is just a
myth-teller, and since he wrote so many lies on known facts, one should
ignore his testimony about unknown places.[42] Such were the alternatives
within a debate that is not concluded today.[43]

It is the same problem with India. When Eratosthenes decided to
change the position of India and locate its northern mountains on the
same parallel as the Taurus mountains, actually the main parallel line of
his map, he was relying on the testimony of Patrokles, who estimated that
from the south to the north of India was a total distance of 15,000 stades,
far less than previous measurements. The astronomer Hipparchus, in his

criticism of Eratosthenes' map, condemned the weakness of such evidence. Strabo is our main source for this polemic:[44] Hipparchus opposed one source to another, the credibility of Deimachus and Megasthenes against the credibility of Patrokles, in order to demonstrate the impossibility of choosing between two different locations of the same mountain when the only data available were written reports and not astronomical observations. The striking fact is that, for Strabo, the only way to put an end to the controversy was not by launching a survey expedition to India and making the necessary astronomical observations, but by checking again the credibility of the sources concerned and calling witnesses (for the prosecution as well as for the defence) to enforce or remove their *a priori* reliability. At the end of such a suit, one would decide whether the total length of India was 15,000, 20,000 or even 30,000 stades, and whether one had to correct the old maps or leave them unchanged, that is to stop making geography. Strabo concluded that Eratosthenes was right, since this was the only way to make geography. If Hipparchus was right on the theoretical level (Strabo does not even admit the possibility), Eratosthenes pragmatically chose to adapt geometrical and astronomical principles to the current status of his documentation and to his whole project, that is, mapping the earth from the Alexandrian Library. D'Anville's dilemma in the eighteenth century was not so different.

There remains to be explained the logic behind Polybius' and Strabo's insistence on the lie (*pseûdos*) as a major perversion of travellers. Eratosthenes' attempt to reform Greek cartography and geography led him to draw a major division between literary and mythical geography, on the one hand, and travel reports and previous geographers, on the other hand. The major consequence was to exclude Homer's poetry from the corpus of geographical sources and to deny the geographical reality of Odysseus' navigation. According to Eratosthenes, it took place beyond the Pillars of Hercules, in the Atlantic Ocean, and as such belonged to fiction, not to geography. It aimed at entertaining listeners, not teaching them geography or any other science.[45] One should not forget that, at the Alexandrian Library, Eratosthenes succeeded Apollonius Rhodius whose major work was the *Argonautica*, devoted to the journey of the ship Argo through the inhabited world. As such, it made use of many geographical materials, mostly archaic itineraries and outdated conceptions. This could explain why Eratosthenes decided to separate geography from this literary and antiquarian scholarship. Adopting such a position against Homer's geography allowed Eratosthenes to avoid a set of *vexatae quaestiones*, such as the place of the Cyclops' land or Calypso's islands and so on.

Such a redefinition of geographical knowledge had far reaching consequences and challenged the cultural dogma of Homer's omniscience,
developed by the allegorical school of Pergamon and by Stoic philosophers. As Stoics, Polybius and Strabo were obviously shocked by
Eratosthenes' expurgation of the geographical field. One of their concerns became to re-establish Homer's authority as a geographical writer
and to demonstrate the historical and empirical background of the
Odyssey. Homer translated his geographical knowledge into the language
of poetry and myth, and his readers should look for the core of truth
beneath the mythical skin.[46] Polybius and Strabo are thus among the most
ancient examples of a hermeneutic trend that led ultimately to Victor
Berard and his attempt to map Odysseus' travels in the Mediterranean
Sea. They concluded that most of Odysseus' navigational steps were to be
located around Sicily and Italy and that Homer was to be considered as a
trustworthy geographical source.[47]

This rehabilitation of Homer had a counterpart, that of pinpointing
the dangers of error and fiction elsewhere, in the corpus of travellers and
explorers who conveyed myths under the form of objective statement and
field reports, for the mere pleasure of deceiving their readers. While
Homer's mythical adornments are immediately identifiable and don't
intentionally cheat the reader, Pytheas, Megasthenes and others lied for
the pleasure of lying and as such they should not be used at all by the map-
maker. Eratosthenes, the armchair map-maker, was thus caught in his
own trap and should rather have relied on Homer's descriptions than
accepted the existence of Thule.

Such a distrust for travellers continued until the Enlightenment age of
scientific explorations, and explains why armchairs cartographers were
sometimes so reluctant to use much of the information provided by
merchants and explorers.

FROM THE GEOGRAPHICAL TEXT TO THE MENTAL MAP

Eratosthenes' lost treatise and lost map were landmarks in the history of
cartography. First, Eratosthenes conceived and made visible new methodological rules, a self-consciousness that changed the nature of map-
making, its links to tradition, to temporality and to progress. Second, he
tried to give geography independence from literature and poetry, reorganizing it through the drawing of a geometrical map and translating
into mathematical relationships and geometrical shapes the data conveyed
by travellers. Along with the map, his treatise encompassed geographical
descriptions, but also, in its first two volumes, an account of the history of

geography and a critical discussion and rectification of older maps. This self-reflexive writing was to be shared by most future authors concerned with geography and cartography, including Polybius, Strabo and Ptolemy.

It is striking that such a redefinition founded not one new tradition, but two. Cartography remained a mathematical and astronomical discipline, technical and esoteric, whose aim was the graphic representation of the earth. Hipparchus (*fl.* second century BC), in his treatise *Against Eratosthenes*, emphazised the necessity of more rigorous astronomically founded data in order to 'rectify' the old maps and change the shape of India. This shift towards mathematics and astronomy led to Marinus of Tyre and to Claudius Ptolemy, during the second century BC. In the latter's *Geographia*, the text as a whole was subordinated to the production of maps, and, as a mere list of locations, it was isomorphic to the set of maps.

Polybius, as the author of a universal history, and Strabo, as the author of a geographical description, both made use of Eratosthenes' work. The Alexandrian map beyond doubt influenced them. But Polybius and Strabo reintroduced the literary tradition, the cultural landscape of the Greek Mediterranean world. (We have, however, lost most of Polybius' Book XXXIV devoted to a systematic geographical description.) Strabo's *Geography* displays an odd divide between its two first books, devoted to the discussion of the Alexandrian map and to the rectification of the geographical tradition, and the later fifteen descriptive books. In the latter, Homer's *Catalogue of Ships* (in the second book of *Iliad*) and its Hellenistic commentators were one of the main sources for the topographical description of Greece (Books VIII–X) under the Roman rule, and the fictional accounts – lies – of travellers inspired most of his description of India (Book XV). And how could Strabo do otherwise? One might claim that he was satisfied with a traditional rewriting of the textual sources, travel reports and regional descriptions available in Alexandrian and Roman libraries under Augustus' reign without submitting them to the geometrical encoding and abstract processing linked to Eratosthenes' map-making. His intended readership was supposed to be wider than the few experts able to use Eratosthenes' and Hipparchus' works. Was this partition between the text and the map therefore an irreconcilable one?

During the second century AD, again in Alexandria, Dionysius Periegetes adapted and described the Alexandrian map in a short didactic poem, in which Eratosthenes and the Stoic philosopher Posidonius were merged with Homer and Apollonius Rhodius: the schoolboy travelled mentally on the map and above the world as a new Odysseus or a new Argonaut. At a time when Claudius Ptolemy was about to write his treatise and perhaps to draw his maps in Alexandria, Dionysius wrote this versified geographical handbook in the sophisticated and artificial language of Alexandrian learned poetry: the text was to be translated into Latin and used in the Byzantine world as well as in the colleges of Renaissance and modern Europe until the nineteenth century.[48] Why did this compilation achieve such a successful reception so quickly? The supremacy of the *logos* over the map it describes, of the literary frame of geography over its visual and mathematical construction, is explained through cultural practices – a written text, a recited poem could reach a far wider audience than any map on a papyrus roll or on a large wooden or stone panel. There was also a well-defined set of scholastic methods that inserted the lesson of geography within the broader frame of a lesson of literature: the key operations were reading, paraphrasing, explaining the erudite allusions, memorizing, reciting. But Dionysius' poem also had visual and imaginary effects of its own. Reading the text was like a methodical travel around and through the earth, organized according to its continents, its countries, its tribes, the catalogue of its place names. This discursive order and the descriptive rhetoric surrounding it, however, were efficient enough to induce visual impressions, to build up a mental map of the world. The poet himself provided his readers with directions for reading his text:[49] 'Now, I shall relate the shape of the whole continental earth, so without having actually seen it, you will get a clear and coherent vision.' How can one look at the world without seeing it, unless through an actual map or an immaterial map in the mind?

Describing geographical shapes though metaphors and geometrical figures, the poet tried to build up, step by step, a verbal map: larger territorial units were outlined first, and then their inner parts were filled in with tribes, rivers, mountains – with names and conventional, sometimes vivid, epithets. An implicit wind rose, the path of the sun, a complex network of contiguities (near, far, beside, above, beyond . . .), as well as a few structural axes drawn from the actual map's meridians and parallels, helped Dionysius' readers to organize the mental picture of the earth. The traditional mnemotechnics involved in the rote recitation of the poem was a dynamic principle: it was a travel as well as a mental drawing process. The reader was the map-maker, following the instructions of the poet. The poetical language allowed the transmission of the cartographical vision, from the poet's mind to those of his readers or listeners. The map, as a whole picture, was the result of a travel, of an evolving process of assemblage, of juxtaposition of shapes, of approximation and of correction.

Dionysius' textual map was not only a fascinating didactic fiction, but also a challenging synthesis of various trends of Alexandrian culture. The geographical library was reunited again, beyond Eratosthenes' anathema against epic poetry. Homer and geometry coexisted again. The map-maker did not rely any more on an infinite chain of mediations and predecessors, manipulating previous texts and maps in order to collect his information and to build up his whole map through the addition and combination of heterogeneous data, of place names, distances and orientations. Instead, the map-maker relied on his direct gaze upon the surface of the earth. The map revealed itself through the map-maker's autopsy. Seen from above, seen from the memory and the imagination, the earth looked like a map, with its lines, its orientations, its place names, its mosaic of lands and seas clearly defined and assembled.

Eratosthenes, in Strabo's account, had to assemble and synthesize a whole library and to purge the travellers' reports of all their sensory and empirical components in order to reach the abstract level of the cartographic diagram. Dionysius' readers share the aerial and immediate vision of the poet, who probably described a map he had under his eyes. Readers and listeners of the poem were at the same time the travellers and the map-makers, the visual observers of singular places and regions, their minds synthesizing words, epithets, metaphors, topographic markers until the whole shape and organization of the *oecumene* were engraved into the tablets of the memory, mere intellectual contemplation beyond all verbal or graphical rendering.

The rhetorical art of description – the *ekphrasis* – had a far-reaching power over the imagination.[50] Literary pleasure was linked to cognitive efficiency. Vision was the foundation of knowledge, and a text, thanks to a specific rhetoric, allowed the encoding and the transmission of this vision, from the writer to his readers. Thus, Dionysius' readers, through a fanciful didactic experience, could share the abstract and surreal vision of the Alexandrian cartographer. Eratosthenes chose to follow the paths of scholarship, geometry and criticism to ascend mentally to a cartographic vantage-point above a schematic and abstract world, a world deserted by gods and heroes. Dionysius' pupils forgot geometry, measures and mediations, and shared the ecstasy of the Muses, of Icarus and of the soul, while slowly flying over the earth's surface, where Ulysses and the Argonauts were still seen travelling, from one poem to another.

The map was as fragile and impressive as a vision of the mind.

2

Mapping Eden: Cartographies of the Earthly Paradise

ALESSANDRO SCAFI

And the Lord God planted a garden eastward in Eden; and there he put the man whom he had formed. And out of the ground made the Lord God to grow every tree that is pleasant to the sight and good for food; the tree of life also in the midst of the garden, and the tree of knowledge of good and evil. And a river went out of Eden to water the garden; and from thence it was parted, and became into four heads.

Genesis 2.8–10

The Bible narrative opens with God placing Adam in the Garden of Eden (Genesis 2.8–15). A theological tradition that, although inaccessible, the Garden continued to exist somewhere on earth remained firmly held in the Middle Ages, and cartographic tradition located the Earthly Paradise on maps of the world. In this essay, I explore some aspects of the cartographic paradox of medieval mapping of Paradise, and reflect on the reasons for its decline in the early modern period.

If we accept maps as some sort of graphic representation 'that facilitates a spatial understanding of things, concepts, conditions, processes, or events in the human world',[1] the appearance on medieval world maps of the Garden of Eden – Earthly Paradise – as one of the 'things' or the 'events' of the human world should not surprise us. In the Middle Ages, as today, mapping was significant in more than one way. It was burdened, though, with theological discourse. And this too should not surprise us, for all mapping involves much more than the drawing of lines. Map construction, no less than writing text, is essentially a social act, one which involves the thoughts and beliefs of both map-maker and culture.[2]

In medieval European culture, philosophical debate about the interrelationship of space and time was profoundly theological. In particular, placing the Garden of Eden on a map of the world had profound theological consequences. To understand the appearance of the Earthly Paradise, in the first place, and, in the second, its precise location, involves the modern thinker in the investigation of one of the most important expressions of belief in Western Christianity. Moreover, a map which shows Paradise as part of the world implicitly acknowledges, by the leap of imagination involved, the limits of human action. A picture of the earth with the Garden of Eden is making visible the divine order of creation. It is at once a confession of the transcendent craft of God operating on terrestrial space, and of the limits of human reasoning. The sort of map-making which engages with theology in this way discloses a vision of the world which goes far beyond the frame of the human domain. Mapping Paradise is an act of faith in the Sacred Text.

And yet there have been many such maps. Surviving cartographic representations date from the sixth-century map of Cosmas Indicopleustes[3] through nearly every mappamundi of the Middle Ages to the fifteenth century. The location as well as the nature of Paradise found expression not only in maps, of course, but also in paintings (for example, Giovanni di Paolo's fifteenth-century cosmogonic image),[4] poetry (notably Dante) and prose (for instance, the fable of Alexander the Great's visit to the Earthly Paradise).[5] By the start of the sixteenth century, however, Paradise had disappeared from maps of the world, remaining only on regional maps. To investigate the reasons for this change involves exploring a significant epistemological shift. The key issues, however, always spring from the same source, the biblical text and its hermeneutics.

MAKING PARADISE VISIBLE

The Book of Genesis clearly describes Eden as an earthly garden with trees and rivers, but has always left biblical commentators with puzzling questions. If the garden of Adam and Eve did indeed exist on earth, as the Bible seems to maintain, where was it located? Was it really in the East, as some versions of the Book of Genesis suggest?[6] What was 'East' and what was the exact position of the region called Eden? Why had no geographer or traveller ever reported finding it? If direct geographical evidence of its existence was lacking, could Paradise on earth still exist? And if it did still exist, what was the function of such a garden: certainly a fit place for God's creatures, but empty since the expulsion of Adam and Eve? Did God create it simply to serve no purpose beyond setting it as the stage for the initial temptation?

To picture the landscape of Eden was also a challenging task. Did it resemble a royal park? What climate did it enjoy? Was it subject to the passing of seasons? Did it rain there? Did frost ever whiten its lawns? Scriptural reference to the trees of life and of knowledge was also enigmatic. Were these material plants or magical trees? Did they have real bark and leaves? Their names seemed to imply that they had spiritual existence. Why should they bear such names and what was the nature of their fruit? Furthermore, according to Scripture, four rivers flowed from a single source within Eden itself (Genesis 2.10–14). Two are easily identified: the Tigris (Hebrew *Hiddekel*) runs along the east side of Assyria, while the Euphrates (Hebrew *Prat*) is the river on which Babylon was built. Both the Tigris and the Euphrates rise somewhere in Armenia and flow through Mesopotamia into the Persian Gulf. The other two rivers, the Pison and the Gihon, however, have never been satisfactorily identified, making any precise geographical location of Eden hypothetical, despite many efforts in Late Antiquity and the Middle Ages to unravel their etymology or identify them with known rivers. The most common interpretation identified the Gihon with the Nile and the Pison with the Ganges.[7] But where on earth is their common spring to be found?

Such questions, generated by the text of the Bible, have preoccupied theologians and exegetes since the texts were first penned. For the purposes of this essay, the import of centuries of controversy and consequent mountains of codices and books can be summarized in three key notions relevant to the cartography of Paradise and accepted in medieval orthodoxy.[8]

The first is the notion that Paradise was a real place on earth. Authorities like the Venerable Bede envisaged Paradise as a straightforward geographical feature: 'There is not any doubt that the place was and is on earth.'[9] Moreover, as many Church Fathers insisted, the Garden of Eden was not a normal place but a divine land, somehow distinguished from heaven itself by its terrestrial location. Second, therefore, is the notion that the Garden of Eden was an intermediate region, something between heaven and earth, a characteristic which makes the relationship between the Earthly Paradise and the inhabited world an ambiguous one. The third notion springs from this duality and attempts to explain a relationship which is at once one of separation and connection. The Earthly Paradise is regarded as beyond the reach of mankind, situated on an inaccessible mountain peak, for instance, or located beyond an impassable ocean. At the same time, it is not entirely disconnected from our world, since the four rivers flow out from the Garden to water the world, and indeed to make life on earth physically possible.

While generations of theologians spilt rivers of ink in their attempts to penetrate the mystery of a Paradise on earth, the map-makers translated theological monochrome into the spectrum of their own visual language. As an exercise of translation, however – from abstract to concrete, from ears to eyes – a map could clarify what was difficult to grasp from the text alone. Visual imagery offered perhaps direct experience of a place and a condition which had always been described as indescribable. In many spiritual traditions direct experience and vision, as opposed to syllogistic reasoning and common sense, are seen as the sole basis of knowing. The visual perception of Paradise by means of a map could thus be taken to be an experience of reality, based as it was on the acceptance of divine revelation and a silencing of the rational mind. In accepting the cartographic paradox of putting Eden on a map of the world, the map-maker was both allowing people to 'see' Paradise and thereby offering direct evidence of scriptural revelation, thus assisting their entry into Paradise itself.

In their commentaries on Genesis and in their lyrics, biblical exegetes and poets have both emphasized the inaccuracy and incompleteness of their descriptions of the Earthly Paradise. For them, 'the map was not the territory'.[10] Their conceptual maps could not fully grasp a reality which transcended human perception. A similar problem was faced by the cartographer who tried to picture the world beyond his own frame of reference. For the latter, however, the map *could* change the territory. By the very act of construction and the implicit recognition of a frame of reference outside the human realm, the cartography of Paradise changed the reality of the world: it incorporated Eden. After all, depiction changes the phenomenon depicted. It can make real something previously unreal. Today physicists penetrate deeper realms of nature only through chains of processes which transform the object of their observation. Modern theories of cartographic communication also acknowledge the agency of cartographic survey and map-making in the real landscape, through the inscription of national boundaries, for instance. Thus, the depiction of Paradise on maps, based upon divine revelation, made the mystery in all its paradoxical nature accessible to the senses. The Garden of Eden became an accepted location of an equal cartographic value to places such as Jerusalem or Rome, measurably distant from the viewer's home town or city. What was previously seen only in the imagination was now visible to the eye; place becomes bound to human experience because the map makes it visible.

MAPPING PARADISE IS A CARTOGRAPHIC PARADOX

Medieval maps show Adam and Eve in the Garden of Eden at a particular moment in time, often that of their Fall. Many versions of the map which illustrated Beatus of Seville's eighth-century *Commentary on the Apocalypse of Saint John* show Adam and Eve covering their shame with

Giovanni Leardo, *Mapa Mondi/Figura Mondi*, 1442.

fig leaves.[11] While the world outside the Garden of Eden suffers the im-
perfections of history, Paradise enjoys a perpetual present: indeed, in the
moment that something 'historical' occurs, such as the disobedience of
our first parents, Paradise disappears. In other words, the Fall is a temporal
and historical barrier beyond which lies a timeless zone. Interestingly, we
are never shown on maps the internal geographical space of Paradise. The
fifteenth-century Leardo map, for instance, hides the landscape of
Paradise behind the fortifications of an impregnable city.[12] Both theologians' texts and map-makers' graphics have consistently emphasized the
impossibility of penetrating the Edenic space.

Nevertheless, the main point of medieval orthodoxy was that the
Garden of Eden was characterized by both time (Adam and Eve experienced life in bliss for a temporal period) and space (it was a material place,
with the trees of life and knowledge and the four rivers). Yet in medieval
manifestations of Paradise, the categories of time and space seem to be
altered. Many medieval legends declare that, while a fortunate pilgrim
experienced Paradise for only a brief instant or a few hours, in the outside
human world many decades or several generations had elapsed. One
fourteenth-century Italian legend relates how three monks, following a
stream, arrived at the Earthly Paradise. They were admitted by a guardian
angel and introduced by Enoch and Elijah to the splendour of the garden.
When the monks asked to be allowed to stay a fortnight, they were told
that they had already been there several hundred years![13] In this liminal
space, time too has a different pace.

Space too becomes relative. A variety of obstacles prevents access to Eden, and it cannot be located or measured precisely. For centuries, theologians sought to make sense of its sacred landscape, yet nobody knew what Paradise looked like. Lacking textual or doctrinal guidance, artists and map-makers were left to depict only a vague countryside, lacking any spatial configuration. According to the Bible, both the tree of knowledge and the tree of life were at the centre of the garden (Genesis 2.9), but how could two trees occupy the same point?

It is helpful in this context to adopt the concepts of *microspace* and *macrospace*:[14] the *microspace* is the empirical known world around us, while the *macrospace* is a cosmological category. We have a good idea of spatial order in our microspace (which includes areas that we think of as being empirically known, even if we have not been there personally), but we have no idea of what life is like in the macrospatial context (for example, the planets in a distant galaxy). As Harrison writes, 'it must be kept in mind that, although macrospatial conceptions often belong to the realm of fantasy and mythology, the actual images of places within macrospace may often be founded on (and thus resemble) well-known microspatial reality'.[15] The Earthly Paradise belongs to an alternative universe somewhere in macrospace but superimposed on microspace. The image of Eden, with trees and rivers, is founded on both literary memories from Scripture and 'microspatial' familiarity with gardens. Still, it remains a fiction, belonging to an alternative universe somewhere in macrospace, having nothing to do with everyday geography. Paradise was a far-away region in macrospace which, even for the most learned men in the Middle Ages, was just as unreachable as if it had been located in a remote galaxy.[16] This is why there are no detailed topographical or chorographical maps of Eden from any period. There may be paintings which define distinct spaces within Eden; for example, the location of the Tree of Knowledge, the quartering of the four rivers, the abundance of peaceable fauna, etc. But this is an intelligible space made visible by the artist, not a sensible geography. Eden is a spatial region fundamentally different from the 'normal' space. In fact, Scripture does not describe the internal geography of Paradise, apart from those two trees in the middle of the garden and the four rivers. There is not an established, 'mappable' space within Eden, and attempts to sketch a spatial structure of Paradise result in a mythical and contradictory geography.[17] In the concept of Paradise itself there is no geography, or, better, there is a different kind of geography. The geographical question about Paradise is: 'where is it?', not 'how are its internal spaces organized?'

A space which had to be shown on maps as finite and limited was in fact a world in itself, a boundless universe paradoxically encapsulated and bounded within a sensible space. In such a context, mapping the location of Paradise and charting its ontologically different time and space on a world map, presents a fascinating cartographic paradox: mapping a place on earth but not of earth.[18]

MAPPING PARADISE IS TO DRAW A CRUCIAL BOUNDARY

In many ancient cosmologies there is a link between creation and separation. In Judeo-Christianity, the creation of the world by God involves differentiating earthly things from the divine. But while separateness seems a fundamental ingredient of being human, the separated elements strive to regain their initial communion with their creator. Like the Creation itself, mapping is an activity of separation and, thus, making. Boundaries are non-existent until made visible, in some way, on a map, if not on the ground. At the same time, differentiating space also means connecting it: any border, however impassable, has two sides.

The boundary *par excellence* is the one that separates humankind from Paradise, a frontier once believed to be guarded by the flaming sword of the Cherubim (Genesis 3.24). The mapping of the Earthly Paradise is also the drawing of that crucial boundary between the post-lapsarian world and the state of perfection before the Fall. It can also be considered as an attempt to reinscribe celestial order on earth's surface and establish a material connection between the divine and human realms. The river which waters the Garden of Eden and exits from it, immediately separating into four streams, represents exactly this role of the border of Paradise in signifying both separation and connection simultaneously.

On maps, the boundary outlining the Earthly Paradise marks also the duality of the Christian attitude towards life on earth. On the one hand, it marks the perfect nature we have lost, the only place where humanity could experience perfection, thus generating a sense of exile into a vale of tears. On the other hand, the mapped Paradise's shared border with other earthly regions sanctifies the physical world and historical human life by indicating the compatibility of human existence with the paradisiacal condition. A map showing Paradise on earth identified the Garden of Eden as described in the Book of Genesis, with its trees of life and knowledge and its four rivers, as a physical place. At the same time, the scene of the Fall defined the temporal line between Eden and the historical world. Human history begins with the Fall, and the thickness of the border as an index of the shift from a perfect to a post-lapsarian state acts as a measure of distance. The more its gravity is emphasized, the wider is the gap between the human and the divine realms.

Placing Paradise on a world map, however, implies a literal reading of the biblical account, meaning that time and space – as well as matter and sexuality, since Adam and Eve had physical bodies in Eden – belonged to a state of perfection. If 'mapping' means to outline, to contour, to frame, in order to disclose the order of reality beyond surface appearance,[19] the literal reading of the biblical account may be considered *ab initio* as a cartographic act. All that is required is to draw the correct boundaries between human perfection and the divine, between heaven and earth, between Eden and the *oecumene*. The critical point in mapping the spatial and the temporal border between Eden and geographic space was the paradox of the relationship between God and nature. Any barrier separating earth from Paradise had to be understood as both division and connection. Paradoxically, the spatial continuum – the link between incommensurate worlds – took the form not of a bridge but of the four rivers of Eden.

PARADISE AS A SPACE–TIME BOUNDARY ZONE

Boundaries are drawn in dimensions of both space and time. A historian puts boundaries across temporal continua, defining different historical ages or periods – the fall of the Roman Empire, the discovery of America, the Congress of Vienna. Here too, to separate is to create: events become significant within the framework of a periodized history even though time itself is a continuum. While historians debate the niceties of each historical boundary, for theologians the Earthly Paradise represents the even more controversial and paradoxical frontier between eternity and time. When did time begin? The very notion of 'beginning' implies the prior existence of time, and the human mind cannot adequately imagine how duration sprang from infinity. The greatest mind of the medieval Latin West, Augustine, strove to resolve this mystery and forged the complex idea of a 'simultaneous creation'.[20] It is a logical absurdity to draw the boundaries of time *within* time.

The line contouring the Earthly Paradise on maps encompasses the mystery of the origin of both space and time since, according to medieval orthodoxy, both existed in Eden. Eden itself thus constitutes a sort of boundary-zone: here space originates and now time begins. Just as many international frontiers were originally zones of transmontane communication rather than clear-cut lines of sharp division, so Paradise seems to constitute a permeable boundary-zone, a place where human space and time mix with divine infinity and eternity. Seen this way, Paradise is itself a boundary.

The Latin for boundary is *fines*, meaning not only 'border' but also 'extremity' and 'region', a space which is defined by its margins. A boundary defines not only the end of a space or the edges of a place, but also the essence and properties of that space or place. The periphery is thus intimately connected to its centre. Centrality and liminality are not opposite concepts but two parts of the same structure.[21] The same may be said about Paradise, which is placed on maps at the edge of the world and yet also superimposed on its centre, the place of the Incarnation of Christ, Jerusalem. *Fines* has also a temporal meaning, indicating the finish of something and, at the same time, its peak, its perfection, its realization. Thus the cartographic border of Paradise defines the limit, essence or full realization of the human realm, a line beyond which lies another time and another space. Paradise was not an ordinary region of the earth; rather, the earth was orientated by reference to Paradise.

Boundaries are also related to the notion of property. Maps have served in territorial disputes at every level, from estate to international scale. It would be tempting to suggest that in superimposing the concept of a space–time boundary-zone over the whole earth, the border of Paradise divides human and divine territories – Earthly Paradise (God's property) from the inhabited world (the sphere of Adam's progeny). However, we must recognize that the Garden of Eden was a place for Creator and creature together, a place fit for humans in communion with God, and that the entire world this side of the Edenic border is also God's property. A strange continuity is marked by a border which is at once a barrier and a portal.[22]

PARADISE AS BOTH INTERNAL AND EXTERNAL REALITY

One of the theological problems in the Christian interpretation of the description of the Garden of Eden in Genesis concerns the Expulsion of Adam and Eve from Paradise. How can Christians overcome the gap separating them from Eden? Regaining Paradise – crossing the border – cannot be achieved through human effort alone, it requires God's help. Bede, whose commentary on Genesis established a paradigm which continued to determine medieval exegesis on this topic long after his death in 735, suggested that a return to the original state of grace could be obtained through baptism and that the four rivers of the Garden of Eden were the ultimate baptismal waters.[23] A similar interpretation was often portrayed in art. In the twelfth-century apsidal mosaic in the church of

San Clemente in Rome, for example, the four rivers of Paradise are shown flowing beneath the cross of Christ, while two harts – representing the human soul as it pants after the living God (Psalm 42) – drink from them. Reassuringly, Bede points out that it does not matter if we remain ignorant of the precise course of the rivers or even of the exact location of Paradise, for the rivers flow from Paradise to sanctify only those chosen by God in ways unknown to man, and will thus reach the chosen.

In the Earthly Paradise, external and internal realities seem to be joined. For the early Church Fathers and later medieval exegetes alike, Paradise was both a spiritual reality and a material fact. Following Augustine, Strabo and Isidore, the *Glossa ordinaria*, the standard medieval commentary on the Bible, explained why the flaming sword that bars the way to Paradise was described as 'removable' (Genesis 3.24):[24] access to the closed Paradise is possible through the cross of Christ, the new tree of life.[25] Geographical space thus became an image for a spiritual journey, one which moreover involved transgressing the border. Metaphorically, the journey meant an inner change, by which men and women may find Paradise in themselves. Geographical space may be crossed simply by the unfolding of time. In this sense, Paradise is at once absent and present, and a point of transition. Situated in this world, it nevertheless belongs to a different dimension; its presence on maps is thus only a footprint, a physical expression of absence.

For an example of the difficulty of talking about an Earthly Paradise which was located both in geographical space and within human spirituality, we can turn to the Late Antique *Hymns on Paradise* by Ephrem Syrus (*fl.* fourth century). According to Ephrem, the Garden of Eden, although an earthly mountain, rises above and surrounds the physical world. It is a high mountain, and 'the summit of every mountain is lower than its summit'.[26] This mountain-island is circular and surrounds the Ocean, the 'Great Sea', which itself circumferences the earth. In this way, Paradise encircles both land and sea. Ephrem claimed to have seen the high mountain of Paradise 'with the eye of the mind',[27] and that Paradise surrounds the whole of creation as the halo of light surrounds the moon. At the same time, to enter Paradise is to enter an inner sanctuary: Paradise is compared to the Holy of Holies, the most hidden part of the Temple.[28]

How might one depict on a map a region which is earthly yet not part of the everyday world, one which is simultaneously at the summit, the periphery and the centre of the universe? Artists and map-makers found ways of portraying all three situations. In Giovanni di Paolo's painting *The Creation of the World and the Expulsion from the Earthly Paradise*

(1445), Paradise was shown at the centre of the universe which occupied
the left side of the canvas, at the very summit of a mountain, stretching
upwards towards heaven. Much earlier, in the sixth century, Cosmas
Indicopleustes had depicted Paradise as the periphery of the world, where
the Ocean surrounds the earth and in its turn is surrounded by Paradise.
Finally, in the version of Beatus of Liebana's map now in Osma (probably
eleventh century), we see the four rivers of Paradise flowing out from a
single, central source to re-emerge on the surface of the earth.[29]

PARADISE ON MAPS

In representing the geography of Paradise, medieval map-makers always
emphasized the *passage* to a dimension different from the time and space
of ordinary human experience. A survey of the iconography of Paradise
on surviving maps dating from the sixth to the end of the fifteenth century
reveals a common and perennial element in the cartography of Paradise:
the use of a visual device to express the duality of relationships between
the Garden of Eden and the known world, their separation and connection. The artist responsible for the extant thirteenth-century Psalter map
(a much-reduced version of something a little older), chose to show the
four rivers of Eden as flowing over the earth, but indicated the separateness of Paradise as a totality by placing it in a vignette, an inset with its
own level of reality, apart and different from ordinary life.[30]

The separation of Paradise was indicated on maps in various ways. It
could be portrayed as an island in the ocean, right on the very edge of the
habitable world, as on the thirteenth-century Hereford *mappamundi*,
where the island is also, for good measure, walled. Within the wall, the
door is firmly closed.[31] Or it could be represented as a garden within the
habitable world but insulated from it by some sort of daunting barrier –
for example, a wall of fire, as on the fourteenth-century world map in
the *Grandes chroniques de Saint Denis du temps de Charles V*, kept in the
library of Sainte-Geneviève, in Paris.[32] On the Borgia map of the world,
made in the fifteenth century and kept in the Vatican Library, the Earthly
Paradise is separated from the rest of the world by a high mountain
chain.[33] Paradise is located in the world but its barriers cannot be
breached. Other ways too were found to express the isolation of the
Earthly Paradise. In the fifteenth century both Andreas Walsperger
(1448)[34] and Hanns Rüst (*c.* 1490)[35] portrayed a fortified castle within the
habitable world, as did, in the same century, the makers of the woodcut
map in the *Rudimentum novitiorum* (1475)[36] and the Leardo map.[37]
Cosmas Indicopleustes, as we have seen, positioned Paradise outside the

Psalter map, *c*.1265.

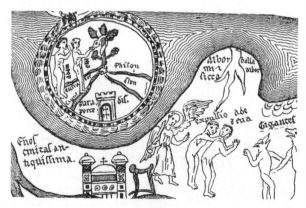

Richard (of Haldingham or of Sleaford), detail showing the Earthly Paradise,
from the Hereford Cathedral map, *c*. 1285.

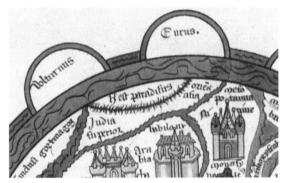

Detail showing the Earthly Paradise from a world map, from *Grandes chroniques de Saint Denis du temps de Charles V* (*c.* 1370).

Hanns Rüst, detail showing the Earthly Paradise from a world map, *c.* 1490, woodcut.

Fra Mauro, detail showing the Earthly Paradise from a world map, 1459.

habitable world, as did Fra Mauro (to whom we shall return below) in the mid-fifteenth century. Whatever visual device was used to indicate the separateness of the Earthly Paradise, care was always taken too to show the connection with our own world. This connectivity could be expressed through the portrayal of the four rivers or by the contiguity of Paradise with the outer Ocean.

PARADISE FOUND: MEDIEVAL *MAPPAEMUNDI*

All the maps so far mentioned are of the same type: namely *mappae-mundi*. This is not accidental. Paradise is shown on no other kind of map in the Middle Ages, and I believe that no other type of map either could deal with the cartographic paradox of mapping Paradise or would have provided an appropriate context for its depiction. Maps drawn for practical purposes or in order to chart a secular geography did not describe the Earthly Paradise, nor had any need to. We do not find the Garden of Eden, for example, on any thirteenth-century portolan chart. Adopting again the concepts of *microspace* and *macrospace*, we may say that the *mappae-mundi* mirrored macrospatial thinking, whereas the portolan charts and the local and regional maps had a practical purpose outside the realm of religion and mythology and reflected microspatial thinking.[38]

The *mappamundi*, it has been well established, was essentially a cartographic encyclopaedia. Its function was to provide a visual synthesis of contemporary knowledge. The makers of *mappaemundi* used texts and images to frame and display Christian history and belief in a geographical setting. As Paul Harvey, David Woodward and Evelyn Edson have all pointed out, geographical exactitude was not the main objective of these maps and it is inappropriate to compare them with later, geometrically precise, map-types.[39] Specifically, David Woodward has remarked on the capacity of medieval *mappaemundi* to combine concepts of both time and space, and has shown how historical events were projected on to a geographical framework. Evelyn Edson has studied the context in which the map-makers produced their work, demonstrating that their world picture incorporated a history of human spiritual development. The space represented on these maps, in other words, was not intended to be cosynchronous but was used to show several events separated by time in the same way as a medieval narrative painting.

A widespread but long-outdated cliché has characterized the Middle Ages as a period of superstition and naïveté: 'they even put monsters and Paradise on maps . . .' Medieval cartography should not, however, be underestimated. However picturesque *mappaemundi* may seem, they cannot be dismissed as devoid of scientific accuracy. On the contrary, the medieval map-maker seems to have been deeply aware of the fact that, if mapping is to express spatial relationships, geographical space cannot exist without time – a sophisticated recognition, and one that is perfectly consistent with the most recent discoveries of modern physics which confirm that space and time are intimately and inseparably connected in a four-dimensional continuum. Most people today are familiar rather with maps which represent a static picture of the earth at a given moment in time. Maps, however, may also consist of records of the events which occurred in that space. By representing a many-layered gathering of historical events as well as points in the geographical space of the world, the medieval *mappamundi* demonstrates a strong intuition for the 'space–time' character of reality.

The *mappamundi*, designed to accommodate space and time within a sort of 'relativistic' framework, offered the perfect answer to the cartographic paradox of showing Paradise on a map of the world. On a *mappamundi*, all measurements involving space and time lose their absolute significance, and the world of everyday life is transcended in a vision of a multi-dimensional reality. We can see this clearly, for example, in the Ebstorf map (*c.* 1239).[40] There are plenty of geographical elements, towns such as Jerusalem, mountains such as the Alps, rivers such as the Po and the Nile. In fact, in the upper right-hand corner of the map, the map-maker makes clear that his work intends to provide guidance for travellers.[41] But there are also scenes from the Bible and ancient history. The burial places of some of the apostles are illustrated, and so are episodes from the myths of Alexander the Great, such as Gog and Magog, confined by the Macedonian, eating human flesh and drinking blood.[42] The map – indeed, the whole world and all space and time – is spanned by a gigantic Christ, with his head in the East, his feet in the West and his arms outstretched along the equator. Not surprisingly, we also find in such a powerful Christian icon a portrayal of the Garden of Eden, shown in the East, close to the head of the Saviour.

We can return to the Psalter map for another example of the way *mappaemundi* should be read simultaneously for both the earthly geography and the spiritual history of the Christian world. The reading takes us through space – from East to West and North to South – and through time – from the Creation to the final triumph of Christ, shown on the Psalter map by the Garden of Eden and the figure of Jesus at the top, flanked by two angels and holding a tripartite orb in his left hand. Again, we see the appropriateness of the representation of Paradise on the Psalter map. A double ring signifies its separateness from the ordinary world, while the four rivers signify its connectedness with earth. Only a map with a frame of reference which goes beyond the human environment and which shows more than secular, Euclidean space – in other words, a four-dimensional map – can show the Garden of Eden or Earthly Paradise.

PARADISE LOST: C. 1500

No medieval scholar pretended to know exactly 'where' Paradise was located. It was sufficient to know that it existed 'somewhere' on earth. It was not difficult to explain, for example, how four rivers as widely separated as the Tigris, Euphrates, Ganges and Nile could have a single source in the Garden of Eden, by suggesting that they travelled underground from a single spring in Paradise before emerging separately into the world.[43] Geography, though, like history, was supposed to confirm the truth of the Bible, and what to the medieval mind was acceptable as a religious mystery was destined, by the sixteenth century, to become a geographical and a rational problem.

Already, in the later Middle Ages, there were questions about the location of the Earthly Paradise, usually, but not consistently, placed in the East. At the same time, this 'East of Eden' was a nowhere. Any attempt, however attractive, to shift the 'Paradise question' onto a purely rational and physical plane – and to identify Paradise with a recognizable geographical location – was destined to fail. The turning point in the history of the Garden of Eden on maps occurred between the fifteenth and the sixteenth centuries. Turn the pages of any collection of printed world maps (for example, *The Mapping of the World* by Rodney Shirley)[44] and one searches in vain on Renaissance world maps for the Earthly Paradise. No Garden of Eden is shown on the world map in Benedetto Bordone's *Isolario* (1528).[45] Sebastian Münster shows no Paradise on the map of the world (1532) decorated by Holbein.[46] What had happened?

Several factors combined to bring about the disappearance of the Garden of Eden from world maps by about 1500. One was the reversal of the trend in theological thinking, which peaked in the twelfth and thirteenth centuries, to interpret the religious mystery of Paradise in terms of rational geography. Fifteenth-century scholastics, although still glossing the traditional views of Peter Lombard and Thomas Aquinas, began to relativize the location of Eden. Gabriel Biel, a German scholastic philosopher, for instance, pointed out that 'east' was a relative notion which depended on the position of the observer, an idea already put forward in the fourteenth century by John Duns Scotus.[47] Another factor sharpening the difficulty of locating the Garden of Eden in the fourteenth and the fifteenth centuries was the increasing number of reports from travellers returning from the East which consistently failed to confirm the material existence of an Earthly Paradise in eastern Asia. A third factor was the rediscovery, in the fifteenth century, of Ptolemy's *Geographia*, with its strictly mathematical approach to the description of the earth's surface.[48]

As a system of coordinates began to appear on world maps during the fifteenth century,[49] the position of Paradise on *mappaemundi* – indeed, the *mappamundi* itself as a genre – began to destabilize. Solutions to the problem of locating the Garden of Eden were offered, including three cartographic solutions. Paradise could continue to be located, as traditionally, in the East. We see this on the Leardo map[50] and other fifteenth-century *mappaemundi* such as the Walsperger (1448)[51] and the map in the *Rudimentum novitiorum* (1475).[52] Alternatively (and with some biblical justification), Paradise could be located in the South. The makers of the Catalan map (*c.* 1450–60)[53] accordingly removed the Garden of Eden from Asia and placed it in Africa, as did Giovanni di Paolo (1445)[54] and Albertin de Virga (*c.* 1411–15).[55] A third option was simply to ignore the question of the location of Paradise. Thus there was no attempt by the Church to 'convert' or Christianize any world map that was being drawn or copied during the fifteenth century for Ptolemy's *Geographia*.

The transition between medieval and Renaissance ways of dealing with the cartographic paradox of Paradise was delicately handled by Fra Mauro (1459).[56] Mauro's *mappamundi* synthesizes European knowledge about the world on the eve of the great discoveries. In it are amalgamated different conceptual frameworks and ideas, drawn from a wide variety of sources, including Ptolemy's *Geographia*, portolan charts, Arabic documents and various travel narratives. His map clearly reveals the shift in process from multi-dimensional medieval mapping towards a modern cartography which is mainly interested in representing measurable space. The map of the earth represents only the inhabited world, in which there is no place for Eden. The Earthly Paradise is relegated, despite its prominence, to one of the eastern corners of the map. It is shown as a circular garden located outside the *oecumene*. At the same time, Mauro adheres closely to tradition in showing that the otherwise inaccessible garden is connected to human reality by the four rivers, the source of all life, which he shows flowing out from the garden to water the whole world. A detailed text on the map refers to the authority of Augustine, Bede and Peter Lombard and offers a summary of theological and geographical debate on the topic. Mauro explains that the Garden of Eden was a real place somewhere in the East, although 'very far from our habitable world and remote from our knowledge'.[57] On Mauro's map, the presence of the Ocean, surrounding both Paradise and the whole earth, together with the four rivers, confirms the earthly existence of the Garden of Eden even if is located in an inaccessible, eastern 'nowhere'.

Fra Mauro's map is still a *mappamundi*, but it is certainly very different from the Ebstorf, the Hereford or the Psalter *mappaemundi*. Simultaneously monastic, nautical and Ptolemaic, Mauro's map presents both the characteristically medieval circular framework and also a number of early Renaissance characteristics, such as its southern orientation (an Arabic influence) and its accurately delineated Mediterranean coastline (taken from portolan charts). Above all, however, this outstanding achievement of later medieval cartography demonstrates a clear tendency towards modern ways of mapping secular contemporary geography.

CONCLUSION

The decline of the *mappaemundi* brought about the decline and fall of the Garden of Eden from maps of the world. Without the *mappaemundi*, Paradise would never have reached a world map. It is absent from the Anglo-Saxon map, for instance, a map of the world in the secular tradition of classical Roman world geography.[58] In their turn, Renaissance maps presented a quite different frame of reference for world geography from the *mappaemundi*. They broke with the tradition of presenting a multi-dimensional image of the world. The European encounter with a new continent made each new map assume a historical and almost accidental dimension, always liable to modification in the light of new geographical discovery.[59] In thus becoming historical objects, maps now excluded any concept of time from within their spaces of representation. They could no longer claim to constitute a comprehensive space–time image of the cosmos, but only to mirror the surface of the earth at a moment in time. The development of a systematic system of coordinates legitimized the inclusion on maps of cosynchronous features only. Space itself became homogeneous, ordered by a geometrical grid; no one point in the map was more important than any other. Cartography would henceforth be concerned only with quantity, based exclusively on measurement.[60]

With quantification, and by asserting the concept of an absolute space, mapping from 1500 certainly gained increasing precision over the whole span of time as well as the whole of earthly space. The price, however, was the loss of the timeless vision offered by the medieval *mappamundi*; mapping's horizon was reduced to three-dimensional Euclidean space and

limited to our ordinary experience of the physical world. On such maps
there was no room for illustrating religious mysteries which would
increasingly be seen as mere decoration. On a map ruled by measurable
coordinates and which treated the universe as transfixed at a certain
moment, there was no room for the ahistorical reality of an Earthly
Paradise, lacking a precise, 'scientific' location.

The loss of Paradise from world maps was no insignificant cartographic omission. It represents a major shift in thought as well as in mapping.[61] The space–time vision of medieval times was broken. And change
in the way Paradise was represented by cartographers coincided also with
a crucial turning point in theological history. While a few scholastic theologians maintained the view that Paradise still existed on earth, the
majority of exegetes came to agree that Paradise had disappeared from
the face of the world at the time of the Flood. This was, for example,
Martin Luther's view in the early sixteenth century.[62]

Imminent changes in mapping and in theological and philosophical
thinking, however, did not mean that around 1500 the Garden of Eden
was not widely believed to exist. For some, discoveries in the Atlantic
reinforced their belief in the Earthly Paradise. It is well known that
Christopher Columbus, touching South America on his third voyage,
thought he had reached the vicinity of the Earthly Paradise:

> I believe that this water may originate from there, though it be far away and may
> come to collect there where I came and may form this lake. These are great indi-
> cations of the earthly paradise, for the situation agrees with the opinion of those
> holy and wise theologians, and also the signs are very much in accord with this
> idea, for I have never read or heard of so great a quantity of fresh water so com-
> ing into and near the salt. And the very mild climate also supports this view . . .[63]

In the event, geographical discoveries disclosed new lands but no biblical Paradise, either in the New World, India, Ceylon, Ethiopia, China or
Japan. The desire to preserve the integrity of a literal and historical explanation of the Garden of Eden as described in Genesis – and thus to support
the authority of Scripture – led Bible commentators to look instead to the
past. Thus, the mysterious region was distanced to the beginning of time.
This change, from Paradise present to Paradise past, is itself mirrored in
maps. Once the notion of a geography inextricably linked to the whole
space–time structure was lost, together with the multi-dimensional mapping of the Christian Middle Ages, the Earthly Paradise was retained only
on explicitly *historical* regional maps. From 1500 onwards, Paradise is
depicted not on maps of the world but on regional maps drawn for the
purpose of biblical exegesis and as reader's aids in printed Bibles.[64]

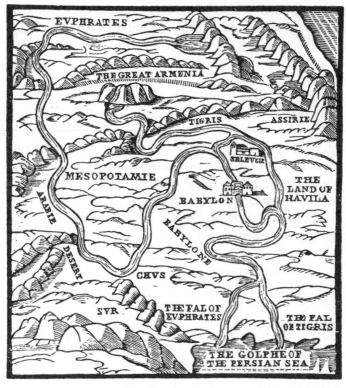

Map of Eden, from T. Tymme's English translation of Calvin's
commentary on Genesis (London, 1578).

The transfer of Eden to regional and historical mapping started with
the Lutheran Bibles of the early sixteenth century and was continued in
the Calvinistic Genevan Bibles from the 1550s. The map from Tymme's
English translation of John Calvin's commentary on Genesis, published
in London in 1578, illustrates Calvin's discussion of the location of the
Earthly Paradise.[65] Note that only the Land of Havilah is marked. Calvin
in fact had no wish to be more precise about the exact site of the Garden
of Eden in Mesopotamia, a geographically well-known region. In his
view, the question of Eden's precise location was not the essential point;
that paled before the events with which it was associated. Increasingly, the
location of Paradise on earth was treated as a purely historical problem,
not as part of the present world.[66] Eden retreated to its origins, as in a
map from John Hopkinson's *Synopsis Paradisi* (1593)[67] or Bishop Pierre-
Daniel Huet's map in the *Treatise of the Situation of the Terrestrial
Paradise* (1691).[68]

Boundaries change. The medieval attitude to the wholeness of human knowledge did not distinguish between cosmographical, philosophical, theological, mythological, historical or geographical knowledge. The legacy of post-Renaissance scientific representation of the world was a separation of Sacred Scripture into its own branch of knowledge. Paradise was mapped only by those interested in constructing its archaeology. The disappearance of the Earthly Paradise from world maps around 1500 represents changes far more profound than mere cartographic tidying up or updating. It points to the shift from medieval to modern thinking, from a holistic to a fragmented view of reality, from a mapping which sought to penetrate the mystery of the whole universe beyond human boundaries to a mapping which is contained strictly within the frameworks of analytical thought and Euclidean geometry, and from cosmography to geography.

3

Terrestrial Globalism: Mapping the Globe in Early Modern Europe

JERRY BROTTON

One particularly telling dimension of recent interest in the social dynamics of globalization has been the reduction of the *image* of the globe itself to what Benedict Anderson has called 'logoization'.[1] The image of the globe becomes the naturalized sign through which discussions of the economic, political and cultural processes of globalism are defined. At the point at which globalism becomes central to contemporary cultural politics, its geographical referent, the image of the terrestrial globe, becomes a residual signifier. The discourse of globalization has been able to chart its development, across the surface of the terrestrial globe, yet this globe is an increasingly inadequate form in representing the rapid and complex transfer of information across its surface. As David Harvey has argued in his highly influential study *The Condition of Postmodernity* (1990), the compression of apprehensions of both time and space has been a defining feature of contemporary postmodern global culture:

As space appears to shrink to a 'global village' of telecommunications and a 'spaceship earth' of economic and ecological interdependencies – to use just two familiar and everyday images – and as time horizons shorten to the point where the present is all there is (the world of the schizophrenic), so we have to learn how to cope with an overwhelming sense of compression of our spatial and temporal worlds.[2]

Harvey uses a simple illustration to emphasize his point, a 'shrinking map of the world through innovations in transport which "annihilate space through time"'.[3] Harvey's circular world map becomes progressively smaller from 1500 onwards, but its shape and contours remain the same. The consequences of this time–space compression not only produce a shrinking of the dimensions of the *terrestrial* globe, they also lead to a reduction of its effectiveness in encompassing the movement of space and passage of time across its surface. I want to suggest that the notion of the terrestrial globe is being rendered residual at precisely the point at which the movement of knowledge and information within what Arjun

Appadurai calls 'the global cultural economy'⁴ becomes *extra*-terrestrial. The terrestrial globe can no longer represent the invisible flow of information technology across its surface. As Michael J. Shapiro has argued, 'global geographies are in flux',⁵ not only at the level of the social and the impact of trans-nationality, but also at the level of representation. What seems to be occurring is a transformation of traditional ways of envisaging the globe and globalization, which makes the appearance of the terrestrial globe increasingly redundant. But to understand this transformation I want to suggest that it is necessary to revisit that other transitional moment in the history of modernity, the early modern period, as the site of the emergence of the image of the terrestrial globe as a socially affective object, to grasp the significance of the current waning of the image of the terrestrial globe under the sign of globalism.

Recent critical attempts to define the nature of globalism in relation to the revolution in information technology question the sustainability of traditional models of geographical representation. Paul Virilio, in his book *The Lost Dimension* (1984), argues that the technological shifts which have taken place in recent decades have led to a revolution in the perception and apprehension of terrestrial space itself. Adumbrating Harvey's discussion of what Virilio terms 'the abolition of distances in time by various means of communications and telecommunications',⁶ Virilio argues:

The communal perception of sensible space was a formation based since Antiquity on the mnemotechnic merits of Euclidean geometry, a geometry of regular plane surfaces regulated by a system of dimensions that dissects a universe in which the measure of superficies dominated the geographic, the urban and rural cadastral, and the architectonic partitioning of constructed elements. Today, on the other hand, the world-view based on orthogonal orthodoxy has given way to a new perception, in which the very concept of physical dimension has progressively lost its meaning and analytical power as a form of dissecting or dismounting perceptive reality. Instead, we find other, electronic means of evaluating space and time, ones which share no common ground with the measuring systems of the past.⁷

For Virilio, the speed of postmodern forms of global electronic communication and information technology undermines the effectiveness with which Euclidean geometry offers a comprehensive understanding and affective visual perception of the theoretical and practical space of the environment which it purports to describe. Expanding on Virilio's arguments, Appadurai has argued for the need to incorporate new ways of apprehending time, space and movement, suggesting that, 'we begin to think of the configuration of cultural forms in today's world as funda-

mentally fractal, that is, as possessing no Euclidean boundaries, structures or regularities'.[8] Whilst Appadurai's argument is not directly concerned with geographical representations of globalism as such, it is
significant that at the point at which he attempts to explain the importance of the concept of globalism in cultural and economic terms, he
should call for the abolition of the founding theoretical development
which allowed for the geographical projection of the globe – namely
Euclidean geometry. Arguably it is this critical development which has led
to the powerful metaphor of 'globalism' within critical theory today, a
metaphor which is increasingly distanced from its referential portrayal of
the terrestrial globe. At the point at which criticism invokes the metaphor
of the globe, its geographical image disappears. The global image which
it represents is at the same time the referent as well as the ultimate point of
departure for the disclosure of the movement of information technology
across the terrestrial globe. The projection of a global image contains no
traces of the impact of the movement of information across its surface;
such information moves instantly and silently, often conducted above the
earth's surface via satellite. The image of the globe is therefore an arresting
symbol, establishing claims to the infinite and truly 'global' accessibility
and reach of information technology, as well as becoming an increasingly
defunct ground across which such information travels. In fact the very
notion of 'travel' becomes an inadequate concept to describe this global
flow of information, as its instantaneous transmission defies standard
perceptions of the temporal and physical expenditure required to travel
across great distances.

This critical development begs the question of what status the global
image itself retains if its very spatial dimensions have collapsed as a result
of the impact of new forms of information technology. If the image of the
globe has suffered what Fredric Jameson might call a 'waning of affect',[9]
then, as Appadurai asks, is it possible, or even advisable, to 'map' the
impact of globalism upon contemporary cultures? What is also of interest to me here is the historical question which such debates fail to address;
if the deployment of the global image is increasingly unable adequately to
reflect the developments of information technology towards the end of
the twentieth century, then was there an identifiable point at which the
terrestrial globe held up such an affect to the cultures which produced it?
My account traces the history of this perception of an affective global
awareness. I want to suggest that this awareness emerges with the
development of geography against which so much recent postmodern
speculation defines itself. The perception of an emergent geography

defining the contours of its own world picture is one which has traditionally been located within the early modern period, from the late fifteenth
century onwards, when the full significance of Euclid's *Geometry* and
Ptolemy's *Geographia* came to influence the geographical imagination of
geographers and map-makers. What follows, therefore, is a genealogy
of present debates around globalism, which locates the first half of the
sixteenth century and its geographical production as defining a perception of the terrestrial globe and its social affectivity, and which can be
seen within the contexts of recent attempts to theorize the 'global postmodern' as only now in the process of dissolution.

Many premodern Western cultures created comprehensive cosmographies which sought to define the limits of their own culture and thus give
shape and meaning to existence. Such cosmographies were consistently
circular in nature, based on the apparent simplicity, unity and perfection
of the image of the circle, and the cyclical characteristics of natural
events. Both early Christian T-O maps and subsequent medieval *mappaemundi* based their deeply symbolic designs upon a sacred topography
which took the figurative and literal body of the Redeemer as constitutive
of their circular design.[10] Whilst the T-O maps offered a tripartite image
of the world, normally taking Jerusalem as its symbolic and iconographic
centre, medieval *mappaemundi* envisaged the world as a literal embodiment of the figure of Christ, whose body defined the limits of the geographical image. Whilst both traditions were rigidly schematic, based on
biblical exegesis rather than on travel and discovery, they offered a particularly holistic and instructive model of their culture's world picture.

However, as David Woodward has pointed out, from as early as the
thirteenth century onwards social and commercial pressures began to
lead to other ways of envisaging the space of the terrestrial world.[11]
Particularly significant within this context was the reception and translation of Ptolemy's *Geographia* from Greek into Latin towards the end of
the fourteenth century.[12] The *Geographia* utilized a concept of abstract,
geometric, homogeneous space based on Euclidean geometry in offering
a theoretical account of how to draw maps of the regions described, and
of the whole known world. As Woodward points out:

By plotting points of known location from perpendicular axes intersecting at an
artificial origin, the cartographer could fit existing surveys into the synthetic
whole; the measurements would thus be less subject to cumulative errors. It was
a shift in thinking away from piecing together local surveys in order to create
a whole – a change from inductive to deductive cartographic thinking ... For
geography, this meant a movement away from local topological concepts toward

Martin Behaim, terrestrial globe, 1492.

those of a finite, spatially referenced spherical earth, a *tabula rasa* on which the achievements of exploration could be cumulatively inscribed.[13]

The result of this shift in perceptions of terrestrial space from one of religious symbolism to the construction of an empty, homogeneous graticule of latitude and longitude, enabled the cumulative mapping of new-found lands within this predetermined spatial grid. It also created the conditions for the development of a geographically comprehensive and all-inclusive apprehension of the early modern world. Ptolemy's third geographical projection, described in the *Geographia*, appeared to suggest the possibility of projecting a spherical terrestrial sphere within an all-encompassing armillary sphere.[14] It was Ptolemy's theoretical models of projecting the world upon a spherical body which were to create the conditions for the production of early modern Europe's first known terrestrial globe, which was produced in Nuremberg in 1492 by the German geographer and merchant Martin Behaim.

Behaim's globe was a remarkable intellectual and practical achievement. The globe defined the scope of geographical knowledge on the eve of Columbus's first voyage, offering a detailed account of the extent of

the Portuguese discoveries throughout the western Atlantic and down the
west coast of Africa. The globe contains extensive legends and detailed
notes on the nature of the spice trade throughout the Indian Ocean, one
of the key factors which motivated the Portuguese voyages. However, the
globe contains no representation of the Americas, offering instead an
erroneously overextended South-East Asia and China, in line with
Columbus's hope of sailing westwards to reach the riches of the East. The
globe also drew heavily on Ptolemy's *Geographia*, not only for its depiction of the tripartite structure of the 'Old World' of Europe, Africa and
Asia, but perhaps even more significantly for its solution to the problem of
how to represent the earth accurately upon a spherical body.[15] Ptolemy's
speculative projections were crucial to Behaim in planning the creation of
his terrestrial globe. Behaim claimed to have studied with the influential
German mathematician and astronomer Regiomontanus (Johann Müller,
1436–1476), whose manuscript treatise on plane and spherical trigonometry, *On Triangles*, built on Ptolemy's calculations in providing
mathematical solutions to the problem of calculating location and distance of points on a sphere whilst taking into account the curvature of its
surface – precisely the type of calculation required to construct a terrestrial globe.[16]

Behaim's terrestrial globe was produced in response to a set of highly
specific requirements necessary to facilitate successful and accurate long-
distance oceanic travel. It also provided a scientifically novel and aesthetically attractive object which celebrated the impact and significance of
Portuguese maritime activity. Whilst the size and scale of Behaim's globe
meant that it was useless for the practical activity of seaborne navigation,
it nevertheless stood as a deeply attractive material manifestation of the
knowledge used to undertake such hydrographically exact practices.
In her discussion of the geographical and cultural expansion of early
modern Europe from the late fifteenth century onwards, the historical
anthropologist Mary Helms has argued that skilfully crafted and intellectually novel material objects were required to apprehend:

the broadened dimensions of temporal and spatial distance that had to be
accommodated especially at the highest levels of European political and ideological life, where, concurrently, new heights of political and religious prominence
and centricity were developing too.[17]

Behaim's terrestrial globe precisely enacted the centricity outlined by
Helms. Whilst the specific mathematical and geometrical knowledge
which made up the globe were put to use within the practical sphere of

seaborne navigation, the Portuguese Crown utilized the symbolism of Behaim's globe both to apprehend the significance of the 'broadened dimensions' of their own world picture, and to announce their own centrality in expanding this world picture. With the royal accession of Dom Manuel I in 1495, the Portuguese Crown adopted the motif of the armillary sphere – the representation of a terrestrial globe encircled by the track of the celestial bodies – as part of its official iconography. At the same point Dom Manuel adopted the title 'Dom Manuel, by the grace of God King of Portugal and Algarve, on this side and beyond the seas in Africa, Lord of Guinea, of the conquest, navigation, and commerce of Ethiopia, Arabia, Persia, and the Indies'.[18] The ability to lay claim to such geographically and culturally distant places was predicated on the concomitant ability to produce prestigious objects like terrestrial globes to signify the legitimacy of Portuguese claims to far-flung places. The armillary sphere was not just a scientifically appropriate symbol of the connection between celestial and terrestrial geography; its appropriation was also symptomatic of a process by which elites gave credence to their claims to territorial expansion. Through the deliberate annexation of the vertical axes of the celestial world, the Portuguese could more convincingly justify their claims to the horizontal extensivity of the terrestrial world across which their pilots and ships moved. Knowledge and possession of the terrestrial was thus legitimated through a highly political redefinition of the celestial, creating what Helms refers to as 'an aura of prestige and awe'[19] amongst those able to comprehend, and also possess, such objects.

The Portuguese Crown utilized the global image as a particularly affective symbol of imperial authority. Invoking the global iconography of imperial Rome,[20] the geographical symbols of the Portuguese empire became both subject and object of their imperial ambitions throughout Africa and Asia, a selective image which they constructed as much as represented.[21] However, the global symbolism of these politically speculative claims to the possession of distant territories was not immediately translated into the political geography of the period, as becomes clear from a closer inspection of the diplomatic history of the period. In the aftermath of Columbus's first voyage, the diplomatic dispute between the crowns of Portugal and Castile over possession of the territories discovered by Columbus was settled under the terms of the Treaty of Tordesillas in 1494 through recourse to a map, not a globe. The terms of the treaty stipulated that a straight line of division between the two crowns should be drawn 370 leagues west of the Cape Verde Islands, and that the dividing line should be drawn 'on all hydrographical maps made hereafter in our king-doms'.[22] The centrifugal force of this imperial division of the world remained deeply indebted to a Ptolemaic vision of the world, which envis-aged a horizontal extension of the Mediterranean-centred *oecumene* from the farthest reaches of Asia in the east to the Pillars of Hercules in the west. This appropriation of Ptolemy's model for mapping the terres-trial world was particularly appropriate for the growing imperial and geographical rivalries of the crowns of Portugal and Castile, as the Portuguese sailed further eastwards towards the Indonesian archipelago, and the Castilian Crown sought to consolidate its fortuitous discoveries in the so-called New World of the Americas to the west.

By the end of the first decade of the sixteenth century, geographers and diplomats began to question the effectiveness of the flat, rectangular map for encompassing the growing dimensions of the terrestrial world. In 1512 the Nuremberg scholar Johannes Cochlaeus reflected a sense that classical geographical perceptions were no longer adequate in describing and representing the proliferation and expansion of newly discovered territories:

And truly the dimension of the earth as now inhabited is much greater than these ancient geographers described it. For beyond the Ganges the immense countries of the Indies stretch out, with the largest island of the East: Japan. Africa is also said to extend far beyond the tropic of Capricorn. Beyond the mouth of the river Don there is also a good deal of inhabited land as far as the Arctic Sea. And what about the new land of Americus, quite recently discovered, which is said to be bigger than the whole of Europe? Hence we must conclude that we must now allow for wider limits, both in longitude and latitude, to the habitable earth than either Aristotle in this book or Strabo in his third book would give it.[23]

Cochlaeus' comments reflected a growing desire to develop geographical solutions adequate to describe and represent this broadened awareness of the scope of the earth, in both its longitude from east to west (as reflected in the Treaty of Tordesillas), but also in its expanding latitudes from north to south.

The immediate response of a range of geographers and cosmographers was to intensify their interest in projecting the earth's surface upon a sphere, rather than a plane surface. Whilst little momentum had initially gathered around Behaim's terrestrial globe of 1492, by the end of the first decade of the sixteenth century scholars developed a renewed and intense interest in terrestrial globalism. In Strasbourg in 1507 the cosmographer Martin Waldseemüller published the *Cosmographiae*

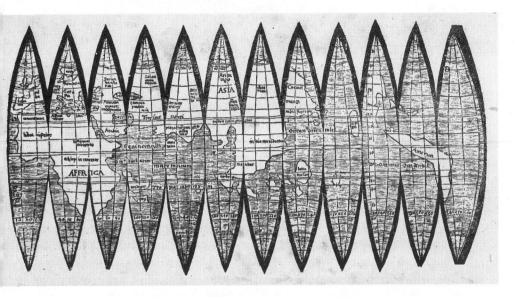

Martin Waldseemüller, woodcut showing terrestrial globe gores, 1507.

introductio ('Introduction to Cosmography'), which offered not only a descriptive book and map of the world, but also a terrestrial globe:

Introduction to cosmography with some important principles of geometry and astronomy; also included are the four sea voyages of Amerigo Vespucci, a map of all the cosmography on a three-dimensional body as well as a flat one, on which are included lands that were unknown to Ptolemy that have been recently discovered.[24]

The *Cosmographiae* proposed to:

write an introduction to the cosmography which we have illustrated in solid form [a globe] as well as on a flat surface [a map]. It is quite reduced in solid form, of course, because of the limited space, but more detailed on the flat surface.[25]

Whilst the terrestrial globe which accompanied the *Cosmographiae* has not survived, a series of globe gores designed to cover a spherical body still exist, attributed to Waldseemüller and dated 1507.[26] Waldseemüller's gores are particularly important as they incorporate the first unequivocal labelling of the New World as America, interestingly projected on Waldseemüller's gores in the eastern hemisphere.[27] Yet perhaps of equal significance is the fact that Waldseemüller's gores were the first *printed* gores designed to constitute a terrestrial globe in the history of European geography. Unlike Behaim, Waldseemüller designed his globe by first drawing a map onto twelve gored sections. Each gore depicted an area of

30 degrees of longitude on both sides of a meridian stretching from pole to pole. This design was then transferred onto woodcut blocks, printed and then applied to the ball to create a terrestrial globe. Subsequent cosmographical studies of the period began to incorporate Waldseemüller's calculations on the projection and construction of terrestrial globes. In 1509 Waldseemüller's printer published three booklets on cosmography which were accompanied by terrestrial globes.[28] Whilst none of these globes survives, the New York Library possesses a terrestrial globe engraved on copper and tentatively dated 1510, the so-called Hunt-Lenox Globe,[29] and the Jagellonicus University Library in Cracow possesses a gilded copper globe which bears a striking resemblance to the Hunt-Lenox Globe, also dated to 1510.[30] The Bibliothèque Nationale in Paris also owns a terrestrial globe known as the Green Globe. Unsigned and undated, this painted wooden globe bears a striking resemblance to an even more important terrestrial globe issued in 1515 (and subsequently lost), that of Johannes Schöner, who published his globe in Nuremberg along with an accompanying manual describing the method by which the globe was constructed.[31] The surviving gores designed to cover Schöner's globe suggest affinities with the Green Globe as well as subsequent globes which began to appear with increasing frequency from the 1520s onwards.

What is so striking about this rapid emergence of terrestrial globes is not only the graphically new geographical perception of the world which they offered, but also the medium which defined their creation. Both Waldseemüller and Schöner, arguably the two most influential globe makers prior to 1520, worked within the medium of print, designing their geographical descriptions for reproduction via the woodcut and, increasingly, copper engraving. Unlike Behaim's globe, which was hand-painted, the gores designed by Waldseemüller and Schöner could be exactly and swiftly reproduced and circulated in substantial numbers amongst scholars, diplomats and merchants throughout early sixteenth-century Europe, establishing and imaginatively defining a particularly global image of the world. The exactly reproducible nature of the printing press also allowed for the rapid distribution of the technical information required to create terrestrial globes, outlined in detail in the manuals produced alongside such globes. This geographical 'blueprinting' allowed scholars with access to printed texts such as those produced by Waldseemüller and Schöner to reproduce such globes, the only variant being the precise degree of geographical information placed upon the surface of the globe.

However, the dissemination of this new global image of the world through the relatively new medium of print cannot alone account for the spectacular development of global geography from the end of the second decade of the sixteenth century. All the globes discussed so far were created in direct response to the proliferation of accounts of the voyages and discoveries of the crowns of Portugal and Castile. Behaim appears to have had first-hand experience of the Portuguese voyages along the west coast of Africa, whilst Waldseemüller utilized his detailed knowledge of Vespucci's voyages to the New World to create the first geographical image of America as a separate continent in his world map dated 1507. Schöner was also intimately connected to the Habsburg-sponsored voyages to the Americas, noting that the New World was not, as Columbus had argued, part of Asia, but was in fact 'a large, independent portion of the earth, in that fourth part of the world'.[32] Yet such globes did not simply emerge in response to the need to map the New World. They also responded to the increasingly global claims to imperial authority made by the Castilian and Portuguese Crowns, as they expanded their own geographical horizons in the aftermath of Columbus's first voyage in 1492. As the two Crowns increasingly came into conflict over claims to the possession of contested territories, the terrestrial globe became a particularly appropriate object with which to lay claim to far-flung territories. The powerful iconography of the globe as an abiding symbol of imperial authority made it a compelling choice for both crowns to define claims to distant domains. In what follows, I want briefly to outline the ways in which this twin mobilization of the terrestrial globe within territorial disputes between the crowns of Castile and Portugal established not only a certain global perception of the early modern world, but also the ways in which it could be represented.

By 1515, when Schöner published his first terrestrial globe, the imperial tensions between Portugal and Castile triggered by Columbus's discovery of land in the West in 1492 had intensified. Whilst the Treaty of Tordesillas had provisionally established a dividing line between the interests of the two crowns in the western Atlantic, it was unclear as to where this line was to be drawn in the eastern hemisphere, should it be extended through 360 degrees around the earth. Unable to perceive the world globally, the diplomats of Castile and Portugal committed their line of demarcation to a flat rectangular map, which was valid only as long as the two crowns remained within its bounds. However, once these bounds were breached, the line of demarcation needed to be seriously reconsidered. The only way that it was possible to do this was to apprehend the world projected on a global scale. By the end of the second decade of the sixteenth century, as Waldseemüller and Schöner tentatively began to produce their own versions of this global perception of the world, the crowns of Portugal and Castile were increasingly straining the limits of the world picture established by the map which defined the terms of the Treaty of Tordesillas. In 1513 the Spaniard Vasco Núñez de Balboa became the first known European to sight the Pacific Ocean. News of Balboa's discovery sparked geographical and diplomatic speculation as to where the line of demarcation agreed at Tordesillas was to be drawn to the west of Balboa's discovery – a west which suddenly and dramatically impinged upon the 'eastern' possessions of the Portuguese in the Indian Ocean.

One man who was particularly aware of the global implications of this situation was the Portuguese naval officer Ferdinand Magellan. Magellan had sailed with the Portuguese fleet throughout the Indian Ocean prior to 1518, and had become convinced that the easternmost sections of the Indonesian archipelago, including the commercially lucrative islands of the Moluccas, lay within the Castilian half of the world, if the Tordesillas line of demarcation were to be plotted not upon a plane chart but upon a terrestrial globe.[33] Magellan therefore defected from the Portuguese Crown and enlisted his services under the Habsburg emperor Charles V. According to contemporary accounts of Magellan's decision, he informed Charles that:

it was not yet clearly ascertained whether Malacca was within the boundaries of the Portuguese or the Castilians, because hitherto its longitude had not been definitely known; but it was an undoubted fact that the Great Gulf and the Chinese nations were within the Castilian limits. They asserted also that it was absolutely certain that the islands called the Moluccas, in which all sorts of spices grow, and from which they were brought to Malacca, were contained in the Western, or Castilian division, and that it would be possible to sail to them and to bring the spices at less trouble and expense from their native soil to Castile.[34]

In devising his plan to sail to the Moluccas westwards via the tip of South America, Magellan also outlined his route to the Emperor whilst in Seville in 1519 with the aid of a globe, rather than a map. Las Casas claimed that: 'Magellan brought with him a well-painted globe showing the entire world, and thereon traced the course he proposed to take.'[35] Whilst such globes were of no significant navigational use, Magellan utilized their spherical representation of the world to persuade Charles of the potential success of a voyage which sailed west rather than east to reach the Moluccas, but still ended up at the same point on the globe.

The success of this calculated display of the globe can be gauged by Magellan's 1519 departure for the Moluccas from Seville with a fleet of five ships.[36] Following Magellan's death in April 1521 and the fleet's arrival in the Moluccas later that year, the remnants of the crew arrived back in Seville in September 1522. The response of geographers throughout Europe to the news of the return of Magellan's fleet was immediate, and the primary object within which the voyage came to be represented with greatest impact was that of the terrestrial globe.[37] In 1523 Schöner wrote a commentary on the voyage, 'dealing with the islands and lands recently discovered upon the instigation of their most Serene Highnesses, the Kings of Castile and Portugal, and a geographical globe for those who desire to follow the sea routes'.[38] This new terrestrial globe, issued in direct response to Magellan's voyage, traced the route of the voyage around its circumference, a vivid depiction of the circumnavigation of the earth which maps and charts were no longer able accurately to represent. The inadequacy of maps in representing both the geographical and political implications of Magellan's voyage was borne out in diplomatic responses to the voyage. In claiming the Moluccas on behalf of the Castilian Crown, Magellan's voyage reignited the imperial dispute between Portugal and Castile which the Treaty of Tordesillas had merely postponed. As the territorial competition between the two crowns became increasingly global, the one object able to mediate these competing claims to imperial possession was the terrestrial globe, as it allowed the geographers and diplomats of both sides graphically to grasp the earth as a spherical rather than a flat domain. When the two crowns met to discuss their respective claims to possession of the Moluccas at Badajoz-Elvas in May 1523, the object over which they fought for possession of the islands and for their respective claims to imperial authority was no longer a map, but a terrestrial globe.

The meeting at Badajoz-Elvas was ostensibly designed to establish the location of the Moluccas, in an attempt to settle ownership of the islands in line with the terms of the Treaty of Tordesillas. However, as the two teams of geographical specialists sat down to dispute the positions of the islands, it became increasingly clear that the introduction of terrestrial globes into the equation undermined the validity of the dividing line established between the two crowns at Tordesillas. Details of the geographical debates between the two negotiating teams makes compelling reading, charting the gradual erosion of the sovereignty of the sea charts used at Tordesillas in favour of terrestrial globes. On 6 May the attorneys 'sent for the sea-charts and globes of each side which each desired. Several examinations were made.'[39] However, by the following day both teams began to make significant distinctions between the charts and the globes:

In the morning the Portuguese representatives said that the sea charts were not so good as the blank globe with meridians as it represents better the shape of the world. Then they discussed the best means of putting the lands, islands and coasts upon it, as they were quite prepared to do this.

The judges for Spain said that they preferred a spherical body, but that the maps and other proper instruments should not be debarred, in order that they might locate the lands better upon the said body.[40]

Whereas Tordesillas had privileged the sea chart as the ultimate arbiter of diplomatic disputation, here both negotiating teams conceded the primacy of terrestrial globes in mediating their differences, to the extent that the sea charts became supplemental to the establishment of the position of the islands upon terrestrial globes. By 28 May both sides had produced independent global geographies outlining their respective claims to contested territory, presenting 'globes showing the whole world, where each nation had placed the distances to suit themselves'.[41] These terrestrial globes did not lead to a resolution of the diplomatic dispute over the Moluccas; in fact they only intensified the gulf between the two crowns, and the talks at Badajoz-Elvas broke down within days of the presentation of the globes. But what the production of these geographically persuasive terrestrial globes provided was an even more rhetorically compelling platform from which to establish claims to global imperial authority, far in excess of sea charts and world maps which were unable to offer a similarly all-encompassing vision of the world in the aftermath of Magellan's voyage.

These debates over the Moluccas permeated subsequent diplomatic discussion concerning claims to disputed overseas territory. In 1527 the English merchant and diplomat Robert Thorne sent Henry VIII a report on the state of the dispute over the islands, entitled 'A Declaration of the Indies'. Thorne also provided Henry with a crude world map which clumsily reproduced not only the line of demarcation in the western Atlantic established under the Treaty of Tordesillas, but also the dividing line between Castile and Portugal through the Indonesian archipelago, reproducing Castile's claim to the Moluccas. In outlining the highly selective and political nature of the geography reproduced by both sides, Thorne also stressed the limitations of the map for encompassing the broadened geographical dimensions over which the two sides were waging their dispute:

For these coastes and situations of the Ilands every one of the Cosmographers and pilots of Portingall and Spayne do set after their purpose. The Spaniards more towards the Orient, because they should appeare to appertaine to the

Emperor [Charles V]: and the Portingalles more toward the Occident, for that they should fall within their jurisdiction.[42]

Lacking the technical skill to project his geographical and diplomatic information upon a terrestrial globe, Thorne could only urge his sovereign Henry to imagine 'that this said carde were set upon a round thing, where the endes should touche by the lines, it would plainely appeare how the Orient part joyneth with the Occident'.[43] Whilst Thorne may have lacked the ability to present Henry with the more geographically and politically affective terrestrial globe, he had grasped the intensely global ramifications of Magellan's voyage for both geography and diplomacy. Magellan's voyage had finally united what Thorne refers to as the westernmost and easternmost limits of his 'carde', or map: the 'Occident' and the 'Orient'. The flat map with which Thorne exhibits such obvious unease could no longer adequately encapsulate the global apprehension of the early modern world's geopolitics exhibited in the response of the Portuguese and Castilian Crowns to Magellan's voyage. The terrestrial globe became the most effective object with which to envisage this apprehension, a fact reflected in the intensification of production in globes and global images from the late 1520s onwards.

If Thorne did not have the technical expertise to provide Henry with a sufficiently global image of the form of the post-Magellan world, the geographers and printers of the Low Countries were perfectly equipped to provide their patrons with just such an image. In 1527, the same year that Thorne produced his world map, the geographer Franciscus Monachus issued his *De orbis situ ac descriptione* ('The Position and Description of the World') alongside a new terrestrial globe of the world. Monachus' frontispiece drew on his terrestrial globe in offering an image of the world divided into two hemispheres, a western (Castilian) sphere and an eastern (Portuguese) sphere.[44] This remarkable image offered a dramatically novel spatial partition of the imperial spheres of interest of both the Portuguese and the Habsburg empires, never previously envisaged by either crown. Monachus' depiction of the world on a circular projection illustrated a new geopolitics, which no longer took place upon the flat surface of a map but across the curved superficies of a terrestrial globe. By 1530 specialized printing presses throughout Europe began to issue terrestrial globes in response to the demand created by princes, scholars, merchants and diplomats. In his *De principis astronomiae et cosmographiae* published in 1530, the geographer Gemma Frisius emphasized the increasingly prominent position accorded terrestrial globes by the ruling elite, claiming:

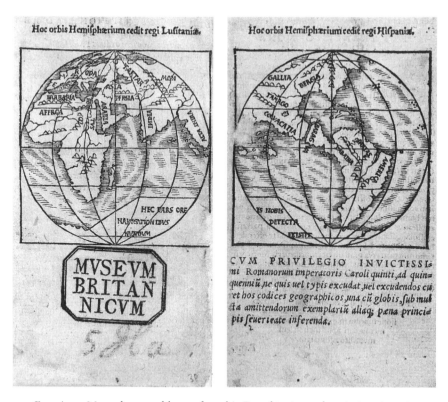

Franciscus Monachus, world map, from his *De orbis situ ac descriptione* (1527).

The utility, the enjoyment and the pleasure of the mounted globe, which is composed with such skill, are hard to believe if one has not tasted the sweetness of the experience. For, certainly, this is the only one of all instruments whose frequent usage delights astronomers, leads geographers, confirms historians, enriches and improves legists [*les legistes*], is admired by grammarians, guides pilots, in short, aside from its beauty, its form is indescribably useful and necessary for everyone.[45]

Frisius underlined his belief in the contemporary significance of terrestrial globes by producing two globes in five years, the first in 1530 and the second in 1535. This latter globe was also produced under the patronage of Charles V, to whom Frisius repaid the compliment by positioning the Moluccas on his globe within the eastern hemisphere claimed by Charles, as well as flying the imperial flag of the Habsburg emperor over the newly acquired city of Tunis.[46] By 1533 terrestrial globes had even reached the court of Henry VIII, just six years after Thorne had failed to provide his sovereign with just such an object to explain the dispute over the

Moluccas. Amongst the array of objects at the centre of Hans Holbein's *The Ambassadors*, painted in London in 1533, a terrestrial globe is rendered with meticulous detail, situated between two eminent French diplomats at the court of Henry VIII, displaying their worldly learning through recourse to objects such as the globe. Holbein's representation of the globe, which depicts French claims to Brazil, is a vivid example of the extent to which the terrestrial globe had become part of the political and intellectual fabric of the early modern world.[47]

The terrestrial globes of the early sixteenth century were the products of a culturally specific perception of globalization envisioned by the imperial crowns of early modern Europe in the aftermath of Magellan's circumnavigation of the globe in 1522. These globes offered a redefinition of the early modern world consonant with the requirements of the fledgling empires of Portugal and Castile, and were accordingly valued for their ability to encapsulate an image of this global space, as well as constructing its coordinates according to the aspirations of self-proclaimed 'emperors' like Charles V and João III. The dispute over the Moluccas resulting from Magellan's circumnavigation of the globe witnessed a profound and enduring shift in the geographical apprehension of the world from that of the flat map to the terrestrial globe. As a result it established the conditions for the emergence of a definitive and perceptibly modern way of representing and perceiving the globe. However, this alone does not adequately explain the intense significance accorded to such globes by scholars, diplomats and artists in the sixteenth century.

Ostensibly the globes produced by Behaim, Monachus and Frisius were of no practical value to either pilots or geographers, as their relatively limited size divested them of any functional value in the pursuit of more accurate navigational or topographical activities. However, their deployment within the field of political dispute and diplomatic negotiation refutes suggestions that they were simply regarded with the passive antiquarian curiosity that characterizes connoisseurship invested in premodern terrestrial globes today. They were rather, in the words of Anthony Grafton and Lisa Jardine, 'studied for action'[48] by the scholars, princes and diplomats who invested so much political and geographical power and authority in them. In drawing up their claims to territorial possession upon the surface of blank globes at Badajoz-Elvas in 1524, the Portuguese and Castilian geographers were not merely producing a politically partial geography. The terrestrial globe was utilized as a socially affective object, whose strength lay in the ideological representation of the world that it purported to describe. Its lack of cognitive specificity was

not its weakness but ultimately its greatest strength, because the very perceptions of distance and space upon which the terrestrial globe rested
stressed speculation and conjecture over the extent and possession of
distant territories. Upon the shape of the terrestrial globe, the crowns
of Portugal and Castile established diplomatically binding agreements
concerning territorial partition and trading rights, themselves ratified
through recourse to the terrestrial globe. Its combination of a highly
contingent but rhetorically persuasive representation of the location of
territory along with an instrumental capacity to define negotiated diplomatic settlement made the globe an ideal object with which to create a
compelling fiction of diplomatic and territorial claims to imperial
authority. The fact that such imperial claims were speculative and illusory
was secondary to the need to establish a particular object which could
bind both sides within diplomatic agreement.[49]

Furthermore, these terrestrial globes established an intimate connection between the representation of terrestrial space and the territorial
ambitions of early modern empires such as Portugal and Castile. Unlike
the perception of social space through which the modern nation-state
came to define itself, the apprehension of territory and its possession
which structured the claims of Portugal and Castile was porous, discontinuous and relentlessly speculative. Power and authority lay precisely in
the quasi-mystical pursuit of not what was knowable and near at hand,
but that which was distant and far away – like the Moluccas. The significance of terrestrial globes throughout the early modern period lay
in their utilization for geographical speculation on the furthest limits of
European political awareness. The Euclidean perception of empty, homogeneous and infinitely extensible space adopted by early sixteenth-
century geography, and which had such a marked influenced on the
makers of early terrestrial globes, was therefore coextensive with the
claims to distant imperial possessions established by the emperors of
Portugal and Castile. It would be anachronistic to interpret this perception through recent perceptions of the imagined community of the modern nation-state, which claims to map every square inch of the territory
across which it attempts to extend its authority.[50] It was precisely this
newer, Enlightenment perception of terrestrial space and its mapping
which was ultimately to supersede the more porous and discontinuous
perception of territory that structured early sixteenth-century
Portuguese and Castilian claims to distant lands.[51] The power of this new
perception of incremental mapping lay in its ability to operate at an infinitesimal level, rendering the speculative claims of the older geography

increasingly outdated. However, as Virilio has argued, contemporary computerized mapping leads to a further intensification of the mapping of the terrestrial world on an incremental basis, an intensification which leads to an abolition of distance which defines the current collapse of the concept of terrestrial space itself:

At this point depth of space – understood as depth of the field of surfaces available to direct observation – vanishes, and is replaced by the depth of time of the indirect recording of numerical data.[52]

It is at this moment that the significance of the image of the terrestrial globe collapses, precisely because it cannot meaningfully render the instantaneous passage of time and the recording of invisible computerized numerical data described by Virilio.

Contemporary perceptions of the waning of this spatiality, based on the contraction of time and space produced by systems of virtual telecommunications moving silently, invisibly and instantaneously, render the ways in which power and authority are speculatively projected across the surface of the terrestrial globe increasingly redundant, as they inhabit an older perception of the transmission of such power and authority, based upon speculation and the laborious passage of time involved in long-distance travel and the transmission of knowledge and information. The terrestrial globe can no longer represent the silent and invisible flow of social communication and virtual interaction across its surface, because the perception of terrestrial space which created the conditions for the creation of the terrestrial globe are no longer valid; Virilio's point is that the virtual transmission of information within globalism is today *extra*-terrestrial. As a result, the image of the world can be at once infinitely reproduced and infinitely reduced, encapsulated in visually arresting images depicting the merging of the world's nations into the single mediator of a microchip. If the sixteenth-century terrestrial globe offers an affective image of a pre-national world picture, then its current waning within the global economy of late twentieth-century capitalism suggests an attempt to chart a new geopolitics which increasingly seeks to erase and supersede national boundaries, in the name of technological innovations as dramatic and profound as those that redefined the world in the first half of the sixteenth century.

4

Mapping Places: Chorography and Vision in the Renaissance

LUCIA NUTI

MEASURE AND PICTURE

Creating recognizable images of the visible features of single parts of the *oecumene*, the inhabited world, was recognized by Ptolemy as the final aim of chorography. A field of vision was thus opened up to the work of the chorographer, who had to demonstrate the skill of a draftsman in rendering ports, countries, villages, rivers and streams. The field of numbers and mathematical abstraction, the sublimity of global knowledge and representation, was restricted to the work of the geographer. As a mathematician, the geographer dealt primarily with points and lines, and pursued resemblance only with respect to the overall shape and form of the *oecumene*. Chorography was therefore intended to convey only a limited knowledge of the earth: an individual part rather than the whole, the secondary rather than the primary, quality rather than quantity.

However, a mistaken connection between geography and painting was established in the sixteenth century owing to a misinterpretation of the Ptolemaic text. The incorrect reading of the opening phrase, 'É geographìa mimesis estì diàgraphès' instead of 'mimesis dià graphès', in its Latin translation 'imitatio picturae', was used by Peter Apian[1] and Wilibald Pirckeimer,[2] and was more widespread than the initial, correct translation by Jacopo d'Angelo: 'Cosmographia designatrix imitatio totius cogniti orbis'. It suggested that Ptolemy himself wanted to establish some kind of relationship between the two disciplines. The unclear and ambiguous expression, in open contradiction to the subsequent text, raised interpretation problems for Ptolemy's Italian editors. In Italian it became 'imitazione di dipintura', or 'imitazione del disegno'. Agrippa of Nettesheim rendered it into English, describing the geographical chart as 'a certaine imitation of paintinge'.[3]

The implications of Ptolemy's distinctions between geography and chorography were fully realized when the overwhelming authority of the rediscovered *Geographia* imposed itself on Renaissance culture. A heritage of unanswered mapping questions fuelled new speculations. A host of questions concerning chorography tantalized the sixteenth-century editors of the *Geographia*, given that Ptolemy, restricting his work to geography, had not proceeded any further, after his initial definition, in tackling the problem of chorographic representation. To which chorographers did Ptolemy refer, and did such practitioners really exist in the ancient word? If so, why did they not leave any record? And how far was the resemblance with the visible world to be pursued by chorographers, and by what means?

There was also a problem of staking out the borders of chorography. Although contemporary use of the term was inconsistent, its range was established on the grounds of contemporary needs and varied from depicting the town,[4] as was the prevailing tradition, to depicting the district.[5] Only occasionally was it extended to the scale of whole regions.

The superiority of geography over chorography, that is the superiority of intellectual and mathematical over pictorial and sensual knowledge, was commonly and consensually acknowledged. Paradoxically, the implications of this basic point came into conflict with another fundamental principle of Ptolemy's system. The attempt to deliver chorography from arbitrary and subjective expression, and to bring it into the world of measurement, thus giving it the full status of science, tended to blur any distinction in cartography between different scales and modes of mapping.

After a vacuum of centuries, Leon Battista Alberti was possibly the first to reconsider urban representation within the terms of mathematical abstraction. The relationship established in his *De re aedificatoria* between the architect and the painter is similar to that expressed by Ptolemy between the geographer and the chorographer. The job of the painter is to represent the visible world. The architect, like the geographer, is a theoretician, using a mathematical knowledge in order to harmonize the building to the structure of the cosmos. Alberti warns the architect not to apply himself to the world of vision and not to entrust his design to pictorial language by using foreshortening. He dismisses pictorial representation as appealing to the eye, but deceptive for correct communication:

Whereas the architect, without any regard to the Shades, makes his Relieves from the Design of his Platform, as one that would have his work valued, not by the apparent Perspective, but by the real Compartments, founded upon Reason.[6]

Human intellect is held to be the addressee of the architect's drawings, not the human eye.

The writer of another contemporary architectural treatise, Filarete, maintains that the architect should not turn to the painter in order to draw the design of a building.[7] Half a century later Raphael reveals the same attitude :

As the architect's mode of drawing is different from the painter's, I will say . . . that in those drawings it is not advisable to use foreshortening to show two prospects together. Because, from a foreshortened line, the architect cannot take any correct measurement, necessary for his art, which requires all measurements to be exact as they are, drawn by parallel lines and not by those that appear and are not.'[8]

'To appear' and 'to be' are regarded as different dimensions of reality.

'A city', Alberti wrote, is 'no more than a great House, and on the other hand a House . . . a little City';[9] both are microcosms, built by the harmonic combination of the single parts. The same principles of thought, design and representation are consequently shared by both. Though it has been convincingly demonstrated that Alberti's *Descriptio urbis Romae* was not a plan, it was undoubtedly not intended as a representational image, but the product of mathematical reason, a construction drawn by points and lines.[10] The drawing of ancient Rome would also have been an abstract image, in whose making Raphael was involved, had the artist ever carried out his intentions.[11]

The well-known plan of Imola drawn by Leonardo at about the same time is possibly the first graphic document to match perfectly the methods described by Raphael and Alberti.[12] Lines, radiating from the centre of the circle[13] in which the town is inscribed, divide it into eight segments, like the directions of the compass.[14] However, despite the two artists' instructions, the worked surface of the sheet is embellished with colour. Is this a mere convention or the desire to create a pictorial illusion? The colouring is as close as possible to sense perception: brick red for buildings, blue for waters, greenish yellow for intramural fields, white lead for streets and squares, straw yellow for the countryside. The impression gained by the observer is that the town appears on the surface of paper as a mimetic image, focused by a powerful lens, which provides the light veiling of its glassy transparency. Actually, the circle, which may appear as the wide eye of the lens, is the transcription onto paper of the dial-like surface of the transit with its eight divisions corresponding to the main winds. Every point, once distances and orientations were recorded, could find its proper place within.

In the late Middle Ages the circular frame around a city was supposed to convey a symbolic meaning of cosmic perfection. At the beginning of the sixteenth century the circular frame is the limit imposed by the surveying instrument for the realization of a rational image of the city. The ambiguity inherent in this solution – appeal to the eye or abstraction from sensory reality – is certainly emblematic of the condition of Renaissance chorography. It lies in-between, subject to suggestions and demands coming from two different epistemologies. Alberti's extreme solution, totally excluding the sense of sight, could not become very popular in a cultural milieu where direct observation was regarded as the primary source of information.[15] Even in mere architectural drawings the will to graphic persuasion, through perspective and shadowing, prevailed over the will to establish a very restricted and sophisticated code amongst architects.[16]

Although the term chorography was discussed in geographical texts and therefore applied to productions which were supposed to be located in the context of geographical descriptions, and sometimes entrusted with rhetorical or autocelebratory tasks, many of the local plans that were produced for practical purposes (boundary disputes, inventories of estates, sales of properties, military operations) seemed to share the concerns of chorography. They all required quantitative information about the land, but information was expressed in pictorial language. Starting from measure, and arriving at visual resemblance: this sums up the challenge, or dilemma, that they had to face.

Some English surveying manuals sought to fill the gap. 'How to draw a perfect drawing of your plot' is the title of one of the final chapters in William Leybourn's *The Compleat Surveyor*, where the author instructs the surveyor how to put the result on paper by colours and shading, once the mathematical survey has been completed.[17] Cristoforo Sorte explains his methods very clearly in describing his chorography of the district around Verona to *cavalier* Vitali:

I orientated the chorography thereof to the prevailing winds. I have drawn it in plan, with its true measures and distances, but the buildings – that is towns, castles and villages with mountains and hills – I have drawn them in elevation, north being at the top, south at the bottom and east and west crosswise; I thought it necessary in order to let people know the sites, because, when it is put that way, one can see all the rivers, the towns, the castles and the villages down across the valleys between the mountains; some of these sites I drew in such a way that peoples who are familiar with their countries can recognize the places without reading the letters of their names.[18]

The value of a total picture, which incorporates measurement but overcomes the limitation of a single language, was therefore widely recognized among scholars and echoed in many sixteenth-century records.[19]

Expressions coupling the two terms such as 'geometrice depinxit'[20] cannot be explained outside this context. It is indeed through the combination of the two 'pingendi rationes' – 'geometrica' and 'perspectiva' – that Georg Braun claimed the superiority of the town images in his books.[21]

The problem of the relationship between measurement and painting, in rendering the abstract structure underlying visual appearances in the world, was a central concern for Renaissance art too.[22] The assumption that the eye is the only arbiter of the picture was widespread and long-lived in Italian culture. 'You need to have the compasses in your eyes and not in your hands, because the hands work and the eyes judge', as Michelangelo put it; and Vasari confirmed: 'You do not need any other measurement better than the judgement of the eye . . .'[23] Vasari, however, is also proud of explaining how he was helped by the compass in drawing the overview of Florence under siege in 1530.[24] The use of technical devices to control the metrical consistency of painted space was usually dismissed by Italian painters because it was thought to interfere with the mental creative process. It was, by contrast, fully accepted and valued in the North.

In the preface to his treatise on perspective Gerard Desargues suggests that a painter should consult a *landmeeter*, or surveyor, to construct his spatial illusions,[25] and that is exactly what many artists, such as Pieter Saenredam and Jan Vermeer, did.[26] On the title page of the same book the concept is effectively expressed by an image: a woman (Picture), holding palette and brushes in her right hand, is working with a measuring device resting on her left hand. An assistant (Measure), wearing a belt marked with numbers, helps her set the plumb line.

If measure is regarded as the maidservant of picture by painters, the relationship is comprehensively inverted by the chorographers. As Egnazio Danti put it, revising Ptolemy's definition, the job of painting in chorography is reduced to the scope of a mechanical art:

thus one recognizes clearly that even though chorography can be practised by a geometer, and is a science subaltern to geometry, it can, as a mechanical art, also be practised by a simple painter; whereas geography can be apprehended only by a geometer, since it does not require painting at all, given that it describes a city with a dot, and a river or a sea coast with a straight or curved line.[27]

The coupling of eye and instrument, engaged in direct observation of nature, seems to have generated a special fascination, attested to by a rich imagery in treatises on perspective and surveying manuals. Here an artist is working on a transparent glass, there a surveyor is taking sightings from several vantage points, as the undulations of the landscape

'Allegory of Painting', from Abraham Bosse, *Algemeene manier van de Hr. Desargues tot de practijck der perspectiven...* (Amsterdam, 1664).

are wrapped in a web of straight lines. 'Measuring by sight' became a pleasurable recreational exercise among the educated class, who were encouraged to participate by an increasing number of works dedicated to practical mathematics.[28] Even measurement operations, that is the construction of the chorography itself, are often accounted for pictorially in a distinctive space within the frame of the map. The metrical key, or scale, is rendered as a ruler, engraved on a stone or a wooden block. The author, sometimes helped by his assistants, is portrayed in the foreground, well dressed, handling an instrument in an attitude of self-conscious authority; beyond him, the result of his work is displayed.

Individual productions turned out quite differently. Among the varied creations that can be classified as chorographies, we can take two to represent the extremes of the spectrum. At one end are the coloured, not to scale, relief maps of parts of Tuscany drawn by Leonardo da Vinci, where a volume of information about river and mountain systems was expressed

zum grund legen. 25

Das Neundte Capitel.

Wie man ein gantzes Land/mit allen seinen
Dörfferen in grund legen soll.

Je du mit disem Instrument oder Brett ein Landschafft
mit seinen Dörfferen in den grund legen solt/ wann dir
nur ein weite von einem Dorff zu dem anderen bekannt
ist/dasselbig kanst du erfahren durch das Instrument/wie ich in
den

Leonhard Zubler, 'Surveying' from *Novum
instrumentum geometricum* (Basel, 1607).

by a skilled use of colour and the illusion of a comprehensive view from
above; at the other end, the rough, flat and uncoloured figure, shaded
with hills and tufts of grass, which William Leybourn offers as an example of how to draw an area of mountainous and uneven land, while
avoiding the risk of losing metric proportion.[29] The first is a triumph of
vision, the second a pale pretence.

To comply with Ptolemy's authority, the chorographer has to observe a
single basic principle of representation, which would determine the language to use. As no comment, or suggestion, was added by Ptolemy about
how to deploy it, 'resemblance with visible features' became a matter of
interpretation. It did not mean automatically that the world pictured on
the sheet must correspond visually to the world seen from a real or hypothetical point of view. The quality of visual space is uniquely created in
the act of making the image.

Variations of scale, viewpoint and expressive level are clearly perceiv-
able within the same picture. The selective eye of the chorographer stares
at single geographical objects and then, working on the paper, renders

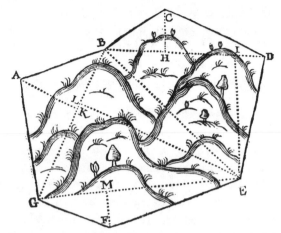

William Leybourn, 'How to draw a mountainous land', from
The compleat surveyor (London, 1653).

them close or distant, two- or three-dimensional, rough or finished, according to his specific needs, his skill and his personal choice. Only 'some sites', and not all, were portrayed in detail, according to Sorte. Each point is focused in the most convenient way, as if a very flexible lens were constantly adjusting angle and moving from one cardinal point to the other. A military interest usually approached the town from a zenithal point to grasp the outline of its fortifications in plan on the ground, while the surrounding hills and mountains stand in profile.[30] Natural elements present themselves, faithfully portrayed (as the mountains in Leonardo's maps of Tuscany), or are used as recognizable symbols (the picture of a tree means a land planted with trees, no matter what species). If grouped, the icons can reinforce the quality of the presence or give it an additional meaning. 'Diverse little trees', according to Leybourn, have to be drawn in the most 'materiall' places. A few trees, surrounded by a ring-fence in John Norden's or Christopher Saxton's chorographies, indicate the extension of enclosures under the Tudors and Stuarts.[31]

The same is true for colours. They can simply be in accordance with nature, recalling immediately the geographical identity of the objects portrayed – river, mountain and so on – or contain more sophisticated information about their historical and human dimension. By means of colour one can distinguish fertile or infertile lands, as Sorte claimed.[32] Going further, William Folkingham laid down subtler correspondences: pale straw colour signifies arable for corn, light green is meadows, deeper green, pasture, darker green, heaths.[33]

Terms drawn from the world of vision are thus variously compounded to make an image that has no interest in attaining a universal credibility as part of the visible world. Disappointment, even visual malaise, might attend the observer who tried to grasp with one glance the varied visual journeys of which the space of the picture is the sum.[34]

THE SEARCH FOR A TOTAL VISION

The only chorographic documents that claim to be considered as views genuinely experienced by an observer are town portraits. One of the most distinctive and popular products of the Renaissance, they had such vitality that they were sold as individual sheets as well as collected in books for about two centuries. Free from strict metric concerns, town portraits could be offered unrestrictedly for the pleasure of the eye.

Geographically speaking, a town covers a sufficiently limited space to be included in a single view. Yet in the Renaissance the vision sought by its representation had a more important quality. For a long time the town had been perceived as a microcosm, both with regard to its architectural structure, as Italian fifteenth-century treatises argue, and to its social and political identity, of which the citizens were conscious and proud. Vision, however, is also part of a historical culture. It provides a pattern for the interpretation and organization of perceived environmental data. As a consequence, modes of representation are not simply sets of formal qualities, but expressions of diverse visual cultures. If the representation of a town 'from life' is at issue, the most trustworthy and significant image of it will undoubtedly be the one that matches most perfectly with the visual culture's mode of relating the observer to the object.

Fascinated by suggestions from Greek geographical culture available from a rediscovered Ptolemy, fifteenth-century Italy initiated a search for an all-embracing view, from an elevated vantage point at a distance, such as surrounding hills, in order to grasp urban form and shape.[35] The alternative at about the same time, which was peculiar to the North, especially to Flanders, consisted in what is commonly called the profile approach – a very low viewpoint taken at a distance, with a wide and open horizon, and with a significant proportion of pictorial space occupied by sky. This choice marks a watershed, or a borderline, between the two visual cultures, because the profile approach is peculiar to the North, especially to Flanders, and is absent from Italian work. The concept of Northern-ness would require a more accurate definition rather than this rather vague or ambiguous expression. I use it deliberately as an undifferentiated whole in order to outline a contrast.

The practice of describing the world in profile and, most of all, the value attributed to the profile view as a form of empirical knowledge, are deeply rooted in a sea-based culture such as that of Flanders. Coastal profiles made their entry in Northern rutters (pilot's sailing books) at the end of the fifteenth century, and this format was later widely applied to landscape and town views, both by painters and topographers.[36] Of course, a geographical factor might be relevant to understanding the fortune of the profile vision in the North. Especially in Flanders and the Netherlands, the appearance of a completely flat land, criss-crossed by numerous waterways, allows the observer to maintain the perception and viewpoint characteristic of the marine view.

This geographical factor, however, seems to reinforce rather than determine the profile approach. If we shift to Italy, the landscape features are indeed so varied that even within the stretch of a few kilometres completely different scenery opens up. Mountains or hills can close the horizon, and at every bend of the climbing road something on a higher or lower level is added or lost. One might claim that it would be difficult to illustrate these in profile. But what about expanses of flat land or flat coasts that are also part of the Italian landscape? Even in front of these, an Italian draftsman seems always to be searching for a natural or artificial higher view point. By contrast, a Northern draftsman coming to Italy can easily reorganize the perceived data under his usual iconographic schema and render the cityscape in a profile view. This is perhaps why Italians had to wait for the printing of a Dutch book of navigation to see the profiles of Italian coasts,[37] and for the work of Northern artists to see their own towns in profile views.

In the collection of maps of small towns in southern Italy that Agostino Rocca made together with their written descriptions, one portrait stands out from the others. The distant profile of Bari, a port town, seen from inland and not from the sea, appears in the middle of the sheet, seen beyond a flat stretch of fields. The text below states: 'Il disegno è di Gaspar Honje fiandrese' ('the drawing is by the Fleming Gaspar Honje').[38] Elsewhere, Bologna is painted as a thin outline seen from beyond its rich countryside by an anonymous Flemish painter, while the Italian portrayals of the same town are always constructed as overall images, in which prominence is given to its distinctive cargo boat shape, which Leandro Alberti described in such detail.[39]

The accepted superiority of mathematical representation lay in its being absolute, abstract and total. Chorography could offer only subjective

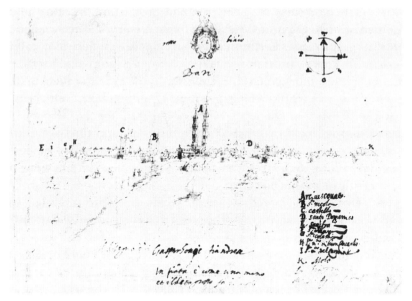

Gaspar Honje, *Bari*, 1583–4.

records of ephemeral reality. Though well aware of this, the Renaissance town view maker longed to achieve totality in the field of visual appearances. He tried to widen his eye and overcome the limited vision of an individual observer, from a single viewpoint, at a prescribed moment in time, in order to depict a total portrait of the urban microcosm. The mirage of a total vision stimulated artists to work out solutions where modes of representation were stretched to the ultimate of their expressive potential and the game of illusion transgressed the bounds of truthfulness. Here too, different visual cultures pursued different routes to totality. The oblique view from an elevated viewpoint, even when successfully achieved as in the famous 'chain map' of Florence, turns out to be limiting. A single, privileged viewpoint unbalances the whole and compresses its more internal parts. The ground level, obscured by the wide building blocks, remains inaccessible to the eye.

The Italian artist abandoned the search for an elevated point from which to view the town and started working on a ground plan in his studio. By the power of intellect alone, he created a vision from an elevated viewpoint that was physically impossible at the time. This newly invented mode, the 'perspective plan', whose first and unrivalled product was the well-known plan of Venice attributed to Jacopo de' Barbari, was presented – and immediately accepted – as the most faithful portrait of a town, because it fulfilled all the needs and expectations of contemporary culture. The ancient human dream of flying above the earth and having such an all-embracing view from above as only God could attain was here satisfied. To the exploration of his located, but intense and penetrating eye, the city holds no secrets: its overall shape, the layout of its streets, the architectonic features of its most prominent buildings are all revealed at a single glance.[40]

In the search for a total vision it is obvious that the profile alone is very limiting. It does not allow one to see anything other than the foreground, where the buildings tend to flatten into a two-dimensional strip. The profile, the ground-level perspective, could be simply developed lengthwise, however, by stitching together partial views drawn from closer viewpoints. The foreground strip was thus rendered in all its details, as it might be seen over the extended time of a slow coastal passage or a walk along the road. In addition, strips of the more internal parts could be superimposed on the foreground within a recessional space, as in the medieval system of additive perspective.

This mode of representation was attempted in a most spectacular way

Melchior Lorichs, *Istanbul*, sect. XI, 1559.

in the imagery of Istanbul at the time of Süleyman the Magnificent. At the beginning of the sixteenth century the city was no longer the ancient Constantinople, but the powerful Islamic capital of a mighty empire, which seemed to present a serious threat to Europe. Although a perspective plan by Giovanni Andrea Vavassore had already shown the partially changed appearance of the town, it is in the second half of the same century that Northern painters, employed in the entourage of imperial ambassadors, scanned it more closely from the coast of Galata.[41] Their portrayals, which were not intended for public circulation at the time, show the still recognizable skyline of the town spread out across the Golden Horn, with all the grandeur of its walls, fountains, gardens, great palaces and mosques, its crowded domes and narrow minarets piercing the horizon.

A film-style iconography was developed in this representation, by combining different techniques of observation from life. The dimensions of the sheets are significant in their own right. If the view (*c.* 1550) by Pierre Coeck, at 86.5 cm in length, is still within the range of a single glance, the watercolour (*c.* 1590) in the Österreichische Nationalbibliothek of Vienna, at 1.5 m long, demands a series of pauses by the observer if the individual monuments are to be appreciated. An anonymous drawing of the same city (*c.* 1566–82) in the Bibliothèque Nationale in Paris is nearly 3 m in length. Finally, the most spectacular example is the 1559 view by Melchior Lorichs, on 11.275 m of drawn paper. Authentic observation from life is claimed by the author, who portrayed himself working with a Turk at the western end of Galata. In 1861 this film-style drawing was cut into 21 separate pieces, so that the continuous narrative was broken into photogrammatic shots. Previously, the image of the town was revealed slowly, as the observer passed before the long strip of paper, as shown on the left-hand side of Jan Cornelisz Woudanus's 1610 engraving hanging on the northern wall of Leiden Library's reading room.[42]

Later, at the opposite end of Europe, another port town, Lisbon, was represented filmically in the same mode, but in quite a different medium. About fifty years before a violent earthquake destroyed so much of the city, the aspect of the old town spread out along the river Tagus was fixed by Gabriel del Barco on a wide surface (1.11 x 2.34 m) of glazed tiles in the palace of the Counts of Tentúgal.[43]

DEVELOPMENTS

It is intriguing to consider how the search for a totalizing image of the town developed after the Renaissance and how the relationship between

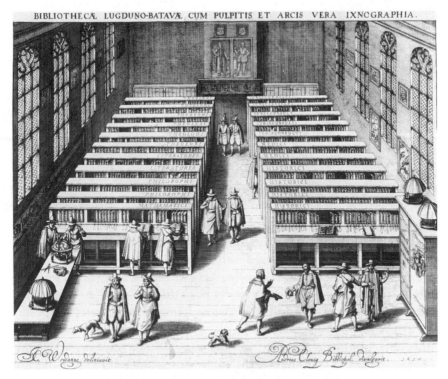

BIBLIOTHECÆ LUGDUNO-BATAVÆ CUM PULPITIS ET ARCIS VERA IXNOGRAPHIA.

Jan Cornelisz Woudanus, engraving from *Bibliothecæ Lugduno-Batavæ cum
pulpitis et arcis vera ichnographia*, 1610.

totality and vision found a new balance in a changed cultural milieu.

The continuing desire for an all-embracing urban view was satisfied
in one of the nineteenth century's most spectacular graphic inventions,
the panorama.[44] The creation of a large-scale panorama required the
achievement of a free horizon from a high viewpoint, such as the top of a
tower or the upper storey of a building. The delineator traced a series of
views in a sequence, scanning through 360 degrees, and then joining them
together. Conceptually, the panorama owes something to both the perspective plan and the profile, but it also diverges from both. The vantage
point is a single elevated one and has to be purposefully chosen, as in the
plan. The vision unrolls in a time-lapse at a constant eye level, as in the
profile, but a significant change occurs in the way the object is focused.
The observer becomes integral to the object and inspection is made from
inside, rather than from a distance. The circular frame of the visual horizon swallows the urban shape, while the urban body is enlarged and
projected towards the infinite.

Luigi Garibbo, *Panorama of Florence, c.* 1840.

This kind of representation reflects a shift in urban culture, at a time when the city was rapidly expanding beyond its centuries-old walls. The loss of interest in a global urban form as a reference mark and the disappearance of the urban borderline as an architectural element are among the first consequences.

Technically, the panorama took advantage of newly available devices, such as the perspective frame, the camera obscura and later the photographic camera itself, which, once installed on a revolving axis, allowed the delineator to fix partial shots. It was still a matter of artistry, as in Renaissance productions, to determine the outcome and to reconstruct the impression of a continuous vision, masking the suture lines. In this case, however, much of the striking effect of the image depended on special viewing conditions: the long strip was bent into a circle and displayed, as for a performance, in specially designed and illuminated spaces. Illusion was not only a game, but a controlling intention in the image's construction.

The search for totalizing knowledge of the town had also developed in a quite opposite direction during the sixteenth and seventeenth centuries. Once it was realized as graphically unattainable in a single image, totality was pursued by multiple views, each exploring a different experience in time or space.

The suggestion came from the North. In opposition to the Italian choice of a single, prime or privileged mode of knowledge and representation, and in opposition to the sustained Italian faith in the perspective plan as the most exhaustive image, the Dutch, and more broadly the

Northern, alternative is a composite sheet on which different images of a town were recorded one beside the other, offering alternative possibilities of knowledge. Both foreign and native traditions are followed. The sailor's perspective offered different possibilities of knowledge than the so-called bird's eye view: both are taken into account, and others also. The town is a complex object. It must be sectioned off, explored and studied by multiple views, in its different modes of being, rather like fruit or flowers in Dutch still-life paintings. The result is a multi-faceted vision of the object, something with which stone-cutters are familiar.

A range of possible combinations was tried out during the sixteenth century and extended further in the seventeenth.[45] The profile, however, is always present, playing a leading role and gaining ground against the perspective plan once more. The first possibility is the combination of two or more frames within the same representation mode: profiles, or views, from several perspectives, as in pilots' sailing books. This solution can be found in the views by Georg Hoefnagel engraved in the last books of the *Civitates*.[46] A more elaborate composition combines two modes of representation, a perspective plan plus a profile, such as the view of Schiedam by Jacob de Gheyn (1598). Finally, the separated worlds of vision and abstraction are combined. The town of the eye and the town of the measuring instrument appear alongside each other on the same sheet, and sometimes in the same hybrid image, such as in the engraving of Amsterdam by Daniël Stalpaert (*c.* 1670). The old city and the new expansion fan out to its ramparted walls. The plan, pushed to the top of the frame, leaves the foreground to coats of arms and allegorical figures, while in the middle there is the profile view of the port crowded with ships.

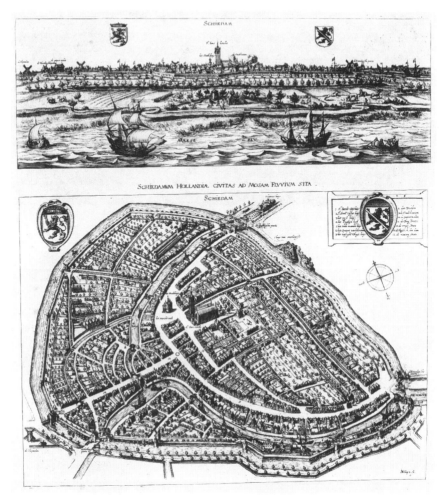

Jacob de Gheyn, *Plan and perspective plan of Schiedam*, 1598.

Publishers experimented further with more complex combinations of plans, profiles, global and partial views, where the various components could be printed from separate plates, so that the whole set or only some parts of it could be assembled. In the eighteenth century the multiple-image portrait seems more appropriate to meet the demands of new tastes and techniques. The profile approach, that is the Northern vision, passes to American culture as the most convincing outline of a town; it is still alive in nineteenth-century American town imagery, eclipsing the primacy that the perspective plan had held in the Renaissance.

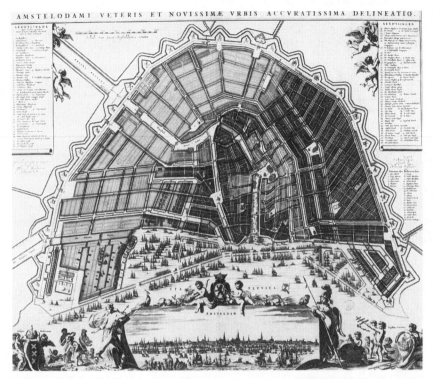

Daniël Stalpaert, *Amstelodami veteris et novissimae ubris . . .* (Amsterdam: Nicolaus
Visscher *c.* 1670).

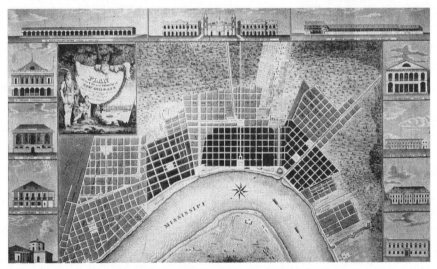

I. Tanesse, *Plan of New Orleans* (New York: C. Del Vecchio and P. Maspero, 1817).

By this time measurement had taken over from pictorial vision, exactitude from lifelikeness, not only in geography, but in chorography too. More and more often, towns were presented as bare plans. However, thin profiles, recalled as mere icons of visual memory, show up in stunning contrast to the strongly emphasized city blocks in maps of gridiron towns, such as those of Mobile (1824) or New Orleans (1817).

CONCLUSION

Despite the fact that information from the sensible world was considered limited, even deceptive, as a guide to full knowledge of the cosmos, vision played an important role in mapping during the Renaissance. Visual evidence was present in maps, as a starting-point, as a source of information to be recorded from life and as a point of arrival, a mode of rendering information lifelike. Vision, however, is not a mere equivalent of sight. The mental process of elaborating what enters through the eyes cannot be divorced from historical and cultural interpretation. Mapping places by means of drawing faithful portraits of the world as seen provides a record of visual choices, cultures and spatialities.

The desire to overcome the limits and subjectivity of sense knowledge developed in different directions from the Renaissance to the nineteenth century: on the one hand it determined a general move towards the expulsion of pictorial language from every kind of map; on the other it fuelled the search for an image capable of expressing totality within the field of vision, the panoramic, all-embracing view of the divine eye.

In the twentieth century we continue to appeal to vision even in abstract urban mapping. We continue to colour geographical charts as if they were records of the world as seen. The relationship between the abstract and the concrete, the mathematical and the visual, the exact and the lifelike, established by the Ptolemaic distinction which lay at the basis of Renaissance geographical culture, is still both present and problematic.

5

Mapping, the Body and Desire:
Christopher Packe's Chorography of Kent

MICHAEL CHARLESWORTH

Christopher Packe published his *A New Philosophico Chorographical Chart of East Kent* in 1743. His chart occupies a small but significant place in the history of mapping, as the first geomorphological map: the first anywhere, that is, to show topographical relief with scientific accuracy.[1] Another important innovation was made in undertaking the work necessary to draw the chart: Packe was the first person to use a barometer to measure the heights above sea level that are shown as points on his chart. Although modern historians of cartography tend to pass over Packe's work once they have noted these facts (made more remarkable by the fact that Packe was not a professional cartographer), more detailed attention to his chart and to his written statements about it can reveal dynamic tensions that illuminate relations between desire, science and art, and between vision and power, in the early modern era.

The chart, measuring five feet square, was published by subscription. In 1736 Packe had presented a paper to the Royal Society in London describing his project and he was sufficiently encouraged by his audience's response to proceed with it. I have yet to find a list of the subscribers to the chart, but we can at least hypothesize that they included two groups – one consisting of Royal Society fellows, led by their President, Sir Hans Sloane, with whom Packe corresponded about the project between 1736 and 1741;[2] and another group in the city of Canterbury, where Packe lived and worked. Packe alludes to interested people in Canterbury when he discusses a problem with the chart's reception:

The Generality of People, even amongst my own Neighbours and Acquaintance have entertain'd so Partial a notion of this CHART, that it has been almost universally look'd upon only as a large *Map* of this little Country; and even in this View, scarcely thought so compleat as it might have been, and as most other Maps are, because it wants the *Roads*.[3]

This quotation comes from the 110-page book that Packe wrote and published in response to such objections. Before we turn to a consideration

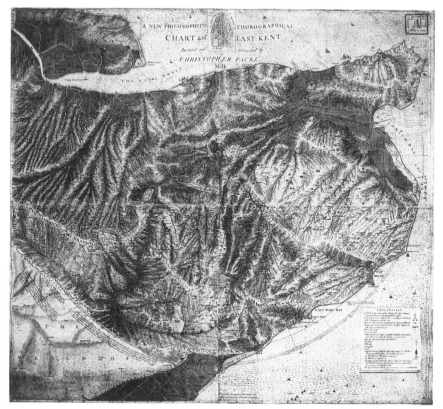

Christopher Packe, *A New Philosophico Chorographical Chart of East Kent*
(Canterbury, 1743).

of this text, however, we must describe his chart, especially since it was
originally published as five feet square in size, but here is reproduced as
just a few inches across. The chart combines different sorts of lines with
shading and words to produce quite a complex semiotic system. One sort
of line traces natural formations, including the coast of Kent and the
rivers and streams that flow down to that coast, describing a delicate den-
dritic pattern resembling frost on the inside of a window-pane. Included
in this type of mark are the rows of small bee-hive shapes signifying
chains of hills, as well as the parts of the chart that designate enclosed
parks, such as those of Chilham and Eastwell which show up clearly,
through contrast, in the western or left-hand half of the chart. In addition
to these lines that represent features of the physical world, another group
of lines are centred on Canterbury Cathedral, a little above the geometrical centre of the chart. These consist of radiating lines and concentric

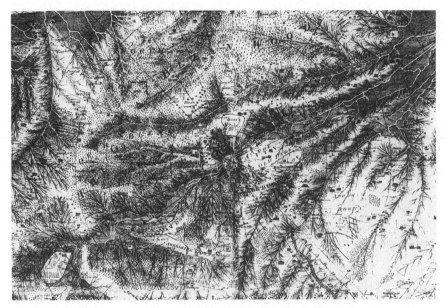

Detail of Packe's Chart showing the group of lines centred on Canterbury Cathedral,
a little above the geometrical centre.

circles that obviously do not represent physical formations. They
correspond, as we shall see, to elements of Christopher Packe's actual
vision. In accordance with well-established practice, the chart also
employs a system of shading. Packe chose lighter shades to stand for
higher altitudes, and darker areas to show places where the soil is deep,
rich and moist, thus promoting a ranker growth of grass. In addition to
these non-verbal signs, there are words written all over the chart. Some
are intended to communicate place names, but others provoke more
thought: what are we to make of this quotation from Psalm 104, written
across the lower reaches of the River Stour? 'They go up by the
Mountains, they go down by the valleys unto the place which thou hast
founded for them' (illus. 3)?

THE CODES OF CULTURE

Packe's work was undertaken and envisaged by him to be of scientific
importance, and just over half of his book is dedicated to explaining it
scientifically. This slim volume is our major source of information about
the project, and its title reveals how its author conceived of his work:
Ancographia, sive convallium descriptio explains that Packe's interest in
the chart was to plot the *valleys* of East Kent. He was intensely interested

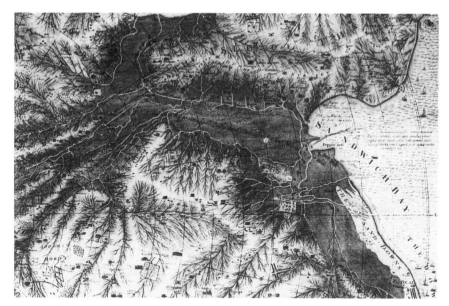

Detail of Packe's Chart showing the quotation from Psalm 104 written across the
lower reaches of the River Stour.

in the hydrological cycle, but although this was paramount in his mind,
his interests were not confined to it alone. A 'Prospectus' for the chart,
reprinted at the end of *Ancographia*, promises the following features:

The Rise and Progress of the Vallies: the Directions of both the Greater Chains of
Hills, and the lesser Ridges; with their several Elevations, or different
Perpendicular Heights, as well *Absolute* from the Sea at Sandwich-Bay as
Relative to one another in many of the most Remarkable Places of the County.
   Also, the Sea, Creeks, Bays and Harbours;
   The Course of Rills, Brooks, [N]Ailbourns and Rivers;
   Springs of Fresh and Medicinal Waters; Pools; Woods; Quarries; Gravel, Sand,
and Chalk Pits; Minerals; Soils.
   To which are added, by way of Ornament, the Churches, the City of
Canterbury, Towns, Villages, Streets, Castles, Camps, Ruins. The Houses of
Noblemen and Gentlemen, with many others of less Note, and other Marks that
are useful in setting off and conducting Vallies from their Rise to their
Determinations.

Despite the justification in the last sentence, whereby such 'ornament' is
brought within the scientific endeavour, we can recognize that an ideological element has entered the project. Those churches and noblemen's
houses, while part of the standard fare of eighteenth-century topographers and antiquaries, are also connected with the accretion and exercise

of power and wealth; a chart that notices such features enters the domain of the ideological. A third element is introduced as the prospectus continues:

Also, Downs, Parks, Groves, Tolls, and Rows of Trees. In fine; whatever is Curious, both in Nature and Art, that Diversifies and adorns the Face of the Earth, is herein presented to the View in their proper Situation and Aspect; that the Exact Harmony of the Whole, and the Beautiful Distinction of the Several Parts of the Country, may appear as in a Landskip, as well as the Main Design of the Work will allow.

The science and ideology, Packe is saying, will be emphatically aestheti-cized, up to a point ('as well as the Main Design . . . will allow'); Packe's language here recalls that used to discuss architectural beauty and pictor-ial aesthetics ('Exact Harmony of the Whole, and the Beautiful Distinction of the . . . Parts') before achieving concretion as a 'Landskip', that is, a landscape drawing or painting.

To realize his chart, Packe built himself a panoramic viewing station and collected the necessary instruments of viewing:

I got made for the purpose a large and very correct Azimuth Compass, inscribed with every thing suitable to my Design, and fitted with a Theodolite . . . and hav-ing obtained leave to erect a Scaffold upon the Top of the great Tower of our Cathedral, I placed the Instrument in its Centre. Here I had so extensive a view of almost the Whole Country, that but few places within my Circle escaped my Sight.[4]

Many of the themes that are brought together in this short passage were already established in mapping practices and look forward to future developments in the charting of terrain: the use of instruments to strengthen and service a conceptual grasp on landscape; the formation of a panoramic seat of vision; and an exultation in the power and overlord-ship enjoyed by the eye – 'few places within my Circle escaped my Sight'. In his reverence for technological development Packe concedes a central position to the 'instrument', making no mention of the human body without which the machine can neither function nor make sense. The his-tory of panoramic representation for strategic purposes is on one level the history of the replacement of the powers of the human body with those of machines: telescopes, balloons, photographic cameras, film cameras, video cameras, spy shuttles, satellites. Even at the outset of this trajectory, Packe's confrontation with terrain was thoroughly mediated and distan-ciated by instruments, not only on top of Canterbury Cathedral, but when out in the fields gathering data through more conventional survey-ing methods. Packe's barometers even incorporated other recently invented scientific implements: 'a sliding Nonius Scale and a Microscope, which divides each tenth of the Inches into ten other parts', allowing him accuracy up to a hundredth of an inch.

From his windswept eyrie nearly four hundred feet above the streets of Canterbury, Packe used his azimuth compass to plot incrementally the angles of his lines of sight. This gave him a sort of base-point from which to begin the process of working out the bearings of places in relation to his centre. His theodolite may also have been equipped with a small telescope, with which Packe could penetrate his immense panorama and isolate details. This viewing process was the prerequisite for drawing the chart; as a result Romney Marsh, for example, was excluded because it was invisible from the tower:

> compare the work within my 16 Mile Circle [of sight] . . . with the Weald of Kent, or Romney Marsh; these, as they are out of my Province, I have only mapped slightly to the extent of my Paper . . . though I have given them a Tinct or Ground over their surfaces, suitable to the general Nature of their Soils; yet how different are their faces . . . to the others, which I profess to finish Philosophically as they lye in Nature. [pp. 3–4]

However, Packe compromised the rigidity of this position somewhat in the cases of the Isles of Sheppey and Thanet, also out of sight from the Cathedral, but which he surveyed exclusively with conventional methods. This indicates a certain gap within his work between the demands of science and the power of panoramic viewing. The chart, as it finally appeared in 1743, was produced from a combination of panoramic observation and field surveys, and it could be argued that, despite Packe's pride in his innovatory viewing station, it was at least equally dependent on his fieldwork.

The scaffolding panorama he constructed was Packe's alone. In contrast to later forms of panorama, this judgement-seat could not be shared with others, and after it had been dismantled the only access to Packe's exhilarating experience was through the intermediate representations provided by the chart itself and *Ancographia*. Packe understood all too well that his project was unique; that no such chart of Kent had ever been seen. In her careful study of the relations between mapping and landscape painting in seventeenth-century Holland, Svetlana Alpers refers to the tradition that map-makers could 'turn to the natives . . . for assistance'.[5] While making his surveys in the field, Packe tried this, but found the attempt unhelpful:

> The Novelty of the Work did not a little enhance its Difficulty . . . without a guide to beat *untrodden* Paths . . . I was to form a Prototype, an *Original*. The Gross or

main part of the Inhabitants, though residing some of them many years, some all their lives on the Spot, never seem'd to have any the least notion of what I was about . . . Neither indeed could any one's Description of any place have given me an Idea of it sufficient for its Delineation . . . but my own eyes must be employed, or my own Observations must be made (and in many places frequently from the same Spot in different Views) before I could Register it in my Chart for Truth. [pp. 103–4]

While nobody could help Packe make the chart, the work's novelty must also have produced considerable difficulties for its first viewers. In *Ancographia*, Packe tries to guide viewers of the chart initially by laying claim to the uniqueness of his own work and differentiating it from other closely related practices. Packe's chart could easily be mistaken for a map, and this possibility was one that he wished to guard against, asserting that there was 'a wide and essential difference between this Chart and a Map'.[6] The differences he defined were both scientific and aesthetic, and give a vivid idea of early eighteenth-century mapping:

What has a *Map* to do with the *Surface* of the Earth more than to afford its several Objects, their Situations? And what is its whole Design more than a collection of the Names of Cities, Towns, Villages, etc. set upon a *Plain* Surface, at a Proper Distance, and in due Bearings to one another; with here and there a few Hills, Trees, and *General Streams* of the Rivers, scattered about in no very exact manner?[7] [p. 3]

In contrast to this haphazard and two-dimensional approach, Packe's chart fills up the course of every valley, and measures the height of the ground, to fulfil his scientific endeavour. But when he states that he will make no apology for a want of roads, an aesthetic concern is to the fore:

And, indeed, what an *Appearance* would the roads here make? How ill it would become this *Picture* to be *scrawled* all over with a Parcel of *double Black Lines*, for ever intersecting one another, and all of them *Foreign* from the Nature of the Work? . . . These roads, if I had put them in, would have been quite needless, and could have had no Effect, but hideously to *Deform* and confound this beautiful *Plan* of more Delicate Delineations. [pp. 4–5]

He argues vigorously because he is aware that by not including roads he could be thought of, in the context of eighteenth-century Kent, as considerably reducing the purely utilitarian value of the chart, or even its iconic value, both of which Packe wishes to situate on a higher, philosophical, level. The beauty that is at issue on the level of immediate effect is only partly the work of the chart-maker: it is inherent in the pattern of East Kent valleys. Producing a twin justification, both scientific and aesthetic, for not marking roads and making a map, enables Packe to defend his unconventional project.

While he excluded roads, Packe allowed into the chart the marks and names of settlements. These are partly to aid the scientific purpose, being 'Marks or Signs by which I set off, and carry on the course of every valley'. They are also in part aesthetic, being 'Ornaments to what would else be a naked System of Philosophy' (p. 3). However, when it comes to the process of naming villages, Packe uses names to distinguish his project from other discourses. He has been:

mindful not to write the names of places according to their true and obscure but their obvious and vulgar pronunciation. [An example is 'Bas'mere' for the village generally now spelled Badlesmere.] I write not as a Conveyancer or Antiquary, but as a Naturalist who desires to be understood by all sorts of Readers; and I think that the best known names best suit my Design. [p. 97]

After this initial disentanglement of his work from rival approaches to mapping, in later passages of *Ancographia* which describe rather than explain East Kent scientifically, Packe can afford to reintroduce alternative discursive frameworks, albeit on his own terms. The first of these is history. Reading earthworks in the Kentish countryside, Packe links them to the invasion by Julius Caesar in 54 BC as described in Caesar's *Gallic Wars*. He identifies the sites of two battles between the Romans and Britons as Chartham Downs (a ridge of high land overlooking the Stour valley on one side and Denge Wood on the other) and Jullaber's Grave (a long barrow on a spur of downland above the River Stour south-east of the village of Chilham). He enjoys an archaeological reflection:

I please myself with the thoughts of having trac'd [Caesar] ... very plainly by his military works from his landing place on the 'Apertum, molle, et planum littus', the open, soft and flat shore, all through this famous Region to Chartham Down, and Jullaber's Tomb; where he gave the conquering Blow, and reduc'd the Kentish Britains to the slavery of the Roman Yoke. [p. 53]

Packe's pleasure in history, however, does not extend much beyond Caesar. A panorama is a broad view that can embrace strongly contrasting elements, and Packe soon announces a shift of interest to other concerns:

After this cursory, dry *Topography* of the Vallies, I can't but stay a little, 'amoenitate loci captus' and indulge myself in the Review of this engaging Country. Its meer *Geographical* Situation affords ample matter for Encomium ... It is the Key to the Commerce, Arms and Arts of Europe. But I shall forebear all Remarks of this Sort, and take only a *Picturesque* Prospect, and regale myself with the Pleasures which our naked Eyes can praesent us with from Barham-Downs or from any other Place of Eminence. [p. 56]

The text has veered towards the political and economic, but Packe steers us back to the aesthetic. His 'Picturesque' is clearly distinguished by its variety, as Packe demonstrates when he begins his 'Review':

The Face of this whole Glebe is lively; its very Aspect has a peculiar Grace and Gaiety . . . vacant, yet not empty; unincumbered, tho' furnish'd; and without Wildness Free. Its Vallies are noble, wide and gentle: they are no where so Retired as to be deform'd with lonely darksome Depths: nor are its Eminences thrown up into ragged mountainous Praecipices . . . it is all a Rural Garden; and the Shallow depressions of its sloping vallies are but so many Ha-ha's. [p. 56]

Both here, and subsequently, the anthropomorphic or prosopopoiac quality in the language is noticeable: 'here all Nature is lightsome, terse and Polite' [p. 57]. In this example the adjectives verge on paradox and oxymoron. The difficulty of being 'terse and polite' at the same time may point to some sort of tension within Packe's perception of the earth's surface.

A long section of a derivative kind ensues, in which Packe views the landscape through pastoral and georgic conventions.[8] His personal voice does not re-emerge strongly in his text until his eye reaches the periphery of vision, beginning with the sea itself:

But what gives us the noblest Idea, and exceeds all description is the Broad, liquid, silver Margin, that mixes its bright Face with Earth and Heaven, and throws its Glittering Arms around almost All its borders; for all this delightful Scene lies in full Prospect of the Sea at Sandwich-Bay, and the Downs. What a new field of Wonders is here! – This at once separates that lovely Region from and connects it with the Universe. To the sprightly Aspect of the Land it joyns the Solemn Air of the Channel, and opens the Short confin'd view of this narrow nook of our Island into a wide extended Plain, bounded at the furthest Ken of the Eye, with the white cliffs of the opposite Kingdom; and enrich'd near Home with the Awful Beauties of the mighty Waters. Here the Floating foundations of the Royal Castles of the British Navy, like so many grand Palaces, gallantly Ride on the glorious surface of the Deep; and the numberless Sail of the Trading-craft, from the rich India-man to the smallest Fisher-boat, make as various an appearance by sea, as the houses of the nobility, the gentry, the farmers, and the cottage[r]s do by land; but with this beautiful improvement that the Still life of the Shore is here nobly Contrasted with the moving Pictures of the watery Plain. Shadows Skim, Winds Ruffle, Billows Rise, the Breakers Foam; Lobsters Crawl, Porpoises Rowl, Sea-Gulls Hover, and the Ships; – some Plough the Surge with a propitious gale, others Dance at anchor to the play of the waves. In fine, for there is no end of Images, the whole strikes you with such an assemblage of Diverse, nay Contrary beauties, which delightfully harmonize into one Ravishing Prospect; and every Thing in This is so Delicately different from the Rougher work of the Other regions, that it seems, as it were to have been made, not by the hands, but by the fingers of the allwise Architect: or rather to be pencill'd out as a

Model of a more enlarged design, as well for the Admiration of the Curious as the Entertainment of the Wise; who would all, if they could choose their lotts, fix their Seats in a Place, that for the conveniences and true delights of Life is an Earthly Paradise. [pp. 58–9]

This remarkable passage abounds with metaphors and similes of pictorial art: still-life, images, a pencilled model, an architectural maquette, even the totally fortuitous 'moving pictures'. Yet, if Packe is a precursor of cinema, he is so only in so far as the grand controlling rhetoric – of panorama – is such a precursor. This verbal panorama, although imagined from Barham Downs, complements that privately enjoyed by Packe from Canterbury Cathedral, and in some sense provides that experience's verbal equivalent. Yet this report of his vision tears down the barrier between what he sees and what he imagines. From Barham Downs he may see his view disintegrating in atmosphere and sea, but he cannot watch lobsters crawling or porpoises rolling (even with the most powerful telescope). These vignettes seem to have an equivalent on the chart itself, in the 'Explanation' or key, in which appear symbols not only for the grand scale of things (high and low tide, the ridges of the hills) but also for the small detail: 'Stacks of hop poles designed to show something near the body of the plantation round this city', for example, and 'Paddocks; where the boars are put up for the making of Brawn'. These details are as much part of the panoramic fabric as the large view. Yet Packe's verbal description is abstracted from the actual grass and bushes of East Kent in much the same way as his chart. Inspired, perhaps, by the excitement of being able to reach 'the furthest Ken of the Eye', Packe penetrates beyond it into a domain of the pure imagination, to envision and allegorize the life of the ocean, which acts as a classic framing device, completing and sealing a description or picture while relating it to some validating external source – in this case, both Britannia's commercial empire and the 'universe'. In this lengthy passage, we see Packe calmly taking his pleasure in culture. He reads East Kent like a text, and finally implies the necessity of imagination to complete the viewing process.

THE CODE OF THE DIVIDED SELF

Yet there is something unruly about Packe's sight. What fuelled him to devote his time and, on the rickety scaffolding above Canterbury Cathedral's Bell Harry Tower, perhaps to risk his life, in order to achieve an innovation that, as we shall see, amounts to the founding act of an entire discourse? A sense of the unruly comes across most clearly from some of the verbal inscriptions on the chart, such as the quotation from

Psalms already noted, and which appear to have little relevance to his scientific project.[9] Yet to what do such phrases testify, if not to the intellectual commitment that Packe sought to fulfil? To answer this question we must turn to the textual equivalent, in *Ancographia*, of the streams and hills marked on the chart to designate the surface of the earth itself. Most of the book describes the countryside of East Kent with particular attention to the flow of water through it, using a strong and immediately noticeable metaphor: 'The vallies of [the Swerdling] District lie in two divisions; one of which fills up all the space of the Duct of the Process from Swerdling to Sham'sford-Bridge; and the Other comes . . . down from the hills thro' Bockholt and Denge Woods into . . . Sinuses on each side of Mysthole' (pp. 39–40). The language (duct, process, sinuses) is that of medical anatomy: it had been learned in the dissection room, for Packe was a physician. Such language comes to a kind of climax after Packe turns his attention to something elusive and baffling in the landscape:

But then there are Other things, even such as I have no weak or imperfect Idea of, that would for ever elude the Description of my Pencil or Pen. There is an Inexpressible Consent, Grandeur and Politeness all over the face of the work, that can never be made to appear in the Chart, as it does in the Grand Book of Nature. The *curvus Anfractus*, the Manner of the Turnings and Windings of the common Sinuses or Ducts of the Vallies; the different way of their *Divarications* on each side of the Ducts with the greater and lesser Sections of their Ramifications, and laterall Exits; the Alternate Osculations and Indentations of the mouths of these Sinuses with the Tongues or low points of land, that separate all the vallies from another on their side, yet refer them to their opposite Neighbour on the other: the Insensible yet Distinct Inosculations of the Capillary Extremities of the evanescent Sections of the Vallies at the top of the hills, that disterminate the two, sometimes three or four Neighbouring Setts from one another; the intimate, deep, and extended Concavitys or Incorporation of whole Groups of Valleys with both their opposite regions, and into the suits of Vallies of the same District . . . These and many more; but above all the surprizing *Turn* of the Whole, that even in the places of its greatest roughness and shade, like a Picture designed for a Distant view, looks easie, harmonious and soft – These are things that though they be the pleasing subjects of my frequent Contemplation, and constant Admiration, they are too high for my expression; nor . . . can I think that the most exquisite Draughtsman could express these subjects in a finished manner to the Life [pp. 100–101]

This long, searching and straining passage, which takes on a distant and hesitant overtone of sexuality ('the Alternate Osculations . . . of the mouths . . . with the Tongues', 'the intimate, deep, and extended Concavitys'), shows that, for Packe at least, there are landscapes of bliss as well as landscapes of pleasure.[10] He is speaking of his motivation here: in part, as his dominant metaphor reveals, he is motivated by pride in his profession; yet on another level his motivation is concealed behind the unspeakability that he admits to in this passage. The edge where real sight becomes inexpressible is the object of Packe's scopic drive.[11] The metaphor from medical science no doubt represents Packe's most profound sense of identity as a working individual, yet it also points to a body as the object which he is attempting to recuperate by acts of looking and representing. He learned the words while contemplating a body in the dissection hall; yet the body that emerges in his written text is not being anatomized; rather, it is being constructed by Packe, who is attempting to bring it into being, to create it. This body's 'face' bears an expression of 'consent, grandeur and politeness', and the facial is a persistent metaphor throughout the book (while the rough parts of the body look miraculously 'easie, harmonious, and soft'). Packe's honest testimony to the elusive quality that fascinates him reveals that his scientific undertaking was found wanting by something unruly in his own sensibility: he searches precisely for what is difficult or impossible to see – such as the archaeological remains that he takes to be traces of Caesar's invasion, or the horizon of sea and sky, attractive and compelling precisely because it cannot be clearly seen and constitutes a boundary. Packe's stubborn truthfulness to his own perceptions allows him to define the inadequacy of the scientific endeavour in which he is formally engaged.[12]

I have indicated a strong unconscious motivation for Packe's project, impelling him towards fashioning an unprecedented image that he conceived of in an extraordinary way. His own comments in *Ancographia* on his conscious motivations are somewhat diffident yet ultimately just as rewarding. He links the chart to his project for writing a 'natural history' of East Kent, which would reveal 'the cause' of the valleys, as well as the 'state of Endemial Diseases' of the area. Although the project's 'materials' have been collected, they have been lain aside (p. 105) and in fact Packe never produced this projected work. As for the cultural value of the chart, a similarly unconvincing tone seems to come into play when he asserts its value to be its 'brevity', as contrasted with verbal descriptions, and when he claims that (in some way he does not specify) everything in it concerns the 'Life and Ease' of the inhabitants of the depicted region. Concerning the future use of his chart he makes a bolder assertion:

And tho' at first sight this may seem to some to be only a Local Draught of this part of Britain, it is really the *Specimen* of a Plan for the study of Nature all over the World. Here Philosophers and Artists, of most sorts, may exercise their talents in their search after natural knowledge; but *Agriculture* and *Physick* stand foremost to our view, and with open arms invite us to their Intimate Acquaintance. [p. 106]

By now, Christopher Packe is looking his most isolated and eccentric. He has deluged his reader with a metaphorical language that serves more to conceal than reveal the countryside of Kent. The connection he advocates between mapping, the practice of medicine and farming seems vague and unconvincing because he leaves unexplained exactly how such philosophico-chorography can benefit, or be benefited by, 'agriculture and physick' and because he wraps the three endeavours within a metaphor of physical intimacy suggestive of love-making ('with open arms invite us to their Intimate Acquaintance'). It seems hardly likely that such a combination of interests synthesized at some historical date to form a new scientific endeavour with spectacular results for human progress. The projected natural history of Kent was probably in the back of his mind as he wrote this passage, but he has explained that the materials for this more cherished project, embracing 'the cause' of the valleys and the state of diseases, have not yet been 'digested', and since the 'natural history' remained unwritten at his death in 1749, it seems that he has found himself incapable of creating a satisfactory synthesis from this tantalizing combination of intellectual interests. He can, however, be rescued from isolation and eccentricity by comparison with the convictions of the eminent twentieth-century scientist James Lovelock:

The waters of the earth, as James Hutton saw long ago, are like the circulation system of an animal. Their ceaseless motions (together with the blowing of the wind) transfer essential nutrient elements from one part to another and carry away the waste products of metabolism.[13]

This remarkable passage, written by the scientist whose inventions were responsible for the detection of the destruction of the ozone layer, and whose theories underpin the concept of the greenhouse effect, enables us to group Christopher Packe with him and with the scientist he mentions, James Hutton, whose life in fact bears out Packe's assertion that 'agriculture and physick' should be closely related to the study of land forms. Hutton studied medicine in Edinburgh, Paris and Leyden from 1744 to 1749, but he never practised as a physician. In 1750 he took up agriculture, living with a farmer in Norfolk from 1752 to 1754 before settling in the latter year on his farm in Berwickshire, a paternal inheritance. From the 1740s onwards he made chemical experiments, and from at least the 1750s onwards journeyed through Britain and into Europe investigating mineralogy and geology. In the history of science, he ranks as 'the independent originator of the modern explanation of the earth's crust by means of changes still in progress'.[14] In 1795 he summarized his findings in his *Theory of the Earth*:

Here is a compound system of things, forming together one whole living world; a world maintaining an almost endless diversity of plants and animals, by the disposition of its various parts, and by the circulation of its different kinds of matter ... that salutary circulation by which provision is so wisely made for the growth and prosperity of plants, and for the life and comfort of its various animals ...

Our solid earth is every where wasted, where exposed to the day. The summits of the mountains are necessarily degraded. The solid and weighty materials of those mountains are every where urged through the valleys, by the force of running water. The soil, which is produced in the destruction of the solid earth, is gradually travelled by the moving water, but is constantly supplying vegetation with its necessary aid. This travelled soil is at last deposited on the coast, where it forms most fertile countries. But the billows of the ocean agitate the loose materials upon the shore, and wear away the coast, with the endless repetitions of this act of power, or this imparted force ...

We are thus led to see a circulation in the matter of this globe, and a system of beautiful economy in the works of nature. This earth, like the body of an animal, is wasted at the same time that it is repaired.[15]

What we have from Packe and Hutton (and Lovelock) is a series of statements, dispersed over a wide conceptual and temporal field, yet related: a *discourse* as defined by Michel Foucault.[16] It is the discourse of *geophysiology*, which is first dependent on the idea that the earth is alive.[17] On one level the relationship between Packe, Hutton and Lovelock can be characterized with regard to the body implied by the discourse. Packe discovers (or creates) a body on the dissecting table, but cannot quite bring it to life. Hutton endows it with a kind of immortality: it becomes a 'super-organism', ever changing, still evolving, a 'living system', a 'living world',[18] and he confides that in the economy of the world 'we find no vestige of a beginning, – no prospect of an end'.[19] It has been the contribution of James Lovelock to grant this body a natural life and, by implication, a possible death: his Gaia hypothesis hinges upon the fact that the sun now emits 25 per cent more heat than it did when life first appeared on earth, and yet, unlike Venus and Mars, the earth is still habitable, indeed, is 'Heaven for the life it bears'.[20] He argues that it is maintained and regulated as a habitable place by the very life that it supports. Much of the urgency of Lovelock's work comes from a realization that, with the ever-increasing output of heat from the sun, or through human interference, this capacity to regulate planetary temperature could cease.

Christopher Packe's endeavour was, as we have seen, panoramic in conception. James Hutton's theory was characterized in similar terms by John Playfair, writing his *Illustrations of the Huttonian Theory of the Earth* in 1802:

The geologist must not content himself with examining the insulated specimens of his cabinet . . . [he] must select, for the places of his observations, those points, from which the variety and gradation of her [nature's] works can be most extensively and accurately explored.[21]

The combination of breadth with accuracy (implying detail) amounts to the panoramic formula. Such an 'exact and comprehensive survey' (and one which in retrospect, through the historical position of geology, we can see as crucial in helping to lay the basis for Darwinian science), according to Playfair, can be assisted by the work of 'other sciences' – sciences to which we have seen Christopher Packe attempting to contribute:

The accurate geographical maps and surveys which are now making; the soundings; the observations of currents; the barometrical measurements, may all combine to ascertain the reality, and to fix the quantity of those changes which terrestrial bodies continually undergo.[22]

Playfair also uses the image of a painting in assessing the lasting foundational value of Hutton's comprehensive theory, and its openness to revision but not obsolescence:

Ages may be required to fill up the bold outline which Dr. Hutton has traced with so masterly a hand; to detach the parts more completely from the general mass; to adjust the size and position of the subordinate members; and to give to the whole piece the exact proportion and true colouring of nature.[23]

Locating his work within geophysiology, and specifying in particular the relations between his thinking and Hutton's, allows us an insight into the sort of intellectual problems with which Packe was trying to come to terms, and the ways in which they might have proved to be obstacles to his thinking. He implies the belief that the valleys have been caused, or carved out, by flowing water; yet he never quite asserts this position directly. Linking the flow of water to valley erosion would have placed him half a century ahead of his time. This remained a point of dispute between Hutton and his critics; indeed, it was Hutton's work that established the truth of the observation.[24] Given this situation, the actual understanding of 'the cause' of the valleys, promised in his projected natural history of East Kent, but never delivered to his readers, may never have been achieved by Packe. For him it might have constituted instead a baffling and eventually insuperable barrier to the intellectual development of his theories.

I have dwelt on Packe – or, more particularly, allowed Packe to speak in his own words – because I believe his work to be a contribution to the discourse of geophysiology, and to be an important element in the re-forming of panoramic fields of vision into specifically modern form. I feel that it is important to understand the work as fully as possible, and therefore to include an understanding of its self-avowed relations with pre-existing mapping, as well as to comprehend the chart as a representation arising from unconscious impulses and motivations. Apart from anything else, such an unconscious investment indicates that desire can create strategic forms for the working-out of its mechanisms.[25]

6

Dark with Excess of Bright:
Mapping the Coastlines of Knowledge

PAUL CARTER

> ... behold
> The Coast how wonderful. Proportions strange,
> And unimaginable forms ...
>
> Charles Harpur, 'A Coast View'[1]

> Shipwreck has, of itself, opened a wide field of geographical knowledge ...
>
> J. G. Dalyell, *Shipwrecks and Disasters at Sea*[2]

If you told an ocean-going yachtsman that coastlines were a construction of the mind, he'd take you for a madman. Likewise any mariner, especially in the shipwreck-prone eighteenth century. Other geographical features – mountains, rivers, even islands – might have a habit of disappearing or relocating themselves as survey methods grew more accurate, but the primary ambition of every marine explorer – *to fall in with land* – lent the coast a privileged position in geographical discourse. The coast not only harboured harbours, the longed-for object of every colonizing expedition, it paraded a variety of geographical objects – those already mentioned, as well as reefs, capes and bays. In a way the coast was an a priori of geographical discourse, a meta-geographical proposition enabling one to say something valuable about the geographical phenomena found along it. A coast was a generalization, an abstraction: but as the medium of connecting isolated objects to one other, it was a condition of knowledge, an analogue of the associative reasoning essential to the orderly progress of reason (and the legitimation of colonialism as the project of bringing formerly isolated peoples into contact with the West – or putting them on the map).

To fulfil these intellectual ambitions, to become an image of reasoning, the coast itself had to be linearized, reconceptualized as a *coastline*. This was as much an intuitive aspect of chart-making as a representation of what had been seen. Matthew Flinders, for instance, who in surveying the coasts of Australia had set himself the task of following the land 'so closely, that the washing of the surf upon it should be visible, and no opening, nor anything of interest escape notice',[3] could not surpass the limitations of his surveying technique. Had he been aware of, and heeded, Dalrymple's and Beautemps-Beaupré's 'violent condemnation of surveying the coastline by a series of magnetic bearings, with an azimuth compass – the method used by Flinders – instead of using the sextant to obtain offshore angles, and fixing the ship with a station-pointer',[4] and had he had reliable timekeepers, he could have avoided 'an infinity of trouble'[5] in determining the position of his reference points – mainly capes – both relative to each other and absolutely on the globe. But nothing would have helped him fill in the gaps between. As Ingleton remarks, 'the intervening coastline between the "fixed" navigational features was usually sketched in by eye'.[6]

Sketching by eye meant to reduce to a line: with a hand-held pen to reduce a sweep of land to a continuous curve. Perhaps the symmetrical concavities ascribed to bays are a relic of pre-Enlightenment gesturalism, as the arm, pivoted on its stationary elbow, naturally describes an arc over the page. But as the command of getting from one place to another without any gaps, the extended line was *logically* a form of knowledge. To assist this illusion, in hand-drawing a chart the cartographer did what he could to eliminate any sign of the line's human source: as a recent text book still suggests, 'Coastlines may be drawn with a crow quill pen or any other fine nib if care is taken to maintain a uniform thickness of line. It is an aid to have the paper loose on the drafting table so that it may be turned around freely and lines drawn towards the cartographer.'[7] Shifted around like this, a seismically sensitive coastline emerges, the trace of a repeated hand–eye passage; and it's not going too far to suggest that its logical appeal is partly aesthetic, its joined-up arabesques suggesting a sympathetic identification between the manual excursions of the cartographer and the mundane voyage of the explorer.

The most spectacular evidence of this psycho-kinetic calligraphic convergence comes from an earlier period – the 68 panoramic drawings of coastlines between Banda and Malacca which Francisco Rodrigues made in 1512–13 apply the same fine nib to the proliferation of aerial arabesques, recalling nothing so much as Albrecht Dürer's exactly contemporary woodcut *The Great Triumphal Car*, also used in capturing the lyrical curvature of the coasts.[8] The scientism of the late eighteenth century might seek to expunge every relic of this anthropomorphism, but it is arguable that aesthetic considerations based on an unacknowledged identification of natural forms with psycho-kinetic movement images continued subtly to influence the appraisal and representation of coasts. It is intriguing in this context to compare Cook's Alaskan charts with those he made of New Zealand and Australia: in contrast with the long sweeps of the latter, the former presented an infinity of inlets or gaps that no running survey could ever hope to fill in.

But unless they could be shown to have a reason of their own, gaps were an offence against logic: only as sources of legitimate speculation, as sites of unbounded advance, could they be recorded. Hence in part the optimistically named Cook's River: renaming it Cook's Inlet after closer examination, George Vancouver regretted that the great navigator's boats had not pushed up a little further 'consequently preventing the indulging of those chimerical speculations concerning its spacious & unbounded extent'.[9] But rivers were coastlines by another name; they were gaps where imagination coincided with reasonable expectation. A coastline that folded back on itself like some marine flagellate, yielding no new body of knowledge, was horrible to contemplate.

An interesting line (as it were) could be drawn from Hogarth's serpentine 'line of beauty' to John Ruskin's 'abstract lines in nature'. Along its axis would be found *inter alia* William Playfair's innovative representation of the National Debt as a continuous mountain-range graph, Ernst Chladni's sound forms (1785), which, by representing vowels as linear patterns, held out the promise of a universal sound writing, and hence the realization of that Royal Society chimaera, a universal language, and Erasmus Darwin's derivation of our idea of beauty from the profile of the female breast, not to mention the mathematician Euler's principle *lineae curvae maximi minimive proprietatibus gaudentes* and the embryologist's concept of orthogenesis.[10] The salient feature of these linearizations of phenomena (no less than of the conventional histories of science and ideas that place them in a progressive line of descent) is that they correspond in the metaphysical sphere to the laws of motion Newton laid down in the physical sphere: they are uniform, dimensionless and self-repeating. They refer to a time which displays no temporal variation, to a space that like the grid of the map projection pretends to have no effect on the objects it contains. Their continuation, their extension in any direction, does not signify an attractive force acting on them locally but an innate propensity to self-reproduction. The result is a geometrical analogue of the doctrine of Progress, an irresistible forward movement which poses as the unchanging repetition of an initial impulse.

This outline history of the line might seem unduly deterministic – after all, 'in both the maps of the Caribou and coastal Eskimo . . . an unbroken line is used to represent coastline or riverbank', and most cultures seem able at the anthropologist's behest to represent where they live lineally. But while this shows a capacity to map, it does not, as Denis Wood emphasizes, 'result in maps'.[11] Or, to put it another way, an ability to inscribe a peripatetically inhabited environment in the form of spatio-mimetic marks is quite different from a cultural propensity to read the line as a sign of space conceived as a bounded blank, uniformly ready for civilizing inscription. The Eskimo line represents a passage, a rate of progress, even a seasonal calendar, and is fat, palpable and regional; the cartographer's line signifies the conquest of environmental memories, the translation of path-finding and performative renewals of place into the blank of a territory metaphysically brought into being by a bounding line that does not belong to it and, being nowhere, cannot be refuted.

Unlike shells, flowers, the human figure and even the trajectories of the planets, the outlines of land masses were not capable of complete definition with the help of elementary mathematics – we have had to await the emergence of a theory of fractals to model the metonymic principle informing their parts. But this did not mean that in principle they could not be reduced to a formula. As early as 1686 Leibniz had taken the case of someone who 'marks a number of points on a sheet of paper entirely at random', and asserted, 'It is possible to find a geometrical line whose motion is constant and uniform in accordance with a certain rule, such that this line shall pass through all the points, and in the same order that they were marked on the pen.' Unintentionally giving a philosophical patent to the pseudo-science of cranioscopy or phrenology later developed by Franz Joseph Gall, Leibniz adds, 'Nor is there any instance of a face whose contour does not form part of a geometrical line, and which cannot be traced at one stroke by a given regulated movement,' although he prudently acknowledges that 'when a rule is very complicated, that which conforms to it passes for being irregular'.[12]

The difficulty of drawing a continuous, dimensionless line is not simply a ticklish problem for the draughtsman: in modest compass it describes the logical paradox inherent in Enlightenment epistemology. A science that claimed to be well founded had *ipso facto* to leave no gaps in its reasoning, but if it were to make any progress it had necessarily to begin somewhere and end somewhere else – without the little *saltus* of imagination, the gift of intellectual wit, or what Vico called *ingenium*, to see relationships and grasp their significance, no progress was possible.[13] But for the gap there was nothing to know, but the scope of knowledge was to eliminate it. And the instrument of elimination is the continuous line. It is a point nicely illustrated in an English treatise on surveying published in 1840, where the apprentice map-maker is warned that is it is an error 'to regard hills as isolated features, as they often appear to the eye; observation, and a knowledge of the outlines of geology, inevitably produce more enlarged ideas respecting their combination; and analogy soon points out where to expect the existence of fords, springs, defiles, and other important features incidental to peculiar formations; and appearances that at one time presented nothing but confusion and irregularity, will, as the eye becomes more experienced, be recognized as the results of general and known laws of nature'.[14] This recalls Goldsmith's confidence in the Linnaean system of classification to 'dissipate the glare' of a 'multiplicity of objects'[15] and cross-fertilizes it with Huttonian uniformitarianism. But Linnaeus proceeded by way of quite fanciful analogy, while Hutton, than whom, his biographer asserts, none was 'more skilful in marking the gradations of nature . . . more diligent in observing the *continuity* of her proceedings', founded his system on an intuition of geological *discontinuity*.[16]

The treatise just quoted suggests another point: that broad paradox of Enlightenment epistemology had a particular incarnation in the different techniques necessarily employed in land mapping and coastal mapping. Edney argues that Foucault was mistaken in identifying the Enlightenment *episteme* with the knowledge of natural history, pointing out that the natural historians themselves 'consistently employed maps and mapping as the trope for their taxonomic systems'.[17] However, the maps in question were the products of trigonometry – no running survey of the coastal kind could accurately map a territory. As Edney comments,

Triangulation defines an exact equivalence between the geographic archive and the world. Triangulation makes it possible to conceive of a map constructed at a scale of 1:1. Not only would this be the same size as the territory it represents, it would *be* the territory. The 'technological fix' offered by triangulation has served to intensify the Enlightenment's 'cartographic illusion' of the 'mimetic map'.[18]

But except in rare cases triangulation was not an option for the coastal surveyor: in theory he could use the same techniques as the land surveyor to fix his geographical latitude and longitude, but in reality he was rarely able to remain in one place long enough in order to make the long run of astronomical and chronometric observations needed to establish his absolute position more or less accurately.

Besides, very few coasts provided the combination of prominent features and long, uninterrupted views needed to establish a baseline. Not only the mountainous Alaskan shores failed to 'afford any convenient situation',[19] the indeterminate flats of the Gulf of Carpentaria were equally inconvenient, the coastal surveyor operating like someone in 'flat uncleared country', unable to see ahead and having to rely on astronomical observations to fix the distances between stations. 'In surveying any extended line of coast, where the interior is not triangulated, no other method presents itself; and a knowledge of practical astronomy therefore becomes indispensable in this, as in all extensive geodesical operations.'[20]

Unable to establish a base line and to triangulate from it, the coastal surveyor no sooner sailed out of sight of the positions previously fixed than he had to begin again the process of fixing his own position, and that of the coastal features in relation to it. Bound to fall back on the rough and ready technique of dead deductive reckoning, where the ship's position was deduced from its direction of sail and an estimate of distance travelled, he proceeded like the land traveller who confined himself to making a route survey; but here too he was at a disadvantage. While the surveyor reconnoitring a new territory could fix the consecutive points of his march by taking the bearing of prominent objects to either side of his course, the surveyor at sea was always to one side of the map he was creating. Hence the pivotal significance of improved timekeepers in late eighteenth-century mapping. Yet these, facilitating a vastly more accurate calculation of longitude, could also contribute to the coastal surveyor's insulation from his object of study: thus, much as Vancouver wanted to set up an observatory during his first Alaskan survey season 'for the purpose of ascertaining the rate and error of our chronometers', he realized that, 'To take the chronometers ashore would mean moving them to an icy, wet, windy place from the shelter of a warm cabin, with probably disastrous consequences for accuracy of the mechanisms.'[21]

In short, the coastal survey stood to one side of the classic ambition of Enlightenment science to map the world, preserving in the awkwardness of its practices a recognition of the refractory nature of the phenomenal world, an awareness of the approximate and constructed nature of its designs. It is telling that in his analysis of maps as signifiers of power Wood nowhere examines the line itself; in a way the line is not a sign in the same sense as the hachured representation of a hill. The geographer's coastline signifies rather the desire of signification, the condition of bringing into circulation the field where power relations will be played out. But the coastline, unlike the conventionally differentiated river or hill or lake, is infinite and folded; it cannot ultimately be mapped and known.

It has no other side – if it reveals one, it becomes detached, turned into an island. It cannot strictly speaking be bounded and possessed; it can provide the ground of knowledge – the suitable place to make astronomical observations; it can provide the limit of knowledge, the horizon as concrete edge; but, itself the sign of elimination, it cannot be eliminated. In this way it resists cartography's inward spiral towards an ultimate classification where every trace of place is neutralized under the aegis of triangulation. By the same token, standing at the threshold of imperial possession, it also stands outside the territorialization of the world; though it bounds a closed figure, remaining recalcitrantly open.

In practice navigators proceeded by way of analogies, and even if these were mistaken, there was no other way. An 'opening . . . observed in the beach' will bear 'every appearance of being the mouth of a rivulet, from the broken and irregular form of the hills behind it'; 'a bright appearance on the horizon' will be confidently interpreted as an indication of the existence of islands 'that seldom failed in being correct, whenever an opportunity offered of proving it'; and so on. These remarks from P. P. King's *Survey of the Intertropical Coasts of Australia*, undertaken between 1818 and 1822,[22] underline the point that whatever the thin ambitions of the cartographer might be, the coast remained *fat* from the point of view of the coastal surveyor and hydrographer. Dismissing a chart purporting to represent Macquarie Harbour in south-west Tasmania, King explained, 'I found it to be merely a delineation of its coast line; without noticing the depth of water, or any of the numerous shoals which crowd the entrance of this extraordinary harbour.'[23]

From the landside, too, the route surveyor, in contrast with the triangulating map-maker, continued to conceive the coast less as a line than as a region, tract or district – much in the sense the term is used in the King James Bible. The explorer E. J. Eyre, making his way round the cliffs of the Great Australian Bight, regularly describes going down to the 'coast' to look for water, where the term implies a distinct transitional zone including sandhills, shore and shallow water.[24] The elusiveness of the coast's definition might have another cause: 'hydrographic charts', we are reminded, 'are made with a datum, or plane of reference, of mean low water, whereas topographic maps are usually made with a datum of mean sea level'.[25] Because of the difficulty of calculating longitude in the eighteenth century north–south coasts in particular could wobble alarmingly on the map: even the extraordinary accuracy achieved by Cook could not overcome this. First Fleet administrators who sited their tents according to the chart were settling in water: perhaps Britain never formally laid claim to *terra australis*.[26]

'The surface is where most of the action is,' writes J. J. Gibson.[27] Geographically, as the journals of Cook, Flinders, King or Stokes attest, the same could be said of coasts: they were where most of the action was. Intellectually, they were an epitome of Enlightenment curiosity; they seemed to concentrate in the greatest density, and in the most accessible form, that multiplicity of objects without which inductive knowledge was helpless to proceed step by step towards universally applicable generalization. King's instructions are telling in this way: 'You will exercise your own discretion as to landing on the several parts of the coast which you may explore; but on all occasions of landing, you will give every facility to the botanist, and the other scientific persons on board to pursue their inquiries.'[28] The coast was primarily conceived as an arena of intellectual enquiry; in this form it was the line that enabled the scientist to draw other lines. On the beach at Hood Canal in Puget Sound during his first expedition to America's north-west coast, Vancouver found himself approached by a group of native people: 'As the Native people drew near, he had a line drawn in the sand between the two groups. He would not allow anyone to cross it without first requesting permission.'[29] So with Enlightenment science generally; it constituted itself as heterology by drawing a line between the observer and the observed. The coast served in this sense as an intellectual base line even when it failed to accommodate the theodolite; as the site of demarcation it brought otherness into the world.

The coast was a pre-emptive clearing; it was a space already extracted and differentiated from the uniformity of nature. It was nature disturbed and ruined, a breach that incubated unimaginable productions that – even if they existed elsewhere – could only be examined here, in this visually-privileged nowhere-place. Its very disarray, the mimic resemblance of its productions to the specimens arranged in a *cabinet de curiosités*, not to mention the antic human behaviours it elicited, suggested it was a museum in the making. The remarkable engraving 'The View of the Island of Ouby from Freshwater Bay on Batchian' from Forrest's *A Voyage to New Guinea and the Moluccas* may pose as an ethnographically inflected picturesque view – in reality it assimilates the coast to the exhibition diorama. Type specimens of a multiplicity of exotic objects present themselves to the scientific gaze, washed-up, exposed, already detached from their environmental matrix, lost it seems unless they can be classified and correctly arranged. The native collectors, handling physically

W. Hamilton, 'The View of the Island of Ouby from Freshwater Bay on Batchian', from
Thomas Forrest, *A Voyage to New Guinea and the Moluccas* (Dublin, 1779).

what the English savant examines mentally, pleasantly flatter the latter's
sense of intellectual superiority.

The coast could be used to demonstrate the continuity of nature precisely because it was a gap, a breach, a discontinuity. To return to James
Hutton and his memorialist, John Playfair – it is not simply that Hutton
made discontinuity a principle of continuity, it is the *mise-en-scène* of
that demonstration that counts. Wanting to draw support for his theory
of 'some expansive force' responsible for 'the immense disturbance ... of
the strata ... elevating those rocks which it had before consolidated', by
appealing, 'Among the marks of disturbance in which the mineral kingdom abounds, [to] those great breaches among rocks, which are filled
with materials different from the rock on either side ...' Hutton and his
companions took a boat from Dunglass and followed the coast round to
the headland of Siccar where, stepping ashore, they found themselves
walking over 'micaceous schistus, in beds nearly vertical, highly in-
durated' towards a perpendicular cliff of sandstone. 'The immediate
contact of the two rocks is not only visible, but is curiously dissected and
laid open by the action of the waves. The rugged tops of the schistus are
seen penetrating into the horizontal beds of sandstone, and the lowest of
these last form a breccia containing fragments of schistus, some round
and others angular, united by an arenaceous cement.'

There follows the famous passage in which, as Playfair contemplates the empirical ground at his feet, 'the millimeters and the shadows of small things', there opens up to him a vast theoretical vision: 'We felt ourselves necessarily carried back to the time when the schistus on which we stood was yet at the bottom of the sea, and when the sandstone before us was only beginning to be deposited, in the shape of sand or mud, from the waters of a superincumbent ocean. An epocha [sic] still more remote presented itself . . . The mind seemed to grow giddy by looking so far into the abyss of time.'[30] The cause of his visionary vertigo is not what is suddenly present to his external eye: it is what passes before his mental eye – *and* the vast discontinuity between the two visions. The source of his wonder is the *lack* of resemblance between the 'palpable evidence' and the 'theoretical speculations' they have occasioned; it is only the ingenuity of Hutton that can persuade him of their ultimate connection. In fact the natural history so persuasively imagined is a vindication of Hutton's metaphysics rather than his physics. It exemplifies Hutton's view that 'there [is] no resemblance between the world without us, and the notions that we form of it.' Yet Hutton's geology may still be a truthful story because, against Berkeley, Hutton holds that, although 'The world . . . as conceived by us, is the creation of the mind itself, [it is] of the mind acted on from without, and receiving information from some external power.' Thus, 'our perceptions being consistent, and regulated by uniform and constant laws, are as much realities to us, as if they were the exact copies of things really existing'.[31]

This inductive conception of knowledge may be described as *coastal*. Much as the coast departs from the uniformity of land and sea, bearing no resemblance to them and yet profoundly mimicking the forces informing their creation, so our knowledge of the world may bear no resemblance to the external world and yet provide us with a genuine insight into its operations. Our perceptions – which, Hutton insists, provide us with a valid account of reality – are Janus-faced, and move back and forth along the littoral of consciousness, endlessly, tidally negotiating the back and forth between inner and outer worlds. And a particular kind of coastal calligraphy is associated with this process of intellection. Hutton's skill as a mineralogist consisted, Playfair considered, in a twofold endowment: in 'an accurate eye for perceiving the characters of natural objects' and 'in equal perfection the power of interpreting their signification, and of decyphering those ancient hieroglyphics which record the revolutions of the globe'.[32] But where did these 'characters' form? What classified them as 'hieroglyphics'? These actions occurred along the littoral where, through the medium of a shared discourse of symbolic forms, the mind had the impression nature was an alphabet, a joined up piece of writing which it was uniquely endowed to decipher.

These coastal cuts were not natural: nor were they environmentally neutral. They were the precondition of an intellectual grasp of the world predicated on the abstraction of things from their places and their reorganization into lines of descent and ascent. Perhaps it is an accident that Aristotle's *De Generatione* and *De Motu Animalium* seem most firmly grounded empirically when describing creatures of the shoreline; but if nothing else they show how walking the beaches of his native Samos was intellectually productive.[33] Ease of peripateia, and step-by-step inductive reasoning: perhaps they were as one on Aegean beaches. Be that as it may, by the time natural history reaches its intellectual climax, in Wallace's *The Malay Archipelago*, the violence that must be done to nature if confusion and irregularity are to be cleared away and her general laws made known is axiomatic. And the environmental metaphor is not idle. It is down jungle trails blazed by timber-getters and mining companies that Wallace ambles with his gun and butterfly-net, around their slash-and-burn fires that he collects, and where obstructive vegetation gets in the way, or the ground is disagreeably steep, he complains as bitterly as any developer.[34]

This disregard of the environment of knowledge characterizes not only Wallace's collecting habits but also the organization of his material: in *The Malay Archipelago* the fragmentary nature of his knowledge of different places and their natural histories, based on a number of brief visits made over an extended period of time, are swept away; instead two geographically adjacent, but biologically isolated, continents are described, a synthesis of data that renders plausible in advance Wallace's thesis – so that like the line his great book is the endless repetition of a point already reached.[35]

Not only in the Pacific but also in the Mediterranean coasts were a condition, and perhaps origin, of colonialism. This was Thucydides' view, and he identified two moments in the process: first, the fact of coastal dwelling which meant that Hellenes and the barbarians of the coast and islands, as communication by sea became more common, were tempted to turn pirates; second, the necessity of reacting to this, which led Minos of Crete to establish a navy with which he 'made himself master of what is now called the Hellenic sea, and ruled over the Cyclades, into most of which he sent the first colonies, expelling the Carians and appointing his sons governors; and thus did his best to put down piracy in those waters'.[36] This rationalization of imperialism was recapitulated in the eighteenth century, where scientists and colonial administrators alike described themselves as clearing up unlawful confusion, and restoring order; a condition of this return is the delineation of a new territory – whether it was the 'Hellenic Sea' or 'Australia' – over which a grid of exclusive authority can be laid.

Coastlines were attractive in many senses: as privileged sites of seeing, they were telescopic. They brought distant things near. Perhaps in proportion to the visualist investment in them, they could also be misty, romantically alluring, emotionally turbulent. Promising the unveiling of riches, they were represented as femininely coy, a Sirenland inhabited, at least in the watercolours of Cox or Bonington, by an amphibious race of mussel-collectors, net-menders and children. The secrecy of the knowledge the coast vouchsafed reached its English apotheosis later in the nineteenth century when Philip Gosse revealed to the world the wonders of its invertebrate crustacea.[37] Coasts kept alive the dialectic between the seen and the unseen whose rationalization was critical to the formulation of Enlightenment epistemology. How did one go from the known to the unknown? – this was the drama the coast played out. 'Behind the cliffy parts of the coast the land assumed a more fertile appearance; and this seemed an almost invariable law in the natural history of this new world,' observed the marine surveyor John Lort Stokes, off the coast adjacent to the Kimberleys in north-west Australia.[38]

Coastlines were tangible horizons making the unattainable attainable; in Stokes's eye their very lack of content might be promising. Encouraging the eye to wander beyond, to pass from the visible into the realms of the as yet invisible, they contracted time as well as space. As a stepping stone, as a gap that presented itself as a featureless continuity, the coast ideally merged into the plain. In this sense the coastal region in the Gulf of Carpentaria Stokes later denominated 'The Plains of Promise' was a continuous coast, an extension made deep. And lo and behold, what is unbroken and uniform begins to differentiate itself: it would not be long, Stokes persuades himself, before 'the now level horizon would be broken by a succession of tapering spires rising from the many Christian hamlets that must ultimately stud this country'.[39]

If, in Australia, the present must telescope the future, along the Siren-infested shores of classical Italy it was the remote past that the coast served to extract from historical mirage and bring into magnified focus. The famous Doric monuments of ancient Poseidonia (modern Paestum) stand on a low plateau of limestone some three kilometres inland in the

Jean-Jacques-François Taurel, *A View of the Temples of Paestum*, 1793.

plain of Salerno, south of Naples. Jean-Jacques-François Taurel's *A View of the Temples of Paestum* (dated 1793) is a tolerably accurate representation of the temples – only in his painting he has moved them down to the coast where they now stand overlooking the Tyrrhenian Sea. His motive? In the offing, in the painting's left-hand foreground, a boatload of scientifically inclined Grand Tourists stand, sketch-book in hand or spyglass to the eye or simply pointing out the enlivening prospect. It is for *their* benefit that the intervening three kilometres of countryside has been abridged and rendered invisible.

To grasp visually these evidences of ancient wisdom, to make of them modern knowledge, the temples have had to be relocated to that museum of the intellectual eye, the coast. To see them properly, as architecture commanding a clearing, the visitors have to remain offshore. Instead of wandering through the bush, getting acquainted with the lie of the land, the climactic moment of revelation depends on cultivating a soothing distance and staying out of touch. It was Berkeley who championed the anti-commensensical view that 'The qualities we experience visually are entirely other than the qualities we experience tangibly, so that there are no means, except that of habitual experience, of working out connections between the two.'[40] But it was later natural philosophers who made it a corollary that the two senses of sight and touch must be divorced, one entirely subordinated to the other, and who, tacitly accepting that 'distance and other spatial properties can be immediately experienced only by touch',[41] tried to eliminate these tactile dimensions of knowledge by relocating the objects of intellectual desire in that zone apparently reserved by nature for seeing.

In reality it was the zone of the blindspot, a construction of the mind. If Berkeley's starting point is that 'sight is a kind of illuminated blindness' and the eye is 'in reality not open to the world [and] therefore cannot see', then something else must show the way ahead. 'It is undeniably the case,' writes Appelbaum paraphrasing Berkeley, 'that as we walk along the road, we are guided by some power, some ability. That power cannot be sensory nor bodily nor organic in origin, since body in itself is mute, dumb, deaf, and mindless.' What then? It must be 'the mind itself that lights up the way. It must be the mind that sees through blind windows of the eyes. It must be intellect that discloses a world through its radiant vision.' The result of this 'diabolical development' is that it 'reduces the exercise of sight to comparative judgment. Nothing fresh enters into the act of seeing, because seeing consists wholly in comparing a current tableau with past ones. Seeing is seeing sameness. Seeing is the same seeing the same.'[42]

In coastal exploration the plausibility of this perverse mentalism, according to which the mind sees through the dead organs of sight and steers them in the direction it wants to go, was reinforced by the mimic motion of the vessel, itself more or less obedient to the cybernaut's commanding will. By extension the coast could be seen as a disclosure of the navigator's own radiant vision, as its profile and outline were the direct offspring of his carefully plotted course and accurate pen. Marine surveyors like King and Stokes, steeped in the picturesque aesthetic, inclined to attribute a face to the country: how else could it be if the coast was the mirror of their own gaze? Its utility, its promise, was in direct proportion to the conformity of its expression to their own expectations.[43]

Hence Stokes's frustration with the environs of Roebuck Bay whose mangrove-ridden tidal reaches offered no decisive break, mappable boundaries, cliff-top points of reference – no definite differentiation between near and far; no progressive narrative or drama of telescopic domination. Instead, a truly in-between zone defied them, one characterized by fleeting appearances, shifting expressions, deceptive depths and equally frustrating shallows:

The face of the country [Mr Usborne] described as exceedingly low, with mud lumps not unlike ant-hills, scattered here and there over the face of it, and several clusters of small trees. Natives also had been seen, though no opportunity of approaching them had occurred, as the moment their restless eyes or quick ears detected our approach, they most rapidly retreated.

To the south-west it was no better. Wickham and the surgeon

visited an inlet near the ship . . . They proceeded to the south-west for about three miles, through a very tortuous channel, dry in many parts at low water, thickly studded with mangrove bushes, over and through which the tide made its way at high water, giving to that part of the country the appearance of an extensive morass.

The only result was to prove 'that no opening to the interior would be found in it'. In returning, Mr Usborne managed to shoot himself. 'The hoped-for river must be sought elsewhere,' Stokes reported disconsolately, christening this zone of non-arrival 'Useless Bay'.[44]

Nowhere did the paradox of sameness manifest itself more disconcertingly than in negotiations with indigenous peoples. To communicate with those people who invariably gathered on the cliff or peered out from the trees wherever the explorer-surveyors landed was the supreme challenge: how to recognize difference, and through the medium of language, to draw these pantomimic creatures into the discourse of reason. But what happened where these figures sidestepped this desire to telescope the distance between them, making themselves instantly *mirrors of their white others?* Of people met at Rockingham Bay, Queensland, in 1819, King noted, 'Everything we said or did was repeated by them with the most exact imitation; and indeed they appeared to think they could not please us better than by mimicking every motion that we made.' But they were no fools, these native ironists: 'Some biscuit was given to them, which they pretended to eat, but on our looking aside were observed to spit it out.'[45]

This was the rule generally: and it could apply the other way. The engraving 'Messrs Fitzmaurice & Keys dancing for their lives' alludes to an incident at Melville island reported in Stokes's narrative, where the ambushed surveyors had the 'happy presence of mind' to mimic the people against whom they trespassed: 'immediately beginning to dance and shout, though in momentary expectation of being pierced by a dozen spears',[46] they saved the situation and escaped. Such encounters were not naive first meetings, but nor were they the transactions of culturally incommensurable automata. Contact events could 'create, albeit briefly, a provisional mode of exchange, a physical and symbolic space inscribed with meaning'.[47] But this depended on having more to offer than one's own gestures of incomprehension or all-too-transparent play-acting.

M.ʳˢ Fitzmaurice & Keys dancing for their lives.

L. R. Fitzmaurice, 'Messrs Fitzmaurice & Keys dancing for their lives',
from John Lort Stokes, *Discoveries in Australia* (London, 1846), vol. II.

Usually, the no-man's-land of the coast was a place where no one met.
The Goulburn Island men who stole King's station-flag did not want
to be surveyed, while Stokes, at Roebuck Bay, north-western Australia,
observed,

Our intercourse with the natives had been necessarily of the most limited character, hardly amounting to anything beyond indulging them with the sight of a new
people, whose very existence, notwithstanding the apathetic indifference with
which they regarded us, must have appeared a prodigy.[48]

Stokes, like Joseph Banks picking out figures on the coast going impas-
sively about their business,[49] cannot believe that the Aborigines do not
share his prurient curiosity to look at everything, to see and be seen. What
will the result of this mutual ignorance be? Alluding to some pistols inad-
vertently left behind on the shore, Stokes imagines the natives making up
a story about them, explaining them as:

the motive for the visit of those white men who came flying upon the water, and
left some of the secret fire upon the peaceful coast: and when again the white sails
of the explorer glisten in the distant horizon, all the imaginary terrors of the
'Boyl-yas' will be invoked to avert the coming of those who bring with them the
unspeakable blessings of Christian civilization.[50]

The coasts of imperial enquiry represented a curious bracketing-off of time and space. As they encouraged panopticism – the visualization of the world in terms of boundaries, confines, classes and divisions – so they encouraged a compensatory desire to dissolve the distances, a misty speculativeness.

The *tabula rasa* of reason provoked its unruly other, the *planchette* or turning-table of the Spiritualists. Cottom suggests that 'Spiritualists were people seized by the tantalizing power that rushes from civilization's representation of itself. They reached out for and were haunted by an imagined origin of communication glimmering through the intentions of disparate individuals to convey particular meanings.'[51] Likewise, endowed with a technology that held out the prospect of a universal knowledge – the representation of civilization in geography's mirror – Stokes was tempted to project onto the behaviour of the peoples he encountered a desire of communication. In this sense the knowledge of the coastal surveyor with its idiosyncratic mingling of obsessively reported empirical detail and metaphysical surmise anticipated that of the medium, offering, as Spiritualism's advocates Balfour Stewart and P. C. Tait claim, 'not merely a bridge between one portion of the visible universe and another, but also . . . a bridge between one order of things and another, forming as it were a species of cement, in virtue of which the various orders of the universe are welded together and made one'.[52]

Just as the debatable land between this world and the next provoked its own culture – the séance – so the controlling line of the Enlightenment coast was home to a strangely detached theatre. It was not only along Australian coasts that ideal lines, representing a design on man (as the Melville Islanders clearly intuited) as well as nature, were being laid out. As Jean Houel's arresting engraving of the Maltese Barrière de la Santé illustrates, a comparable geometrical hieroglyphic also served to symbolize territorial arrangements around the Mediterranean basin. Houel's explanation of the curious design on the beach is comprehensive – anyone deemed free of plague may come ashore and proceed by way of the paths marked with wooden posts to the Quarantine Offices. The posts are joined by rails so as to form pathways, each of which has its own special destination depending on whether it is for foreigners or residents of the place. AA indicates the spot where merchandise must be deposited before being carried successively to points BB and CC; in the spare spaces are separately laid out the different kinds of merchandise. Foreign merchants stop behind the barrier DD and can here do their bargaining with the merchants of the island who stand behind the barrier EE (which being

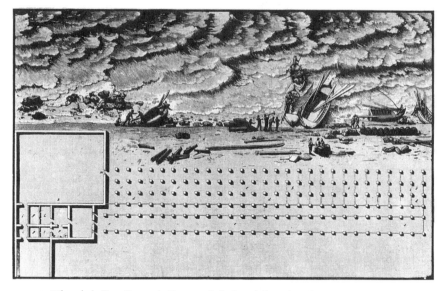

'Plan de la Barrière et du Bureau de la Santé, à Malte', from Jean Houel,
Voyage pittoresque des isles de Sicile, de Malte et de Lipani
(Paris, 1782).

some 200 paces long can accommodate 150 people). Between the path
marked D and that marked E is a space nine paces wide, so as to prevent
infection crossing from one side to the other while at the same time allowing the merchants to view the goods on offer.[53] It is as if the bacchanals of
the coast have here been tamed, fitted out with a respectable, if altogether
absurd, choreography. Human intercourse is reduced to a system of triangulation; a kind of *ballet mécanique* is the result.

A cultural triangulation can be constructed between the quarantine
station, the coastal survey and the (admittedly later) cult of the séance.
The physical resemblances between the regimes they established pre-
supposed shared metaphysical assumptions. All three, for example,
cultivated a science of *surroundings*, and detached observation from
historical precedent or environmental memory. A corollary of this was
the internalization of desire, its cathexis into various forms of self-
perpetuating activity which operated in parallel with events occurring in
the historical world. As Spiritualists entertained a 'quasi-Pentecostal trust'
that in any group of six or eight persons gathered together one or more
would prove to be a medium capable of other-worldly communication,[54]
so the quarantine station was predicated on the assumption that in any
similar group one or more would be infectious. The coast was similarly

contagious: there ordinary distances were swallowed up and one stood, as Playfair supposed, on the edge of an abyss.

At the mercy of circumstances, it was natural to counter panic with various displacement activities: the higher arcana of table-rapping had its scarcely less mysterious counterpart in the quarantine station's rituals of expurgation. In Malta, we learn, letters from infected zones were 'dropped in vinegar, and then put into a case, and laid for about a quarter of an hour on wire grates, under which straw and perfumes had been burnt'. There were different methods of 'expurgation' for different classes of goods: in Venice wool, flax, feathers and similar materials were aired for 40 days by removing them from their containers and mixing and turn-ing over the heaps twice a day by porters working with hands and arms bared. Woollen and linen cloths were regularly unfolded and refolded and sometimes hung on a cord for better exposure to the air. Furs, considered especially dangerous were, we learn, 'very often waved and shaken'. Articles like beeswax, sponges and candles were purged by immersion in salt-water for 48 hours. Salted hides, salts and minerals, however, were considered non-infectable.[55]

Meanwhile along the coastlines of empire proceedings were equally self-referential: after leaving Madeira, Banks and Solander hastily set about drawing and describing the plants they had collected there. Then, 'When a longer absence from land had exhausted the supply of fresh sub-jects, we finished the former descriptions and added synonyms from the books that we had carried along with us.'[56] But this way of killing time, by a system of synonyms putting every object in its place, was geography by another name. Edney mentions the intriguing case of the *émigré* French nobleman Joseph de Maimeux who, around 1800, reversing the method by which maps were made, 'created tables for a uniform script, in which each word was located by coordinates, specifically analogous to latitude and longitude, each table constituting a "topographic map of the domain of thought"'.[57] This is not far removed from the organization of the Maltese barrier. In both cases a system of substitutions is proposed, a mental geography that will control every aspect of human life. And the medium of this translation is the continuous line.

From here it is but a short step to remove the native people from the unnamed land where they resist the graticule of classification, and to relo-cate them along the mental coastline of empire, in that nowhere-place where they can be usefully connected into a continuous chain and made to perform. It is no accident that the founder of New Lanark and proponent of the rational displacement of people, Robert Owen, was also an ardent

Spiritualist. His silent monitor, which Owen likened to 'the supposed recording angel marking the good and bad deeds of poor human nature', was an analogue of the coastline. It asserted its control by virtue of its continuity: nowhere, it was everywhere; like the electrical telegraph, a line communicating presence, it yet remained invisible.[58]

In the Pacific an additional cross-cultural blindspot hampered understanding. It might be true that English seamen had, in contrast with their Mediterranean counterparts, a tradition of coastal navigation well adapted to the tide-prone coasts of Australasia and Polynesia; we are told that, 'Because of the ever-present problem of depth of water and because the flux and reflux of the tides cause powerful tidal streams of ever varying speed and direction whenever they flow, tidal lore loomed large in the Atlantic seaman's life.'[59] Still this shouldn't disguise the incompetence and ineptitude inherent in the imperial project of *getting ashore*, emblemized in its design of ships fitted only to moor, that is to pose as stationary fortresses anchored in a moving medium. It seemed like (and it was) a life-and-death matter to come ashore safely: yet from a non-European cultural perspective the drama of arrival might be entirely invisible, a non-event. If the Tahitian canoeists steered their light craft in and out of reefs 'in all appearance intirely unmov'd by the neighbourhood of so remarkable an object' (to transplant Banks's phrase)[60] as *Cook's Resolution* foundering on a reef, this was no mere affectation: they simply didn't see the problem. J. R. Forster noted, 'The Natives, who were all gone towards night, fished during night on the reefs, with fires, & came early in the morning again alongside the Ship.' And, perhaps grasping the cultural specificity of his nautical crisis, he commented, 'Their boats often overset, but this is no harm to them for Men & Women swim most excellently, & I saw several dive for a single bead, & bring it up from a great distance under Water.'[61]

This lack of comprehension could operate in the other direction. The canoe, with or without outrigger, was the coastal vessel par excellence, perfectly adapted for the agile navigation of that morass where water and land promiscuously mingled, and shallows, bars, reefs and sandbanks were the rule rather than the exception. But the English navigators, proud of their copper-bottomed 'coffins', leaking water at the rate of an inch an hour, could not see this. 'The only vehicle, by which these savages transport their families and chattels across the water, is a log of wood,' King noted; '[it] may be called a *marine-velocipede* . . . the extreme case of the poverty of savage boat-building all round the world.' King attributed its poverty to a paucity of suitable canoe-building timber, and concluded, sanguinely enough, that it was nevertheless proof 'that man is naturally a navigating animal'.[62]

But that proof was, as it were, poisoned. One of the strongest material arguments for the diffusionist theory of cultural and racial development was the canoe: the distance of a culture from its original home could, it was argued, be measured by the sophistication of its boat-building techniques. The geographical origin of the canoe might be disputed but the primitiveness of the Australian version of it proved that the idea originated elsewhere. Just as Grey attributed the rock-paintings he found in the Kimberleys to a canoe-culture visiting Australia from overseas, because he could not reconcile their sophistication with the poverty of the local people's material culture,[63] so with their canoes – they must have been adopted from somewhere else, from the single-tree canoe of the Andamaners, perhaps, or from the Malay sampan.[64] In the genealogical delirium which was late eighteenth- and early nineteenth-century ethnography, canoes were signs of geographical and historical filiation; and it was an odd consequence of this logic that those who had sailed furthest from their putative racial home, were also the most primitive, the most forgetful. That there existed amphibious cultures, equally at home on land and sea and free of any nostalgia to locate their origins on one side of a line or the other, never seems to have occurred to the map-makers looking for harbours, and in the meantime spinning their logical barriers.

In the end, to return to our yachtsman, shipwreck was inevitable. The coastlines of the eighteenth century were cultural artifacts, like the vessels that fell in with them. They were loci of epistemological confusion as well as physical danger. To map them was to bring into being the *terra firma* without which accurate surveys were impossible: but, in an eighteenth-century anticipation of Gödel's theorem, the inner consistency of the map depended on presupposing a proposition that could not be proved within that system. Not surprisingly, the irrational ground of cartographic reason attracted to itself images of unreason. Henri Corbin engagingly reports the early nineteenth-century practice of therapeutically dunking young ladies in the waves: 'The female bathers held in the arms of powerful men and awaiting penetration into the liquid element, the feeling of suffocation, and the little cries that accompanied it all so obviously suggested copulation that Dr Le Coeur was afraid the similarity would render bathing indecent.'[65]

To the evangelical mind coastlines suggested spiritual immersion or baptism. The Reverend John Paton, author of *Missionary to the New*

Hebrides, describes a memorable shipwreck on the island of Tanna: 'I sprang for the reef, and ran for a man half-wading, half-swimming to reach us; and God so ordered it, that just as the next wave broke against the silvery rock of coral, the man caught me and partly swam with me through its surf, partly carried me till I was safely set on shore.'[66] In the midst of peril the coral appear *silvery*: to escape the roaring sea is not simply to get ashore, it is to experience self-transcendence, to consign oneself to the mercy of a greater power, to die to the old self and to put on the vestment of a new being. And once ashore, it is the impossibility of following the coastline that brings him self-knowledge, for, coming to a mighty rock he cannot climb, the shipwrecked man of God has no choice but to let himself over the edge of the cliff and seek to continue his journey on the shore below:

I lay down at the top on my back, feet foremost, holding my head downwards on my breast to keep it from striking on the rock; then, after one cry to my Saviour, having let myself down as far as possible by a branch, I at last let go, throwing my arms forward and trying to keep my feet well up. A giddy swirl, as if flying through the air, took possession of me . . .[67]

Surviving his fall, Paton naturally gives thanks to God, besides invoking the New Testament's master of shipwrecks, St Paul. But the 'giddy swirl', close emotional kin to Playfair's giddiness on looking so far into the abyss of time, is also the gap in reason, that necessary difference that cannot be reduced to sameness, which haunted the Enlightenment mind. It describes the shipwreck of the mind that imagines it can illuminate the way ahead by the power of its own reason, but it also evokes the birthplace of *ingenium*, the speculative genius that connects disparate things. Interestingly, Paton attributes his salvation to spiritual grace, yet the descent into darkness which renews his faith depends on re-entering his body, against Cartesian mentalism allowing back into the metaphysical picture a psycho-kinetic identity inseparable from the lie of the land.

The Enlightenment coastline not only represented a technical challenge to late eighteenth-century map-makers. A necessary construction of Enlightenment reason, it dramatized the limitations and contradictions inherent in the Enlightenment project. As a surface where most of the cultural action was – not only geographically but to an increasing degree, socially, intellectually and imaginatively – the coastline suggested that the optimistic anticipation of mapping the world, classifying its products and ordering their relations, was founded on a myth. Experienced as a radical discontinuity, as a breach in time and space, the coast could be construed as the necessary other of reason – without its prospect of stripped-bare nature the mind would lack the raw material whose orderly collection constituted its *raison d'être*. Yet, even when its products had been threaded along taxonomic lines, the coast remained obstinately discontinuous, abyssal, anti-rational, impossible to fix. To represent it as a line was to paper over a crack – and the image is suggestive, as the nightmare represented by the coast consisted in the fact that it resembled reason so closely.

Writing of 'The deceptious appearances that are frequently observed at sea, such as the reflection of the sun, ripplings occasioned by the meetings of two opposite currents, whales asleep upon the suface of the water, shoals of fish, fog-banks, and the extraordinary effect of mirage [which] have given birth to many . . . non-existing islands and shoals,' King commented that if all of these were laid down in charts, 'the navigator would be in a constant fever of anxiety and alarm for the safety of his vessel'.[68] But along the coast this was normal: where the known and unknown resembled each other, and might so easily collapse into the blindness of the same, no wonder dark and light, anxiety and boredom, land and sea seemed distinguished by only the narrowest of lines. Where the sun shone most brightly 'in the direction of our course', there the greatest danger was in 'running thus "dark with excess of bright" upon any rocks or shoals that might be in our way'.[69] No wonder that 'crossing the line' was, as Kant observed, a euphemism for insanity, the shipwreck of reason.[70]

7

Mapping Tropical Waters: British Views and Visions of Rio de Janeiro

LUCIANA DE LIMA MARTINS

Two centuries ago the city of Rio de Janeiro in Brazil was relatively closer to the Orient and the South Seas than it is today. To explain this shift in geographical relations, we must map ourselves into a late eighteenth-century world in which sailing vessels were the only means of inter-continental communication. Sailing itself demanded a combination of maritime knowledge and practical skills to deal with the forces of nature: reef-strewn oceans, winds, storms and currents. To some extent self-contained 'wooden worlds', ships nevertheless required regular access to shore facilities. In order to stay at sea for months, their crews needed fresh water and, ideally, supplies of fresh food. The ships themselves required regular attention, especially when sailing in tropical waters, for the com-bination of sun and salt ravaged their topsides while prolonged voyages took a toll of their gear, not to mention the constant danger of under water fouling.[1] A network of ports of call was thus a prerequisite for any successful maritime enterprise, and navigation was all the more safe and efficient when the qualities of a safe harbour, a place for refit and repair, and a provisioning depot were combined in one port.

In addition to the elements, there were two further hazards to be nego-tiated at sea in the early nineteenth century: the threat of piracy and vast blanks of uncharted oceans. In his history of British naval hydrography during the nineteenth century, George S. Ritchie summarizes the British policy of securing the 'freedom and safety of the seas', concluding that 'the Royal Navy set about removing the pirates and making the charts'.[2] In this essay, I am more concerned with mapping waters than combating pirates; or, more precisely, with the visual culture of the British maritime geographical imagination in the early nineteenth century. In his study of British maritime ascendancy, Gerald Graham claims that 'with the "inevitability of gradualness" the *geography of the sea . . .* shaped Brit-ain's destiny'.[3] As I show here, however, Britain's influence in shaping a geography of the sea was probably stronger than vice versa. The ability to establish a network of island bases and mainland trading stations, tied together commercially and strategically by communication routes connected to the mother country, was a key source of Britain's power. By the close of the eighteenth century, British routes had been traced not only to the African coasts and the Baltic, but also to the South Atlantic and South Pacific, to the Indian Ocean and China. It needs to be stressed, however, that though it was 'gradual', this pattern of influence was not 'inevitable'. Imperial policy in the southern ocean, for example, 'was usually initiated in response to immediate problems such as strategic or penal deficiencies, or to outside pressures such as that from the southern whalers'.[4]

How, then, was this network established and maintained throughout the nineteenth century? What kinds of practices were involved? According to Simon Schaffer, 'the imperial vision hinged on reliable and potent knowledge'.[5] But knowledge of the world far beyond the limits of both Europe and the British Empire required authoritative observations from people who had actually laid eyes on these territories. I shall focus here on the role that seamen played in rendering this 'other world' visible and above all recognizable for the British navigators and hydrographers, for it was their work which helped to shape the British 'geography of the sea'. Exotic and unfamiliar landscapes were sketched, painted and charted by British seamen throughout the nineteenth century. Gradually, a vocabulary of images from those distant places was constructed and put into circulation. Through charts, views and pictures, polar and tropical regions were brought back home, not only images from places actually under the British flag, but from all corners of the globe.[6]

My particular concern is with the role of maritime routes and life at sea in navigators' 'mapping' of the tropics as recorded in graphic images of the harbour of Rio de Janeiro. A distinctive feature of the European vision of the tropics was the commercial project to relocate plants between different tropical territories in the Americas, Africa, Asia and the Pacific, an exchange feasible only by sea. Images of landscapes, together with exotic species and commodities, circulated through the tropics, resulting in the composition of 'hybrid' tropical landscapes and a more generalized idea of tropicality.[7] In order to investigate how these images were mapped out, I begin by considering the place of Rio within the broader network of Royal Navy strategic and logistical planning. I then turn to the increasingly significant role of graphic images in improving and enlarging the geographical imagination of the Royal Navy. These two sections provide the context for a detailed consideration of the graphic representations of tropical Rio produced by British mariners in the early nineteenth century.

RIO DE JANEIRO AND THE MARITIME ROUTES

In the early nineteenth century, Rio de Janeiro became increasingly significant to British commercial and strategic interests. Rio was a safe harbour, 'easy of access, readily known by the remarkable land about it', and 'very commodious', as James Horsburgh, a hydrographer of the East India Company, described it in 1809.[8] Having become the capital of Brazil in 1763, the city was enjoying rapid growth in both population and trade. At this time, Rio was – after Lisbon – the second most important naval and commercial centre in the Portuguese empire.[9] It was a good place for any necessary refit and repair, as vessels were provided with fresh drinking water flowing directly from the mountains behind the city, wood from its forests, and a variety of necessary provisions.[10] Because of these facilities, Rio became a common port of call for many foreign vessels.

In the decades around 1800, the 'tedious' journey across the Atlantic from Britain to Rio lasted between about 55 and 80 days.[11] As a vessel approached the port, the imposing entrance to the harbour dominated by the Sugar Loaf mountain afforded a welcome sight for mariners. Ready access to Rio and its services served to advance British interests in India and protected the commercial routes to Calcutta, Bombay and Canton.[12] Even the colonization of Australia benefited from its role as a provisioning depot. From Rio, the sailing time to Cape Town was between 30 and 50 days; to India, 105 to 150 days; to China, 120 to 180 days; and to Australia, 70 to 90 days.[13]

This pattern of sailing routes was a function of wind and current patterns in the South Atlantic, as originally established by Portuguese navigators. Bartholomeu Dias, followed by Vasco da Gama, had found that these patterns favoured westbound routes for southern passages. When da Gama rounded the Cape of Good Hope in November 1497, he was not only the first seaman in history to complete a voyage to India of some 9,000 miles, but also the first to establish an efficient triangular route from Europe via South America and then around the Cape.[14]

Rio's role as a port of call for British vessels was not merely a product of favourable winds and currents. During the late eighteenth and early nineteenth centuries, British trade was expanding globally. Closer links with Portugal benefited British merchants, shippers, industrialists and the Admiralty. The rights to utilize the Brazilian ports of Rio de Janeiro, Salvador and Recife had been secured by Britain in seventeenth-century

Anglo-Portuguese treaties.[15] By the end of the eighteenth century, the extension of commercial influence in the Portuguese colonies increasingly attracted British attention, especially as relations with Spain and Spanish America were delicate and complex.[16] Through the sheer extent of its industrial and commercial power, Britain came indirectly to dominate Brazilian trade.

In 1807 the Portuguese royal family sailed from the Tagus to Rio in order to escape Napoleon's conquest. With their arrival in March 1808, the city became the new capital of the Portuguese empire. These events reinforced the association of British diplomacy and Portuguese interests, for it was a small British squadron that afforded security to the Portuguese fleet. In 1808 Rio became also the headquarters of the Royal Navy's South American station. Rear-Admiral Sir William Sidney Smith was appointed first Commander-in-Chief of the squadron to be stationed off the Brazilian coast.[17] What exactly did it mean to be a 'station' of the British Navy?

In order to secure its maritime interests, the British government maintained ships-of-war at several foreign stations: 'each station had an area or zone to patrol, a squadron of ships, and a headquarters or base of operations'.[18] Yet 'British interests' were never monolithic. The defence policy of the Admiralty was very often eclipsed by 'haphazard political opportunism in the face of specific problems', or 'in the gloom of Treasury account'.[19] The rapidity with which the limits of the stations were defined and redefined is indicative of the lack of a fixed imperial design. From 1810 to 1844, for example, the Cape of Good Hope station had its limits changed no less than 18 times, including many inclusions in, and exclusions from, the South American and West African stations.[20]

The main duty of the Royal Navy ships on the coasts of South America was to protect British shipping against interference from either governments or pirates. In addition, the Navy was also to become involved in the campaign against the slave trade. Little direct influence by British statesmen can be detected in the events that led to the independence of Brazil in 1822, though British diplomacy was crucial three years later in securing the recognition of Brazil by Portugal. 'To give countenance and protection to this extensive commerce, and to support the influence of British interests in these countries is the just and indispensable duty of the Squadron placed under your command',[21] to quote the words of one captain's instructions in 1831, was precisely the role of the Navy in South America. With increasing British political influence and maritime trade beyond Cape Horn, the South American station was split in 1837 into the

'Pacific' and the 'Brazils' stations: the former ran along the West coast of the Americas and out as far 170° west, while the latter covered the eastern coast of South America.[22] From Valparaiso – the headquarters of the new Pacific station – men-of-war not only protected British interests on the west coasts of Latin America, but also carried treasure from ports as far as the Gulf of California.[23]

Besides policing the seas against piracy and the slave trade, the Royal Navy's most significant duty on foreign stations was to obtain more reliable information for British navigators. The relatively few charts from the southern seas which existed in the mid-eighteenth century were commonly described as inadequate for safe navigation.[24] According to Commodore John Byron, writing in October 1764, dangers even lurked within Rio harbour: 'if we had followed the Portugueze pilot's advice, who was frightened out of his Senses we [would have] lost the ship'.[25] In this case, the inaccuracy of the charts was held to have been far from accidental; moreover, John Hawkesworth, the contemporary editor of Byron's journal, claimed that Portuguese merchants practised 'every artifice in their power to entice away the crew' in order to protect their commercial interests.[26]

In order to overcome such problems, real or imagined, the British began to organize the production of their own charts. But there were political difficulties to negotiate: taking soundings and making surveys ran the risk of infringing the territorial rights of sovereign states. In an Admiralty letter presumed to have been issued around 1760, the following instructions regarding the provision of hydrographic information can be found:

You are to comply with the aforegoing Directions, not only with respect to the Coasts, Harbours, Roads, and Places belonging to all Foreign Potentates, but likewise with respect to all the Coasts, Ports, Bays and Roads, of Great-Britain and Ireland, and their adjacent Islands; and moreover with respect to the British Islands, Colonies, Settlements, and Plantations, in all Parts: And you are to appoint your Master, with such Officers and Youths of your Quarter-Deck as you shall find best disposed and qualified to make the Surveys and Observations above-mentioned; taking however particular Care, when in Foreign Parts, not to do any thing to give Umbrage or Offence to the Governors, or Inhabitants, of Places in Friendship with the King.[27]

When the *Endeavour* visited Rio in 1768, for example, Captain Cook carried out a sketch survey of part of the bay. He complained that a 'strict watch' was kept over him and his crew during their whole stay, hindering them 'from taking so accurate a Survey as [he] wished to have done'.[28] In this context, coastal sketches would have compensated for the lack of precise measurements. Such work required trained men. Yet Captain Cook remarked in 1770 that 'he did not know many seamen who were capable of drawing a chart or sketch of a sea coast'.[29] From this date, marine survey was to become increasingly important in the work of the Royal Navy.

'EYES AND EARS OPEN': THE CONSTRUCTION OF MARITIME KNOWLEDGE

The need to acquire knowledge of the outer world increased as British horizons broadened. Given the Admiralty's drive for knowledge of the East, 'serving officers, however junior, were encouraged to *keep their eyes and ears open*, and to take notes on the manners and customs of the native people they might encounter. Governments of the day were largely dependent on the observations of intelligent travellers.'[30] But intelligence alone would not guarantee the success of the enterprise. According to Graham, the average sailor was 'rarely excited by the sights and sounds and smells of distant places'; they 'found few enchantments in exotic landscapes, and saw little beauty in either the customs or the monuments of Asian races'.[31] However, as I shall show, there is material evidence that a visual sensitivity was in the process of being developed even among ordinary seamen from the eighteenth century onwards.

For practical purposes of navigation, the description of coastlines through drawing was considered superior to any written account. These views were intended to impress on the mariner's eye the characteristic outline of particular landmarks. They were especially helpful when navigating in poor visibility, or along unfamiliar coasts. The first printed sailing directions which included illustrations of coastal profiles date back to the sixteenth century: *Le grant routtier* by Pierre Garcie, published in 1520. As D. W. Waters emphasizes, the crude woodcuts of Garcie's work aimed 'to caricature important features so that seamen would find each illustration a reflection of the terse verbal description and immediately recognize, in consequence, the particular stretch of coast'.[32] It is worth remarking in this context that recognition is a social event, that is, it transcends the mere act of perception. While the latter implies a solitary sensory experience, the former relies on the activation of codes that 'are learnt by interaction with others, in the acquisition of human culture'.[33] To depict a place in order to make it recognizable is, then, a process that involves learning codes of recognition, the visual alphabet which allows communication. To 'represent' a distant place is to make it present for those who have not been there.

From the later seventeenth century, according to Bernard Smith, 'the practical value of drawing for recording information became widely accepted', with the support of men like Sir Christopher Wren, Samuel Pepys and John Locke.[34] Both military and maritime surveys thus required the training of skilful draughtsmen. In the Royal Mathematical School of Christ's Hospital, where students were trained in the art of navigation, great emphasis was placed on marine surveying and drawing.[35] The aim was not to produce professional artists, but to provide ordinary seamen and trainee officers with basic drawing skills, which would enable them to record coastlines, harbours, fortifications and topographical detail as quickly and accurately as possible. Alexander Cozens was one of the talented drawing masters at this School, working there from January 1750 to May 1754.[36] Cozens was familiar with the process of navigation, for his father and grandfather had been important shipbuilders in Russia's new, British-run navy for 35 years.[37] As a painter, he was an expert in marine views, and coastal profiles were particularly prominent in his work. It is not surprising that the drawing techniques of coastal profiles were taught by an artist who elaborated a perceptive landscape theory, based on recognition of forms, by individualization of the essential characters and their immediate interpretation, skills that were demanded in the art of navigation.

The relevance of drawing to marine surveying was emphasized in late eighteenth-century treatises. Murdoch Mackenzie, a maritime surveyor 'in his Majesty's Service', compiled a list of ten types of draughts and surveys.[38] Two of them deserve particular attention here, for they explicitly refer to geography as a particular kind of mapping knowledge: the 'Memorial Sketch' and the 'Eye-Sketch'. According to Mackenzie,

A Memorial Sketch, is a delineation of a harbour, or any part of a coast, from the memory only, without notes, or immediate sight. When such a sketch is made by one who has been often in the place, or who has *viewed* it with particular attention, it may convey a *general idea* of a bay, harbour, or island, fit to gratify curiosity, or enlarge geography, by *shewing that some such places are there.*[39]

'An Eye-Sketch', in contrast,

is a delineation of any harbour, or part of a coast, done by the eye at one station, without measuring distances; and drawn according to the *apparent shape and dimensions of the land* ... Such a sketch is soon made by one moderately skilled in drawing: and if skilful officers, in places unknown, or not surveyed, did take such sketches, it would be of some service both to navigation and geography.[40]

Even when made by memory, sketches would provide geographic information, 'shewing that some such places are there'; 'geography' for Mackenzie meant a particular kind of mapping, that is, a knowledge related primarily to the sense of sight and distinct from a mere curiosity.

The relevance of recording information graphically was also emphasized by Alexander Dalrymple, hydrographer of the East India Company. In his influential *Essay on Nautical Surveying* of 1771, Dalrymple was especially concerned with the visual aspects of the land:

I must also strenuously recommend, to the expert Navigator, to omit no opportunity of taking *Views* of the *Land*. It is obvious no *Plan* can be well *constructed* without having a *View* of the *Land*, at least in the *mind's eye*; and therefore much better to have it recorded, and always present to refer to . . . *Views* are useful, not only in giving the most competent description of the Country, but in pointing out the proper places for *landing, watering, wooding, fishing,* &c.[41]

Dalrymple not only recommended that navigators should draw coastal views, but himself drew and published sheets of coastal views. He also worked extensively on historical collections of voyages and discoveries in the southern seas. He was particularly concerned with the problem of naming places, as difficulties arose from the tendency of successive navigators to use different names for the same places. When it was not possible to use native names – a practice that Dalrymple approved of – he suggested that 'the fittest names are descriptive'.[42] It would then be easier to verify whether the navigators were referring to the same coastline or not. The instruction to 'be descriptive', however, is itself open to interpretation, as the traveller could refer to a feature, a point of view, or his own personal experience. Paul Carter neatly illustrates this point in reference to Captain Cook's place names in Australia which included names Cook used more than once and names that 'did not generalize or classify, but denoted particulars alone'.[43] Carter links this vagueness to the practice of exploration itself, for,

while discovery rests on the assumption of a world of facts waiting to be found, collected and classified, a world in which the neutral observer is not implicated, exploration lays stress on the observer's active engagement with his environment: it recognizes phenomena as offspring of his intention to explore.[44]

Dalrymple, however, was in a rather more ambiguous position, in between the place of the sedentary map-user and that of the voyaging map-maker. As a hydrographer, he was actively involved in the planning and execution of future expeditions; indeed, he had the 'greatest ambition to be the navigator who investigated his own theories'.[45] Despite acknowledging, as did Cook, that place names could be used as tools of travelling, Dalrymple desired them also as fruits of travelling. As a collector, he wanted to map the blank spaces of his geographical knowledge. But Dalrymple had been passed over in favour of Cook for the Royal Society's 1769 expedition to Tahiti to observe the Transit of Venus. His ambitions were cut back by a power struggle between the Royal Navy and the Royal Society for the overall control of this voyage of scientific exploration.

Surveying, then, like navigating, demanded experience as well as theory. As emphasized in Mackenzie's *Treatise on Surveying* of 1774:

Previous to undertaking a geometrical survey of the sea-coast, a proficiency in drawing will be found of advantage; at least so much of it, as to be capable of shading with India ink, or etching with a pen, *hills, rocks, cliffs, miniature buildings*, and the *coast-line* of a *map*; of sketching, from nature, the *out-lines* of them; and of taking distant views of the land, from sea. This can only be attained by practice, aided by a few instructions from a drawing-master. A surveyor who is not capable of sketching readily, and shading with some neatness, ought to have a draughtsman with him for that purpose.[46]

Practice could only be acquired with the mobilization of financial resources. In order to provide accurate charts and navigation information of world-wide scope for the Royal Navy, there was a need for something more material: money, manpower and ships. Well aware of the development of hydrographic science in other maritime countries, the Admiralty established its own Hydrographic Office in 1795, appointing Dalrymple as its first hydrographer.[47] In his work at the Hydrographic Office, Dalrymple took advantage of his experience as a collector and publisher of charts and coastal views. Being a civilian, his work primarily consisted of compilations from existing charts, for he did not have the resources to order new surveys. Nevertheless, in 1804, when the Admiralty instructions on the keeping of Remark Books were updated, Dalrymple was able to offer advice on the draft of an Admiralty letter directing Royal Navy officers to transmit hydrographic information.[48]

Rather than narrating the development of the Hydrographic Office, I shall outline some distinctions between the graphic images produced by maritime surveyors and hydrographers. Broadly speaking, printed charts depict small-scale coastal outlines. They may be associated with navigation, the science of directing a ship by astronomy, geometry and the use of instruments. Plans (large-scale cartographic representations of harbours and islands), coastal views and sailing directions relate more specifically to pilotage, that is, the skill involved in steering a vessel into or out of port.[49] The significance of drawings 'on the spot' also deserves attention in this context. While such illustrations provided potentially useful information about coastlines and offshore hazards associated with hydrographic surveys, they were often also used as sources for illustrations to written accounts of maritime voyages. As Bernard Smith has pointed out, while such illustrations relied upon field studies, they also drew 'upon the words of an associated text and upon the memory of the illustrator'.[50] On other occasions, seamen used pen and brush as modern sailors use a camera, to record incidents and landscapes as a personal record of their voyages. Rather than being coastal views in the nautical sense, these graphic images illustrated the navigators' adventures, and were not necessarily accompanied by a text. Broadly speaking, then, it is possible to identify three main 'types' of drawings by mariners (though the boundaries between them were often blurred): coastal views and plans associated with hydrographic surveys; illustrations for official accounts of maritime expeditions; and drawings intended as a personal record of the voyage.[51] In what follows I examine a number of graphic images of Rio produced by British mariners and hydrographers in order to understand the interrelationship between these different types of drawing in the process of mapping tropical waters.

IMAGES OF RIO DE JANEIRO

Rio de Janeiro was a port of a sovereign country. Since the uninvited surveying of foreign coasts was generally held to be beyond the remit of the British Navy, Admiralty and commercial charts of Rio were of necessity based on existing surveys, with additional information about the Brazilian harbour provided by British navigators incorporated where possible. Inset views of the coastlines increasingly came to be superimposed on the blank spaces of the unexplored continental interiors. We have only to compare the chart in the *Brazil Pilot*, translated from the Portuguese of Manoel Pimentel, dated 1809, with the one in *The African Pilot*, from about 1784, to see the difference. While the former may provide useful information to navigate but little help to pilotage, the latter combined three graphic tools for sailors: a chart of the South American coast, a plan of the Rio harbour and coastal views, depicting the striking profile of the mountains. The *Plan of the Bay and Harbour of Rio-Janeiro on the Coast of Brasil* (1794) in the British Library provides a further example: manuscript additions have been made in red ink on a proof impression of the chart by Laurie and Whittle, which is itself based on a French chart by M. D'Après. Improved 'from the Observations

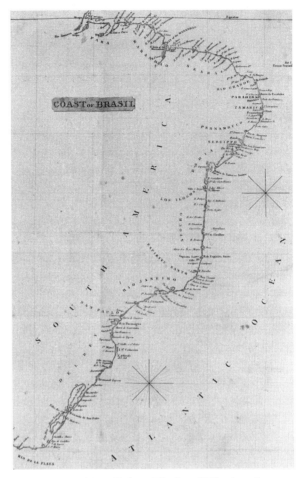

'Coast of Brasil', from *The Brazil Pilot* (1809).

of Sampson Hull and other Navigators', the additions include, among other details, two 'Appearances of the Land'. In this and subsequent charts, the 'British imprint' on foreign surveys consisted of a mosaic of inset coastal plans and views.

As noted above, views were essential if navigators were to recognize unknown coastlines. On printed charts, they highlighted topographic features; together with harbour plans, they provided sailors with a tool to check the exact position of the vessel. Drawings of ships provided visual scale reference, while names and numbers helped to make the necessary connections with the sailing directions. Trees, buildings and lighthouses were represented as iconic images, like symbols in charts. Weather

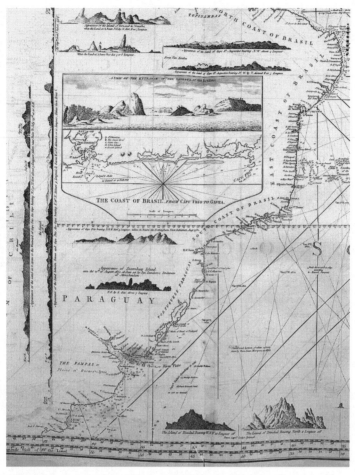

'The Atlantic and Ethiopic Oceans', from *The African Pilot* (1806 edn).

remarks – clouds above all – were occasionally and timidly inserted in these small framed maritime landscapes, as if the insertion of more 'artistic' elements would sully the scientific purity of the Admiralty charts. The varied information recorded by naval official surveyors in foreign lands was thus filtered; more precisely filtered a second time as, in the offices at home, hydrographers translated personal recording styles into a single graphic language.[52]

The practice of drawing associated with navigation favoured the production of a number of graphic images that extended the purely nautical provision of hydrographic information. Although relatively insignificant in the development of either hydrography or maritime art, some of the

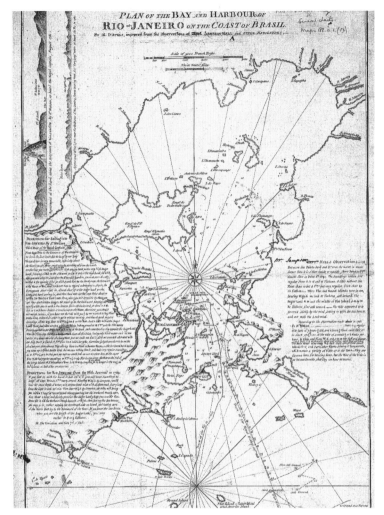

*Plan of the Bay and Harbour of Rio-Janeiro
on the Coast of Brasil*, 1794.

personal drawings produced by mariners offer a valuable source for
understanding aspects of the shipboard community's geographical imagination in the early nineteenth century, aspects which cannot be fully
recovered from the more literary traces of naval officers and hydrographers. A fascinating illustration is offered by a group of images of Rio
bequeathed to us by a midshipman (later lieutenant), Charles William
Browne.

Charles Browne joined HMS *Alceste* on 17 December 1815.[53] In

Charles William Browne, *Aqueduct – Rio de Janeiro*, 1818.

February 1816 the frigate sailed from Spithead, transporting Lord Amherst's embassy to China. Although it was not a survey expedition *per se*, the voyage provided an opportunity to explore a poorly charted area of the tropical world. There were about 160 men on board ship; among them, Murray Maxwell (the captain), William Havell (official artist to the embassy), Dr Clarke Abel (expedition surgeon and naturalist) and John M'Leod (another surgeon). After calling at Madeira, the *Alceste* made for Rio de Janeiro, following the standard trans-Atlantic route on her way to the Cape. On 21 March the visitors were received on the quayside by the leading members of the British community in Brazil. The *Alceste* remained in Rio for ten days before proceeding to the East Indies.[54] After various calls at Chinese ports, the frigate sailed from Macao on January 1817, but she was wrecked in the Gaspar Straits, with the loss of most of the embassy's possessions. This probably accounts for the production of the sketchbook entitled 'Sketches from Memory, made in Jan. and Feb. 1818, by C. W. Browne, R.N. of His Majesty's late Ships, *Alceste* and *Julia*', now held in the National Maritime Museum London. As a pencil note on the cover informs, the drawings were made during the course of a voyage in HMS *Eden* in 1818–19.[55]

The first image of Browne's sketchbook is an illustration of the *Alceste* and four small vessels. The ship deserved the front page, for she was the instrument which made possible the adventure of travelling to distant lands. *Aqueduct – Rio de Janeiro* is the second image; drinkable water was, after all, one of the main reasons for calling at Rio. Despite the lack

C. W. Browne, *Rio de Janeiro*, 1818.

of buildings, the dreamlike sketch *Rio de Janeiro* that follows could well illustrate surgeon M'Leod's description of the harbour:

The numerous islets appearing on this extensive *sheet of water*, – its richly-wooded banks, rising like an amphitheatre on either hand, studded with villages and country seats, – added to the *distant view of lofty and picturesque moun-tains*, – form, altogether, a very unusual and noble landscape.[56]

Continuing through Browne's sketchbook, though, we find a whole series of maritime landscapes: images of the Cape of Good Hope, Java, Corea, Canton and so on. As a Brazilian familiar with Rio, I am quick to identify Charles Browne's sketches of the city. Yet, even allowing for the passage of time, there are some aspects of these images which are unfamiliar. Examining Browne's images, we identify a hybrid combination of Chinese and Brazilian elements of vegetation and graphic conventions. As is evident from some of the illustrations in Captain Basil Hall's work, *Voyage of Discovery to the West Coast of Corea, and the Great Loo-Choo Island* (1818), drawn by William Havell from Browne's sketches, the midshipman had learned how to depict the floral patterns of Chinese fabrics.[57] Two, probably later, drawings signed by Browne, now in the Royal Geographical Society in London, evoke a similar strangeness. Both are attached to a manuscript account of a surveying expedition to explore the river Zambezi, West Africa, undertaken by officers of HMS *Leven* in July 1823.[58] Browne was in charge of this expedition, in which he and all the other Europeans died. Lacking hydrographic significance, these draw-ings could have remained Browne's personal property. In the first one,

C. W. Browne, *View from Lake of Mountain.*

called simply *View from Lake of Mountain* – which appears to be of Corcovado mountain at Rio from the Rodrigo de Freitas lagoon – the vegetation that clothes the mountain slopes seems to owe more to those Chinese patterns than to the intricate mass of the Brazilian vegetation. In the second, entitled *Corcovado and Gloria Church* , his church resembles more an Indian temple than the baroque architecture of colonial Rio. We should remember that, between 1818 and 1821, Browne was on board the *Eden*, whose voyage included numerous calls at Indian harbours.[59]

This graphic strangeness is significant not because of the accuracy or otherwise of his representations of Rio, but rather because it reveals the extent to which Browne's hands and eyes were influenced by the experience of navigating the globe, and how these faculties in turn helped to shape his memory of tropical landscapes. More specifically, it highlights the connections between memory and mapping. The orthodox scientific view by the mid-nineteenth century was that in the description of nature, nothing could be trusted to memory alone. Field observations 'should be noted down on the spot', according to W. J. Hamilton's instructions in the

Admiralty's *Manual of Scientific Enquiry* first published in 1849.[60] As Darwin put it, on the basis of his experience during the *Beagle* voyage, 'trust nothing to the memory; for the memory becomes a fickle guardian when one interesting object is succeeded by another still more interesting'.[61] The same advice could be read in 'Hints to Travellers', a body of instructions to aspiring explorers published by the Royal Geographical Society in 1854, in which it was stressed that the 'less left to memory the better'.[62] Instant material record of what was seen 'on the spot' increasingly became regarded as a necessary condition of truthfulness. The observer, it was argued, simply could not trust his own memory to render the knowledge available for future explorers.

Browne's drawings, though, provide some clues to the sources of these anxieties about observation and memory. Recalling the short stay in Rio in his account of the voyage, Dr Clarke Abel (the surgeon and naturalist on board the *Alceste*) stressed the overwhelming experience of being in front of 'the glorious productions of a tropical climate in their native soil',[63] an impression shared by M'Leod.[64] The naturalist also mentioned some excursions to places nearby 'with two of the officers of the *Alceste*'. Charles Browne could well have accompanied this party. William Havell made some sketches during the party's short stay in the city.[65] What is at issue in the present context is what Charles Browne could have learned by observing the artist working, or even by hearing the naturalist's awed descriptions of Brazilian nature. As Browne's sketches of the *Alceste's* voyage were made 'from memory' nearly two years later, a question thus arises: did his memory record the place itself, or the sketches drawn by Havell, or the impressions of the naturalist Abel and the surgeon M'Leod?

For those who mistrust such visual evidence, however, there is written proof of the collaborative work of both men, Browne and Havell. The preface to Captain Basil Hall's work notes: 'the drawings of scenery and costume were made by Mr. William Havell, the eminent artist who accompanied the Embassy, from sketches taken on the spot, by Mr. C. W. Browne, midshipman of the Alceste, and myself'.[66] Moreover, Havell stayed in India from 1816 to 1826, where he earned his living by painting portraits of East India Company and Army officers, as well as colourful landscapes.[67] Comparing the careful composition of Browne's drawing *Corcovado and Gloria Church* with Havell's oil painting *On the Coromandel Coast, South India*, it is possible to infer that Browne was aware of Havell's work: compositionally both images punctuate space

C. W. Browne, *Corcovado and Gloria Church*.

William Havell, *On the Coromandel Coast, South India*, 1821.

with a boat and some seagulls in the foreground, a ship in the middle distance and the coastline in the background.

Browne's depictions of Rio can help us to understand what fearsome 'tricks' memory was supposed to play. The blind belief in the sketch 'on the spot' presupposes a mind freed from memory, where what is seen is directly recorded by means of the observer's hands (and later on, through the medium of a camera), neglects the fact that to forget is as complex a feat as to remember. Facing unknown landscapes, with pencil in hand, on what else other than their memories would seamen rely for the graphic vocabulary to depict such views? Contemporary anxieties about the role of memory in observation reflected an empiricist presupposition: 'the suspicion that beneath words, beneath ideas, the ultimate reference in the mind is the image, the impression of outward experience printed, painted, or reflected in the surface of consciousness'.[68]

Many mariners' images of tropical landscapes worked as frames for the representation of ships. As in portraiture, they served to confirm the 'presence' of the vessel. In the second part of *Liber nauticus* (1805), a didactic work concerned with the visual representation of the 'floating monuments of British power', Dominic Serres recommends the representation of background scenes taken from nature in order to render the vessels 'still farther interesting'.[69] The lesson was learned by many naval officers, including Harry Edmund Edgell, George Lothian Hall and Owen Stanley, all of whom depicted Rio as background to the Royal Navy ships which transported them. However, as I have attempted to show through a study of Charles Browne's drawings, representing background scenes 'taken from nature' was not as straightforward a process as Dominic Serres believed.

Coastal sketches were designed, above all, to render unknown forms recognizable for future navigators. A common means of achieving this mapping goal was to resort to comparison with known forms, in order to memorize them. The coast of Rio, for example, was commonly imagined by navigators as 'a man lying on his back'. *The Brasilian Navigator* by John Purdy (1844) thus quotes Baron Roussin's description of the 'peculiar figure of the land' visible from the approaches to the harbour:

When coming in from the offing, between the E.S.E. and S.W., the configuration of their summits presents, in a very remarkable manner, the figure of a man lying on his back from W.S.W. to E.N.E.; whereof the Gavia forms the head, and the Sugar-loaf the feet. When the tops of these mountains are free from clouds or mists, it is almost impossible not to be struck with this appearance.

It is equally impossible to know how many seamen were indeed struck by such an appearance, for the 'man lying on his back' reclined in Baron Roussin's mind, not along the coastline. Presumably, many would have recognized the coast from this powerful description, and indeed the image was quoted in many other navigating manuals.[70] The French artist J. B. Debret used it to illustrate his own account of a voyage to Brazil. Debret was aware of the colloquial description of the view used by navigators.[71] In this example, the means by which unknown forms are rendered recognizable is very evident. Amateur artists employed more subtle schemes, but the principle at work was the same: by rendering alien forms familiar, they could reference a common geographical imagination. Unknown forms were moulded into a hybrid landscape composed of interchangeable tropical elements of the British maritime way of seeing. Architectural features and elements of vegetation were interchangeable within the hybrid landscapes of this tropical zone.

MAPPING THE ABSENT

The 'outer world' which British seamen encountered during the eighteenth and nineteenth centuries stimulated their minds and bodies in a variety of ways. They alone could feel the relief of arriving at a safe and luxuriant harbour after two months at sea, drinking fresh water from the mountains, or experiencing a night on solid ground under the southern sky cooled by the sea breeze. In general terms, the slow process by which a body of representational practices was established for the composition of their coastal surveys can be ascribed to the difficulties of mapping the absent. By these means, British officers and men at sea and at home could work on images, look at charts and establish the limits of a station, a route or, through a sketch, clarify what dangers or marvels might confront future expeditions.

My emphasis on sketchbooks is intended to bring us closer to the complex knowledge of navigators in the early nineteenth century. Like finished paintings, printed charts and official accounts of voyages are designed for particular audiences; very often they tell us more about these audiences than the work involved in producing them. This is not to claim that unfinished images are free from convention – far from it – it is simply that they are less polished, more open, performances. They also allow different sorts of people a voice, not just a social or scientific elite. As Anne Secord remarks in a different context, 'one of the functions of scientific texts is to obscure the work involved in the production of knowledge in order to render such knowledge objective'.[72] When science, art and imperial interests are joined, as they evidently were in the work of maritime surveyors, the task of interpretation becomes still more complex.

The geography of British maritime enterprise is portrayed here less as a triumphal expression of imperial power than as a practical means for mapping and recording the circulation of mariners and their images of tropical landscapes around the globe. Construction of British maritime knowledge in the early nineteenth century was the result of a constant negotiation between conventions established in the inner spaces of the Navy offices and the representations of outer spaces by people who had actually laid eyes on distant lands. Rather than merely passive providers of data to official maritime cartographers and officers, seamen helped to shape the British geographical imagination of that outer world. The necessarily communal character of life at sea could not but influence the technical output of British maritime surveyors. Everyday life in sailing vessels demanded a degree of sociability among the travellers and crew thrown together for lengthy voyages. Even within the naval hierarchy, the social worlds of officers, sailors, diplomats, naturalists, artists and others could not remain entirely distinct.

The hybrid landscapes considered here also draw our attention to some obsolete meanings of the English words 'commerce' ('to communicate physically') and 'trade' (the 'course or track' of a ship).[73] British sailing vessels mapped tracks across the globe; not only in the charts elaborated in hydrographic offices at home, but in the actual places they visited. Sailing out with the trades and back in the westerlies, these vessels enabled the exchange of images of landscapes, as well as commodities and exotic species, through a wider tropical world.

8

Mapping Modernity:
Utopia and Communications Networks

ARMAND MATTELART

The image of the communication net is the paradigmatic representation of those interactions and transactions which are now reorganizing the world. Responsibility for the network's reticular pattern, which is at once symbol and tool of economic and social relations, is claimed by both management theorists seeking competitive edge and by a new kind of citizenship seeking to coordinate the organization of civil society in response to the worldwide scale of its various problems.

The network of cyberspace networks is an object of reverie. Many see in it the promise of a new society, one in which current socio-economic imbalances might be solved. Belief in the redemptive power of communication techniques and networks is by no means new. It re-emerges with every technological advance. However, the impulse to find in networks a magical solution to social and economic crisis is not matched by the reality of strategies and the politics of their implementation. The macro-applications of communication networks have been, are and will remain the object of contradictory claims: they lie at the heart of confrontations for global control. The objective of this essay is to map a broad genealogy of the imagery surrounding the figure of the communication network. Both the network and cartography are modern concepts, and their development is mutually intertwined.

FROM THE FORTIFICATIONS MAP TO THE NETWORK

The contribution of French thought to the construction of the network concept is critical. A cursory count of book titles is sufficient to reveal that, as early as the nineteenth century, the network concept and metaphor have been more successfully promoted in France than in other countries and languages.

In Diderot and Alembert's *Encyclopaedia*, to be sure, the entry 'network' makes no reference to communication; nor does the word appear under the entry dealing with 'roads, routes and paths'. In 1765, when the work was published, the meanings of network still revolved exclusively around the use of thread in the silk trade. It was defined as a 'plain needle-work of gold, silver or silk thread, woven in such a way as to obtain stitches and openings'. It is only at the beginning of the following century that the word network was used in the French language to denote the spatial form of a communication system. To understand the genesis of the word's meanings, however, we have to go beyond noting its formal absence. Indeed, since the second half of the seventeenth century, well before its endorsement in official taxonomy, the image of the network had been gaining ground in two ways.

The first is the more general, deriving from the practices of French engineers, philosophers and scientists, and admitted into common language through the historical importance of words and meanings in the construction of French culture. This first set of meanings relates to metaphors of the living organism, and especially those taken from the circulation of the blood. The living organism was regarded as the archetype of rationality. The image of the body, viewed as a system where each part sustains a determined function enabling the reproduction of the whole, served to represent the connections which organically united the sovereign power and its subjects through the channels of wealth production, consumption and distribution. After all, 'political arithmetic', the ancestor of political economy, was defined as an anatomy. It was physicians who in effect enabled the transition of meaning by shifting the word 'network' from the exclusive domain of the weaving industry. The transplantation was particularly the work of the Italian naturalist and physician Marcello Malpighi (1628–1694). 'Reticular body' is the expression given by this precursor of microscopic anatomy (what came to be histology) to the tangle of lines he noticed on the epiderm. The application of 'network' to channel patterns invisible to the eye was a consequence of new observation methods in a science which, since Bacon, valued experience and facts.[1]

The second course of reticular representation is more typically French. It develops from the progress of fortifications science and military cartography. One individual played a key role in this: Vauban (1633–1707), Louis XIV's principal military engineer, who constructed the fortifications which served to stabilize France's national borders. Vauban used reticular representation within his practice in two ways. The first was in 'methods for attacking and defending fortified towns' which Vauban perfected in his technique of 'mine and countermine'. The mine technique consisted in approaching the walls of enemy strongpoints by means of underground passages leading to a chamber filled with gunpowder which

Sébastien le Prestre de Vauban, Relief plan of city and fortifications at
Besançon, 1706.

would be detonated below their foundations. The countermine technique
dealt with similar underground techniques intended to destroy enemy
mines during a siege of one's own strongpoint. These techniques were
defined as a complex system of 'arteries' and, in the case of countermines,
of 'listening arteries'.

Vauban became deeply concerned with cartography as an aid to this
science of siege. His individual fortresses, such as Neuf Brissac in Alsace,
were part of the broader construction of fortress France. The frontiers on
which he built his military constructions were France's front lines. His
conception of military defence – continuous defended frontiers for a
strategically conceived national space, and defence in depth – all
demanded exact maps. Thus a graphic map was drawn up as a part of
each fortification project, a synthesis of information for its defenders.
The topographic model at a scale of 1:600 represented not only entire
towns and their fortifications but also the surrounding countryside, with
special care taken over communication lines over a very wide area, sometimes up to twenty times the surface area of the town. Building fortifications and drawing up the map were part of the same process. Thus 'the

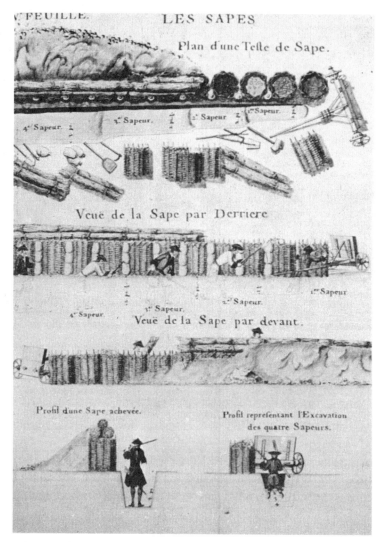

Underground mining operations, from Vauban, *Traité de l'attaque des places*.

relief map is sometimes used as a model and sometimes as a portrait'.[2] In addition, given that the absence at this time of a connected and coherent communication system constituted a major obstacle to the organization of French national space, Vauban instituted a fluvial topography by beginning an inventory of the rivers of the kingdom, appraising the possibilities of rendering each one navigable, if necessary by means of canals, in order 'to connect fluvial navigation'.[3] The official priority in transport

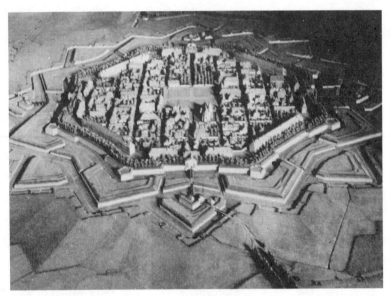

Relief plan of Neuf Brissac (designed by Vauban) on the Rhine border, 1706.

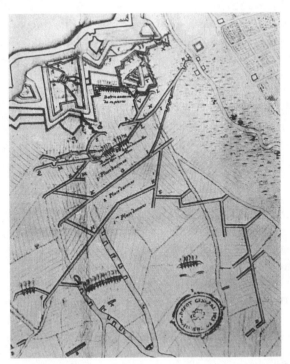

Network plan of attack on the fortifications at Maastricht.

policy under Louis XIV was for water rather than land communications; these navigation works rested with the recently created and highly talented Royal Engineers, initially under the authority of Vauban himself.

The appearance of the word 'network' in the first quarter of the nineteenth century was the logical product of the convergence of these two semantic manoeuvres. In 1802 Vauban's biographer, Pierre-Alexandre Allent (1772–1837), Royal Engineer and future general, inaugurated modern representation of the network in his *Essay on Military Reconnaissance* by referring to the hydrological network whose topography resembles the roots and branches of a tree. In 1825 the Corps of Engineers sanctioned use of the term 'network' to describe an articulated system of fortifications, underground passages and communication lines.[4]

The other contributor to the changing meaning of network was Claude Henri de Saint Simon (1760–1825), inventor of 'social physiology', the precursor of sociology. This second relationship became established by rendering the technical network in biomorphic imagery. At the same time as modern histology and its methods were being determined, social sciences figured their own renewal through organic metaphors. Saint Simon extrapolated observations made by the physiologist Xavier Bichat (1771–1802) on the 'weave of tissues' which reveals the composition and organizational structures of an organ. This histological vision of the connections which constitute tissue as the foundation of life was transferred to the social sphere. The natural organism mapped onto the organization of human societies as 'the product of an artificial network'. Thus appeared the metaphor of the 'organism-network'.[5] As a contestant for the status of exact science, 'social physiology' set itself the goal of 'reorganizing the body politic'. The history of the communication network as social utopia could now begin.

THE IDEAL OF THE EXCHANGE

Why was French culture and language so obsessed by the 'network'? A first explanation is to be found in Enlightenment ideals of exchange as a creator of values. The principle was put into practice during the seventeenth century by the *Ancien Régime*'s Corps des Ponts et Chaussées, the first to formalize a problematics of communication, centred on the organization of national space and on the construction of an internal market through canals and roads. By designing bridges and planning roads, they sought to achieve the goals of Reason. By taming 'evil nature' – the irrational – which separates people and prevents them from 'helping one another', they believed they were assisting the triumph of a 'good nature'

– the rational – which links, unites and guarantees the free flow of people and goods.[6]

To this first explanation, we should add the historian Fernand Braudel's suggestion that France's slowness in achieving national unity also played an important role:

Given the huge dimensions of France, it is clear that progress in transportation was crucial to the unification of the country, though it was by no means adequate at this stage, as has been pointed out with reference to periods closer to our own time by the historian Jean Bouvier (who maintains that national markets did not exist in France before the completion of the railway network) and the economist Pierre Uri (who goes even further, claiming categorically that present-day France will only be a true economic unity when the telephone system has reached 'American-style perfection'). They are no doubt right. But the admirable engineers of the Ponts et Chaussées who built the eighteenth-century roads were certainly responsible for progress towards a French national market.[7]

By contrast, Braudel observes, by the the early eighteenth century in England, the question of transportation and communication was no longer the object of theoretical debate. It was already integral to the reality of a home market, generating connections and exchanges accelerated by the Irish campaign and the conquest of Scotland. The kingdom was quick to abolish tolls and other internal barriers and to establish a national communication system. Substantial investment in the first quarter of the eighteenth century perfected a navigable river network of 1,160 miles, placing most of the country no more than 15 miles from water transport.

French delay at each succeeding stage in the evolution of communication networks (material and immaterial) explains why the communication network became such an important symbol. It represented a means of overcoming the shortcomings revealed by reality, and of making a project more credible. Claude-Henri de Saint Simon's disciples, the first utopists to exploit the concept of the communication network, well understood this. In 1837, on return from his tours of the USA and Great Britain, undertaken officially to study the impact of railway networks, the Saint-Simonist Michel Chevalier wrote: 'while in Paris people still discuss railways, here they build them . . . While English capitalists embark upon this great venture, Parisian capitalists remain unmoved . . .'[8] Whatever the case, the fact remains that the image of a map criss-crossed by free-flowing communication networks inspired many French authors of social utopias during the nineteenth century, who made explicit reference to the perfection of the English model. In his 'philosophical and social novel'

Voyage en Icarie (1840), Etienne Cabet (1788–1856), a disciple of Robert
Owen and an advocate of a form of communism intended to recover the
'primitive purity' of Christianity, celebrates in his character Lord
Carisdall the perfection of communication networks in this lost communal paradise, presided over by the sage Icar, whom he visits:

> The major railways are in red, minor ones in yellow, tramways in blue and all
> other roads in black. You can see also all the canals, big and small, all the naviga-
> ble and canalized rivers. Here are all the working mines and quarries. Notice also
> the local roads on this map of the provinces and the communal paths on this
> parish map. Now tell me if you know of a more sophisticated and efficient com-
> munication system. *I was amazed because it was even better than in England . . .*[9]

THE CULT OF THE NETWORK

From their earliest social applications, networks based on technical support invariably appeared to be the basis of new types of exchange between
people, of a new democracy. Their ramifications appeared to irrigate a
vast community, overcoming isolation, parochialism and the vagaries of
climate. Such a belief is already apparent in 1794 with the installation
in revolutionary France of the first optical and signal telegraph line,
invented by the Chappe brothers. Some revolutionaries dreamed of
putting the future lines 'at the service of the great democratic republics'.
Capable of 'communicating their information and their intentions over
great distances, so to speak, instantaneously', the citizens could revive the
agora, but were no longer limited as in Athens to the public square.

Disillusion was quick to set in. In reality, the optical telegraph was put
to use in the service of those in power. The technique quickly proved its
strategic utility by connecting Paris to its fortresses and revolutionary
armies in the north, then besieged by the coalition of European powers.
Claude Chappe suggested a three-fold civil use for his invention: the
transmission of commercial and industrial information, the launch of a
small telegraphic gazette and finally the transmission of lottery results.
Only the last of these recommendations was accepted by the Consul, the
future emperor Napoleon I, as a means of ending the speculative advantage made possible by the delay in mail transmission of lottery results
between Paris and the provinces.[10] The French optical telegraph network
– the densest in the world with about 550 stations and covering almost
5,000 kilometers – was designed by engineers of the Ponts et Chaussées
according to the same Paris-centred star-shaped model as the road
system. For more than fifty years, it remained the exclusive domain of the
Interior and War ministries. The public would only gain access to

Inauguration of the optical telegraph (1794), from *Le Petit Journal*,
1 December 1901.

telegraphic communication in 1852, some fifteen years after William Cooke and Samuel Morse's 1837 invention of the electric telegraph.

The significance of the optical telegraph as forerunner should not be overlooked. It established what was to become a recurrent feature of reticular utopias for the next two centuries and a key to visions of the third millennium. In the construction of communication images, Greek democracy was used repeatedly to illustrate the new social era promised by technical advance. What such reference to the Greek archetype obscures, however, is not only the fact that the promise has always remained unrealized, but also that the very possibility of an *agora*, of equal exchange among those placed at the hub, depended in the Attic cities on social relations themselves predicated upon an unequal exchange with the rest of society. The gap between prophecies based on the democratic potential of networks and the trajectory of realpolitik in their establishment is thus a permanent aspect of communication history.

The railway gave rise to the formulation of a primary doctrine, based on the thaumaturgic virtues of communication networks. Saint-Simonianism inspired a genuine 'cult of the network'. By contrast, to the great despair of Alexis de Tocqueville, the French government and business class of the 1830s remained reluctant to throw themselves into the rail adventure. Army officials were deeply sceptical about the strategic benefits of the new means of transport, objecting that it would 'weaken the troops' and 'make them lose their stamina for the long marches which have played such an important role in the triumph of our armies'.[11] In 1832, as a challenge to this gloomy attitude, the Saint-Simonian Michel Chevalier (1806–1879) published a series of visionary articles in the Saint-Simonian journal *Le Globe* on 'The System of the Mediterranean'. Two years earlier, England had inaugurated the first true railway line, widening the technical gap with France. France was to pass its fundamental rail legislation only in 1842, initiating a system which, like the road and telegraph networks, would be centred on Paris.

In his somewhat lyrical texts, Michel Chevalier, an engineer educated at the Ecole Polytechnique and the Ecole des Mines, pinned his hopes on the belief that the 'railway is the symbol of universal brotherhood', in a grandiose conception of reconciling East and West around the Mediterranean, as the first step towards world peace. He mapped an imaginary network connecting railways with river and sea routes and telegraphic lines. Thus Chevalier took his reader through Spain, Italy, Germany, Turkey, Russia, Asia and Africa. In the seven-league boots of the network, he leapt from the Bosphorus to the Persian Gulf, and from there to the Caspian Sea; from Elephantine Island to Alexandria. Of Russia he wrote:

If ever there were a country where railway can powerfully influence civilization, it has to be Russia. Everything about its inhabitants remains dormant; they die having vegetated rather than lived, never losing sight of their ancestral homes, like molluscs anchored by their shells to a rock. As for politics, the most efficient way to rouse them from their slumber will be to locate near them examples of extraordinary movement, to excite them by the spectacle of prodigious speed and to invite them to join the currents which swirl around their door.[12]

In much the same ways that technical communications reduce physical distances, Chevalier believed that the railway network would decrease the distance between social groups. It would act as a democracy. To change the world, you have to 'interlace it with steam and electricity!'. In 1837 Chevalier returned from the States more messianic than ever, to claim that 'reactionaries are only too well aware of it: they are as suspicious of an engineer from the Ponts et Chaussées as they are of Voltaire's publisher'.[13]

Like religion, the vocation of networks is to *religare*, to create the universal bond. This is true of both spiritual networks (or financial networks) and material networks (or transportation networks). Thanks to them, industrialists, guided by scientists, will manage the nation and its relations with other nations like a 'great industrial concern'. By introducing the biomorphic metaphor into the doctrines of social reorganization, Saint-Simonianism placed in the structuring power of the network all its hopes of saving Europe from the organizational crisis into which the collapse of Christian unity had plunged it, and of banishing forever the spectre of a military society.

Once the Church of Saint-Simonianism was over its brief militant period, its belief in the structuring force of the network provided the basis for a more managerial conception of society, feeding the French spirit of enterprise in the second half of the nineteenth century. Faith in technical determinism guided the new captains of industry in constructing great railway companies and bank networks across the world. It governed the establishment of transatlantic shipping lines and the great interoceanic routes, whose crown jewel was the Suez Canal. Finally, it offered a philosophy of progress to the commissioners of the Great Universal Exhibitions, in many of which Michel Chevalier himself participated, held successively in Paris following London's initiation of the first at Crystal Palace in 1851.

For over half a century, the miniaturized version of the globe represented by the universal exhibition shared the same image with the communication network, 'girdling' the macrocosm, the same quest for a lost paradise of human community and communication. They mutually reinforced their common belief in the mythical construction of an invisible universal bond. The great hymns to technical innovation through communication would merge with the rhetoric of exhibition promoters about the brotherhood of man brought about at these 'great reunions of Progress'. The London Exhibition witnessed the inauguration the first underwater cable between Dover and Calais (and between the Paris Bourse and the London Stock Exchange), a symbol of this common quest for 'universal brotherhood'. In 1889, at the centenary of the French Revolution, Elisée Reclus's monumental treatise on universal geography held pride of place at the Universal Exhibition in Paris. Under his supervision, an entire pavilion was constructed around a metallic globe. The 1900 Paris Exhibition ended the century by publicizing cinematography, the Lumière brothers' invention of 1895, incorporating the nascent motion picture within the redeeming image of technology encircling the globe. 'Animated images', wrote Jack London (1876–1916),

tear down the barriers of poverty and environment which bar access to education, and disseminate knowledge in a language everyone can understand . . . Time and distance have been annihilitated by the magic of film, uniting the peoples of the world . . . Thanks to this magic, the extremes of society can take a step towards the inevitable rebalancing of human condition.[14]

On the eve of the Great War, each new technical advance – electric telegraph, telephone, radio communications, even aviation – had had its own antiphon in praise of its capacity to organize humans in one great family in pursuit of the same objective: the establishment of a concord that transcended social and national division. Each of these communication networks had become the symbol of an international community, a great body of interdependent members. This is how two early twentieth-century French geographers defined the globe in their text, *Les principales puissances du monde*:

The earth is a kind of organism where all the parts are mutually dependent; the features of its surface are, one might say, interconnected, presenting a series of actions and influences, of causes and effects, wherein effects react back upon causes, as in the case of a well-organized body.[15]

Several socialist and anarchist writers constructed utopias celebrating the emancipatory capacity of networks in contrast to the forces of obscurantism and the centralizing tendencies of industrialization with respect to people and wealth. Peter Kropotkin (1842–1921) saw electricity as the

means of escape from the paleotechnic age of imperial mechanics and
logic. Its flexibility, its immateriality in today's parlance, announced a
neotechnic world governed by decentralization and the disappearance of
sprawling towns, the end of the separation between town and countryside, between manual and mental work, the principal sources of social
division.[16] New urban utopias together with regional planning were born
out of such ideas, inspiring architects and town planners for a very long
period. Resistance to the common-sense political consensus on technicist
progress was rare, as were those expressing worries about the ascendancy
of technology over social organization. Jules Verne's novel, *Paris au XXe
siècle*, in which the reader is transported to the 1960s, condemns outright
an emerging technical society in which facsimile transmission already
exists, but it is exceptional, out of tune with other science fiction works
between 1860 and 1906. Rejected by his publisher in the 1860s, the manuscript was only published in 1995. In his other novels, Verne, like most of
his contemporaries, is fascinated by the imaginary networks mapped
out by flight, specifically aeroplanes which he defended even at the
experimental stage against the supporters of balloon flight. His novel
Robur-le-Conquérant – a work which clearly reveals his affinity with
Saint-Simonian belief in a society saved by scientists and technologists –
teems with fictional tele-descriptions. From the platform of the aircraft
Albatross, the narrator surveys the regions of the world over which he
flies:

At two o'clock, the *Albatross* passed over Omaha on the Nebraska border;
Omaha City, the true terminus of the Pacific Railway, a fifteen hundred league
line of steel stretching from New York to San Francisco. For an instant, the yellow
waters of the Missouri appeared, followed by the wood and brick houses of the
town, set at the heart of this fertile basin like a buckle on the iron belt that circles
the continental waist of North America.[17]

The English liberal Samuel Butler (1835–1902) remains one of the most
interesting 'science fiction' writers because he addressed a contemporary
technicism, adopting an opposite perspective to the general belief in the
liberating exploits of machines which measured and conquered space and
time. In *Erewhon* (1872), an anagram of 'nowhere' (ou-topos in Greek),
Butler breaks with the instrumentalist vision of technology, envisaging in
his utopia the changes that a mechanized world was likely to have on
people, on ways of thinking and feeling, on their subjectivity.[18]

Paradoxically, radio communications, perfected by Marconi as early as
1896, had to await the end of the Great War to be exploited in the civil
domain; indeed it was this first 'total conflict' that produced decisive

Aerial navigators survey the terrestrial scene, from the first edition
of Jules Verne's *Robur-le-Conquérant* (Paris, 1886).

progress in communication techniques. It also spawned the earliest documentary films, and cryptology evolved into a science of secret coding; the
telephone also became more mobile thanks to the portable switchboards
used by US expeditionary forces.

AVOIDING BARBARISM

The Treaty of Versailles together with the creation of the League of
Nations and the International Labour Office embodied attempts to realize the ideals of peace which had gathered pace over the second half of the
nineteenth century, despite armed conflict and the inability of governments to agree on a common representative body and rule of law. Ideals of

universal communication and the network were intimately associated with this process of institutionalizing new peace mechanisms. Primarily, the aim of the League of Nations was to create a 'forum for public debate', as the American president Thomas Woodrow Wilson, one of its most ardent founders, put it. At a secondary level, it was deemed to offer an institutional model for intergovernmental understanding.

And this seems only natural when we recall that the establishment in 1865 of the electric telegraph network gave rise to the organization of the first joint action between modern states. The International Telegraph Union mapped out the first space for cross-border electric connections and served as a model for the numerous intergovernmental organizations which proliferated in the years preceding the conflict. During the signing of the founding act of the Union by about twenty states (from which Great Britain excluded itself because its telegraphic services depended uniquely on private companies) the French Foreign Minister made a speech which attached to the new technique the unbounded hopes of the signatories:

We are gathered here in a genuine congress of peace. If it is true that war more often than not is born out of misunderstanding, are we not removing one of its causes by facilitating the exchange of ideas between people and by placing at their disposal this amazing transmission system, this electric wire through which thought can travel across space at the speed of lightning, and which permits swift and uninterrupted dialogue between the scattered members of the human family?[19]

The United States refused to take part in this 'forum for public debate', taking refuge in isolationism. As early as 1933, national socialism exploited the incapacity of governments to agree a convention for the peaceful use of radio and respect for international sovereignty. Short-wave programmes from Nazi Germany reached the American continent. By orchestrating a 'psychological war' (a recurring theme in *Mein Kampf*) German radio had already been instrumental in the fall of the Austrian Chancellor Dollfuss. The spectre of conflict dampened those, like the historian Lewis Mumford in 1934, who remained convinced that radio broadcasts offered humanity the opportunity to recover a political unity lost since the days of Attica's tiny cities.[20]

Sensing the threatened stranglehold of macro-systems, whether of technology or of the Leviathan state, the 'dystopians' or 'counter-utopians' challenged the ethical claims of technology and the network. In 1918 the Russian émigré Evgeni Zamyatin, reflecting on his experience of daily life in England, foresaw a robot-like humanity driven by mechanical inevitability. In his novel *Islanders, or the Fisher of Men*, this 'steam-train' humanity was propelled 'along the tracks' laid down by 'axioms of compulsory redemption', punctuating, numbering and timetabling all human activities.[21] In 1920, back in his native country, he wrote *We*, an account of the aberrations, not only of the state as a self-serving organization, but of the machine to whose deification we have all contributed, thereby attracting the wrath of the censors. A Bolshevist, and later a dissident, Zamyatin died in exile in Paris in 1937. *We* describes a hydra-headed organism in which no one has a name, where everyone is identified by a number and indeed rejoices in their molecular status: each an atom, a phagocyte. Inside every lobotomized individual with his gramophone-like voice ticks an invisible metronome. The illness is rooted in imagination.[22] *We* anticipates Aldous Huxley's *Brave New World* (1932) and George Orwell's telescreen society of *1984* (1949).

The Second World War in its turn mobilized the totality of communication technologies. It witnessed the birth of the great electronic calculators which themselves anticipated computerized networks and the mathematical science of cybernetics. In 1948 Norbert Wiener, the founder of cybernetics, diagnosed the structuring power of the 'information' network; he was convinced that future society would be organized around it. If humanity wished to avoid a return to the barbarism of the war, which had so traumatized Wiener, it had to appropriate that power. While the mathematician's ideal was incarnated in the 'information society', he warned the public against the dangers of abusing it. Its principal enemy was entropy, or the tendancy in nature to destroy the orderly and to hasten biological deterioration and social disorder. 'The amount of information in a system is the measure of its degree of organization; and the one is simply the negative of the other.'[23] Information, the machines which process it and the network they create were the only things which could resist blockage to circulation, which is exactly what entropy produces. An information society must be a society where information circulates freely. It is by definition incompatible with restriction and secrecy, with inequality of access and the transformation of circulation into commodity. To encourage these is to promote entropy, to hinder human progress.

In analysing the mechanisms of power, the cyberneticist must implacably identify obstacles to the vital free circulation of information:

One of the lessons of the present book is that any organism is held together in this action by the possession of means for the acquisition, use, retention and transmission of information. In a society too large for the direct contact of its members, these means are the press, both as it concerns books and as it concerns newspapers, the radio, the telephone system, the telegraph, the postals, the theater, the movies, the schools and church . . . Thus on all sides we have a triple constriction of the means of communication: the elimination of the less profit-able means in favor of the more profitable ones; the fact that these means are in the hand of the very limited class of wealthy men, and thus naturally express the opinions of that class; and the further fact that, as one of the chief avenues to political and personal power, they attract above all those ambitious for such power. That system which more than all others should contribute to social home-ostasis is thrown directly into the hands of those most concerned in the game of power and money.[24]

Transparency, rejecting social exclusion, challenging the logic of the market – these are three questions found in the works of the inventor of the 'information society'. Too often, they would be evaded by other prophetic enthusiasts for the total computerization of society.

THE 'INFORMATION AGORA'

Norbert Wiener's extraordinary vision of a future 'information society' remained for a long time in the realm of fantasy. The information and communication technologies born out of the Second World War would evolve through other conflicts. They developed initially in the context of the law and national security, under the auspices of contracts between university research centres, the electronic and aerospace industries, the Pentagon and NASA. The Cold War, the moon landings and the arms race as well as war in Asia mapped out the field of technical innovation and prioritized its application. In 1950, at the request of the US Air Force, the continental defence network SAGE (Semi-Automatic Ground Environment) was established. By linking computers to radar tracking devices and by connecting all the computers of the system by telephone, real time data transmission or 'teleprocessing' came into being. In 1968 a further application appeared which brought us even closer to the end of the century: the ARPANET (Advanced Research Project Agency), a network which linked those university computer centres under contract with the Pentagon. This would become the model for the World Wide Web some twenty years later.

Latent in the theoretical discussions of a 'post-industrial' or 'tertiary' society in the United States in the 1960s, the term 'information society' re-emerged strongly a decade later when speculation occurred about the role of computer networks within economic globalization. In the West the agenda became dominated by the watchword of civil conversion and by how information and communication technology could serve the 'needs of society' rather than those of national security. In 1972 NASA launched the first civilian earth observation satellite, ERTS-1 (Earth Resources Technology Satellite), later renamed Landsat-1.

Meanwhile, in the late 1960s, the Canadian Marshall McLuhan's utopian vision of a 'global village' or 'planetary tribal village' constructed by television emerged.[25] Although born of the small screen, this simply recycled for the electronic age the well-worn determinist conception of a necessary social development through communications technology, extending it unproblematically into the network era promised for the third millennium.

One of the most important texts to locate the problematics of the communication network permanently within the new era of an 'informational agora' was the report entitled *L'informatisation de la société* (1978) drawn up by Simon Nora and Alain Minc at the request of President Valéry Giscard d'Estaing. Translated into several languages, it was one of the first documents through which a major industrial country reflected on 'how best to handle the computerization of society'. 'Telematics', a neologism denoting the convergence of computers, television and telecommunications, was explicitly envisaged by the authors as a tool for resolving the political and economic crisis affecting French society, a crisis they unhesitatingly characterized as a 'a crisis of civilization'. They believed that a network of computerized communication was the guarantee of a 'new global mode of social regulation'. These two top civil servants, both inspectors of finance, were concerned about the hegemony of American data banks:

Leaving to others – i.e. to American data banks – the responsibility for organizing this 'collective memory', while being content to plumb it, is to accept a form of cultural alienation. Installing data banks is our imperative of national sovereignty.

A country which neglects this responsibility risks being deprived of the 'capacity to control its destiny'. They therefore suggested an industrial strategy aiming at national independence in this field. Politically, they saw telematics as part of a project of resoldering the bonds of social cohesion. Massive computerization of society could create a new 'network' in which each homogeneous community would communicate with both fellow communities and the centre. They concluded that 'language and its rituals brought stability to the village. Computerized conversation and its codes must recreate an "information agora" reaching to the limits of the modern nation.'[26]

In 1980 Jean-Jacques Servan-Schreiber, author of the famous *Défi américain (American Challenge)*, published in the 1960s, grappled with another challenge in a new book: *Le Défi mondial*, published simultaneously in about twenty languages. Servan-Schreiber's central thesis is captured in the following:

All attempts to help the Third World in the past thirty years have failed . . . The West can only emerge from the current crisis and evolve towards full use of every individual's capacities by developing the Third World as a whole.[27]

The 'bare foot computer', an image dear to the author, symbolized the alliance between the farmer and a reticular tool which providentially permits a jump in the stages of social development to direct attainment of post-industrialism. To support his argument, Servan-Schreiber turned to the work of the American Alvin Toffler whose *The Third Wave* spoke of 'great struggles of tomorrow' not in terms of rich and poor nor between the East and the West but between 'those seeking to maintain and safeguard industrial society and those already willing to supercede it: between "Archaics" and "Moderns"'.[28]

What did the future hold for the diagnostics of crisis management in the 1980s? Let us turn first to Eric Le Boucher, specialist of such questions at *Le Monde*, taking stock of the situation in 1986:

The Nora-Minc report was written at a time when the values of the Left still held ideological centre stage. It was predicated upon a broad political vision of the future. Such is no longer the case. Nobody undertakes such exercises anymore. Today, "pragmatism" replaces reflection. On left and right the blueprint is the same: the more computerized the country, the more "modern", the more likely it is to "win" over other countries in battling the crisis. There is no alternative.[29]

As for J.-J. Servan-Schreiber's generous projects, they were enthusiastically welcomed by the Elysée which, during the first few months of François Mitterand's presidency, resolutely supported initiatives to create a worldwide centre of computer science in Paris. Servan-Schreiber wasted no time in recruiting renowned scientists to the project, including the Americans Seymour Papert and Nicholas Negroponte, both based at the Massachusetts Institute of Technology Media Lab (founded by the latter in 1979), as well as a number of researchers from Pittsburgh University. But despite such brilliant assistance, this scientific and intellectual adventure lasted no more than two years.

TOWARDS THE DEREGULATION OF THE CONCEPT

The depths of shame were plumbed when computing, marketing, design, advertising, all the communications disciplines, seized upon the word 'concept' itself:
this is our business, we are the creative people, we are *conceptual*! . . . It is profoundly depressing to learn that 'concept' now designates a service and computer
engineering society.[30]

Thus the philosopher Gilles Deleuze and the psychiatrist Félix Guattari
justified their 1991 project to restate the importance of reflexive work in
the face of the growing authority of new usages 'stupid and impudent
rivals' - emerging out of puerile management-speak in its 'frantic dash to
universalize communication so as to produce a marketable form of any
concept'. Distinguishing three stages in the evolution of each concept
the *encyclopaedic*, the *pedagogical* and the *commercial-professional*,
Deleuze and Guattari argued that only the second of these could prevent
it from plummeting from the heights of the first stage to the bathos of the
third, 'an unmitigated disaster for thought'.

The commodification of the world of communications which took
place in the 1980s did not fail to impact upon the language of networks.
One might go so far as to state that the deregulation of systems corresponded to a veritable deregulation of the concepts we use to designate
the reticular world. With privatization and deregulation, first in broad-
casting and later in the break-up of public telecommunications monopo-
lies, contradictions in the constant call by those in power for social benefit
through technological revolution were quickly apparent. Welfare systems
nationally and internationally have been subordinated to technical and
financial logics. Geo-economics protagonists have superseded geopolitical actors, until recently sovereign in the enunciation of macro-strategies
for network expansion. The former basically await the latters' removal of
the final legal barriers to the construction of a totally fluid global market.

The crisis faced by the great tradition of political utopia has stimulated
the exponential rise of the techno-utopia. In 1994 the US Vice-President,
Al Gore, presented to the International Telecommunications Union
(ITU) delegates, gathered in Buenos Aires, his plan for the Information
Superhighway:

The Global Information Infrastructure (GII) will be an assemblage of local,
national and regional networks . . . This GII will circle the globe with information superhighways on which all people can travel . . . The GII will be a metaphor
for democracy itself . . . The GII will not only be a metaphor for a functioning
democracy; it will in fact promote the functioning of democracy by greatly

enhancing the participation of citizens in decision-making. And it will greatly promote the ability of nations to cooperate with each other . . . I see a new Athenian Age of democracy forged in the fora the GII will create.[31]

Gore's messianic vision of technology was peppered with literary references, taken from Jules Verne's science-fiction novels. This geopolitical speech, delivered by a hegemonic power, catalogued the arguments favouring the orthopaedic virtues of a global cybervillage. Symbolically delivered in the capital of a country aspiring to join the 'first world' by adopting the neo-liberal path, the speech dwelt at length on the role of the information highway in education and health. But it neglected the appalling exclusions forced by the structural adjustment policies of the World Bank and International Monetary Fund on working people and the impoverished middle classes in the South. Painting a glowing picture of the benefits to be expected from the progress of telephonics was insufficient to pay off the debts incurred by addressing their underequipment. Fifteen per cent of the world's inhabitants monopolize two thirds of its phone lines. As though seeking to align himself more closely with the problematics of the 'development', he expressed his desire to convert the Peace Corps, that organization of young volunteers created by the Kennedy administration, to digital technology. But he forgot to add that the conditions of their mission had radically changed with the decline of welfarism and its effects on the South. There is a marked contrast between anachronistic musings such as these, vague reminiscences of a charitable era when aid and assistance policies were conjugated with the national security dictates of the Cold War, and the fundamental message of Gore's speech: only opening national telecommunication systems to the logic of the market, that is their privatization, secures development. Future 'cooperation between peoples' and the viability of 'global conversation' between citizens depends on adjustment to the norms of a *global democratic marketplace*. This egalitarian representation of a 'global village' that aggregates people in a common participation in the symbols of Modernity is in constant conflict with the reality of living standards among the vast majority of humans. The dynamic of economic models of globalization risks leading towards a 'ghettoized' world, organized around a small number of megacities and regions, concentrated mainly in the 'North', with outliers in the 'South', serving as the nerve centres of worldwide markets and flows.

By the end of February 1995, the hegemonic rhetoric of *participatory democracy* through the 'assemblage of local, national and regional networks' was no longer on the agenda of the first G7 summit to discuss the construction of the global information society. Gathered in Brussels, in the presence of Al Gore and 40 delegates from major American, European and Japanese electronic and aerospatial companies, and protected from the public gaze, the self-styled industrial giants abandoned, on grounds of pragmatism, the construction of the information highway to corporate initiative. In July 1997 President Bill Clinton no longer sought to disguise the realpolitik underlying the rhetoric of global democracy. Flanked by Vice-President Gore, the Chairman of IBM and other cyber-businessmen, he announced the adoption of a 'general framework for global electronic commerce' with a view to establishing a 'global zone of free-exchange'.

The time when technical prophecy seemed the monopoly of 'world-makers' or utopian reformers is long past. At the century's close, futurology has become a veritable profession. Global space strategists are convinced of the strategic importance of elaborating the art of 'propagandizing' the future. The production of legitimizing discourse is even more crucial while global arteries remain more promise than actuality, and while media announcements remain the only means of convincing us that these techniques for overcoming 'centrality', 'territoriality' and 'materiality' already govern the planet.

Techno-utopia has become an ideological weapon of the first order in trading influence to sustain a free-market vision of global order. Despite proclamations which periodically sign the death warrant of the nation state, together with history and ideology, this remains the enemy whose prerogatives have to be challenged well beyond its complicity in deregulation. Techno-utopia gives birth to the dream of unmediated planetarism. The two single players would be global economic units and a 'global civil society' brought into being by the cybernetic network. Only techno-libertarians are shortsighted enough to support such a planetary populism that seizes upon the simplistic vision of an abstract and evil state opposed by an idealized civil society, a liberated space of free communication between fully sovereign individuals.

So, contrary to McLuhan's predictions, the future still has its gurus and its best-sellers, and paper remains an essential ingredient in the digital era. Gutenberg's invention even enabled *Wired* magazine, bible of the cyberpunks, to establish a newspaper group among whose 1996 acquisitions was the Global Business Network which specializes in selling scenarios on the digital future to corporations! Such books as Nicholas Negroponte's *Being Digital* or Bill Gates's *The Road Ahead*, both from 1995, are examples of the overlap.

Digital information is a 'force of nature'; there is no way to 'stop' or 'curb' its progress, according to MIT Professor Nicholas Negroponte and shareholder in *Wired*, in line with the neo-Darwinist fetishizing of technology. Connect or perish: this force 'decentralizes', 'globalizes', 'harmonizes' and 'totally empowers'. Thanks to these four cardinal virtues, continues this American researcher,

in the same ways that hypertext removes the limitations of the printed page, the post-information age will remove the limitations of geography. Digital living will include less and less dependence upon being in a specific place at a specific time, and the transmission of place itself will start to become possible.[32]

Bill Gates, chairman of Microsoft, goes straight to the point, freely admitting that the prime objective of this network of networks is the 'ultimate market', generating a 'frictionless capitalism . . . In the great planetary market place, we as social creatures will sell, negotiate, invest, bargain, choose, discuss, stroll, meet.'[33] According to Gates, the image of a segmented planet of virtual communities merges with the pragmatism of transnational 'consumption communities'. Such communities, segmented and targeted according to purchasing power, divide the planet into creditworthy ghettos within national territories: north and south, east and west. The map of the global market is an archipelago of minorities.

Living standards replace geographic proximity. As formulated by global advertising networks, it looks something like this:

sophisticated marketeers recognize greater social differences between midtown Manhattan and the Bronx, two sectors within the same city, than between midtown Manhattan and the Seventh Arrondissement of Paris or London's Mayfair. This means that when manufacturers contemplate business expansion, demographic and consumption preference rather than geographic location maps increasingly determine the decisions ... All this underlines the economic logic of globalism.[34]

Combining globalization and segmentation, the marketing industry has gradually appropriated the concept of 'socio-cultural mapping' to refer to its transnational consumption typologies. By facilitating the compilation of ever more sophisticated data banks on the socio-cultural profile of consumers, computing has offered industry a qualitative leap. If on the one hand global maps of market segments appear in all the advertisement and marketing manuals, on the other, the precise methods of conducting surveys and collecting data on trans-border consumers remain absolutely impenetrable. Questions concerning the legitimacy of consumer tracking were openly addressed in 1995 when the European Union proposed data protection legislation to protect private individuals. The US government reacted immediately by accusing the Europeans in the World Trade Organization of breaking the principles of free trade.

Thus the shift in regulation regimes towards privileging the market and private enterprise values marks a turning point in the modernist history of constructing the 'individual measure' and in the orthopaedic application of socio-cultural mapping. It is a history which opened about 1835 when the Belgian astronomer and mathematician Adolphe Quételet (1796–1874) launched his work on 'social physics' with the express intention of equipping public authorities with the necessary quantitative tools to regulate the uncertainty produced by 'disruptive forces', that is: 'all those things which influence men morally and prompt them to act in one way rather than another'. Collectively, these threaten the stability of society.[35] As a pioneer in the standardization of international statistical systems, Quételet was also the first person to measure and classify the probability of a given individual to commit a crime, evaluating the relative influence of season, sex, age, social class, nationality and geographic location; and to map delinquency and suicide rates against other measures of social instability. The historical associations between the image of the network and mappings of social ecology are thus more profound than any of their supposed geographical connections.

9

The Uses of Cartographic Literacy: Mapping, Survey and Citizenship in Twentieth-Century Britain

DAVID MATLESS

INTRODUCTION: A COMMON OBJECT

Critical analyses of cartography have aligned maps with an impulse to dominate: land, people, things, properties, colonies. The cartographic eye is equated with the eye of power-as-domination. Alternatively maps are claimed as a vehicle of resistance, a language whereby rights to place may be asserted or through which non-dominatory representations might be cultivated. Here, mapping appears more benign, exercising a more 'human' cartographic eye.[1] This essay takes a somewhat different tack, acknowledging these various political and aesthetic possibilties of mapping but wary of an approach which reads it simply for signs of either oppression or liberation. I address rather the politics and aesthetics of common cartographic literacy, considering a place and time where the map emerges as an ordinary, even banal document, a common object. My focus is an influential movement for regional and local survey in Britain in the early twentieth century, a movement constituted through a preoccupation with what Michel Foucault would term the 'power-knowledge' of the map.

Power-knowledge implies both that 'power' is not exhausted by domination and that 'knowledge' cannot be assessed for essential qualities of liberty: 'it is not the activity of the subject of knowledge that produces a corpus of knowledge, useful or resistant to power, but power-knowledge, the processes and struggles that traverse it and of which it is made up, that determines the forms and possible domains of knowledge'.[2] One could argue that such an approach is especially necessary for any study of mapping in the twentieth-century West. The form of survey considered here emerges at a time when cartography was becoming subject to mechanical reproduction and mass use, and the issue of cartographic literacy was expanding from an argument over access to possessable, containable,

privileged knowledge, to a question of the nature and purpose of common geographical knowledge. Writing on 'Cartography, Ethics and
Social Theory', Brian Harley argued, 'it is only the topographical map
that can inscribe the gestalt of the ordinary landscapes of the world. It is
only the topographical map that is intelligible and available to a larger
proportion of its citizenry.' The topographic map is placed on the side of
what Harley terms a 'democratic and humanistic form of geographical
knowledge',[3] working against academic forms of mapping which objec-
tify the world in the service of the powerful. My approach here, by contrast, does not necessarily assume an alignment of cartographic literacy
and social opportunity and improvement. Rather, I trace the map's emergence as a popular document through specific formulations of cartographic literacy, concerning how the map should be used, who is able to
use it, what forms of knowledge it should register, what kinds of citizenship it could cultivate. I have discussed elsewhere the place of the map
within early twentieth-century cultures of landscape and leisure; themes
of citizenship and anti-citizenship, knowledge and pleasure, orientation
and power, recur in this essay.[4]

My title alludes to Richard Hoggart's 1957 study *The Uses of Literacy*,
an often jaundiced account of the effects of new 'mass' forms of media on
working-class culture.[5] Hoggart's stated aim was to bridge a dangerous
divide of mutual incomprehension between the languages of self-styled
'mass' and 'expert' cultures. Whatever Hoggart's normative reading of
traditional cultural integrity and modern cultural decline, his study has
the virtue of raising questions regarding the cultural constitution of 'literacy' and the effects of appealing to the 'popular'.[6] Such work should
caution against us taking an easy turn to, say, a language of 'cognitive
mapping' or 'social cartography' as an escape route from postmodern
disorientation.[7] The cultural history of cartographic literacy would show
a far more complex aesthetic and political field, with the map partici-
pating in processes of subjectification which work through assumptions
concerning the nature and value of popular and educated knowledge. In
this essay we shall find cartographic literacy figured as basic to a form of
citizenship, to a geographical self, whereby people could know their place
– in all senses of that term. The map as a common object thus assumes a
key role in a story of what Nikolas Rose terms the 'genealogy of subjectification', those histories of conduct whereby human beings produce
themselves through spatio-temporal relations with human and nonhuman
subjects and objects.[8] As the regional surveyors Fagg and Hutchings put
it, maps, walks and observations made up a 'technique of living'.[9]

MAPS AND SURVEYS

The second part of this essay will consider the forms of citizenship cultivated through survey. We begin, however, by addressing the general purposes of regional survey and the central role played by the map.

Survey: vision, boredom and power

> A new age, a new enthusiasm, a new enlightenment are already dawning... Regional Survey and its applications . . . are destined to become master-thoughts and practical ambitions for the opening generation.[10]

Regional survey emerges in the early twentieth century, organizing itself around the work of sociologist-geographer-biologist-educationalist Patrick Geddes as an ordering device, simultaneously epistemological, social and economic, and geared around the study of the interrelationships between 'place, work and folk'. The role of regional survey in the discipline of geography and economic '(ad)venture capitalism' has been considered in detail elsewhere; here my focus is on the centrality of mapping in survey.[11] The key figures in the story are Geddes, his chief collaborator Victor Branford, and C. C. Fagg and Geoffrey Hutchings, authors of the standard 1930 text *Introduction to Regional Surveying*. Two diagrams in Fagg and Hutchings's book can serve to indicate the scope of survey. The 'conspectus' diagram maps knowledge onto place, making survey an exercise in both regional and epistemological synthesis. Physical, biological and social environments and their respective sciences interact to make local study a human ecology. Fagg and Hutchings suggested the conspectus was best understood alongside a transect diagram of the region, which showed what 'roughly would be revealed if it were possible to take a gigantic knife, make a clean vertical cut through the country . . . and turn up the cut edge to look at'.[12] A network of knowledge translates into a formally layered vision of regional life, with land a necessary ground of life and thought. The diagrams together suggest that the mind can be mapped onto, and mapped from, an orderly transect of any region. The themes of both images will recur through this essay.

Despite, or perhaps because of, their visionary ambition, surveyors expressed regular concern that their practice might prove dull. As Branford put it: 'Survey – the word is not a blessed one.'[13] Speaking in Eastbourne in June 1920, Fagg assured his audience that his topic was not boring: 'a rapid surface utilisation survey is not so puerile a performance as it may appear at first sight to be'.[14] If survey was to make the visionary out of the mundane, surveyors worried that the latter might take over.

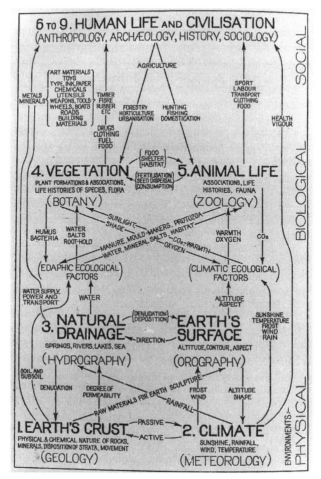

The regional survey conspectus diagram, from C. C. Fagg and G. E. Hutchings,
Introduction to Regional Surveying (Cambridge, 1930).

Conversely we find attempts to head off potentially awkward associations of power. In *Interpretations and Forecasts*, Branford anticipates
Harley's recent analyses, tracing the emergence of the Ordnance Survey
to the British state response to Jacobite and Napoleonic threats, and registering the connection of mapping and legal record, estate improvement
and tax gathering. Associations of power, however, lead him not to reject
the map but to assert its potential as 'a social process modifying our
knowledge of our whole environment, guiding our use of it also, and thus
a real piece of contemporary social evolution'.[15] The map is reclaimed
from military use for 'the education of pupils in knowledge and com-

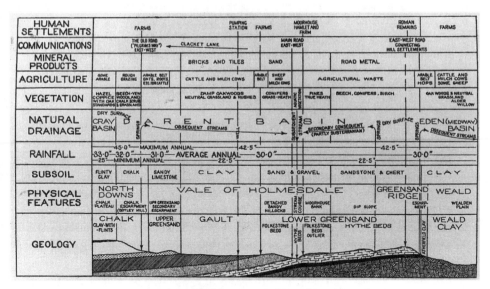

A specimen transect diagram, from Fagg and Hutchings, *Introduction to Regional Surveying.*

mand of their region'.[16] Healthy command is the desired state, with 'the citizen as sociologist' pursuing 'the science of looking around, and the art of creating eutopias'.[17]

The map as the key mirror in an orderly kaleidoscope

> We need scarcely add that those interested in regional survey should never leave copies of old Ordnance Survey maps in the possession of second-hand booksellers.[18]

Survey worked through a range of media, visual and textual, including photographs, books, postcards, lantern slides and regional relief models. All were offered as keys to the 'Regional Drama': 'Such is the stream of events, each and all charged with its elements of drama, and continuously visible through this changeful, yet orderly, kaleidoscope of the regional and civic outlook.'[19] The key survey document was the map: 'we cannot too strongly emphasise the fact that whenever possible the most satisfactory method of recording regional observations is on a map'.[20] If survey was an 'orderly kaleidoscope', the map was more than one mirror among many; it was a visual binding agent. Fagg and Hutchings listed 160 possible maps following the conspectus structure, and arranged for Messrs Winsor and Newton to produce a special set of 'Regional Survey Colours', allowing a colour standardization of output.[21] This was not to say that the map was sacrosanct. Noting how large maps could be awkward in the field, Fagg and Hutchings suggested the reader 'cut up all maps, of whatever scale, into sections measuring 9" x 6"', to be mounted on thin card and numbered.[22] The map was both the 'essential foundation'[23] of survey and something to cut and paste in the field.

The map was also a model of thought. Branford and Geddes presented mappability as the reason for the superiority of nineteenth-century French sociologist Frederic Le Play over Karl Marx, who failed the 'one invariable test in all such matters: Can the data and the results be graphically set down, concretely mapped?'[24] This may seem a churlish positivist dismissal of Marx, and it paralleled a rejection of his revolutionary rather than 'evolutionary' politics, but mapping does not here denote a simple empiricism. Rather, the map as a document is always at once concrete and abstract, fitting Geddes's requirement that a synthesizing vision of the region demanded literal as well as conceptual overview: 'Large views in the abstract ... depend upon large views in the concrete.'[25] The plan view offered by the map therefore manifested survey's epistemology as well as its methodology. By a 'rigorous insistence on mapping' the observer was 'saved from the besetting temptation of general talk, and yet he comes in time to have generalizations as well as particulars', which in their turn were open to verification or criticism:

There is an orderly progress; and from fact to image, and from image to symbol, there is, or should be, no break; and similarly for the return from symbol to fact. Thus the social sciences begin to form their first commencements of 'conceptual shorthand,' and from this they may go on to represent and co-ordinate for man's thought and benefit, not only the world without but even the world within.[26]

Thinking is like making and using a map, and mapping is necessary for thought.

Viewpoints

The map was presented on active service, working in the field as a portable object. Here regional survey echoed the emerging and interlinked promotion of open-air leisure, youth culture and geographical fieldwork, emphasizing an 'outlook geography' of seeing from highpoints, with the unfolding of the map enabling a reading of the country.[27] Branford and Geddes singled out Hilaire Belloc's walking literature as providing an exemplary engagement with landscape, calling Belloc 'one of the very best of our regional geographers'.[28] In *The Path to Rome*, a hike-cum-Catholic-pilgrimage across Europe, Belloc had ruled a line on a

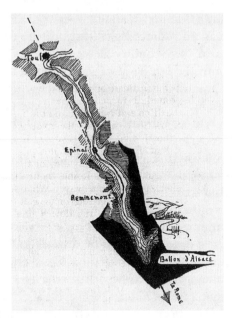

Hilaire Belloc's route map from his *Path to Rome* (London, 1902).

map from Toul on the upper Moselle to Rome, and set out to walk along it.[29] Belloc's directness appealed to survey in its echo of the transect, and its movement beyond obvious valley routes to attain highpoints:

this is the peculiar virtue of walking to a far place, and especially of walking there in a straight line, that one gets these visions of the world from hill-tops.

When I call up for myself this great march I see it all mapped out in landscapes, each of which I caught from some mountain, and each of which joins on to that before and to that after it, till I can piece together the whole road.[30]

While the rail or bicycle traveller was denied the perspective of the ridge and therefore missed the 'full picture',[31] a walk could be punctuated by the summit command of space:

they furnish at one point (that is, at the summit) what ordinary roads going through passes can never give you: a moment of domination. From their climax you look over the whole world, and you feel your journey to be adventurous and your advance to have taken some great definite step from one province and people to another.[32]

Belloc provides a stark example of what Mary Louise Pratt terms the 'seeing-man',[33] a traveller expressing an imperious mode of visual topographic power, the view from the height embodying a masculine and imperial possession of the landscape. I would not, however, follow Pratt in labelling such seeing as 'a purely passive experience'. Similarly, survey's motif of the world as an orderly kaleidoscope suggests a complexity beyond her analysis of 'promontory descriptions' as assuming static scenes.[34] Order remains the key trope of survey, but it is a more shifting field demanding a plurality of methods and viewpoints. And while Belloc's writing in *The Path to Rome* can certainly be understood in terms of an assertive masculinity in the landscape, one should be cautious about extending this label to all regional survey work. Much of this was carried out by and written up by women, and while one certainly finds in this period equations of topographic overview and masculine power, the open air is also asserted as a space of equal access for women and men where restrictive definitions of feminine conduct could be overcome; I return to this point below.[35] Summit domination must also be placed within longer narratives of ascent and descent, a form of situated knowledge working alongside others gathered on the way up the hill and after coming down, all of which go to make up the document of survey. The summit becomes a key point only through its location within a broader narrative. As the school survey leaflet *Discovery* put it in its outline of methods for local study: 'BIRD'S EYE VIEW – Climb to the top of a hill, tower or high building to get a bird's eye view of your district . . . Come down from the height and begin work.'[36]

Regional and open-air surveyors certainly echoed Belloc in registering the purpose and pleasures of topographic overview. In a 1924 essay on Hastings, Branford described going up a local hill: 'Reaching the flat-topped summit, we look around and see the rolling ups and downs of the land and the gleaming expanse of sea. This panorama is Geography.'[37] Fagg and Hutchings proposed local 'orientation charts' on vantage points, three concentric circles indicating visible points within 1.5 miles, landmarks within 51.5 miles and the direction of more distant cities. Location would be brought home:

If we can stand upon an eminence and say 'Athens is straight over there' or 'Cape Town is precisely in that direction' these places with all their associations immediately become more real to us. We gain a vivid impression of the fact that they do exist on this same earth and have a geographical relationship to the intimate details of our own town or village as depicted in the centre of the chart.[38]

To take one interwar example, archaeologist Sir Arthur Evans and the Oxford Preservation Trust sponsored the construction of Jarn Mound, with a chart on top, on Boar's Hill above Oxford, adding to the existing height to obtain a panoramic view. Slippage problems brought down the first heap, but a 50-foot-high mound was completed in November 1931.

Jarn Mound, from Sir Arthur Evans, *Jarn Mound* (Oxford, 1933).

While not formally part of the regional survey movement, Jarn Mound makes sense within a culture of landscape seeking an overview of country. Local elite literary associations concerning Matthew Arnold's view over Oxford also drove the mound upward. To the east the Chilterns, to the south the Berkshire Downs, to the west the Cotswolds, and Oxford close by: 'Of the view itself that here opens out it can certainly be said that it is far and away the most spacious to be found in this part of England.'[39] Today the hilltop trees have grown, as trees do, and while Oxford is just about visible, you have to imagine the rest.

Institutional frames

Survey was cultivated in various institutional frames. Much early activity centred on the Outlook Tower in Edinburgh, established by Geddes in the 1890s on Castle Hill and known for its exhibitions, camera obscura and view of the city embodying principles of direct observation, synoptic vision and scientific synthesis.[40] Branford saw the Tower as the intellectual equivalent of a city's central telephone exchange, with the many voices in a place unable to converse adequately without it.[41]

A more significant institution in the interwar period was the Regional Survey Section of the South-Eastern Union of Scientific Societies, set up in 1915 through Fagg's efforts, to work alongside existing Union sections on botany, geology and photography: 'Our various sections are too often water-tight compartments . . . the regional survey provides a living tie between them all.'[42] Fagg was Honorary Secretary from 1915 to 1923, remaining a dominant influence through the 1920s. A survey in 1925–6 recorded ten societies in the region conducting 'organised regional surveys', with others keeping local or specialist records. Woolwich, Tunbridge Wells, Croydon and Saffron Walden were the major centres.[43] The Section presidents through the 1920s included Branford, Geddes, Fagg, Hutchings, Alexander Farquarson, George Pepler, Herbert Fleure and Harold Peake.[44] In 1928 Fagg used the Union's journal, the *South-Eastern Naturalist*, to provide the first history of the movement, presenting survey as a mature practice.[45] The Section mounted displays in the Annual Congress museum, and from the late 1920s held field meetings, some in 'rustic' locations, others in 'civic' centres. In November 1931 a Regional Survey conference at Dartford included two rambles along the route of the proposed Thames Tunnel approach road, with discussion on questions of regional planning.[46] The Hill Farm field centre at Stockbury, a 'centre for open-air education' run by Christine Pugh, provided a regular rural venue. In 1928 Pugh and Hutchings produced *Stockbury: A Regional Study in North-East Kent*, outlining geology, vegetation, animal life and historical geography, and linking physical and sociological features. Hutchings drew the maps and transects. The book concluded by comparing surveyors to upland smallholders:

They have been drawn hither by the instinct, strongest perhaps in the primitive hunter and his modern prototype, which has urged men to spread over the earth and everywhere subdue their environment. Moved by the same impulse the student of Nature seeks out these uplands and finds the reward of his journey in the quiet woods and wide open spaces of the Downs.[47]

THE MAPPING CITIZEN

Survey and mapping can be understood in terms of cultivating a particular model of citizenship, with educated open-air experience a source of intellectual, spiritual and physical improvement. The remainder of the essay explores the nature of this cartographically literate citizen. We can approach this issue through a consideration of the psychoecology of regional survey.

Psychoecology: purse/piss and vir supremus

Regional survey presented itself as a modern practice but with primitive connection; mapping was regarded as an essential part of being human:

We might say that the subject of regional survey is modern but that the function of regional surveying is as old as animal life; for every young organism must, according to its individual needs and limitations, investigate its environment as

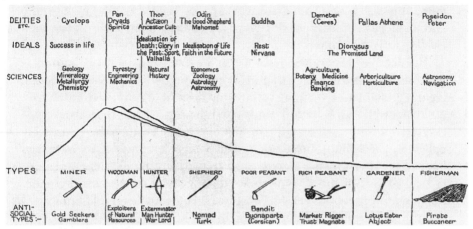

The 'Valley Section' with rustic types, from Fagg and Hutchings,
Introduction to Regional Surveying.

part of the technique of living; and this investigation of environment, whether it
be by caterpillar or child, is the very essence of regional survey.[48]

Regional survey becomes a psychoecology in two senses. Firstly different psychological types are mapped onto Geddes's archetypal regional
diagram, the 'Valley Section'. Pugh and Hutchings's comment on the
hunter and naturalist makes sense in terms of an argument for the correspondence of contemporary branches of knowledge and archetypal
'nature occupations', resident in different zones of the region and at
the root of differences within the human psyche. Branford and Geddes
imagined an aerial view of the ideal valley as a chessboard, with 'each
occupational type upon its native square, . . . its character determined and
consequently its role conditioned according to the formula: Place-Work-
Folk'.[49] The region and the human is constituted through a psycho-social
ecology, with a corresponding anti-social ecology of supposedly im-
moral occupations and practices, sometimes given a specific ethnicity.[50]
Citizenship again makes sense only in relation to an anti-citizenship symbolically located underground, low against the deities on high. The valley
section defines a vertical and horizontal moral geography.

Secondly, regional survey can appear as a means to cultivate a new psychological type. Fagg produced two substantive essays on psychoanalysis
and Geddesian evolutionary theory, one for his 1923 Presidential Address
to the Croydon Natural History and Scientific Society, the other for a 1933
talk to the British Psychological Society. Fagg concluded of Freud that, 'by
fearlessly investigating the Oedipus complex he has given us hope that we

may someday be able to make a world fit for children to live in; a family
and social environment in which our already abundant super-babies may
develop into super-men'.[51]

The detail of his argument for a eugenic town and country planning is
beyond this essay, but Fagg's figure of the superman approximates to the
ideal regional surveyor. Fagg isolates two psychological types to suggest
their possible sublimation and combination. The 'Inspector' type
exhibits 'purse pride', reacting to 'repressed anal erotism' by obsessively
collecting, recording, inspecting: 'Often actually myopic, its members
have no great vision, but a great capacity for learning the rules and regu-
lations.' The 'Bohemian' type shows 'piss pride', being creative, artistic,
dreamy, ambitious and exhibitionist, subservient to 'urethral libido':

 Pride they have in abundance, but it is in their exhibitionistic conquests. It corresponds to 'piss pride', the term by which Tommies styled the morning erection . . .
In this connection it is interesting to recall the folk description of the shower at
sunrise as 'the pride of the morning'.[52]

The Inspector type had been 'chiefly responsible for the development of
civilization', but 'left to themselves they would produce at best some kind
of a "Brave New World"'.[53] It is not hard to connect fears of the 'puerile'
and dull nature of survey to Fagg's Inspector analysis. Perhaps regional
survey needed to be more Bohemian?

The Bohemian type, however, also troubled Fagg:

My view is that most so-called genital erotism has a urethral basis, and for object,
so far as the male is concerned, it is often, and particularly in fetishism, unconsciously directed towards an anus, not necessarily male. I find this view thrust
upon me with the persistence of a paranoid delusion. For this reason I have
regarded it with suspicion, but I still adhere to it.[54]

Surveying with his 160 possible types of map, concerned about purse-
puerility on the one hand, and urine and the anus on the other, Fagg
looked to a sublime merger of Inspector and Bohemian:

the needs of humanity . . . require the emergence of a higher type, capable of
exploiting the qualities of these two species and of man in the interests of all.
This type, if it comes, will merit further generic distinction and may be called in
anticipation *Vir supremus* . . . He will spring from such members of *Homo
Sapiens* who, instead of specializing in the direction of anabolic security or kata-
bolic dissipation, conserve the metabolic balance . . . I can see no brilliant future
for humanity apart from the emergence of *Vir supremus*, but I believe that sooner
or later he may arrive.[55]

It may be reasonable to conclude that for Fagg *Vir supremus* would be a
model regional surveyor; visionary yet meticulous, happy to record every-

Girls with map, from Harry Roberts, *The Practical Way
to Keep Fit* (London, 1942).

thing and file it away yet always conscious of being part of a creative
process of co-operative social evolution, a figure of metabolic balance.
Regional survey can become a healthy means for channelling the 'striving
for increased control over environment . . . the primary impulse of living
organisms, that is of each organism individually. It is the easily perverted
or compromised dynamic principle in organic evolution.'[56] Regional survey as a non-perverted form of field pleasure providing a psychological
template for the superman?

Regional survey, like the promotion of open-air leisure, worked
through a delicate mix of elitism and populism, and in Fagg's later
writings we find the former becoming predominant. Generally, though,
tensions between elite and popular practice are resolved through an ideal
of the educated citizen, appreciative of beauty, responsible in conduct and
defined against a residual anti-citizen who transgresses social and aesthetic codes, either through malice or ignorance.[57] The map is central to
this educated citizenship: an image from open-air enthusiast and health
commentator Harry Roberts's *The Practical Way to Keep Fit* can conclude this section. Pictures of girls with maps were common in open-air

literature, with walking styled as a progressive activity for both male and female, conducted in progressive clothing. In Roberts's book the image illustrates a psychological argument concerning 'The Problems of Adolescence'. For Roberts, single-sex education and shared interests meant that the young, with their developing 'sexual instinct', preferred 'their own sex' for close emotional ties. Such affections were, however, 'in the nature of a safety-valve', and should be transient; lasting homosexual regard reflected a lingering 'childish state'.[58] The map is considered an appropriate technology for controlled self-development, centring an image of adolescent navigation, holding the figures together yet apart, guiding them to adulthood where they might healthily map with new companions.

The controlled release of the map into the community

If the map touched basic human psychology, it needed careful handling. Surveyors saw danger in both the aesthetics and politics of mapping, risks of loose pleasure and controversy. Aesthetically the solution was to stress the controlled nature of cartographic pleasure. Journalist C. E. Montague's essay 'When the Map is in Tune' was a key reference point, presenting citizen, map and landscape in concert, producing a harmonious revelation of place: 'The notation once learnt, the map conveys its own import with an immediateness and vivacity comparable with those of the score or the poem.'[59] Cartography was to be non-dissonant yet also, in Fagg's terminology, non-anal: 'Geography, in such a guise, is quite a different muse from the pedantic harridan who used to plague the spirit of youth with lists of chief towns, rivers and lakes, and statistics of leather, hardware and jute.'[60] Inspector and Bohemian are reconciled through a certain excitement.

Care was also taken over the politics of mapping. Addressing the South-Eastern Union, Fagg guarded against the political associations of social enquiry:

The crude suggestion that sociology and socialism are synonymous terms is not worthy of discussion, but the fear expressed by some that sociology will lead us into political and religious controversy does perhaps merit a few words of comment. If the danger were a real one I should certainly seek to avoid it, for the introduction of political or religious controversy into our societies would greatly impair their value as scientific institutions.

Fagg counters with an assumed mutual exclusivity of science and politics, with survey on the side of the former: 'Sociology after all is but a study of the natural history of society, and as such is amenable to scientific methods.'[61] Natural history suggests both a mode of observation and a society formed through human-environment relations. Political questions may be addressed only when translatable into observational science. Thus in 1929 H. J. Fleure could legitimately consider the politics of head shape in the South Wales coalfield:

in an industrial district where the crowd psychology is what in politics is called red, or at least pink, the short dark longhead will be likely to vote on the left side of the electorate and may use his traditional oratorical powers to no little purpose.[62]

If political attitudes had a biological basis, then politics was a question for regional science.

Local study: a new knowledge of the familiar

In choosing our survey area we have staked out a claim, so to speak, and we wish to find out and record all there is to be known about it . . . The regional surveyor has indeed a voracious appetite for the books that have been written about his region, but he does not respect their bindings. In effect, if not literally, he will tear off their covers and re-arrange their pages with those of other books, and with gleanings from any and every source.[63]

Just as local maps could be cut and pasted, so could local books. Regional survey sought to cultivate citizenship through a new form of local knowledge, stressing observation over book-learning, and departing from more traditional conceptions of local knowledge as folklore. The latter becomes one object of study among many rather than the unique source of local insight. Indeed C. V. Butler suggested that the study of folklore might be awkwardly reflexive: 'It is not always easy for boys and girls to go far in collecting material dealing with local folk-lore and everyday social life, without becoming self-conscious as to their own and their families' doings and sayings.'[64] Adequate local knowledge was generally assumed to be lacking. The making of local citizens entailed criticism of their current state. Addressing the South-Eastern Union at Guildford in 1924, Sir Francis Ogilvie argued, 'even to-day the average man's knowledge of his home area is scrappy; his mind-map has many blanks . . . it is entirely unsatisfactory for a grown person in the area, who has ordinary powers of locomotion and normally developed curiosity'.[65] Ogilvie suggested an exploration of the local River Wey with a map as 'best friend and guide':

I guarantee that with such a programme for recreation, mental and physical, 1924 would rank for each self-appointed 'explorer' as among the richest of years . . . For the Basin of the Wey is an ideal area for regional study . . . And the Basin of the Wey is the Guildford Region . . . By the end of his first season, he will have doubled his seeing power and far more than doubled the field in which he will find delight in seeing, wondering, watching and learning.[66]

Seeing power and delight were the aim of publications produced by the Sociological Society and the Le Play Society in the 1920s to 1940s. The journal *Observation* contained exemplary stories by Fagg, Branford and others to encourage young readers, while the leaflets *Exploration and Discovery* outlined methods for local study.[67] We can gather the details of such work through two examples of local school study, one rural and one urban.[68] In the early 1920s in Oxfordshire and Berkshire, C. V. Butler coordinated *Village Survey Making* to foster 'constructive local patrio- tism' through 'a natural and open-air approach both to communal ser- vice, and to the study of "civics", a much-abused term and subject'.[69] Butler quoted Kipling's *Puck of Pook's Hill* on the 'joyous venture' of local study: 'even when they are tracing a map of the local water-system or making a list of the village pigs'.[70] Children surveyed field names, parish boundaries, farm stock, occupations, communications, adminis- tration and history (documentary and oral), all of which was recorded on maps under categories of 'Place, Work, Folk, their relations and reac- tions'. Tracings enabled superimposition such that 'the connection, or *lack* of connection', between factors could be grasped:

they are, from the standpoint of professional research, a humble and incomplete contribution to the study of man and his environment in quite unimportant localities. Their preparation, however, has caused so much pleasure to those con- cerned (including the small boy who found recently that this 'new kind of geog- raphy' allowed him to prepare for his home-work a list of the tame rabbits of the village), that their makers would like to recruit others to share their enjoyment, and to help to get down records of their own district.[71]

Again, though, there is a warning against survey becoming:

too factual and too local, degenerating . . . into the mere compilation of lists (of rabbits, etc.), and of neat map-tracings . . . or . . . into too lasting a contemplation of local affairs, the parish pump and the village policeman. Neither of the latter is necessarily very inspiring or elevating per se, though both are full of interest if considered as representing man's control over nature (e.g. with regard to water supply), or the 'sanctions' of government in the civilised state, or if correlated with 'general' history and geography.[72]

Abstraction from the concrete was necessary to escape factual banality. The Inspector type again haunts the study.

In North London Miss E. C. Mathews had worked on similar lines in 'Field Work in the Brent Valley': 'The open country lay not far from our doors, and the electric trams and the Metropolitan Railway afforded easy access to it.'[73] Mathews's study of 'Home Geography', in both location and tone, uncannily anticipates Patrick Keiller's recent film *London*, a documentary fiction in which laconic commentary runs over still shots, allowing the eye to migrate across the scene to take in local detail.[74] *London* includes an exploration of the 'River Brent' through Neasden, Perivale, Hanwell, Brentford. Mathews's children studied a map to define the same valley, and took excursions to highpoints where sketch maps could be drawn: 'As soon as our destination was reached the class scattered, inspired with the spirit of the explorer.' Keiller's narrator, Paul Schofield, might have intoned Mathews's description of a summer's work, as the class converse by the water:

Sitting on the grass, we talked of the various uses of rivers; of the advantages and disadvantages of the presence or absence of trees; of the changes in volume rivers undergo. Many such topics were apt to arise on the spot.

Width, depth and flow differed upstream and downstream of the Brent reservoir: 'This we saw at Neasden.' Other matters arose at crossing points: 'Here we considered the position of cities.' Vehicles also gave opportunities for outlook geography: 'On the top of the electric tramcar we saw that we topped a low ridge', 'We took the electric tram to Edgware . . . we were upon the ancient Watling Street . . . for a considerable distance, we were carried north-west in a line of remarkable straightness.' The whole of Home Geography was reviewed from a viewpoint on Hampstead Heath, and the course culminated in the construction of a contoured map: 'All this covered rather more than a summer's work.'

Intimacy with the unknown

Survey could also offer a new knowledge of the unfamiliar. In the 1920s and 1930s Le Play House and the Le Play Society organized trips to locations across Europe, selecting a region, generally one of peasant economy and society where relations of place-work-folk were evident in a rural setting, and producing a report on return. Destinations included Poland, Sweden, Romania (twice), Slovenia, Sardinia and Jersey. The people were themselves investigated, their culture, physique and customs studied, their head shapes tabulated and racial types identified.[75] Here also fieldwork appears as educated tourism, a different kind of holiday, with trips led by male academic geographers, attended mainly by women, and offering an experience of place distinct from bookish reflection, cultured antiquarianism or vulgar tripping: 'original expert observation on the spot'.[76]

Survey not only generates knowledge but acts as a practice of cultural distinction. For Fagg and Hutchings the survey could give:

a fairly intimate acquaintance with an unknown district . . . in a surprisingly short time. A few years ago . . . the authors set out, equipped only with the 6-inch maps, the 1-inch geological map and a note book, to survey together 24 square miles of country including a small town in a county unknown to them. They completed the surface utilisation survey in three fairly strenuous days and acquired in the process an intimate and detailed knowledge of the district that astonished themselves no less than the natives of the place.[77]

Fagg and Hutchings achieve a three-day intimacy with the unknown. Survey astonishes surveyors and surprises locals unaware of the new local knowledge.

Understanding the unfamiliar is central to two volumes produced by Geddes and Branford in their 'Making of the Future' series. In *The Coming Polity* in 1917 and *Our Social Inheritance* in 1919, programmes of 'country walks' and 'city walks' are outlined for 'rustic' and 'civic' survey.[78] A particular form of place experience is offered as the route to citizenship. In such work, as in the Le Play Society excursions or Fagg and Hutchings's country trips, survey provides a template of knowledge which can apply whether the destination is domestic or foreign, wherever the citizen is travelling. If in its component parts each place is like any other, then the form if not the precise content of local knowledge can translate across places and people. Survey becomes an international language of region and locality. *The Coming Polity* imagined a French regionalist arriving in Dover to see southern England. In order to gain a regional perspective the traveller ascends the Downs for 'a pilgrimage of watersheds',[79] with occasional valley excursions. The traveller's purpose is 'aesthetic and geographic': 'his object is to seek out and reach certain vantage points, where the moorland itself sinks into mere foreground, and there rise into full view stretches of the river valley that meanders below'.[80] Outlook geography blends with attention to history and legend, 'combining mythopoesy with interpretative travel',[81] with walking the key to the regional outlook. While the roadway gives 'a succession of detached impressions', producing an 'analytic' and 'abstract' view, and the railway encourages people to read rather than look at the landscape, the 'hillway traveller' sees 'the glory, the wonder and the variety of the world. He sees it region by region and so observes it as a natural whole. In other words, he is acquiring the regional outlook, and he correspondingly develops the synthetic habit of mind'.[82]

In *Our Social Inheritance*, walking prompts a composed civic outlook:

Let it not be thought that Civics is a dull and ponderous study. On the contrary, its first object is to see and enjoy the beauty and the wonder of cities. It is an open-air study, suffused with life and delight. Consequently, Civics is well adapted to restore health and tone to a mind depressed or wearied. It is essentially recreative ... a mode of spiritual healing.[83]

Five city walks are outlined through Westminster, providing 'A City Survey For Disoriented Citizens',[84] with each following an identified spirit of locale – theatricality in St James's, art and wealth in Mayfair: 'What we have to observe and interpret is the mode of life in this habitat.'[85] Connections are occasionally made to other parts of the city: Westminster Cathedral set off against the adjacent slums of Pimlico, Oxford Street contrasted to 'the source of shopping commodities', the East End.[86] The aim is to put urban life into controlled perspective, encouraging balanced citizenship. Describing Trafalgar Square and the Strand, Branford and Geddes acknowledge the possible liquid imagery of the city only to fix on something solid: 'the pedestrian, even amid the whirlpool of traffic, may seize and dwell upon the triple-spired perspective, of which St. Mary's is dominant'.[87] Walks mix movement and 'repose' in order to produce:

a rhythm or melody of healing. Further developed, the melody acquires the more tonic qualities of harmony. This civic harmony emerges from the subtle interaction between the personality of the Citizen and the individuality of the City.[88]

In the immediate post-war context Branford and Geddes offer the modern city as a potential environment of recuperation and self-reconstruction. Walking, as a technique synoptic and composed, is to generate the requisite self for the making of the future.

CONCLUSION: SKY-SITUATED KNOWLEDGE

Cartographic literacy has run through this essay not only in formulations of citizenship on the part of regional surveyors, but also in the ways in which those surveyors exhibited their own theoretical literacy regarding cartography. Current critiques of mapping are anticipated in this material, with regional surveyors self-consciously reflecting on its spatialities: how cartography could constitute particular senses of place, embody specific forms of power over space and cultivate certain forms of belonging. We also find an awareness of the historicity of survey. Branford and Geddes regarded their overviewing practice as appropriate to an age where progress was signified by powered flight. Air travel, they suggested, promised to:

reverse the railway tendency towards the de-regionalizing and de-spiritualizing of travel. For the airman sees again the natural regions of the world, and these more than ever of old, in broad and synoptic vision, which again is intensified by the ecstasy of flight, to inner clarity and unity. By a strangely appropriate turn in the whirligig of time, the 'highways' of the airmen would seem again to be con-centrating towards Salisbury Plain.

If walking gave a regional outlook, so too did flying. Branford and Geddes speculate that the focus of transport will again be pulled away from the metropolis: 'The call of Stonehenge will surely be renewed in the nascent age of aerial locomotion.'[89]

Mapping might further be taken for granted if perching in mid-air became a common experience. Flying is evidently a socially restricted activity in this period, and Branford and Geddes's appeal is very much to the pioneering male airman, but the implication is that the coming polity will see a social extension of the aerial view.[90] With the map moving into mass reproduction and the people moving into the air, a conjunction of mapping, survey and citizenship might be further cemented. In terms of recent intellectual alignments of mapping with domination, the key point is that the aerial view is here not a god's-eye view, a position of anonymous, remote and objectifying power, but a specific human posi-tion produced through new kinds of travel, whether via aeroplane or by a revival of walking to highpoints for a bird's eye view. This is less what Donna Haraway refers to as a totalizing visual 'god-trick', a 'conquering gaze from nowhere',[91] than a sky-situated knowledge, whereby the strange planar realism of the map corresponds to common experience, becoming a document at once abstract and empirical. None of this is to suggest that the map does not embody particular relations of power-knowledge, but as that term implies, this is not a story of power-as-domi-nation clashing with a resistant view from below. The map emerges in the early twentieth century as a common object embodying hill-situated and sky-situated knowledge, making sense through particular formulations of mapping as cartographic literacy.

The Agency of Mapping: Speculation, Critique and Invention

JAMES CORNER

Mapping is a fantastic cultural project, creating and building the world as much as measuring and describing it. Long affiliated with the planning and design of cities, landscapes and buildings, mapping is particularly instrumental in the construing and constructing of lived space. In this active sense, the function of mapping is less to mirror reality than to engender the re-shaping of the worlds in which people live. While there are countless examples of authoritarian, simplistic, erroneous and coercive acts of mapping, with reductive effects upon both individuals and environments, I focus in this essay upon more optimistic revisions of mapping practices.[1] These revisions situate mapping as a collective enabling enterprise, a project that both reveals and realizes hidden potential. Hence, in describing the 'agency' of mapping, I do not mean to invoke agendas of imperialist technocracy and control but rather to suggest ways in which mapping acts may emancipate potentials, enrich experiences and diversify worlds. We have been adequately cautioned about mapping as a means of projecting power-knowledge, but what about mapping as a productive and liberating instrument, a world-enriching agent, especially in the design and planning arts?

As a creative practice, mapping precipitates its most productive effects through a finding that is also a founding; its agency lies in neither reproduction nor imposition but rather in uncovering realities previously unseen or unimagined, even across seemingly exhausted grounds. Thus, mapping *unfolds* potential; it re-makes territory over and over again, each time with new and diverse consequences. Not all maps accomplish this, however; some simply reproduce what is already known. These are more 'tracings' than maps, delineating patterns but revealing nothing new. In describing and advocating more open-ended forms of creativity, philosophers Gilles Deleuze and Félix Guattari declare: 'Make a map not a tracing!' They continue:

What distinguishes the map from the tracing is that it is entirely oriented toward an experimentation in contact with the real. The map does not reproduce an unconscious closed in upon itself; it constructs the unconscious. It fosters connections between fields, the removal of blockages on bodies without organs, the maximum opening of bodies without organs onto a plane of consistency . . . The map has to do with *performance*, whereas the tracing always involves an 'alleged competence'.[2]

The distinction here is between mapping as equal to what is ('tracing') and mapping as equal to what is *and* to what is not yet. In other words, the unfolding agency of mapping is most effective when its capacity for description also sets the conditions for new eidetic and physical worlds to emerge. Unlike tracings, which propagate redundancies, mappings discover new worlds within past and present ones; they inaugurate new grounds upon the hidden traces of a living context. The capacity to reformulate what already exists is the important step. And what already exists is more than just the physical attributes of terrain (topography, rivers, roads, buildings) but includes also the various hidden forces that underlie the workings of a given place. These include natural processes, such as wind and sun; historical events and local stories; economic and legislative conditions; even political interests, regulatory mechanisms and programmatic structures. Through rendering visible multiple and sometimes disparate field conditions, mapping allows for an understanding of terrain as only the surface expression of a complex and dynamic imbroglio of social and natural processes. In visualizing these interrelationships and interactions, mapping itself participates in any future unfoldings. Thus, given the increased complexity and contentiousness that surrounds landscape and urbanism today, creative advances in mapping promise designers and planners greater efficacy in intervening in spatial and social processes. Avoiding the failure of universalist approaches toward master-planning and the imposition of state-controlled schemes, the unfolding agency of mapping may allow designers and planners not only to see certain possibilities in the complexity and contradiction of what already exists but also to *actualize* that potential. This instrumental function is particularly important in a world where it is becoming increasingly difficult to both *imagine* and actually to *create* anything outside of the normative.

THE AGENCY OF MAPPING

Mappings have agency because of the double-sided characteristic of all maps. First, their surfaces are directly *analogous* to actual ground conditions; as horizontal planes, they record the surface of the earth as direct impressions. As in the casting of shadows, walks and sightings across land may be literally *projected* onto paper through a geometrical graticule of points and lines drawn by ruler and pen. Conversely, one can put one's finger on a map and trace out a particular route or itinerary, the map projecting a mental image into the spatial imagination. Because of this directness, maps are taken to be 'true' and 'objective' measures of the world, and are accorded a kind of benign neutrality. By contrast, the other side of this analogous characteristic is the inevitable *abstractness* of maps, the result of selection, omission, isolation, distance and codification. Map devices such as frame, scale, orientation, projection, indexing and naming reveal artificial geographies that remain unavailable to human eyes. Maps present only one version of the earth's surface, an eidetic fiction constructed from factual observation. As both analogue and abstraction, then, the surface of the map functions like an operating table, a staging ground or a theatre of operations upon which the mapper collects, combines, connects, marks, masks, relates and generally explores. These surfaces are massive collection, sorting and transfer sites, great fields upon which real material conditions are isolated, indexed and placed within an assortment of relational structures.

The analogous-abstract character of the map surface means that it is doubly projective: it both captures the projected elements off the ground and projects back a variety of effects through use. The strategic use of this double function has, of course, a long alliance with the history of mapping, and not only militaristically (*reconnaissances militaires*) but also ideologically.[3] Surprisingly, however, the strategic, constitutive and inventive capacities of mapping are not widely recognized in the urban design and planning arts, even though cartography and planning have enjoyed a long and mutually influential relationship since the fifteenth century.[4] Throughout the twentieth century, mapping in design and planning has been undertaken conventionally as a quantitative and analytical survey of existing conditions made prior to the making of a new project. These survey maps are both spatial and statistical, inventorying a range of social, economic, ecological and aesthetic conditions. As expertly produced, measured representations, such maps are conventionally taken to be stable, accurate, indisputable mirrors of reality, providing the logical basis for future decision making as well as the means for later projecting a designed plan back onto the ground. It is generally assumed that if the survey is quantitative, objective and rational, it is also true and neutral, thereby helping to legitimize and enact future plans and decisions.[5] Thus, mapping typically precedes planning because it is assumed that the map will objectively identify and make visible the terms around which a planning project may then be rationally developed, evaluated and built.[6]

What remains overlooked in this sequence, however, is the fact that maps are highly artificial and fallible constructions, virtual abstractions that possess great force in terms of how people see and act. One of the reasons for this oversight derives from a prevalent tendency to view maps in terms of what they represent rather than what they do. As with art historical analyses of drawings and paintings, considerations of maps as a successive series of paradigmatic types and representations overlook the durational experiences and effects of mapping. That mappings are constructed from a set of internal instruments, codes, techniques and conventions, and that the worlds they describe and project derive only from those aspects of reality that are susceptible to these techniques, are dimensions of mapping still barely understood by the contemporary planner. Instead, most designers and planners consider mapping a rather unimaginative, analytical practice, at least compared to the presumed 'inventiveness' of the designing activities that occur *after* all the relevant maps have been made (often with the contents of the maps ignored or forgotten). An unfortunate consequence of these attitudes is that the various techniques and procedures of mapping have not been subjects of inquiry, research or criticism. Instead, they have become codified, naturalized and taken for granted as institutional conventions. Thus, critical experimentation with new and alternative forms of mapping remains largely underdeveloped if not significantly repressed.[7] The 'alleged competence' of the tracing effectively dominates the exploratory inventiveness integral to acts of mapping.

This indifference towards mapping is particularly puzzling when one considers that the very basis upon which projects are imagined and realized derives precisely from how maps are made. The conditions around which a project develops originate with what is selected and prioritized in the map, what is subsequently left aside or ignored, how the chosen material is schematized, indexed and framed, and how the synthesis of the graphic field invokes semantic, symbolic and instrumental content. Thus, the various cartographic procedures of selection, schematization and synthesis make the map *already* a project in the making.[8] This is why mapping is never neutral, passive or without consequence; on the contrary, mapping is perhaps the most formative and creative act of any design process, first disclosing and then staging the conditions for the emergence of new realities.

In what follows, I discuss mapping as an active agent of cultural inter-vention. Because my interests lie in the various processes and effects of mapping, I am less concerned with what mapping *means* than with what it actually *does*. Thus, I am less interested in maps as finished artifacts than I am in mapping as a creative *activity*. It is in this participatory sense that I believe new and speculative techniques of mapping may generate new practices of creativity, practices that are expressed not in the inven-tion of novel form but in the productive reformulation of what is already given. By showing the world in new ways, unexpected solutions and effects may emerge. However, given the importance of representational technique in the creative process, it is surprising that whilst there has been no shortage of new ideas and theories in design and planning there has been so little advancement and invention of those specific tools and tech-niques – including mapping – that are so crucial for the effective construal and construction of new worlds.[9]

THE EFFICACY OF TECHNIQUE

A comparison between Mercator's projection of the earth's surface and Buckminster Fuller's Dymaxion projection reveals radically different spa-tial and socio-political structures. The same planet, the same places, and yet significantly dissimilar relationships are revealed or, more precisely, *constructed*. The Mercator map stretches the surface of the globe with-out excision onto a flat surface, oriented 'upwards' to the north. The com-pass directions are made parallel, leading to gross distortions of land area and shape, especially as one moves towards the poles. The northern hemi-sphere dominates, with Greenland more than twice the size of Australia, even though the southern island is in fact greater than three times the land area of the northern. Needless to say, this view has well suited the self-image of Europeans and North Americans in an era of Western political hegemony. By contrast, Fuller's Dymaxion Airocean World Map of 1943 cuts the earth into triangular facets that are then unfolded as a flat poly-hedron. Both the north and south poles are presented frontally and equally, with little distortion, although the typical viewer is at first likely to be disoriented by this unusual, poly-directional arrangement of coun-tries. Only the graphic graticule of latitude and longitude allows the reader to comprehend the relative orientation of any one location.[10]

Interestingly, the Dymaxion structure can be unfolded and re-oriented in any number of different ways, depending on the thematics of one's point of view. The polyhedral geometry provides a remarkably flexible and adaptive system wherein different locations and regions can be placed

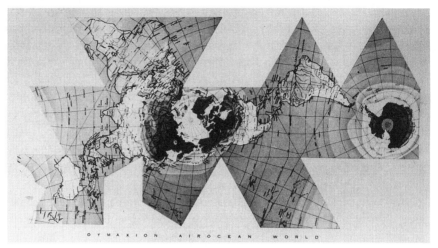

R. Buckminster Fuller and Shoji Sadao, *Dymaxion Airocean World Map*, 1954.

into significantly different sets of relationship. Precisely where the map is cut and folded determines how the parts are seen in relationship to each other, each time in radically altered, yet equally true, configurations. Potentially at least, each arrangement possesses great efficacy with regard to certain socio-political, strategic and imaginative possibilities.

Unlike the scientific objectivism that guides most modern cartographers, artists have been more conscious of the essentially fictional status of maps and the power they possess for construing and constructing worlds.[11] In the same year as Fuller's projection, the Uruguayan artist Joaquín Torres-García drew the *Inverted Map of South America* with a very distinct 'S' at the top of the drawing. This remarkable image reminds us of the ways in which habitual conventions (in this case the unquestioned domination of north on top) condition spatial hierarchies and power relations. The convention of orienting the map to the north first arose early in the global and economic expansion of Northern Europe and in response to practices of navigation. But there are many instances of other societies at different times orienting their maps towards one of the other cardinal points, or making them circular without top and bottom (the Dymaxion map is perhaps one of the few modern instances where singular orientation is not a prerequisite). Maps of this sort are still legible and 'correct' in their depiction of spatial relationship, but the reader must first learn the relevant mapping codes and conventions.

Another instance of critique and invention of the modern map is Waltercio Caldas's *Japão*, of 1972.[12] Here, the artist is mapping a territory

ONE CONTINENT
Bottom of the Areonautical Ocean

EAST BY STEAM TO THE ORIENT VIA SUEZ

ONE OCEAN
Admiral Mahan named it.
The British discovered and used it.

EAST BY SAIL—TO THE ORIENT VIA GOOD HOPE
From the Spanish Main via the Piratical Indian Waters.
12,000-mile great circle route from New York to Australia.

STRATOSPHERE STRATEGIC
European triangle controls the altitude merry-go-round.

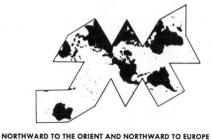

NORTHWARD TO THE ORIENT AND NORTHWARD TO EUROPE
Old and new worlds on either hand.
Russia overhead and McKinder's World Island trisected.

R. Buckminster Fuller, *Alternative Sectional Arrangements of the
Airocean World Map*, 1943.

that is foreign, or 'unimaginable' for many in the West. Rather than colonizing this territory through survey and inventory, typically Western techniques of power-knowledge, Caldas simply marks an otherwise empty
map surface with very small inscriptions and numbers. These are contained by a very prominent, classical cartographic frame. There are no
other outlines, shapes or forms, just small type and a few scribbles. There
is no scale, no identifiable marks, no graticule of orientation, just a square

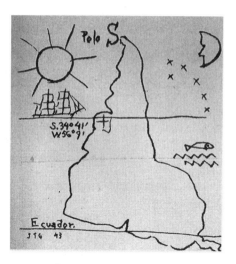

Joaquín Torres-García, *Inverted Map
of South America*, 1943.

ink frame. In this stark, minimal cartographic field, Caldas presents an
elusive geography, an open and indeterminate field of figures that returns
terra incognita to an otherwise excessively mapped planet. The image is
also a commentary on the cage-like power of the imperializing frame: the
graphic square surrounds, captures and holds its quarry, but at the same
time its contents remain foreign, evasive and autonomous. This blank,
non-figured space raises both anxiety and a certain promise – promise
because its potential efficacy lies in the emancipation of its contents. The
autonomous, abstract structure suggests how mystery and desire might
be returned to a world of places and things that have been otherwise
excessively classified and structured. In Caldas's image, such places are
liberated through precisely the same measures that first captured them.

Whereas certain artists have engaged creatively with cartographic
techniques, planners and designers have been less ambitious.[13] Techniques of aerial-oblique and zenithal views – planimetry, ichnography,
and triangulation – were most developed during the early sixteenth century, and have since become the primary tools with which cities and landscapes are analysed, planned and constructed. Quantitative and thematic
mapping techniques originated with the Enlightenment enthusiasm for
rational progress and social reform, and these were later complemented
by various statistical, comparative and 'zoning' techniques during the late
nineteenth and early twentieth centuries.[14] Some advances in these techniques have occurred over the past 30 years with the rise of satellite and

remote-sensing capabilities, together with new computer technologies such as Geographic Information Systems, but in principle they remain unchanged. These techniques remain largely unquestioned, conventional devices of inventory, quantitative analysis and legitimization of future plans. Issues of selectivity, schematization and synthesis remain generally oriented around the same conventions used a hundred years ago. With only a handful of exceptions, the relationship of maps to world-making is surprisingly under-thought. The limitations of this condition are extremely unfortunate; as the late geographer J. B. Harley argues:

One effect of accelerated technological change – as manifest in digital cartography and geographical information systems – has been to strengthen its positivist assumptions and [to breed] a new arrogance in geography about its supposed value as a mode of access to reality. If it is true that new fictions of factual representation are daily being foisted upon us, then the case for introducing a social dimension into modern cartography is especially strong. Maps are too important to be left to cartographers alone.[15]

In what follows, I suggest ways in which the social, imaginative and critical dimensions of mapping may be re-established in modern cartography, especially in mapping for urban and landscape planning and design. First, I discuss three points of clarification: the map's relationship to reality; the changing nature of time–space relations; and an insistence on equality of importance amongst mapping actions (techniques), mapping effects (consequences) and maps themselves. These will underpin my outline of a number of alternative mapping practices that play actively constitutive roles in forging culture, space and place.

MAPS AND REALITY

Jorge Luis Borges's tale of a fully detailed and life-sized map that eventually tore and weathered to shreds across the actual territory it covered is frequently quoted in essays on mapping.[16] Not only does the tale beautifully capture the cartographic imagination, it goes to the heart of a tension between reality and representation, between the territory and the map. Equally referenced is Lewis Carroll's tale in *Sylvie and Bruno*, also of a life-sized map, in this case folded, thus preventing it being unfolded for practical application. The map was useless, allowing Carroll's character Mein Herr to conclude, 'so now we use the country itself, as its own map, and I assure you it does nearly as well'. In these two fables, not only is the map an inferior, secondary representation of territory, but the more detailed and life-like the map strives to be, the more redundant or unnecessary it becomes. Unlike paintings or photographs, which have the capacity to bear a direct resemblance to the things they depict, maps must by necessity be abstract if they are to sustain meaning and utility. And such abstraction, the bane of untrained map-readers, is not at all a failing of maps but rather their virtue.

Jean Baudrillard reverses Borges's tale to make another point:

Simulation is no longer that of a territory, a referential being or substance. It is the generation by models of a real without origin or reality: a hyper-real. The territory no longer precedes the map, nor survives it. Henceforth, it is the map that precedes the territory.[17]

Arguably, of course, the map *always* precedes the territory, in that space only becomes territory through acts of bounding and making visible, which are primary functions of mapping. But Baudrillard is going one step further here, claiming that late twentieth-century communication and information technologies have produced such a blurring of what is real and what is a representation that the two can no longer be distinguished. He inverts Borges's fable to proclaim that 'it is the real and not the map whose vestiges subsist here and there'.[18] Here, Baudrillard is careful to explain that this reversal does not mean that the world is scarcely more than a vast simulacrum, but rather that the act of differentiating between the real and the representation is no longer meaningful.

The dissolution of difference between reality and representation can also be approached through studies of spatial perception and cognition, especially those of child psychologists such as Jean Piaget, Edith Cobb and Donald Winnicott. Winnicott, for example, discusses the necessity of play for the maturing of psychological selfhood, describing how children relate to the external world of things and spaces in extremely fluid and labile ways. In discussing the importance of engagement and discovery through playing, he describes 'transitional objects' as those that are so possessed by the imagination that they are neither fully part of the self nor explicitly external. Emphasizing the creativity afforded by play, Winnicott argues that the space of play must remain beyond the reach of the empiricist question, 'Did you find that (in the world) or did you make it up?'[19] To distinguish so completely an external, *a priori*, 'real world' from a constructed and participatory one would not only deny imagination but also be incongruent with humankind's innate capacity to structure reciprocal relationships with its surroundings.

If for Borges and Carroll the territory itself wins out over the map, and for Baudrillard the map has come to both precede and construct the territory, Winnicott points to the futility of trying to make any distinction between the two, or indeed to accord primacy to either. And, whereas Baudrillard writes about the dissolution of difference with regard to the world of contemporary culture and its various systems of production, and Winnicott is more concerned with psychological development in relation to the phenomenal world, both authors recognize the conflation of cultural invention with found nature.

Reality, then, as in concepts such as 'landscape' or 'space', is not something external and 'given' for our apprehension; rather it is constituted, or 'formed', through our participation with things: material objects, images, values, cultural codes, places, cognitive schemata, events and maps. As the philosopher of science Jacob Bronowski pointedly observes, 'there are no appearances to be photographed, no experiences to be copied, in which we do not take part. Science, like art, is not a copy of nature but a re-creation of her.'[20] This mediated mode of being is more fully described by the philosopher Ernst Cassirer:

In truth . . . what we call the world of our perception is not simple, not given and self-evident from the outset, but 'is' only insofar as it has gone through certain basic theoretical acts by which it is apprehended and specified. This universal relationship is perhaps most evident in the intuitive form of our perceptual world, in its spatial form. The relations of 'together,' 'separate,' 'side-by-side,' are not just 'given' along with our 'simple' sensations, the sensuous matter that is order in space; they are a highly complex, thoroughly *mediated* product of empirical thought. When we attribute a certain size, position, and distance to things in space, we are not thereby expressing a simple datum of sensation but are situating the sensory data in a relationship and system, which proves ultimately to be nothing other than a relationship of pure judgement.[21]

The application of judgement, subjectively constituted, is precisely what makes a map more a project than a 'mere' empirical description. The still widely held assumption that maps are mute, utilitarian tools, of secondary significance to the *milieu* they represent, and lacking in power, agency or effects beyond simple, objective description, is to grossly misconstrue their capacity for shaping reality. Both maps and territories are 'thoroughly mediated products' and the nature of their exchange is far from neutral or uncomplicated.

I offer this sketch of maps and reality because it charts out what I think remains markedly under-thought (or, more precisely, *under-practised*) in current cultural projects. The implications of a world derived more from cultural invention than from a pre-formed 'nature' have barely begun to be explored, let alone accepted, at the level of cartographic practice. While contemporary scholars have begun to demonstrate how even the most objective descriptions of reality are culturally 'situated', and that 'nature' is perhaps the most situated yet shifting construction of all, few have dared to develop and practise techniques for realizing the potential offered by such an emancipated (even playful and promiscuous) world of constructions.

Whereas the architectural and planning arts ought to be leading such an exploration, they are still largely entrenched with the tools of thought passed down from Enlightenment and modernist paradigms: orthography, axonometry, perspective, maps as quantitative surveys and inventories, and plans as rational, self-contained ideals. Although these conventions are closely aligned with procedures of translation and construction, they are also technical instruments that enable the utopian renovation of huge tracts of urban fabric (stylistic issues notwithstanding). Sites are treated either as blank areas (*tabulae rasae*) or as simple geometrical figures to be manipulated from high above. The synoptic 'master-plan' governs, while mapping, and all its potential for engaging and evolving local intricacy, is relegated to the relatively trivial role of marking location, inventorying resources and justifying future policies.

In recent years, however, much greater attention has been paid in the landscape and architectural arts to the specificity of site and context. Also, there has been a corresponding interest in developing more discreet and local modes of intervention as distinct from universal planning. Hence the resurgence of interest in mapping by a generation of young landscape architects, architects and urban planners. For them, mapping refers to more than inventory and geometrical measure, and no presumption is made of innocence, neutrality or inertia in its construction. Instead, the map is first employed as a *means* of 'finding' and then 'founding' new projects, effectively re-working what already exists. Thus, the *processes* of mapping, together with their varied informational and semantic scope, are valued for both their revelatory and productive potential. Consequently, concepts of 'site' are shifting from that of simply a geometrically defined parcel of land to that of a much larger and more active *milieu*.

Milieu is a French term that means 'surroundings', 'medium' and 'middle'. *Milieu* has neither beginning nor end, but is surrounded by other middles, in a field of connections, relationships, extensions and potentials. In this sense, then, a grounded site, locally situated, invokes a host of 'other' places, including all the maps, drawings, ideas, references, other worlds and places that are invoked during the making of a project. 'Site' today is a multiplicitous and complex affair, comprising a potentially boundless field of phenomena, some palpable and some imaginary. In making visible what is otherwise hidden and inaccessible, maps provide a working table for identifying and reworking polyvalent conditions; their analogous-abstract surfaces enable the accumulation, organization and restructuring of the various strata that comprise an ever-emerging *milieu*.

These ideas return us to the opening concern of this essay for the role of maps within the landscape and architectural imagination. For the landscape architect and urban planner, maps are sites for the imaging and projecting of alternative worlds. Thus maps are in-between the virtual and the real. Here, Winnicott's question, 'Did you find that in the world or did you make it up?' denotes an irrelevant distinction. More important is how the map permits a kind of excavation (downward) and extension (outward) to expose, reveal and construct latent possibilities within a greater *milieu*. The map 'gathers' and 'shows' things presently (and always) invisible, things which may appear incongruous or untimely but which may also harbour enormous potential for the unfolding of alternative events. In this regard, maps have very little to do with representation as depiction. After all, maps look nothing like their subject, not only because of their vantage point but also because they present all parts at once, with an immediacy unavailable to the grounded individual. But more than this, the function of maps is not to depict but to enable, to precipitate a set of effects in time. Thus, mappings do not *represent geographies* or ideas; rather they *effect* their actualization.

Mapping is neither secondary nor representational but doubly operative: digging, finding and exposing on the one hand, and relating, connecting and structuring on the other. Through visual disclosure, mapping both sets up and puts into effect complex sets of relationship that remain to be more fully actualized. Thus mapping is not subsequent to but prior to landscape and urban formations. In this sense, mapping is returned to its origins as a process of exploration, discovery and enablement. This is less a case of mapping to assert authority, stability and control, and more one of searching, disclosing and engendering new sets of possibility. Like a nomadic grazer, the exploratory mapper detours around the obvious so as to engage what remains hidden.

SPACE AND TIME TODAY

A creative view of mapping in the context of architectural, landscape and urban production is rendered all the more relevant by the changing nature of spatial and temporal structures in today's world. Events occur with such speed and complexity that nothing remains certain. Large numbers live in a world where local economies and cultures are tightly bound into global ones, through which effects ripple with enormous velocity and consequence. Surrounded by media images and an excess of communication that makes the far seem near and the shocking merely normal, local cultures have become fully networked around the world. Air travel and other modes of rapid transportation have become so accessible that localities can be more closely connected to sites thousands of miles away than to their immediate surroundings. Today, structures of community life are shifting from spatial stability towards shifting, temporal coordination. Public life is now scheduled and allocated more by time than centred according to place, while the circulation of capital demands an ever-more mobile and migratory workforce. Ten-mile linear cities are built in South-East Asia in a matter of months, seemingly constructed out of nothing according to modes of agreement that are neither democratic nor authoritarian, merely expedient. And finally, perhaps, the near-conquest of both the Genome and the Universe proclaim the end of earthly limits and coherence. Such fantastic play across the world's various surfaces is characterized not only by a fertile heterogeneity but also by conceptual elements coming loose from their traditional moorings. The boundaries between different foundational realities have become so blurred, in fact, that it is practically impossible in a cyber-world to distinguish between what is information and what is concrete, what is fact and what is fiction, what is space and what is time.

Mapping and contemporary spatial design techniques more generally have yet to find adequate ways to engage creatively with the dynamic and promiscuous character of time and space today. Most design and planning operations appear somewhat outmoded, overwhelmed or incongruent in comparison to the rapidly metabolizing processes of urbanization and communication. In celebrating the urban freedoms and pleasures of Los Angeles, for example, the urbanist Reyner Banham goes to great lengths to explain the complex array of forces that led to the city's development, with planners and designers playing a distinctly minor role.[22] He questions whether or not Los Angeles would be as rich and modern a city if planners had exercised more of their authority – a point often made about London in comparison to Paris. While not everyone may share Banham's enthusiasm for the contemporary metropolis, his point is that new and productive forms of socialization and spatial arrangement are evolving without the aid, direction or involvement of planners and designers. Moreover, Banham suggests that to assume this is a bad and negligent thing is to adopt a somewhat naïve and insular, even elitist, position. This point is also argued by Rem Koolhaas in his discussion of 'the generic city', or those identity-less areas that today comprise the bulk of the sprawling urban fabric where most people live. In criticizing a continued fascination of architects and planners with the 'old identities' of traditional city centres such as Paris or Berlin, Koolhaas argues that there is a much more current and urgent urban condition that is being neglected. He argues that there might be certain virtues in these generic regions, such as their complete lack of memory or tradition that then liberates the urban planner from a whole series of conventional obligations, models and assumptions. 'The stronger identity, the more it imprisons, the more it resists expansion, interpretation, renewal, contradiction,' he writes. 'The generic city presents the final death of planning. Why? Not because it is unplanned . . . [but because] planning makes no difference whatsoever.'[23]

Through such urbanists as Reyner Banham, Edward Soja, David Harvey, Rem Koolhaas and Bernard Tschumi, anthropologists such as Marc Auge, or philosophers such as Henri Lefebvre or Gilles Deleuze, it is becoming clearer to architects and planners that 'space' is more complex and dynamic than previous formal models allowed. Ideas about spatiality are moving away from physical objects and forms towards the variety of territorial, political and psychological social processes that flow through space. The *interrelationships* amongst things in space, as well as the *effects* that are produced through such dynamic interactions, are becoming of greater significance for intervening in urban landscapes than the solely compositional arrangement of objects and surfaces.

The experiences of space cannot be separated from the events that happen in it; space is situated, contingent and differentiated. It is remade continuously every time it is encountered by different people, every time it is represented through another medium, every time its surroundings change, every time new affiliations are forged. Thus, as David Harvey has argued, planners and architects have been barking up the wrong tree in believing that new spatial structures alone would yield new patterns of socialization. The struggle for designers and planners, Harvey insists, lies not with spatial form and aesthetic appearances alone (the city as a thing) but with the advancement of more liberating processes and interactions in time (urbanization). Multiple processes of urbanization in time are what produce 'a distinctive mix of spatialized permanences in relation to one another';[24] hence the urban project ought to be less about spatial determinism and more about reshaping those urbanization processes that are 'fundamental to the construction of the things that contain them'.[25]

Thus, in criticizing the formalism of both the modernist utopia and the sentimental, communitarian 'new urbanism', Harvey argues that the dynamic multiplicity of urban processes cannot be contained within a singular, fixed spatial frame, especially when that frame neither derives from, nor itself redirects, those processes moving through it. He writes:

The issue is not one of gazing into some crystal ball or imposing some classic form of utopian scheme in which a dead spatiality is made to rule over history and process. The problem is to enlist in the struggle to advance a more socially just and emancipatory mix of spatio-temporal production processes rather than to acquiesce to those imposed by finance capital, the World Bank and the generally class-bound inequalities internalized within any system of uncontrolled capital accumulation.[26]

Harvey's point is that projecting new urban and regional futures must derive less from a utopia of form and more from a *utopia of process* – how things work, interact and inter-relate in space and time. Thus, the emphasis shifts from static object–space to the space–time of relational systems. And, it is here, in this complex and shifty *milieu*, that *maps*, not *plans*, achieve a new instrumental significance.

MAPPING

'To plan a city is both to think the very plurality of the real and to make that way of thinking effective,' writes the philosopher of the everyday Michel de Certeau: 'it is to know how to articulate it and be able to do it.'[27] Mapping is key here for it entails processes of gathering, working, reworking, assembling, relating, revealing, sifting and speculating. In turn, these activities enable the inclusion of massive amounts of information that, when articulated, allow certain sets of possibility to become actual. In containing multiple modes of spatio-temporal description, mapping precipitates fresh insights and enables effective actions to be taken. Thus mapping differs from 'planning' in that it entails searching, finding and unfolding complex and latent forces in the existing *milieu* rather than imposing a more-or-less idealized project from on high. Moreover, the synoptic imposition of the 'plan' implies a consumption (or extinguishing) of contextual potential, wherein all that is available is subsumed into the making of the project. Mapping, by contrast, discloses, stages and even adds potential for later acts and events to unfold. Whereas the plan leads to an end, the map provides a generative means, a suggestive vehicle that 'points' but does not overly determine.

A particularly important aspect of mapping in this regard is the acknowledgement of the maker's own participation and engagement with the cartographic process. In studying the development of spatial perception in children, Jean Piaget has written:

Geometrical intuition is essentially active in character. It consists primarily of virtual actions, abridgements or schemata of past, or anticipatory schemata of future actions, and if the action itself is inadequate, intuition breaks down.[28]

In describing the mental imaging of various relational processes, such as cutting, folding, rotating and enlarging, Piaget writes:

Spatial concepts can only effectively predict these results by becoming active themselves, by operating on physical objects, and not simply evoking memory images of them. To arrange objects mentally is not merely to imagine a series of things already set in order, nor even to imagine the action of arranging them. It means arranging the series just as positively and actively as if the action were physical.[29]

Actions precede conceptions; order is the outcome of the act of ordering. Thus mapping precedes the map, to the degree that it cannot properly anticipate its final form. Robinson and Petchenik claim that 'in mapping, one objective is to discover (by seeing) meaningful physical and intellectual shape organizations in the *milieu*, structures that are likely to remain hidden until they have been mapped . . . plotting out or mapping is a method for searching for such meaningful designs'.[30] In other words, there are some phenomena that can *only* achieve visibility through representation rather than through direct experience. Furthermore, mapping engenders new and meaningful relationships amongst otherwise disparate parts. The resultant relational structure is not something already 'out-there', but rather something constructed, bodied forth through the act of mapping. As the philosopher Brand Blanshard observes, 'space is simply a relation of systematized outsideness, by itself neither sensible nor imaginable';[31] it is *created* in the process of mapping.

MAPPING OPERATIONS

The operational structure of mapping might be schematized as consisting of 'fields', 'extracts' and 'plottings'. The field is the continuous surface, the flat-bed, the paper or the table itself, schematically the analogical equivalent to the actual ground, albeit flat and scaled. The field is also the graphic *system* within which the extracts will later be organized. The system includes the frame, orientation, coordinates, scale, units of measure and the graphic projection (oblique, zenithal, isometric, anamorphic, folded, etc.). The design and set-up of the field is perhaps one of the most creative acts in mapping, for as a prior system of organization it will inevitably condition how and what observations are made and presented. Enlarging the frame, reducing the scale, shifting the projection or combining one system with another are all actions that significantly affect what is seen and how these findings are organized. Obviously, a field that has multiple frameworks and entryways is likely to be more inclusive than a singular, closed system. Also, a field that breaks with convention is more likely to precipitate new findings than one that is more habitual and routine. And third, a field that is designed to be as non-hierarchical and inclusive as possible – more 'neutral' – is likely to bring a greater range of conditions into play than a field of restrictive scope.

Extracts are the things that are then observed within a given *milieu* and drawn onto the graphic field. We call them extracts because they are always selected, isolated and pulled-out from their original seamlessness with other things; they are effectively 'de-territorialized'. They include objects but also other informational data: quantities, velocities, forces, trajectories. Once detached they may be studied, manipulated and networked with other figures in the field. As described above, different field systems will lead to different arrangements of the extracts, revealing alternative patterns and possibilities.

Plotting entails the 'drawing out' of new and latent relationships that can be seen amongst the various extracts within the field. There are, of course, an infinite number of relationships that can be drawn depending upon one's criteria or agenda. Richard Long, for example, who has made an art-form of walking, may plot a line upon a map to connect the highest to the lowest summit in sequential order, for example, revealing a latent structural line across a given terrain. Upon the same map, however, it is possible to plot a line that connects all south-facing aspects in sequential order from large to small areas, or to find a range of wet conditions that can then be set into relationship by plotting a comparative index of water characteristics. In addition to geometrical and spatial plotting, taxonomic and genealogical procedures of relating, indexing and naming can often be extremely productive in revealing latent structures. Such techniques may produce insights that have both utility and metaphoricity. In either case, plotting entails an active and creative interpretation of the map to reveal, construct and engender latent sets of possibility. Plotting is *not* simply the indiscriminate listing and inventorying of conditions, as in a tracing, a table or a chart, but rather a strategic and imaginative drawing-out of relational structures. To plot is to track, to trace, to set-in-relation, to find and to found. In this sense, plotting produces a 're-territorialization' of sites.

Thus we can identify three essential operations in mapping: first, the creation of a field, the setting of rules and the establishment of a system; second, the extraction, isolation or 'de-territorialization' of parts and data; and third, the plotting, the drawing-out, the setting-up of relationships, or the 're-territorialization' of the parts. At each stage, choices and judgements are made, with the construing and constructing of the map alternating between processes of accumulation, disassembly and reassembly. By virtue of the map-maker's awareness of the innately rhetorical nature of the map's construction as well as of personal authorship and intent, these operations differ from the mute, empirical documentation of terrain so often assumed by cartographers.

We may now identify four thematic ways in which new practices of mapping are emerging in contemporary design and planning, each producing certain effects upon perceptions and practices of space. I label these techniques 'drift', 'layering', 'game-board' and 'rhizome'.

Drift

The Situationists were a European group of artists and activists in the 1950s and 1960s. They aimed somehow to disrupt any form of what they took to be the dominant regime or capitalist power. Drawing from various Dadaist practices, and later influencing other conceptual art movements such as Fluxus and Performance Art, the Situationists advocated a series of works that increased public consciousness and promoted direct action and systematic participation in everyday life. They were less interested in art objects and stylistic concerns than with the engaging life situations and social formations.[32]

Guy Debord, a key Situationist theorist, made a series of maps, or 'psycho-geographic guides', of Paris. These were made after Debord had walked aimlessly around the streets and alleys of the city, turning here and there wherever the fancy took him. Recording these wanderings, Debord would cut up and reconfigure a standard Paris map as a series of turns and detours. The resultant map reflected subjective, street-level desires and perceptions rather than a synoptic totality of the city's fabric. More a form of cognitive mapping than mimetic description of the cityscape, Debord's maps located his own play and representation within the recessive nooks and crannies of everyday life. Such activity became known as the *dérive*, or the dream-like drift through the city, mapping alternative itineraries and subverting dominant readings and authoritarian regimes.

What is interesting about the *dérive* is the way in which the contingent, the ephemeral, the vague, fugitive eventfulness of spatial experience

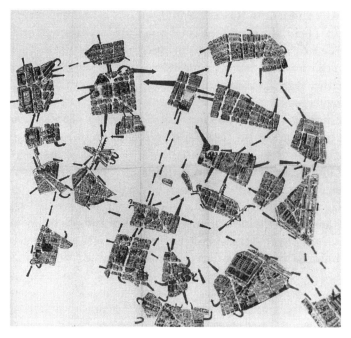

Guy Debord, *Discours sur les Passions de l'amour*, 1957.

becomes foregrounded in place of the dominant, ocular gaze. As de Certeau writes:

The ordinary practitioners of the city live 'down below', below the threshold at which visibility begins. They walk – an elementary form of this experience of the city: they are walkers, *Wandersmänner*, whose bodies follow the thicks and thins of an urban 'text' they are able to write without being able to read it.[33]

The political and moral underpinnings of this view gesture towards the valorization of individual participation within a seemingly repressive apparatus of state or bureaucratic power. In describing the importance of such cognitive mapping in relation to urban space, Frederic Jameson writes:

Disalienation in the traditional city . . . involves the practical reconquest of a sense of place and the construction or reconstruction of an articulated ensemble which can be retained in memory and which the individual subject can map and remap along the moments of mobile, alternative trajectories.[34]

If mapping had been traditionally assigned to the colonizing agency of survey and control, the Situationists were attempting to return the map to everyday life and to the unexplored, repressed topographies of the city. In this regard, Fluxus founder George Maciunas organized a series of 'Free Flux Tours' around Manhattan in 1976, which included an 'Aleatoric Tour', a 'Subterranean Tour', an 'Exotic Sites' itinerary and an 'All the Way Around and Back Again' trip. The art 'object' here was the city itself, the map's role to facilitate alternative impressions of and interventions in the urban *milieu*. There are similar instances of such work – Daniel Buren's *Seven Ballets in Manhattan*, or Yoko Ono's urban 'scores', for example – but the essential characteristic shared by all these projects is an ambition to contest and destabilize any fixed, dominant image of the city by incorporating the nomadic, transitive and shifting character of urban experience into spatial representation.[35]

Although earth-artist Richard Long shares little of the political and strategic agenda of the Situationists, his systematic play with maps and landscapes is very much in the same vein as *dérive*. Long works closely with maps in planning and then recording his walks.[36] Sometimes he will simply draw an arrow-straight line across a terrain and embark on the mission of walking it in actuality. The line may have a particular unit of measure (a mile, sixty minutes or seven days) to which he will adhere, or it may assume a geometrical configuration such as a circle, a square or a spiral, superimposed upon a variegated terrain. At other times, the line might follow a particular topographic condition, tracing the highest to the lowest point, following a lake edge or bisecting human boundaries. He links together river beds, mountain tops, wind directions, left turns, dead ends or any number of other topographic itineraries in an effort both to experience the land through what is an 'unusual' walk or journey and to trace upon it (albeit lightly, or even only in memory) an alternative gesture.

It is important to understand that the primacy of both Long's and the Situationist's use of maps belongs to the their *performative* aspects, that is to the way in which mapping directs and enacts a particular set of events, events that derive from a given milieu. But, of course, there are the recordings that come after the proceedings, and these are neither passive nor neutral in their effects either. In Long's *A Seven Day Circle of Ground – Seven Days Walking Within an Imaginary Circle 5½ Miles Wide* (1984), for example, the extremely selective choice of place names (spaced locationally) are brought into a unique associational relationship *simply* by the straightforward and laconic recording of the performance, recorded by the word 'tent' and the array of seven 'midday' points contained within a circular frame. The circle itself, like other lines and figures in Long's work, is not visible on the ground; it exercises its effect through its

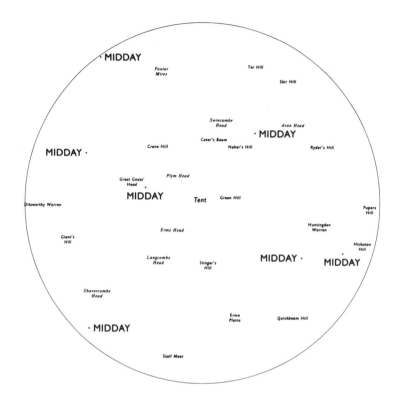

A SEVEN DAY CIRCLE OF GROUND

SEVEN DAYS WALKING WITHIN AN IMAGINARY CIRCLE 5½ MILES WIDE

DARTMOOR ENGLAND 1984

Richard Long, printed text from *A Seven Day Circle of Ground* . . .

(arbitrary) delineation on the map. Like a frame or graticule, the circle is an imaginary figure that holds otherwise inchoate things in a field of relationship. This, in turn, points towards various alternative readings and actions that might then be exercised upon a particular landscape.

These various practices of 'drift' use maps as instruments for establishing and aligning otherwise disparate, repressed or unavailable topographies; they are 'set-ups' that both derive from and precipitate a series of interpretative and participatory acts. Their highly personal and constructive agency make them quite unlike the detached work of conventional map-makers. They are openly cognitive, mental maps, rendering new images of space and relationship. Moreover, the drift permits a *critique* of contemporary circumstances, not from outside and above (as a master-plan) but from participation *within* the very contours and fabric of political and institutional reality. The field, the extracts and the plottings are played out not only upon the surface of the map but also upon the physical terrain itself, leaving an entire corpus of interventions and effects behind. Thus, drift discloses hidden topographies within ruling, dominant structures in an attempt to re-territorialize seemingly repressed or spent ground.[37]

Layering

A relatively new development in the design of large-scale urban and landscape fabrics has been 'layering'. This involves the superimposition of various independent layers one upon the other to produce a heterogeneous and 'thickened' surface. Architects Bernard Tschumi and Rem Koolhaas were amongst the first to develop layering strategies in design and planning in their respective proposals for the Parc de la Villette in Paris, 1983.[38] Generally, these projects dismantle the programmatic and logistical aspects of the park into a series of layers, each of which is then considered independently from the other layers. There is an internal logic, content and system of organization to each layer, depending on its function or intended purpose. The layers are not mappings of an existing site or context, but of the complexity of the intended programme for the site. In both analysing and synthesizing the enormously complex array of data and technical requirements surrounding the programme for the new park, these mappings also array an enabling geometry. When these separate layers are overlaid together, a stratified amalgam of relationships amongst parts appears. The resulting structure is a complex fabric, without centre, hierarchy or single organizing principle. The composite field is instead one of multiple parts and elements, cohesive at one layer but disjunct in relation to others. Such richness and complexity cannot be gained by the limited scope of the single master-plan or the zoning plan, both of which group, hierarchicalize and isolate their component parts. Unlike the clear order of the compositional plan, the layering of independently structured conditions leads to a mosaic-like field of multiple orders, not unlike the combination of different coloured paint delineations for the playing of games superimposed on a gymnasium floor. One layer becomes legible only through the lens of the game or rules of use that apply to it. But, of course, the possibility of 'hybrid' games becomes possible here too – not only may things occur simultaneously side-by-side, but they may also merge as a new event structure (as in many children's games

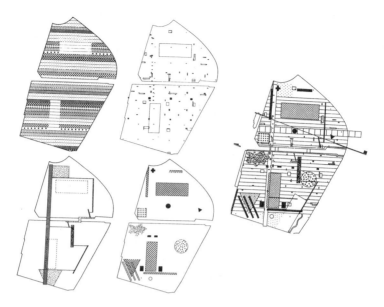

Rem Koolhaas/Office for Metropolitan Architecture, *Layer Diagrams for the Parc de la Villette*, 1983.

where throwing, hitting, passing and running are combined into a new system of play).

The same effects of multiplicity, montage and hybridization are found in similar layering techniques used in some contemporary rock music genres. Several autonomous mixes may be simultaneously run together to develop a polyrhythmic and cross-cultural condition. The music escapes any single interpretation, as a range of cultural and genre sources come into radically new fields of combination. Caribbean rhythms are overlaid with country-and-western and techno-dance music, often producing a frenzied cacophony of associations and new possibilities. Significantly, though, this effect is performative not representational; it engenders new possibilities out of old, and does not simply array its extracts as a muted archaeology.

Another way one can characterize the multiplying functions of layering is in terms of indeterminacy. Unlike a traditional plan, the layered field remains open to any number of interpretations, uses and transformations in time. Just as upon the gymnasium floor, almost anything can happen; the layered structure provides little restraint or imposition. Unlike traditional plans, maps share this open-ended characteristic. Maps are not prescriptive but infinitely promising. Thus, as constructed projects, mapping

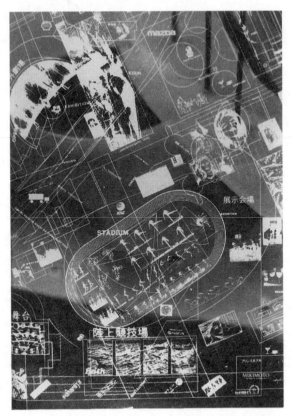

Rem Koolhaas/Office for Metropolitan Architecture,
Program Map, Yokohama, 1992.

strategies propose organizational field-systems that both instigate and sustain a range of activities and interpretations in time.

Another architect who has worked with strata in the formation of projects is Peter Eisenman. In his proposal for a new Art Museum at the California State University at Long Beach, California, developed in collaboration with landscape architect Laurie Olin, a whole series of local maps are drawn upon and transformed into a new composite assembly.[39] In the resulting design, landscape and building are merged into one large fractured ground-plane, evoking both the excavations typical of archaeological sites as well as the strata of historical and projective time that are often visible in maps but not on the ground.

In documenting the site, the designers found a number of significant historic moments: the Gold Rush settlement of California in 1849, the creation of the campus in 1949 and the anticipated 'rediscovery' of the

Peter Eisenman with Laurie Olin, *Sketch Site Plan, phase 4, University Art Museum of the State University at Long Beach California*, 1986.

museum in 2049, two hundred years after its initial marking. Seven key 'figures' emerge from this: 'ranch', 'campus', 'fault-lines', 'land-division grids', 'river', 'channel' and 'coastline'. An archival search through historical maps enables these primary figures to be identified and drawn out as discrete shapes. Each figure is considered a separate layer, and can be either shrunk, enlarged or rotated according to the designer's syntactical code. 'Scaling', for instance, is a significant step in Eisenman's work.[40] This involves the displacement, reduction/enlargement and multiplication of prominent textual figures (shape-forms derived from topographical maps) so as to remove any fixed or stable reading. The trace of the faultlines, for instance, is not intended to represent or even invoke a geological condition, but rather to produce a new, de-territorialized figure through extraction and scaling. In both defamiliarizing and systematizing the landscape through such a series of mapping operations, Eisenman eliminates the traditionally assumed causal relationship between form and intention while also avoiding the limitations of purely autonomous, self-referential procedures of composition. He argues that in manipulating mappings of the site and its larger milieu, the project can 'evolve' a future form out of specific and unique local histories.

In tracing out several iterations of the scaled overlays, Eisenman searches for new analogic relationships; for example, amongst the 'ranch', the 'campus' and the 'faultline'. He finally settles on what he believes to be the most poignant composition of combination and relationship. As he says, 'the overlapping registration of several maps . . . are combined in such a way that none of the notations takes precedence over any other, and so as to textualize coincidental overlaps by subjective interpretation'.[41] The composite quarry reveals certain relationships that were never visible, as if the ground itself were now a constructed map, or text, albeit infinitely interpretable. Constructed fragments of information become 'marks of intelligence, glimpses of the way the culture organized itself,' writes Eisenman, continuing: 'One recognizes in this project that architecture is about telling stories, and this stone text that is being written, this fiction, might tell a very different story about Long Beach than has ever been recorded before.'[42] In other words, the way in which the narrative is assembled, the relating or registering of one thing to another, constructs a radically new fiction out of old facts.

Whereas Koolhaas and Tschumi's strategic layers are drawn from and anticipate future programmes, Eisenman's layers are site and textual in origin. They are less intended to accommodate a variety of changing activities than they are to produce new formal arrangements. In both cases, however, the practice of superimposing otherwise independent layers of information is aimed towards the production of a constructed *milieu* that is heterogeneous and multiple in its effects. In other words, traditional notions of centring, bounding, imparting meaning and asserting finish or completion are here banished in favour of more plural, open-ended 'performances' of the project-in-time. In this context, mapping is no longer restricted to preliminary site surveys or data collection but rather extends *generatively* into the formation of the design itself, analytically transforming the originating referents into new figures and coordinates.

Game-board

A third thematic development of mapping in contemporary design practice, and one related to the notions of performance mentioned above, has been the projection of 'game-board' map structures. These are conceived as shared working surfaces upon which various competing constituencies are invited to meet to work out their differences. As a representation of contested territory, the map assumes an enabling or facilitating status for otherwise adversarial groups to try and find common ground while 'playing out' various scenarios. Ideas of drift and layering are developed here, as the former allows for personal engagement between mapper and constituents, while the latter permits the analytical separation of multiple issues and agendas.

Raoul Bunschoten is a London-based architect who has engaged with a number of complex and contentious urban regions in Europe, and has developed a number of innovative mapping techniques for working with such sites.[43] For Bunschoten, cities are dynamic and multiple; they comprise a vast range of 'players' and 'agents' whose 'effects' flow through the system, continually reworking the variety of urban spaces in any given field. His approach is aimed first towards identifying and then redirecting the temporal play of these various forces. Consequently, urban design is practised less as spatial composition and more as orchestrating the conditions around which processes in the city may be brought into relationship and 'put into effect'. Bunschoten calls this 'stirring'.

A key principle in Bunschoten's work is the idea of 'proto-urban conditions'. These are the range of potentially productive situations in a given *milieu*. But whereas the conventional planner's list of possibilities derive more from some overall governing authority, proto-urban conditions are 'drawn out' from existing structures and potentials, and, thus, are already invested with local, emotive force. 'Proto-urban conditions are like emotions in human beings,' writes Bunschoten, 'subliminal conditions that strongly affect physical states and behavior. These conditions form a metaphoric space in the city, a space that is in need of appropriate forms of expression.'[44] In order to employ and operationalize these various conditions, they must first be made visible. Bunschoten accomplishes this by setting up a number of map-frames, within which certain processes or conditions are graphically identified. He is careful to link the various cultural aspirations of each group to a physical space or territory, distinguishing amongst 'local authorities' who anchor conditions into specific institutions or places, 'actors' who participate with stated desires and 'agents' who have the power and capacity to make things happen. Each frame permits the play of certain thematic conditions (preservation, ecology, economic development or cultural memory, for instance), whilst the composite overlay of all of the frames more accurately conveys the plural and interacting nature of the urban theatre.

In Bunschoten's proposal for Bucharest, Romania, the city is clearly

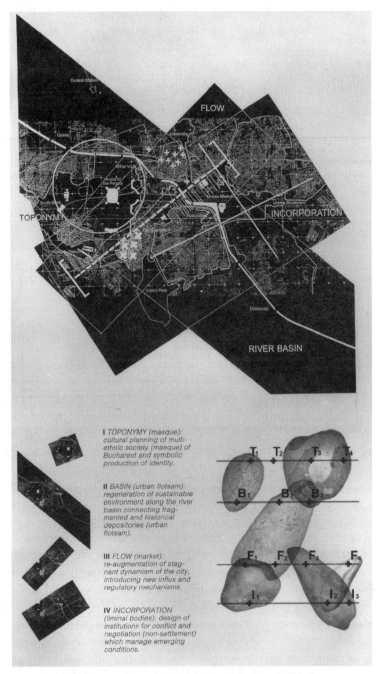

Raoul Bunschoten/CHORA, *Four Planning Fields for Bucharest, Romania*, 1996.

Raoul Bunschoten/CHORA, *Toponymy,*
Alexandrov, Russia, 1995.

mapped into the larger context of the Black Sea basin with respect to the
various social, political and physical changes that have affected the city's
development. 'In this way, the Black Sea is a large-scale object that relates
to cultural identification,' writes Bunschoten, 'but, importantly, it is also
virtually a "dead sea", a cause for international concern that engenders a
kind of operational power and creates the possibility of linking global
economy to urban planning propositions within the context of cultural
and ecological planning.'[45] In other words, through situating the city in its
larger geographical and political-economic region – linking Bucharest
with Russia, Central Asia, Western Europe and the Middle East –
Bunschoten develops a cartographic 'stage' upon which various interests
and agents can be identified and brought together for mutual benefit.

To clarify the process further, Bunschoten itemizes four fields:
'toponymy' refers to the deployment of the colourful, cultural and ethnic
diversity that characterizes Bucharest; 'basin' refers to the desire to regen-
erate the various ecologies and historical sites of the river basin; 'flow'
refers to both the regulatory mechanisms and the physical venues for market and economic exchange in the city; and 'incorporation' refers to the
specific design of new institutions and small-scale self-organizational
forms that permit public negotiation. When the layers are superimposed,

there are revealed a number of vertical correspondences, or 'stepping stones', that are conceived by Bunschoten to permit decisions and actions on one plane to have effects upon the others. He writes:

The overall aim of the project is to provide a cultural planning concept that acts as a model for interested parties in Bucharest. It is a rule-based plan for developing and advancing possible scenarios of urbanization, a type of game structure. The game suggests a mode of planning based on temporal structures that evolve independently and yet may intertwine with fruitful effects. This requires players, acting both in the city and at a distance. Both model and game are based on an understanding of as many different proto-urban conditions as possible.[46]

The graphic map provides the game-board for playing out a range of urban futures. Identified players and actors are brought together to try to work out complex urban issues within an open-ended generative structure. Diverse forms of negotiation are promoted as the survival strategies of each player unfold and become interwoven with others in reaction to changing interests and situations. Thus the maps themselves are evolving structures, drawn and redrawn by the urban planner so as to permit the game to continue while also generating the necessary conditions for the emergence of an enterprising urbanity.

This tactical kind of mapping is not to be confused with the simple inventory and empirical presentation of resources. First, its data is not indiscriminately derived from the usual statistical and quantifiable sources and represented in the form of tracings; rather, data is knowingly selected and arrayed according to local knowledge of and direct participation within the field itself. These maps are informed by a kind of street-level ethnography that is often highly personalized and peculiar to places and individuals. In this way, the field-worker/mapper gains a remarkably detailed and socially colourful sense of local dynamics and desires.[47] Moreover, game-board mapping is more purposefully active and rhetorical than the passivity and neutrality assumed by a GIS engineer. The game-board mapper exercises shrewd judgement in designing the map structure, incorporating and engaging the various imaginations of all the relevant parties. In devising the map (constructing field frames, naming, indexing, graphic iconography and so on), the designer 'sets up' the game-board in a very specific way, not in order to predetermine or prefigure the outcome but rather to instigate, support and enable social forms of interaction, affiliation and negotiation. And in this sense, one can see the similarity of Bunschoten's approach to the revitalization of urban fields to that of the Situationists. In neither case is it believed that a single authority, or a single directive, can ever really produce a rich form of urbanism. It is recognized instead that multiple *processes* of urbanization must be engaged and artfully, yet indeterminately, choreographed in relation to evolving and open-ended spatial formations.

Rhizome

Open-ended and indeterminate characteristics can be likened to the process-form of the rhizome. 'Unlike trees or their roots,' write Deleuze and Guattari, 'the rhizome connects any point to any other point . . . It has neither beginning nor end, but always a middle (*milieu*) from which it grows and overspills, [constituting] linear mulitiplicities.'[48] In contrast to centric or tree-like, hierarchical systems, the rhizome is acentred, non-hierarchical and continually expanding across multiplicitous terrains. 'Rats are rhizomes. Burrows too, in all of their functions of shelter, supply, movement, evasion, and breakout.'[49]

As mentioned earlier in this essay, Deleuze and Guattari draw an important distinction between 'maps' and 'tracings', describing the former as open, connectable, 'experimentations with the real', and the latter as repetitive redundancies that 'always come back to "the same"'. Hence, tracings belong to hierarchical systems of order that ultimately limit any hope of innovation – 'all of tree logic is a logic of tracing and reproduction'.[50] By contrast, the infinitely open, rhizomatic nature of mapping affords many diverse entryways, exits and 'lines of flight', each of which allows for a plurality of readings, uses and effects.

The significance of the rhizome for mapping is encapsulated in Deleuze and Guattari's belief that 'the book' (and we might equally say the map, the city or the landscape) 'has no object. As an assemblage [it] has only itself, in connection with other assemblages and in relation to other bodies without organs.' Thus, they conclude:

We will never ask what a book means, as signifier or signified; we will not look for anything to understand in it. We will ask what it functions with, in connection with what other things it does or does not transmit intensities, in which other multiplicities its own are inserted and metamorphosed, and with what other bodies it makes its own converge.[51]

This viewpoint privileges actions and effects over representation and meaning; the concern is for how things work and what they do. Moreover, there is an explicit interest here for new kinds of affiliative relationship and interconnection. The argument emphasizes probing practices of interpretation that extend previous products of culture (maps and landscapes, for instance) towards more diverse and interconnected fields of possibility, their 'becoming' bodied-forth through various acts of mapping and relating.

One especially important principle with regard to mapping as a rhizomatic (burrowing and extending) activity is what Deleuze and Guattari refer to as the 'plane of consistency'. While this assumes a rich and complex array of meanings for the authors, I shall summarize plane of consistency here as a surface that is both inclusive (even of things that may not normally fit or 'belong' to any given scheme, including arbitrary 'debris') and *structuring* of new and open-ended series of relationships. Obviously, if such a surface is both inclusive and structuring, the techniques and modes of representation must be both multiple and flexible. Several different graphic and notational systems have to come into play so that diverse and even 'unmappable' aspects of a *milieu* are revealed. All of this must be brought to bear on one plane, one fully inclusive, non-differentiated surface (as many architects are fond of saying, if one cannot see it all right in front of one's eyes, as a visual synthesis, then one cannot properly formulate a proposition). The devised systems of collection and array cannot be closed; they must remain open, fostering endless chains of possibility and insight. Rather than limiting reality, the rhizomatic map opens reality up to a host of new and alternative possibilities. The process is not unlike working with bits of arbitrarily found matter upon a dissecting table – a mode of work integral to collage, and with all the similar experiences of discovery, revelation and pleasure. Unlike collage, however, which functions mostly connotatively (by suggestion), mapping typically *systematizes* its material into more analytical and denotative schemas. Where mappings may become more inclusive and suggestive, then, is less through collage, which works with fragments, and more through a form of systematic montage, where multiple and independent layers are incorporated as a synthetic composite.

A useful example of multiple and inclusive synthesis of complex information is the French engineer Charles Joseph Minard's narrative map of the fate of Napoleon's army in Russia during the winter of 1812–13.[52] Moving from the left on the Polish–Russian border, the thick band shows the size of the army (422,000 men) in June 1812. Its width diminishes as the size of the army is reduced through casualties. When the army reaches Moscow (to the east/right) in September there are only 100,000 men who must begin their retreat west through the winter months. The retreat line is in solid tone and can be read in conjunction with location and temperature readings. The army returned to Poland with a mere 10,000 survivors. Minard's graphic describes a complex and tragic human story in an enlightening and eloquent way. But more than telling a story, the map conditions how places on the land have come to exist in new relationships precisely through the vector of an event.

Minard's map very elegantly synthesizes a complex amalgam of facts and interrelationships (the size of the army, the locations and times of battle, vectors of movement, topography, place names, weather and temperature, and the passage of time). These events in time assume particular geometrical shape-forms, vectors, densities and patterns of effect. It is no small feat to encode graphically complex and multivariate temporal events in direct relationship to geography, but even more impressive is how the mapping visually layers and embeds the network relationships amongst all of the variables. If the chart were to be animated in a computer program, its shape-forms would change significantly if any one of the many variables were altered. Thus the map depicts a *systemic* field of interrelationships; it is dynamic performance of interacting parts, mapping 'shaping forces' as much as spatial terrain.[53] This is akin to what the Dutch urbanist Winy Maas calls a 'datascape', that is a spatial visualization of otherwise invisible flows and forces that exercise enormous effects across terrain.[54]

At the same time, however, Minard's datascape is far from the rhizomatic plane of consistency outlined above because it is a closed system. It only depicts the facts that are relevant to its narrative theme, and it must therefore be read in a linear way. There is a clear intention of thematic communication in this map, together with a sequential, narrational reading, common to itinerary maps. The map offers clues for rhizomatic mappings because of its overlay and structural incorporation of different space–time systems of analysis, but at the same time it is not at all rhizomatic because of its focused content and single, linear reading. A more rhizomatic map would be much more multi-variate and open. Indeed, such a map might not 'represent' any one thing at all; rather, it might simply array a complex combination of things that provides a framework for many different uses, readings, projections and effects, rather like a thesaurus, without beginning, end, limit or single meaning.

Of course, regular Ordnance Survey and United States Geological Survey maps are 'open' in the sense described above. They contain many different layers of information, with multiple entryways, diverse uses and applications, infinite routes and networks, and potentially endless surfaces of engagement. Richard Long's drifts might be considered rhizomatic exploitations of these 'neutral' planes. What these maps do not show, however, are time structures – local stories, histories, events and

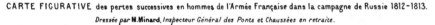

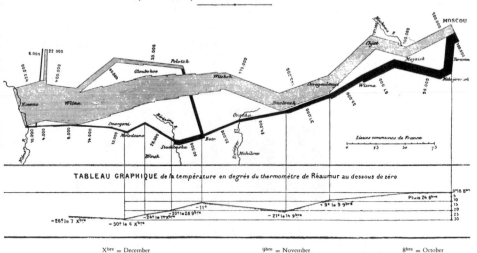

Charles Joseph Minard, *Carte figurative des pertes successives en hommes de l'armée Française dans la campagne de Russie 1812–13*, from E. J. Marey, *La Méthode graphique* (Paris, 1885).

issues on the one hand, and local processes such as capital flows or seasonal hydrological patterns on the other. In some of my own mappings of the larger, working American landscape, I have purposefully used and subverted the conventions of USGS maps, and incorporated into them other systems of notation that are intended to 'open' and further 'extend' the field.[55] In *Pivot Irrigators I*, for instance, the USGS map is cut as a circle without scale, place names or geographical coordinates visible; the cropping and reframing effectively de-territorializes the map and its referent (illus. 12). Incorporated into this frame are other fragments of images such as underground aquifer maps – which are allied with the irrigation landscapes of the West – and infra-red satellite photographs which capture the circular forms of different fields as temperature traces (the more recently irrigated fields coolest and therefore lightest). Satellites too use these temperature 'fixes' to register their own location in space, and thus another circular construction is drawn to invoke both the planetary geometry of fixing location as well as the engineered geometry of the pivot-irrigator field. Similarly, in *Windmill Topography*, the de-territorialized map is framed as an egg-like ellipse (the shape of both a turbine gear and a wind-shadow) and combined with a topographical section

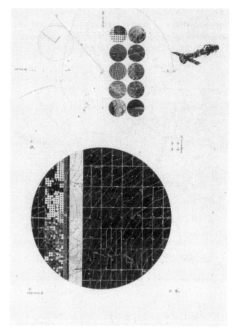

James Corner, *Pivot Irrigators I*, 1994.

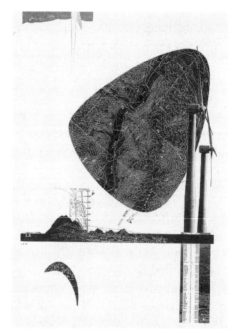

James Corner, *Windmill Topography (Los Angeles, CA)*, 1994.

that depicts the mountain range, air temperature, air-pressure and wind velocity charts. Together, the composite parts of the map construct an ideographic, synaesthetic image of the vast windmill territories east of Los Angeles while also arraying the various shaping forces and conditions that undergird the genesis of this still evolving landscape. There are similar mappings in this project: the poly-oriented and calendrical maps of the Hopi, the multi-scaled maps of the Very Large Array radio telescope installation in New Mexico, or the various 'field plots' of contour farming in the mid-west or dry-strip farming across the northern plains. In each, the codes and conventions of the USGS maps (frame, scale, orientation, colour-separation, numerical coordinates, grid measures and indexes) are co-opted, enhanced and subverted. There is an attempt to represent and describe certain geographical conditions and processes of landscape formation whilst also to suggest new foundations for future work. In a sense, these mappings construct 'planes of consistency' that present analytical information while also allowing for suggestive readings/projections. They 'draw out' of common maps and landscapes certain figural and processual relationships that might occasion new landscapes. Admittedly, these mappings are not as open or rhizomatic as they might be, owing to their thematic focus, but their inclusion and incorporation (synthesis) of diverse kinds of information and possibility, as well as their utilization and subversion of dominant conventions, illustrates two important ways in which mapping might move towards more polymorphous and creative ends. They are also suggestive of how temporal, systemic, performance networks can be rendered distinct from traditional cartographic concerns with static space.

Performance networks are multiple systems of interconnection which liberate elements while also fostering non-hierarchical communication and relationship amongst otherwise disparate parts. 'To network' means to work one's way into a field of opportunity, mapping the various players and sites whilst remaining an active a player in the field. Cities and landscapes are becoming increasingly dependent upon network spaces and processes; as Paul Virilio puts it:

The essence of what we insist on calling urbanism is composed/decomposed by these transfer, transit, and transmission systems, these transport and transmigration networks whose immaterial configuration reiterates the cadastral organization and the building of monuments.[56]

In other words, the experience of spatial life today is as much immaterial as it is physical, as much bound into time and relational connections as it is to traditional notions of enclosure and 'place.' By extension, the principle of rhizomatic planes of consistency – together with the above-mentioned and closely allied themes of drift, *dérive*, layering, scaling, *milieu* and game-board structures – provides a useful model for mapping as a creative form of spatio-temporal practice in urban planning and design. In this way, we move away from urbanistic projects as authoritative master-plans, concerned solely with the composition and order of static parts, toward practices of self-reflexive organization. Mapping as an extensive and rhizomatic set of field operations precipitates, unfolds and supports hidden conditions, desires and possibilities nested within a *milieu*. Here, the concern becomes less about the design of form and space *per se*, and more about engaging, accelerating and networking interactions amongst forces in time. Instead of designing relatively closed systems of order, rhizomatic mappings provide an infinite series of connections, switches, relays and circuits for activating matter and information. Hence *mapping*, as an open and inclusive process of disclosure and enablement, comes to replace the reduction of *planning*.

CONCLUSION

'All perceiving is also thinking, all reasoning is also intuition, all observation is also invention,' wrote Rudolf Arnheim.[57] Moreover, these activities are not without effect; they have great force in shaping the world. It is in this inter-subjective and active sense that mappings are not transparent, neutral or passive devices of spatial measurement and description. They are instead extremely opaque, imaginative, operational instruments. Although drawn from measured observations in the world, mappings are neither depictions nor representations but mental constructs, *ideas* that enable and effect change. In describing and visualizing otherwise hidden facts, maps set the stage for future work. Mapping is always already a project in the making.

If maps are essentially subjective, interpretative and fictional constructs of facts, constructs that influence decisions, actions and cultural values generally, then why not embrace the profound efficacy of mapping in exploring and shaping new realities? Why not embrace the fact that the potentially infinite capacity of mapping to find and found new conditions might enable more socially engaging modes of exchange within larger *milieux*? The notion that mapping should be restricted to empirical data-sorting and array diminishes the profound social and orienting sway of the cartographic enterprise. And yet the power of 'objective analysis' in building consensus and representing collective responsibility is not something to be abandoned for a free-form 'subjectivity'; this would be both naïve and ineffective. The power of maps resides in their facticity. The analytical measure of factual objectivity (and the credibility that it brings to collective discourse) is a characteristic of mapping that ought to be embraced, co-opted and *used* as the means by which critical projects can be realized.[58] After all, it is the apparent rigour of objective analysis and logical argument that possesses the greatest efficacy in a pluralistic, democratic society. Analytical research through mapping enables the designer to *construct* an argument, to embed it within the dominant practices of a rational culture, and ultimately to turn those practices towards more productive and collective ends. In this sense, mapping is not the indiscriminate, blinkered accumulation and endless array of data, but rather an extremely shrewd and tactical enterprise, a practice of relational reasoning that intelligently unfolds new realities out of existing constraints, quantities, facts and conditions.[59] The artistry lies in the use of the technique, in the way in which things are framed and set up. Through reformulating things differently, novel and inventive possibilities emerge. Thus mapping innovates; it derives neither from logical possibility (projection) nor necessity (utility) but from logical *force*. The agency of mapping lies in its cunning exposure and engendering of new sets of possibility.[60]

This discussion of mapping also implies a parallel with contemporary practices in urban design and planning. The bureaucratic regime of city and landscape planning, with its traditional focus on objects and functions, has failed to embrace the full complexity and fluidity of urbanism, and of culture generally. This failing results in large measure from the inadequacy of techniques and instruments to imaginatively incorporate the rich interplay of processes that shape the world. In asserting authority and closure, current techniques have also failed to embrace the contingency, improvisation, error and uncertainty that inevitably circulate in urbanism. Given the complex nature of late capitalist culture, together with the increased array of competing interest groups and forces, it is becoming ever more difficult for urban designers and planners to play a role in the development of cities and regions beyond scenographic or environmental amelioration. There is a kind of inertia and levelling of possibilities as it becomes politically impossible in a mass democracy to do anything out of the ordinary. While there is no shortage of theories and ideas for addressing this condition more critically, there has been very little development of new operational techniques for actualizing them. In other words, the difficulty today is less a crisis of *what* to do than of *how* to do anything at all. It is precisely at the strategic and rhetorical level of operation, then, that mappings hold great value.

Instances of drift, strata, game-board and rhizome represent only a handful of techniques that mapping practices might assume if they are to play more creative roles in design and planning, and in culture more generally. These techniques presuppose any number of variations and enhancements as issues of framing, scaling, orientation, projection, indexing and coding become more flexible and open-ended, especially in the context of powerful new digital and animation media. As we are freed from the old limits of frame and boundary – preconditions for the survey and 'colonization' of wilderness areas – the role of mapping will become less one of tracing and re-tracing already known worlds, and more one of inaugurating new worlds out of old. Instead of mapping as a means of appropriation, we might begin to see it as a means of emancipation and enablement, liberating phenomena and potential from the encasements of convention and habit. What remains unseen and unrealized across seemingly exhausted grounds becomes actualized anew with the liberating efficacy of creatively aligned cartographic procedures. Mapping may thus retain its original entrepreneurial and exploratory character, actualizing within its virtual spaces new territories and prospects out of pervasive yet dormant conditions.

Mapping and the Expanded Field of Contemporary Art

WYSTAN CURNOW

What prompted my interest in mapping and art was the approach of the 150th anniversary of the 1840 signing of the Treaty of Waitangi. This was the document by which Maori, the indigenous inhabitants of what has come to be known as New Zealand, ceded their sovereignty to the British Crown. Looking again at publications on the early years of New Zealand's European art history, my eye was caught by a peculiar feature of a 1848 watercolour landscape by Sir William Fox. There, smack in the middle of the sky, hovering high above a natural harbour, was the rubber stamp of the New Zealand Company, the London-based company whose business was the organized British settlement of these islands in the South Pacific. It raised a question: was this in fact a picture, one for framing, and hanging on the parlour walls of the Fox family home before its eventual donation to the nation? Or rather was it a document, included in one of Sir William's reports to his superiors, for studying, tabling and filing in the Company's offices before its donation to the nation? *Bird's Eye View of Waitohi*, I discovered, was indeed painted to provide topographic information to the Company, much as a map would, about areas of the South Island suitable for purchase and settlement. It is interesting to note that only since the 1950s and '60s has Fox's work – and similarly topographical documents produced by draughtsmen and surveyors as part of their employment by the New Zealand Company and various provincial governments – been regarded as they are now, as foundation works in the nation's art history.

Differences between art and cartography are not always self-evident or fixed; and examining or shifting the boundary can affect the understanding of either or both. Bird's eye views and panoramas, coastal profiles even, can plausibly be interpreted as landscape painting genres and assigned a place in the making of a local tradition. However, such a project risks obscuring the role that mapping played in the processes of colonial appropriation and settlement. To take another example, Svetlana Alpers, in her book *The Art of Describing*, has changed the way seventeenth-century Dutch painting is understood by restoring to the art historical account what she argued was its originally close relationship to mapping and other descriptive techniques of the day.[1] Alpers singled out the panorama and the topographic city view as particularly map-like in source and nature. Her work suggested there are histories to be written not only of mapping's relation to the whole landscape tradition – from Philips Koninck to Sir William Fox – but also of the relation of both to the course of European expansion. In theory such histories would link Jan Vermeer's *The Art of Painting* (1662), Isaac Gilsemann's coastal profile, sketched from the deck of Abel Tasman's ship following its first sighting of New Zealand (1742), and Fox's bird's eye view just over a century later.

In 1989, as a contribution to the Treaty anniversary, I curated an exhibition, *Putting the Land on the Map: Art and Cartography in New Zealand since 1840*, which was divided into three segments: nineteenth-century topographical landscapes and related maps, contemporary art works incorporating maps, and examples of Maori oral mapping on audiotape. Oral maps? What are those? So far as etymology is concerned there is no such thing; 'cartography' and 'map' belong to the vocabulary of writing cultures, and denote the paper or cloth on which inscription takes place. Our proposed histories of European expansion, however, have to recognize a fact our ancestors either ignored or were ignorant of: that all cultures map. A few years ago a tribunal, set up to adjudicate outstanding land disputes between Maori and the Crown, addressed itself to a long-standing disagreement over the terms of the sale of much of the South Island of New Zealand by Ngai Tahu to the Crown. The disagreement was one that stemmed directly from the inability of either party to recognize the other's mapping code, and the assumptions that informed its use. Commonly Europeans took the absence of written maps as an endorsement of the 'emptiness' of the land, as further evidence of its lack of 'cultivation'. Unmapped land was land unoccupied, and to that extent unpossessed. The 'uncharted' territories that Europeans mapped commonly already had their maps, complex oral maps embedded in genealogy, legend and ideology, and sustained by memory and ritual, which took literary rather than visual form. The inscribed map registered and itself hastened dispossession, replacing and silencing what had gone before.

Putting the Land on the Map was, however, mainly contemporary art – paintings, sculptures, installations, photographs, audio and video tapes – concerned with mapping. At the time I put it together there had been only one or two exhibitions like it. Since then there have been many, a develop-ment that attests to a new art world interest in the subject of mapping as well as to its wide relevance to current art practices. Almost 50 artists were involved in *Tierra de Nadie*, curated by Jose Lehrero Stals, in Granada, 1992, only four of whom were among Robert Storr's selection of 30 artists for his *Mapping* two years later at the Museum of Modern Art in New York. Storr's show provoked a small but very rich gathering of more than 50 artists, curated by Peter Fend; *Mapping: A Response to MoMA* opened at American Fine Arts, New York, early the following year. The two shows had only one artist in common. In 1996, *Under Capricorn/The World Over*, which addressed issues of globalization from opposite ends of the earth – the Stedelijk Museum of Modern Art, Amsterdam, and the City Gallery, Wellington – and on a website, was put together by Dorine Mignot and myself. Last year, Zelimir Koscevic's *Cartographers: Geo-gnostic Projection for the 21st Century* opened at the Museum of Contemporary Art in Zagreb, and travelled from there to Warsaw, Budapest and Maribor. This was another substantial exhibition, and yet only a handful of its 50 artists had appeared in the shows just named. The smaller *Atlas Mapping*, 1997, curated by Paolo Bianchi and Sabine Folie, for the OK Center for Contemporary Art in Linz, also had a central European focus.

Since *Putting the Land on the Map*, the sudden collapse of the Soviet empire has given new and urgent meanings to the post-colonial concerns represented in that show, abruptly re-structuring global space, and dramatically casting the history of Western expansion in a new light, a history with which the modern map is so closely identified. The recent rush of exhibitions of map-based art is surely a reflection of these momentous political changes, although the works themselves represent a wide variety of impulses, and the most important map-based individual practices date back 30 years, to the time of the last significant shift in direction of the century's art.

CONCEPTUAL ART AND THE MAP: ROBERT SMITHSON

Before the advent of conceptual art in the mid-1960s and early 1970s, artists interested in mapping were few and far between. Conceptual art supplied a crucial dispensation, under which all manner of new forms and media, found objects, common activities and documents such as maps entered art's discursive terrain. For a new generation, painting, as a vehicle for thought and its distribution, had come to a standstill, hopelessly compromised by narrow and increasingly challenged codes of practice. As a result of this repudiation, the idea or concept of the work now determined the materials and procedures of the work, rather than the other way around. As one of the leading conceptual artists, Sol LeWitt, put it, 'The idea becomes a machine that makes the art.' And those materials and procedures commonly belonged more to the world than to the art gallery or the studio.

Since Western cartography shared with painting its project of representing the three-dimensional world on a two-dimensional surface, its terms of entry into this new art discourse were to that extent circumscribed, and so by contrast with the convergence of painting and cartography in seventeenth-century Holland, the new art did not endorse the authority of the inscribed map. On the other hand, conceptual artists were extremely interested in the activity of mapping. In so far as an activity, or 'performance', outside the studio and the gallery, replaced the traditional art object, their work frequently amounted to a kind of mapping, generating new forms of thinking and feeling about space. And no matter how problematic the conventional map may have seemed to some artists, they occurred often as one of several ways of documenting art's new activities.

Peter Fend 'responded' to MoMA's *Mapping* show largely because it obscured the conceptualist position. Storr's exhibition, he wrote, was just

about paintings, sculptures, or drawings which happen to include maps. It has nothing to do with mapping . . . But the task of a show called *Mapping* is to deal with an action of charting or planning a domain or space, within which action would take place – *real* world actions, or at least performed actions.[2]

In the early 1960s, in Amsterdam, Stanley Brouwn would stop someone in the street and ask directions. He has subsequently exhibited the maps drawn for him under the generic title *This Way Brouwn*. In London, in 1967, Richard Long walked back and forth along a line across some lawn until his footsteps had made a line in the grass. He photographed it and exhibited it as *A Line Made by Walking*. Since that time Long, and his compatriot Hamish Fulton, have taken hundreds of walks over longer distances than *A Line Made by Walking* – 'no walk, no work' is Fulton's motto – in many parts of the world, adding as they go to their impressive individual atlases. Two years later, in New York, Vito Acconci carried out his *Following Piece*; every day for 23 days he randomly chose a person in the street to follow for as long or as far as that person travelled in public space. This work was presented as a series of photographs. In 1968 Lawrence Weiner announced his version of the conceptualist dispensation: 'With relation to the various manners of use: 1. The artist may construct the piece. 2. The piece may be fabricated. 3. The piece need not be built. Each being equal and consistent with the intent of the artist the decision as to condition rests with the receiver upon the occasion of receivership.' Weiner composes written statements which would document the activities to be undertaken, such as these simple verbal maps from 1969: *The Joining of France Germany and Switzerland by Rope, The Arctic Circle Shattered* and *Floatable Objects Thrown into Inland Waterways One Each Month for 7 Years.*

The one artist to be included in both Storr's and Fend's exhibition was Robert Smithson; for though he died in 1974, it is hard to make a show concerned with mapping without him. In 1968 Smithson was working on two distinct groups of works, both dedicated to the wittily perverse project of making three-dimensional art based on graphic systems for representing three dimensions in two: the perspectival and the cartographic. He considered such systems obsolete – codes that had had their say and their day. *Pointless Vanishing Point* is an eight-foot-long segment of a set of converging perspective lines – there is no vanishing point, it is literally as well as figuratively pointless – rendered as a solid, in fibreglass. *Leaning Strata* is a solid which hybridizes the grids of global projection and linear perspective. Painted white, not quite big enough to be monumental, these pristine but somewhat disconsolate solids seek a home in a space other than that from which they have mistakenly emerged.

With the second group, the *Site/Nonsite* installations, Smithson comes up with such a space; one which is, however, more rather than less problematic. A 'nonsite', *Pine Barrens, New Jersey*, consists of a photostat of a topographical map of Pine Barrens (the 'site') and an arrangement of trapezoid bins containing sand from it. Similarly, another 'nonsite', *Franklin, New Jersey*, is an aerial photograph of the site plus an arrangement of trapezoid bins containing mineral samples from it. On the photostat there is a note which says 'Tours between the "Nonsite" and the "site" are possible. The red dot on the map is the place where the sand was collected.' Both the map and the arrangement of bins are hexagonally shaped and divided by a grid, so that once again we have a 'pointless' combination of systems, a polar projection and a set of vanishing points. As Smithson himself said, the 'nonsite' is a three-dimensional map of the site.

But it is also an endlessly problematic map. The opposition of 'site' and 'nonsite' produces a stream of ambiguities and contradictions, and a dialectical argument which is without resolution. Like landscape paintings, the installations represent specific places. However, despite the proffered tour, these 'sites' are hardly sights one would to go out of one's way for. Yet that appears to be what recommends them to the artist. They are barren, unsightly (nonsitely?) wastelands distinguished by little more than their geology. As if to point up the wilfulness of his cartographic purposes, Smithson chooses bedrock places in which to practise his arts of mapping. The 'nonsites' signify the 'sites' in two distinct ways, through the mixed codes of the map, and indexically by way of samples from it, which the installation sets out to confuse one with another and both with the code of perspectival depiction. But the 'nonsite/nonsight' pun reminds us (again) that representation is only that, and further, there is the logic peculiar to language which arbitrarily throws up the occasional short-circuit. Smithson gave this account of his dialectics:

The range of convergence between Site and Nonsite consists of a course of hazards, a double path made up of signs, photographs, and maps that belong to both sides of the dialectic at once. Both sides are present and absent at the same time ... Two-dimensional and three-dimensional things trade places with each other in the range of convergence. Large scale becomes small. Small scale becomes large ... Is the Site a reflection of the Nonsite (mirror), or is it the other way around? The rules of this network of signs are discovered as you go along uncertain trails both mental and physical.[3]

Smithson's richly deconstructive treatment of the languages of mapping and perspective characterize more effectively than any other conceptual practice art's 'spatial turn' in the late 1960s.

PERFORMING THE MAP. ARTISTS WHO WALK: RICHARD LONG AND HAMISH FULTON

Since he, too, makes installations of rocks and stones, and uses photographs, diagrams and words to represent mainly out of the way places, Richard Long appears to have much in common with Robert Smithson. But his purposes, and those of Hamish Fulton, are different. Both base their art on the activity of walking and its representation. The simplicity of the walk-works and the variety of the forms that they take is in sharp contrast to the complexities and incompatibilities of each of Smithson's *Site/Nonsite* works. Rather than deconstructing the inscribed map, they revive a mode of mapping which predates it, and implicitly contests its authority. Theirs are maps structured by the journey or itinerary, and they give voice to what, as J. B. Harley noted,[4] the pages of contemporary road atlases silence: the variety of nature, the history of the landscape, and the space–time experience of it.

As Rudi Fuchs has pointed out, knowledge gained from walking differs not only from that offered by the road atlas but also from that gained just from looking at the landscape. With *Eight Walks* (1974) Long (mis)takes the Ordnance Survey for a road map; walking its graticule as if it were a set of paths, he traverses an area eight times: four north to south, four west to east. What is exhibited is the Survey map with Long's routes over-scored and the elapsed times noted. The variation in time 'is a precise reflection and transference, into time, of the particular differences of each line of ground, at a constant walking pace'.[5] Similarly represented on a map is *A Six Day Walk Over All Roads, Lanes and Double Tracks Inside a Six Mile Wide Circle Centred on the Giant of Cerne Abbas* (1975); in this case Long's route follows well-worn social and historical paths. In *Dartmoor Riverbeds* (1978), a marked topographical map is accompanied by six photographs. 'Choosing the high area of Dartmoor which contains the sources of streams flowing in all directions . . . he used the riverbeds as footpaths. Following the water really involved following the lie of the land, which he had, up to that point, gathered by walking his own abstractly conceived lines and circles.'[6]

Besides photographs which sample what is to be seen, or marked-up maps, Long and Fulton use texts to document walks. Some represent by re-enacting the activity in language. For example, *A Moved Line* consists of the title, the idea or instruction 'Picking up carrying placing/one thing to another/along a straight 22 mile walk' and then the following narrative:

Moss to Wool/Wool to Root/Root to Peat/Peat to Sheep's Horn/Sheep's Horn to Stone/Stone to Lichen/Lichen to Toadstool/Toadstool to Bone/Bone to Feather/Feather to Stick/Stick to Jawbone/Jawbone to Stone/Stone to Frog/Frog to Wool/Wool to Bone/Bone to Bird Pellet/Bird Pellet to Stone/Stone to Sheep's Horn/Sheep's Horn to Pine Cone/Pine Cone to Bark/Bark to Beech Nut/Beech Nut to Stone/Stone to End of the Walk.[7]

It is followed by a place and a date: 'Dartmoor 1983'. There is a scale: the distance from noun to noun equals one mile. The reader travels this distance, following the words to the end of the line. It is a journey of discovery (marked by acts of finding/naming: 'I hereby name this place Bird Pellet') and attention, whose nondescript but companionable talismans embody the walker's absorption in the surfaces of the landscape traversed. The reader's recitation of the text transforms the walker's slow progress into a rapidly rhythmic incantation, whose force derives less obviously from the work than its translation into text.

Fulton's *A non-stop 82 mile walk lasting a day a night and three quarters of a day roads and paths fields and woods Kent August moon 1978*[8] has the walker looking up instead of down. The names of birds in red or black type are scattered across a double-page spread; not so many at the top – skylark, heron, hawk – mostly smaller ones at the bottom – sparrow, bullfinch, wren – as though the page were a landscape and a chart on which representative observations of these birds had been plotted. On the other hand, *A Seventeen Day Walk in the Rocky Mountains of Alberta Autumn 1984*, also a double-page text piece, consists of 28 four-letter nouns arranged in four contiguous columns of seven words. The reader can take two routes, reading down: 'snow/twig/howl/ rain/ eyes/frog/ dawn' or across the columns: 'snow/lake/leaf/star/twig/hawk/ crow/fish'. The choice of only four-letter nouns has nothing to do with the walk, but everything to do with producing a text that will activate the reader. Fulton insists that the text does not represent the walk, and the walk does not illustrate the text; his word maps move towards poetry, emerging as much out of their own textuality as out of a given walk.[9] Thus the texts of both Long and Fulton acknowledge Korzybski's adage: 'The map is not the territory, and the name is not the thing.'

As the collective walks of Long and Fulton lightly criss-cross more and more of the earth's surface, their retrospective exhibitions, the catalogues of these, books of texts such as Fulton's *One Hundred Walks* and *Standing Smoke*, assume the character of world atlases. Long says, 'My art is about working in the wide world, wherever, on the surface of the earth.' By 1989 Fulton had 'walked over 12,000 miles in Nepal, India, Bolivia, Canada, Peru, Iceland, England, Scotland, Wales, Ireland, the United States, Mexico, Australia, Switzerland, France, Portugal, Spain, Japan and Lapland'.[10] However, neither artist works to a programme, a global plan according to which he decides where next to walk. Their atlases are not organized geographically, nor do they observe strict chronology; the walks are self-justifying. And yet the preference of both artists for walking in remote and austere landscapes, empty and barren landscapes bounded by wide and distant skylines, wastelands and wilderness areas, some of which are to this day unmapped, has produced a register of areas in those countries as yet untouched by the depredations of real estate agents, developers, industrialists or tourist operators. These are anti-atlases, which in documenting their authors' 'manners of use' of the territory outside of 'limited economy', as Bataille calls it,[11] raise questions as to the manners of use of those within it, questions ideologically beyond the brief of the normal atlas. Both Long and Fulton are concerned with the health of the overall 'general economy', that which combines the economy of nature and of man, and those manners of use of the planet which will best sustain it.

THE SIGN OF THE ABJECT GLOBE

The first images of the planet transmitted from cameras aboard Apollo 7 to television sets on earth left viewers awestruck; like the astronauts themselves, we were both thrilled and frightened by this extra-terrestrial view; the power of sight so trained upon the earth revealed our celestial solitude. The global transmission, reproduction and dissemination of that image – technological processes that are part and parcel of that power of sight – have, however, reduced its sublimity to abjection. Ironically it has become one of the most ubiquitous and banal images of our time. Through repetition, and through appropriation for all manner of commercial use, it comes close to being 'just' a sign, an empty signifier. Australia's international airline, QANTAS, uses it in its latest advertising campaign with the slogan: 'Our World for Sale'. Not only a sign of the global, this image has become itself an instrument of globalization. It is, of course, a symptom of and a sign for the growing intrusion of signs into the space of everyday life. That visual artists should be increasingly aware of semiotics and be producing representations of representations is not surprising. Nor is it a surprise that the abject globe is a new subject in contemporary art. John Miller, an artist in MOMA's *Mapping* show, made a model of the Sherwin-Williams logo which shows a bucket of paint being poured over the globe – the slogan goes: 'We Cover the Earth' – except that his world has been 'generously coated with the colour of lustrous excrement'.[12] Laurie Simmons is an artist who specializes in staged photographs; in her *Bending Globe*, the exposed haunches of a white, spotlit figure – half globe, half human – are tensed and expecting the worst. Globes have been a much favoured prop in Boyd Webb's melancholy photographic satires for some years; *Chattels* shows a plastic blow-up toy giraffe swimming for dear life, bearing a barely inflated globe on the back of its neck. Dimly visible beneath the still surface of this strangely yellow sea are the drowned bodies of giraffes who perished in this catastrophe.

Especially since the early 1980s, fears for the environmental, economic and political state of the globe have found urgent expression in often ironic and sometimes fiercely satirical works like these. The starting-point is frequently some challenge to, or disruption of, the cartographic image and its codes. In this context the commonly held but naïve view of the map as semiotically transparent, as a culturally neutral vehicle for the objective representation of the earth, rather than a set of codes which are historically and culturally determined both in their nature and applications, has served as a provocation. This view was not only implicit in mass

Laurie Simmons, *Bending Globe*, 1991, cibachrome photograph.

media usage, but also, in the 1980s, still received wisdom among most cartographers. It was while working on *Putting the Land on the Map*, that I
first read Wood and Fels's 1986 structuralist essay 'Designs on Signs/Myth
and Meaning in Maps',[13] and was struck by the belatedness of its challenge to conventional views, for the contemporary artists I was interested
in seemed to have already taken the point, whether or not they had read
Saussure or Barthes. Certainly Ruth Watson, a New Zealand artist who
was included in both Koscevic's *Cartographers* and *Under Capricorn/The
World Over* had read them, and more. She has a special interest in the
history of global projections, and over a ten-year period has returned
periodically to the task of elaborating on and exposing their ideological
subtexts. Sixteenth- and seventeenth-century projections represent for
her an apotheosis of disembodied vision; her simulations involve additions and subtractions which blatantly foist on them unwonted psychological and physiological meanings. Specifically, Watson insinuates signs
of the excluded 'subject', particularly the female Subject, into the designs
of the world map. In her *Map of the World*, based on a Johannes Schöner
gored azimuthal projection of the southern hemisphere, she replaces
Terra Australis Incognita (Antarctica) with a strange brain-like object
which is ironically more accurate than the German cartographer's 1515
estimate. Engraved images of a speculum, an ear and an eye multiply the
body references, while signs of modern northern cities and diagrams of

Ruth Watson, *Lingua Geographica*, 1996, cibachrome photo installation.

subatomic particles further disrupt the continuity of its geographical and historical references. In *The Soul is the Prison of the Body*, 1989, Watson simulates Martin Waldseemüller's 1507 lemon peel projection, the first world map to bear the name America; its woodcut striations which signify waves she misrenders as the lines of a vast fingerprint describing the movements of the oceans. *Lingua Geographica*, 1996, derives from another early sixteenth-century projection, the Stab–Werner heart-shaped projection. Watson used it for two world maps, each a jigsaw of fragments of colour photo enlargements of the surface – not of the heart, but of the tongue – pinned directly to the museum wall. Made for *Under Capricorn/The World Over*, one was installed in the southern hemisphere, in Wellington, with the north pole at the top, an orientation 'downunder' viewers are accustomed to. The other, in the northern hemisphere, in Amsterdam, had the south pole on top, which for 'upover' viewers was mildly disorienting. The title is the medical name for what is commonly called 'cracked tongue', presumably because of its landscape appearance. *Lingua Geographica* is held together by pins, but also by visual puns and verbal figures. The semiotic coincidences of map and heart, of tongue and landscape, are fortuitous only to those who are of a mind to think them so. Watson asks us to piece together out of these image fragments and fractured codes a picture of what might be called the cartographic unconscious of Western expansion.

Immediately recognizable cartographic icons of national identity receive similar treatment by conceptual artists. They are subjected to a variety of indignities and distortions which foist upon them unwonted meanings. Mistaking usages of scale and orientation, Robert Longo has upended the United States, making of his native land a Gargantuan child's toy, a great shit-coloured slab on wheels. While Tony Cragg, in *Britain Viewed from the North*, tips his country on to its side in a wall-mounted image comprising bits of cheap and often broken plastic. The most subtle and extensive body of this kind of work is Luciano Fabro's *Italia* series, which he began in the 1960s. Fabro is associated with Arte Povera, the European 'movement' which coincided with and shared some concerns with conceptual art. What links the series is the outline shape of the country. An early work, cut from a sheet of iron, has Italy hung upside down from the ceiling by a steel cord. Germano Celant writes of it like this:

Dangling topsy-turvy, subjected to the play of air, Italy loses its weight, its iconic gravity, to become a buoyant rhetorical 'ornatus' on which we can hang the shifting varieties of our formal and material imaginations . . . On the floor or on the wall, made out of leather or lead, glass or netting, fur or gold, brass or steel, Italy can be smooth or curly, whole or broken, folded or crumpled. The titles that accompany her are both true and false, glorious or banal, permitting illustrious or vulgar associations.[14]

Ringing the changes on the material base of the cartographic sign in such a manner is like committing the written word to speech, so that it acquires a series of unique voicings, individual combinations of timbres, tones, volumes, intonations, rhythms which it was not thought to have. Although in all other respects their work is dissimilar, Watson and Fabro are united in the challenge their work poses to the highly disembodied nature of the cartographic sign. For Long and Fulton, in so far as the walk is the work, they don't feel called upon to make such a challenge; in so far as their work is a text, however, they seek to embody the walk with the activity of the text.

INSTALLATION AND THE POST-COLONIAL MAP: LOTHAR BAUMGARTEN

If contemporary artists' mapping began as performance art, as an activity that took place outside of the museum which was subsequently (or simultaneously) documented there, it has tended to develop as site-specific installation art, that is, an arrangement of materials and information whose support is neither a canvas nor a pedestal but the literal architecture of the museum. Both Long and Fulton have used the gallery wall as a page for texts whose enlargement enhances the activity of reading. Smithson's 'site' is an installation; he himself pointed out that his trapezoid bins are containers within the container of the art gallery, and his proffered tours to the 'nonsite' insist on the fact that its space is literally continuous with that of the 'site'. Installations map through being site-specific, through indexing their materials and information with those of the museum and its location in physical and social space.

The questions some conceptual art has raised about the neutrality, transparency and objectivity of the map have also been directed at the museum, and its white cube interior decoration. The emergence of per-formance and installation art has been accompanied by a re-negotiation of art's place in the museum. A major positive outcome has been the conversion of disused factories, railroad stations, castles, churches, ware-houses or schools into contemporary art museums. Such conversions do not try to suppress the broad character of the buildings; on the contrary, traces of their former uses are often seen as offering exciting prospects for context-sensitive art practices and viewer experiences, prospects that the traditional purpose-built museum neither delivered nor countenanced.

The Castello di Rivoli is an outstanding example of this tendency. A partially restored eighteenth-century mansion on the outskirts of Turin, it began its present life as a museum of contemporary art in 1984. At its opening exhibition it was hardly possible to view any works exhibited there in isolation, so intrusive was the decor. In a sense all the works became installation art whether intended as that or not. The one explic-itly spite-specific work was *Stanza di Rheinsberg*, by the German artist Lothar Baumgarten. On the walls of what was once the nursery, between the original (if worse for wear) ceiling and baseboard frescoes depicting local domestic animals and gardens of the period, Baumgarten placed the names of South American flora and fauna over a ground of intense blue pigment, broken here and there by a brilliant orange feather. His addi-tions made a map of the Atlantic hemisphere, inscribing back onto the Old World the 'New' that it so presumptuously 'discovered'. Most of these names are obscure, as are the languages to which they belong. The historical givens of the site speak of loss: there are no longer fields or gardens around here, the children are ghosts, their lessons long lost. Baumgarten has prepared a lesson, but there is no one here – except art lovers.

America. Invention, 1993, on the other hand, took place in that New World – 'invention' being italicized as if to say 'not discovered, but

Lothar Baumgarten, *America. Invention*, installation in
the Guggenheim Museum, New York, 1993.

invented' – and as a temporary installation in the apparently purpose-
built Guggenheim Museum in New York. However, far from being
regarded as neutral, it has been considered a difficult if not downright
unfriendly place to exhibit art from the day its doors opened. Its architect, Frank Lloyd Wright, wanted to create an American architecture.
According to Herbert Muschamp, 'If in architecture the American scale
of space had been successfully captured only by the skyscraper and the
highway, the Guggenheim's interior held its own with both by turning the
scale upside down and inward.'[15] The building was already America;
Baumgarten's installation took the opportunity to carry on where Wright
left off, elaborating and correcting the building's meaning as he went. He
decorated the interior of the main rotunda with the names of the native
societies of the Americas. Many of these were familiar, many not; but
standing on the ground floor and gazing around and up at the red and
grey names, it was clear that north was up and south was down: *Innuit* on
the top level, *Cherokee* on the lowest. The names were organized so that
the rotunda was transformed into the interior of a hemisphere. What
about South America? It was there to be discovered, a few names at a time,
on the journey up the spiralling ramp – the southern hemisphere inverted
inside the northern. Moreover, to ascend the ramp was to head south to
where at the top, under the dome, Tierra del Fuego met up with Alaska.
What this folding, this implicating of one hemisphere in another, served
to disturb was the identification of polarity and orientation with hierarchy.
That such identifications are neither necessary nor immutable was very

much the point of his installation. To further confront the viewer with a politics of orientation, Baumgarten inverted every second name so that the experience of reading them, especially while on the ramp, was conceptually, if not to say physically, dizzying.

On the wall of the 'high gallery', an alcove space off the lower end of the ramp, there were lists of past participles drawn from books on New World colonization, arranged in gore shapes derived from the same projection of Martin Waldseemüller that was used by Ruth Watson. Here is one of the lists: 'Seized changed disciplined depoliticised pitied mourned invaded researched tricked devastated'. And here is another: 'Respected beaten infantilised ravaged expelled rejected hunted stigmatized protected defamed'. In this vocabulary of violence, such words as 'respected', 'researched', 'mourned' and 'protected seem all of a piece with 'beaten', 'ravaged' and 'tricked'. If Baumgarten thus captured the Guggenheim for one term of his cartographic metaphor, if he thereby compromised Frank Lloyd Wright's famous building, his hold on it was intentionally temporary and tactical. The artist was in fact aesthetically sensitive to the architect's design; his choice of vendome, a French typeface invented around the time the museum was built, which subtly echoed the combinations of shallow curves with straight lines found throughout Wright's building, was typical of his sympathetic engagement with the building. In sharp contrasting typeface (Haas Grotesk condensed bold), colour and arrangement was the announcement (or was it an offer?) on the main floor of the museum: 'borrowed land for sale'. Here was a bottom line, one which grounded the geographic decoration above on Lenape land, and squeezed the present, constructed 'moment' between the site's alienated past and its necessarily compromised future.

The word-installations Baumgarten presented in *Under Capricorn/ The World Over* were again made up of lists, this time of river names. In Amsterdam (*Watershed*) the rivers of La Gran Sabana region which covers adjacent parts of Venezula, Surinam and Brazil; in Wellington (*From North to South*) New Zealand rivers. The South American names were in Pemon, the New Zealand in Maori. These river works – and there are more like them – show how vestiges of lost languages and cultures, or of those in retreat from dominating cultures, are more likely to survive in the names of rivers because they are not property.

Baumgarten has been installing texts like these, visual meditations on the power of names in mapping, especially as it has affected and still affects the South American continent, for more than twenty years. Like Long, Fulton and Watson, he has developed a large and significant body of work shaped by a wholehearted engagement with the activity of mapping. There are, of course, others of whom the same might be said – David Tremlett, Alfredo Jaar, John Hurrell and Clifford Possum Tjapalt-jarri come to mind. And while today a large number of artists have taken a passing interest in the subject, artists who make up the numbers in the large exhibitions I noted at the outset of this discussion, without the contribution of those for whom the subject has determined the way they make their art and the directions their oeuvres have taken, what contemporary art has to say about it would also be only of passing interest. They are the artists who have most tellingly challenged the transparency of the map, its claims to semiotic and social innocence and objectivity; they are the artists who have most thoroughly questioned the hegemony of the visual implicit in the inscribed map, and have sought to restore to mapping the task of articulating the kinds of spaces it saw fit to silence. And it is they who have looked for an ethics of mapping through their adoption, in the arts of performance and installation, of exemplary manners of use.

References

Denis Cosgrove: Introduction: Mapping Meaning

1 Brian Harley and David Woodward, *History of Cartography* (Chicago and London, 1987–). The journal *Imago Mundi* which began publishing in 1935 celebrated its 50th issue in 1998, with an editorial which notes the breadth of current interest in the history of cartography: *Imago Mundi*, 50 (1998), pp. 7–10.

2 Christian Jacob, 'Toward a Cultural History of Cartography', *Imago Mundi*, 48 (1996), pp. 191–8.

3 Christian Jacob, *L'Empire des cartes: approche théorique de la cartographie à travers l'histoire* (Paris, 1992).

4 Roger Starling, 'Rethinking the Power of Maps: Some Reflections on Paper Landscapes', *Ecumene*, 5 (1998), pp. 105–8; John Gillies, *Shakespeare and the Geography of Difference* (Cambridge, 1994); Richard Helgerson, 'The Land Speaks: Cartography, Chorography and Subversion in Renaissance England', *Representations*, 16 (1986), pp. 51–85.

5 Robert Storr, *Mapping* (New York, 1994).

6 Jacques Lévy, 'A-t-on encore (vraiment) besoin du territoire?', *Espaces et Temps*, 51–2 (1991), pp. 102–42.

7 David Woodward, *Art and Cartography: Six Historical Essays* (Chicago and London, 1987).

8 Kevin Lynch, *The Image of the City* (Cambridge, MA, 1960); Peter Gould and Rodney White, *Mental Maps* (Harmondsworth, 1974).

9 Harley and Woodward, *History of Cartography*, vol. I, 'Introduction' (Chicago, 1987); von Humboldt's use of Jomard's maps is discussed in Claudio Greppi, ed., *Alexander von Humboldt: l'invenzione del Nuovo Mondo. Critica della Conoscenza Geografica* (Florence, 1992), pp. xxxi–liv.

10 A.E. Nordenskiöld, *Periplus* (Stockholm, 1897). Nordenskiöld's work is discussed in Harley and Woodward, *History of Cartography*, vol. I, 'Introduction'; Roberto Almagià reproduced and commented upon a number of Italy's great archival map collections, including those of the Vatican and the Venetian Republic, in the first half of the twentieth century. See, for example, his *Monumenta Italiae cartographica* (Florence, 1929).

11 Jacob, 'Toward a Cultural History', p. 195.

12 Lisa Jardine, *Worldly Goods: A New History of the Renaissance* (London, 1996) challenges this interpretation of Renaissance culture, devoting considerable attention to cartography's role in negotiating fifteenth-century globalism. See also Jerry Brotton, *Trading Territories* (London, 1997); Leslie Cormack, *Charting an Empire: Geography at the English Universities 1580–1620* (Chicago, 1997); and, for a broader critique of the enduring spatial concepts that have been inherited from this historiography and

geographicity, Martin Lewis and Karen Wigen, *The Myth of Continents: A Critique of Metageography* (Berkeley, Los Angeles and London, 1997).

13 J. Brian Harley, 'Re-reading the Maps of the Columbian Encounter', *Annals, Association of American Geographers*, 82 (1992), pp. 522–42.

14 Printed editions of *The Divine Comedy* over the course of the sixteenth century sought to illustrate Antonio Manetti's investigations into the site, shape and size of Dante's cosmography, mapping and measuring the underground spaces of Hell in a series of engravings which progress from the crude woodcuts of the Giuntina edition of 1506 to the carefully mensurated, 'scientific' diagram produced by the Accademia della Crusca in 1595 (see http:/www.nd.edu/~italnet/Dante/text/Hell.html).

15 See, for example, the discussion in Phillip Edwards, *Sea Mark: The Metaphorical Voyage, Spenser to Milton* (Liverpool, 1997), pp. 69–98.

16 Jonathan Sawday, *The Body Emblazoned: Dissection and the Human Body in Renaissance Culture* (London, 1995); idem, 'Self and Selfhood in the Sixteenth Century', in Roy Porter, ed., *Rewriting the Self: Histories from the Renaissance to the Present* (London, 1997), pp. 29–48.

17 L. Benevolo, *The European City*, (Oxford, 1994), pp. 85ff.

18 Ola Söderström, 'Paper Cities: Visual Thinking in Urban Planning', *Ecumene*, 3 (1996), pp. 249–81.

19 The continuing settlement of aboriginal land claims since the Mabo judgement overturned the legal assumption of Australia as *terra nullius*, declared at the time of British colonial appropriation, depends upon acceptance of a wide range of 'cartographic' documents, ranging from conventional Western cadastral and property maps to rock markings and oral mappings attested by group memory through storytelling.

20 Frank Lestringant, *Mapping the Renaissance World: The Geographical Imagination in the Age of Discovery* (Oxford, 1994).

1 *Christian Jacob: Mapping in the Mind: The Earth from Ancient Alexandria*

1 Large-scale maps, too, are never mere reproductions of the visible. They render visible a range of information invisible in the real territory. But their limited spatial extent makes possible an empirical control, through observation, through journeys and so on.

2 As defined by J. B. Harley and D. Woodward, 'Preface', and J. B. Harley, 'The Map and the Development of the History Cartography', in *History of Cartography*, vol. I: *Cartography in Prehistoric, Ancient, and Medieval Europe and the Mediterranean*, ed. J. B. Harley and D. Woodward (Chicago and London, 1987), pp. xv–xxi and 1–42.

3 For a general survey of extant evidence and sources and of the history of ancient Greek cartography in English, see O.A.W. Dilke, *Greek and Roman Maps* (London, 1985); also the contributions of O.A.W. Dilke and G. Aujac in Harley and Woodward, eds, *History of Cartography*, vol. I, pp. 130–279.

4 It is beyond the scope of this paper to give even a general survey of the transmission of Ptolemy's *Geographia*.

5 See C. Jacob, *Géographie et ethnographie en Grèce ancienne* (Paris, 1990); 'Quand les cartes réfléchissent . . .', in *Penser/Figurer: L'espace comme langage dans les sciences sociales, Espaces/Temps*, 62–3 (1996), pp. 36–49; 'Premières géographies. Poésie, cartes et périégèse en Grèce (VIIIe–fin VIe siècle avant J.-C.)', in A. Sérandour, ed., *Des Sumériens aux Romains d'orient: la perception géographique du monde. Espaces et territoires au proche-orient ancien*, Actes de la table ronde du 16 novembre 1996 (Paris, 1997), pp. 157–76.

6 Herodotus, *Histories* V.49–51 and Plutarch, *Life of Nicias* XII.1; *Life of Alcibiades* XVII.3–4 should be used with caution in order to estimate the familiarity of fifth-century BC Greeks with cartography.

7 We should be aware that its form, contents and purposes were different from today. The Alexandrian map-makers excepted, no one in ancient Greece would claim to study 'geography'. There were other words and categories. See F. Prontera, 'Prima di Strabone: materiali per uno studio della geografia antica come genere letterario', in F. Prontera, ed., *Strabone: contributi allo studio della personalità e dell'opera* (Perugia, 1984), pp. 186–259.

8 Such is the case, for instance, with the *Description of the Inhabited Earth* by Dionysius Periegetes (second century AD), a poetical handbook for schoolboys. See C. Jacob, *La description de la terre habitée de Denys d'Alexandrie ou la leçon de géographie* (Paris, 1989).

9 The English reader could use the translation by H. L. Jones (Loeb Classical Library, Harvard and London, 8 volumes).

10 For the cultural frame of Alexandria, see P. M. Fraser, *Ptolemaic Alexandria* (Oxford, 1972, repr. 1998), 3 vols; by the same author, see 'Eratosthenes of Cyrene', *Proceedings of the British Academy*, LVI (1970), pp. 175–207. Eratosthenes' fragments are edited by H. Berger, *Die geographischen Fragmente des Eratosthenes* (Leipzig, 1880; repr. Amsterdam, 1964).

11 See C. H. Kahn, *Anaximander and the Origins of the Greek Cosmology* (New York, 1960).

12 But we know nothing about the way such information was encoded. It was probably only a linear drawing, with shores and main rivers. Nothing suggests that Anaximander wrote a 'geographical treatise' as a 'companion book' to his map.

13 Edited (but not translated) by F. Jacoby, *Die Fragmente der griechischen Historiker* (= FGrHist), I.

14 Diogenes Laertius V.51.

15 This metaphor appears in Strabo's *Geography* II.5.6 C 113, II.5.9 C 116, II.5.14 C 118–19, II.5.18 C 121–2. It is debatable whether this image should be attributed to Eratosthenes. On Alexandria's shape: Strabo XVII.1.8 C 793.

16 See F. Hartog, *The Mirror of Herodotus: The Representation of the Other in the Writing of History*, transl. J. Lloyd (Berkeley, Los Angeles and London, 1988).

17 Strabo II.5.11 C 117 (transl. Jones).

18 For a general discussion of these effects of the Alexandrian Library, see C. Jacob, 'Navigations alexandrines: lire pour écrire', in M. Baratin and C. Jacob, eds, *Le pouvoir des bibliothèques: la mémoire des livres en occident* (Paris, 1996), pp. 47–83.

19 See B. Latour, *Science in Action* (Cambridge, MA, 1983).

20 The standard way of reading books in the ancient Greek world was to read them aloud.

21 Strabo II.1.5 C 69.

22 Probably not, since what we call 'geography' today did not exist as such in Antiquity, but covered several fields, including history and mathematics. It seems Eratosthenes was the first to use the word 'geographia' in relation to map-making.

23 On the bematists, see P. M. Fraser, *Cities of Alexander the Great* (Oxford, 1996), ch. 4. On the scientific activity linked to Alexander's exploration, see L. Bodson, 'Alexander the Great and the Scientific Exploration of the Oriental Part of his Empire: An Overview of the Background, Trends and Results', *Ancient Society*, XXII (1991), pp. 127–38.

24 *Epitome peripli Menippei*, 3 (*Geographi Graeci minores*, I, p. 566).

25 See S. Maqbul Ahmad, 'Cartography of al-Sharif al-Idrisi', in J. B. Harley and D. Woodward, eds, *History of Cartography*, vol. II, Book One: *Cartography in the South Traditional Islamic and South Asian Societies* (Chicago and London, 1992), pp. 156–74.

26 See N. Broc, *La géographie des philosophes, géographes et voyageurs français au*

XVIIIe siècle (Paris, 1975), pp. 31–6; A. Godlewska, 'Traditions, Crisis, and New Paradigms in the Rise of the Modern French Discipline of Geography 1760–1850', *Annals of American Geographers*, LXXIX/2 (1989), pp. 192–213.

27 See J. B. d'Anville, *Traité des mesures itinéraires anciennes et modernes*, 1769, reprinted in: *Oeuvres de d'Anville publiées par M. de Manne*, tome 1er (Paris, 1834).

28 Paris, Bibliothèque Nationale de France, Dépt. des Manuscrits, Fr. Nouv. Acq. 6502-03.

29 This map brought major improvements to the shape and the proportions of Italy.

30 In Strabo's *Geography*, we do not find a single longitude established through an astronomical observation. In Ptolemy's *Geographia*, we find confirmation of the scarcity of such data, and only one example: the measure of the distance between Arbeles and Carthage, calculated during a lunar eclipse: I.4.

31 Eratosthenes' measurement of the circumference of earth is one of the rare examples of such a fully controlled scientific process. Observing the shade inclination of a gnomon in Alexandria when the sun was at the zenith above Syene, and, knowing the distance between Syene and Alexandria, it was possible, through a trigonometrical calculation, to calculate the circumference of earth.

32 A systematic description, such as Strabo's *Geography*, had the same effect.

33 Ptolemy's primary meridian was set at the Canary Islands.

34 For a general survey of ancient Greek philology, see R. Pfeiffer, *History of Classical Scholarship from the Beginnings to the End of the Hellenistic Age* (Oxford, 1968).

35 Polybius III.59.3; XXXIV.5.1–6, B–W (= Strabo II.4.1 C 104); Strabo I.2.1 C 14, II.1.11 C 71; Ptolemy, *Geographia* I.5, I.6.1.

36 Strabo I.2.1 C 14, I.3.1 C 47; Polybius III.59.1.

37 Such criteria in the field of epistemology recall the tragical divide between involuntary fault and voluntary crime: see Aristotle, *Poetics* III.53a, 7. It was also an important category of rhetorics and ethics. See Aristotle, *Rhetoric* I.1374b, 7–11; *idem., Rhet. ad Alex.*, 1427a, 30–43. The criticism of sources thus relied on a more general model of the 'fault through ignorance' as opposed to the intentional offence.

38 See Strabo I.2.12 C 22, I.3.1 C 47, I.3.23 C 62.

39 Polybius IV.42.7. See Ptolemy (quoting Marinus of Tyre), *Geographia* I.11.7: lies about distances.

40 Strabo, I.2.23 C 30. See also Polybius III.58.9.

41 Polybius III.38.3.

42 Strabo, I.4.3 C 63, II.4.1–2 C 104.

43 See G. E. Broche, *Pythéas le massaliote* (Marseille, 1936); H. J. Mette, *Pytheas von Massalia* (Berlin, 1952); about the modern tradition, see M. Mund-Dopchie, 'La survie littéraire de la Thulé de Pythéas: un exemple de la permanence de schémas antiques dans la culture européenne', *L'Antiquité Classique*, LIX (1990), pp. 79–97; 'L'"Ultima Thule" de Pythéas dans les textes de la Renaissance et du XVIIe siècle: la réalité et le rêve', *Humanistica Lovaniensia. Journal of Neo-Latin Studies*, XLI (1992), pp. 134–58.

44 Strabo II.1.2–5 C 68–9.

45 *Ibid*. I.1.10 C 6–7, I.2.3 C 5–6, I.2.15 C 24.

46 *Ibid*. I.2.7-8 C 18–19, I.2.11 C 21–2.

47 See the discussion in Strabo I.2.11 C 21–I.2.20 C 27.

48 See Jacob, *La description de la terre*.

49 Dionysius Periegetes, *Description of the Earth*, vv. 170–71.

50 *Ekphrasis* was a key feature of Imperial Greek culture. Handbooks of rhetoric explained the technical principles of this kind of description, while such writers as Philostratus, Lucianus, Ps.-Longinus and Pausanias provide us with vivid examples of such developments.

2 *Alessandro Scafi: Mapping Eden: Cartographies of the Earthly Paradise*

* This essay is part of a forthcoming book on the mapping of Paradise for British
   Library Publications. I am grateful to Catherine Delano-Smith and Jill Kraye for their
   help and advice. I am also thankful to Evelyn Edson, David Fletcher, Moshe Idel, Meir
   Shahar and David Woodward for their insights. I finally wish to express my gratitude
   to the following bodies for their financial support: Accademia Nazionale dei Lincei,
   British Academy, Warburg Institute, Università Cattolica di Milano, Mishkenot
   Sha'ananim of Jerusalem.

1 J. B. Harley and D. Woodward, eds, *History of Cartography* (Chicago, 1987), vol. 1, p.
   xvi.

2 D. F. McKenzie, *Bibliography and the Sociology of Text*, The Panizzi Lectures 1985
   (London, 1986), p. 34.

3 Cosmas's map appears in the three surviving manuscripts of his *Christian
   Topography*: Rome, Biblioteca Apostolica Vaticana, MS Greek 699 (ninth century,
   Costantinople); St Catherine's of Mt Sinai, MS Greek 1186 (eleventh century,
   Cappadocia); Florence, Biblioteca Laurenziana, Plut. IX.28 (eleventh century, Mt
   Athos). See W. Wolska-Conus, *Cosmas Indicopleustès: topographie chrétienne* (Paris,
   1968); J. W. McCrindle, *The Christian Topography of Cosmas, an Egyptian Monk*
   (London 1987); D. Woodward, 'Medieval *Mappaemundi*', in Harley and Woodward,
   eds, *The History of Cartography*, vol. 1, pp. 261–3 (reproduction p. 262); C. R. Beazley,
   Dawn of Modern Geography (London, 1987), vol. 1, pp. 273–303; E. Edson, *Mapping
   Time and Space: How Medieval Map-makers Viewed their World* (London, 1997), pp.
   145–9.

4 *The Creation of the World and the Expulsion from the Earthly Paradise*, now in the
   Metropolitan Museum, New York, dated 1445. See J. Pope-Hennessy, *Giovanni di
   Paolo* (New York, 1988), pp. 14–17; L. Baránsky-Jób, 'The Problems and Meaning of
   Giovanni di Paolo's Expulsion from Paradise', *Marsyas*, VIII (1957–9), pp. 1–6; L. S.
   Dixon, 'Giovanni di Paolo's Cosmology', *Art Bulletin*, LXVI/4 (December 1985), pp.
   604–61; K. Lippincott, 'Giovanni di Paolo's "Creation of the World" and the Tradition
   of the "Thera Mundi" in Late Medieval and Renaissance Art', *Burlington Magazine*,
   CXXXII/1048 (July 1990), pp. 460–68.

5 The most important version of this story is a brief text in Latin, *Alexandri Magni iter
   ad Paradisum*. See L. P. G. Peckham and M. S. La Du, *La Prise de Defur and Le Voyage
   d'Alexandre au Paradis Terrestre* (Princeton, 1935), pp. xli–xlviii, and D. J. A. Ross,
   Alexander Historiatus (Frankfurt am Main, 1988), pp. 35–6.

6 For example, both the Septuagint, the Greek version available in the third century BC
   in Egypt for Greek-speaking Jews, and the *Vetus latina*, a version derived from fragmentary early Latin translations, stated that Paradise was planted by God in the East
   (Genesis 2.8).

7 See, for example, Flavius Josephus, *Jewish Antiquities* I.37–9, ed. T. E. Page *et al.*,
   Loeb Classical Library (London, 1930), vol. IV, pp. 18–21.

8 The full complexity of the theological issues involved only emerges from a rigorous
   study of the individual authors. Here suffice it to say that after a period of debate
   between the allegorical and the literal interpretation of the text, Augustine favoured
   the interpretation of the Garden of Eden as both material fact and spiritual allegory,
   and that all later exegetes, including Isidore of Seville, Bede, Rabanus Maurus, Peter
   Lombard and Thomas Aquinas, followed his view.

9 Bede, *Hexaemeron sive libri quatuor in principium Genesis usque ad nativitatem
   Isaac et electionem Ismaelis*, ed. C. W. Jones, Corpus Christianorum Series Latina,
   CXVIIIa (Turnhout, 1967), I.1449–50, p. 46: 'nos tamen locum hunc fuisse et esse
   terrenum dubitare non licet'.

10 A. Korzybski, *Science and Sanity*, 4th edition (Lakeville, CN, 1958), p. 750.

11 For a complete list of the manuscripts containing Beatus' commentary, see A. M. Mundo and M. Sanchez Mariana, *El comentario de Beato al Apocalipsis: catálogo de los códices* (Madrid, 1976); for the illustrations, see J. Williams, *The Illustrated Beatus: A Corpus of Illustrations of the Commentary on the Apocalypse* (London, 1994), 3 vols, with 2 more to come.

12 Three world maps, all signed by Giovanni Leardo and dated respectively 1442, 1448 and 1452, survive: they are kept in the Biblioteca Civica of Verona; the Biblioteca Civica Bertoliana of Vicenza; the American Geographical Society Collection of the University of Wisconsin, Milwaukee. See Woodward, 'Medieval *Mappaemundi*', pp. 316–17 (plate 20).

13 See A. Graf, *Miti, leggende e superstizioni del medio evo* (Florence and Rome, 1892), vol. I, pp. 87–8, and H. R. Patch, *The Other World, According to Descriptions in Medieval Literature* (Cambridge, MA, 1950), pp. 165–6.

14 These concepts are developed by D. Harrison, *Medieval Space: The Extent of Microspatial Knowledge in Western Europe during the Middle Ages* (Lund, 1996).

15 *Ibid.*, p. 2.

16 *Ibid.*, p. 9.

17 For example, Ephrem the Syrian, whom I shall mention later. See note 26.

18 M. Shahar, in his paper 'Blissful Realms in Medieval China', presented at the Inaugural Conference of the Mishkenot Encounters for Religion and Culture, *Visions of Paradise* (Jerusalem, 27 April–3 May 1997, Acts forthcoming), discusses the relativity of space and time and the immanence and transcendence of Chinese medieval Paradise, qualities which, in my view, may be found also in the Western Christian tradition.

19 D. Cosgrove, *Geography and Vision*, an Inaugural Lecture presented at Royal Holloway, University of London (Egham, Surrey, 1996).

20 Augustine, *De Genesi ad litteram*, I–VIII, Patrologia Latina XXXIV, ed. J. P. Migne (Paris, 1887), cols 247–394.

21 On the centre model and the boundary model see Harrison, *Medieval Space*, pp. 13–14. As Harrison points out, notions of taboo and of invisible power were associated in the Middle Ages with the idea of liminality, and 'the most conspicuous part of the centre was often the area where it met the periphery'. Indeed, as Harrison mentions, Lagazzi, *Segni sulla terra: determinazioni dei confini e percezione dello spazio nell'alto medioevo* (Bologna, 1991), pp. 31–43 and 87–8, noted that in early medieval Italy a space within boundaries is defined just as an area developing around a centre (in the case he studied, a monastery).

22 I am grateful to Catherine Delano-Smith and David Fletcher for having discussed with me the notion of boundary in cartography.

23 Bede, *Hexaemeron* I.1579–91, p. 50.

24 The standard Latin version of the Bible, the Vulgate, compiled by St Jerome at the end of the fourth century, has *versatilem*.

25 *Biblia latina cum glossa ordinaria*, facsimile of the *editio princeps* ... (Strasbourg, 1480/81), ed. M. T. Gibson and K. Fröhlich, vol. I (Turnhout, 1992), p. 30.

26 Ephrem the Syrian, *Hymns on Paradise*, ed. S. Brock (Crestwood, NY, 1990), I.4, p. 78.

27 *Ibid.*

28 The writings of Ephrem are a very good example of the intellectual and theological complexities involved in the Paradise question. See S. Brock, 'Introduction' to Ephrem the Syrian, *Hymns on Paradise*, pp. 49–74.

29 For reproductions of Giovanni di Paolo's painting, see note 4; for Cosmos, see note 3; a reproducton of the Osma map (Burgo de Osma, *Arch. de la Catedral*, Cod. 1, fols 34v–35) can be found in Williams, *The Illustrated Beatus*, I, p. 51.

30 London, British Library, Add. MS 28261, fol. 9r. On the Psalter map, see Edson, *Mapping Time and Space*, pp. 135–7 (plate VI).

31 On the wall map of Hereford Cathedral, see P.D.A. Harvey, *Mappa Mundi: The Hereford World Map* (London, 1996) and Edson, *Mapping Time and Space*, pp. 139–44 (plates VII–X).

32 See M. F. de Barros e Sousa, Viscont of Santarém, *Atlas composé de mappemondes, de portulans et de cartes hydrographiques et historiques depuis le VIe jusqu'au XVIIIe siècle* (Paris, 1849), pl. XXXVIII; and *Essai sur l'histoire de la cosmographie et de la cartographie pendant le Moyen-Age et sur le progrès de la géographie après les grandes découvertes du XVe siècle*, vol. III (Paris, 1852), p. 214.

33 Rome, Biblioteca Apostolica Vaticana, Borgiano XVI (gallerie); see R. Almagià, *Monumenta cartographica vaticana*, vol. I (Vatican City, 1944), pp. 27–9 (reproduction in plate XI) and M. Destombes, ed., *Mappamondes, AD 1200–1500: catalogue préparé par la Commission des Cartes Anciennes de l'Union Géographique Internationale* (Amsterdam, 1964), pp. 239–41.

34 Rome, Biblioteca Apostolica Vaticana, Cod. Palat. Lat. 1362 b; see Almagià, *Monumenta cartographica vaticana*, vol. I, pp. 30–31 (reproduction in plate XII) and Destombes, *Mappamondes*, pp. 212–14.

35 See L. Bagrow and R. A. Skelton, *History of Cartography* (London, 1964), pp. 100–101 (reproduction in plate LI).

36 *Ibid.*, pp. 99–100, with reproduction.

37 See note 12.

38 Harrison, *Medieval Space*, p. 9.

39 P. D. A. Harvey, *Medieval Maps* (London, 1991); D. Woodward, 'Reality, Symbolism, Time, and Space in Medieval World Maps', *Annals of the Association of American Geographers*, LXXV (1985), pp. 510–21; idem, 'Medieval *Mappaemundi*', pp. 288–90, 326–30; Edson, *Mapping Time and Space*.

40 The Ebstorf map, once in Hannover, was destroyed in an air raid in 1943. A reproduction may be found in W. Rosien, *Die Ebstorfer Weltkarte* (Hannover, 1952); Woodward, 'Medieval *Mappaemundi*', fig. 18.19; and Bagrow and Skelton, *History of Cartography*, plate XXII, E. See Woodward, 'Medieval *Mappaemundi*', pp. 307–9.

41 Rosien, *Die Ebstorfer Weltkarte*, p. 80: 'Que scilicet non parvam prestat legentibus utilitatem, viantibus directionem rerumque viarum gratissime speculationis directionem'. Woodward, 'Medieval *Mappaemundi*', p. 309: 'It can be seen that [this work] is of no small utility to its readers, giving directions for travellers, and the things on the way that most pleasantly delight the eye.'

42 See Bagrow and Skelton, *History of Cartography*, plate XXII.

43 Already Philo (c. 20 BC – c. AD 50), a Jewish thinker and exegete from Alexandria, speculated that 'perhaps Paradise is in some distant place far from our inhabited world, and has a river flowing under the earth': *Questions and Answers on Genesis* I.12, ed. R. Marcus, Loeb Classical Library (London, 1953), supplement I, p. 8. This view was later confirmed by Augustine (*De Genesi ad litteram* VIII.7.14, PL XXXIV, col. 378) and held throughout the Middle Ages.

44 R. W. Shirley, *The Mapping of the World: Early Printed World Maps 1472–1700*, 3rd edition (London, 1993).

45 *Ibid.*, pp. 64–5. Benedetto Bordone, *Libro ... de tutte l'isole del mondo* (Venice, 1528), Book 2, XLII v.

46 Shirley, *The Mapping of the World*, pp. 74–5. The attribution to Holbein is not beyond question.

47 Gabriel Biel, *Collectorium circa quattuor libros sententiarum*, ed. W. Werbeck and U. Hohman, vol. II (Tübingen, 1984), d. 17, q. 2, pp. 404–5; John Duns Scotus, *Quaestiones in libros II sententiarium*, *Opera Omnia*, vol. VII (Lyons, 1639), p. 789.

48 Fred Plaut discusses the disappearance of Paradise from medieval maps in 'General Gordon's Map of Paradise', *Encounter* (June/July 1982), pp. 20–32 and 'Where is Paradise? The Mapping of a Myth', *Map Collector*, 29 (December 1984), pp. 2–7. See also J. Delumeau, *Une histoire du paradis: le jardin des délices* (Paris, 1992), pp. 81–97.

49 Woodward, 'Medieval *Mappaemundi*', pp. 314–18 describes this period as 'transitional'.

50 See note 12.

51 See note 31.

52 See note 33.

53 See Destombes, *Mappamondes*, pp. 217–21, reproduction in plate W.

54 See note 4.

55 See Destombes, *Mappamondes*, pp. 205–7, reproduction in plate Q.

56 On Fra Mauro's map, now in the Biblioteca Nazionale Marciana, Venice, see Almagià, *Monumenta cartographica vaticana*, vol. i, pp. 32–40; T. Gasparrini Leporace, *Il mappamondo di Fra Mauro* (Rome, 1956); I. Wojciech, 'Entre l'espace ptolémaïque et l'empirie: les cartes de Fra Mauro', *Médiévales*, xviii (1990), pp. 53–68; Destombes, *Mappamondes*, pp. 223–6; Woodward, 'Medieval *Mappaemundi*', pp. 286–370. See also my forthcoming entry in *Medieval Trade, Travel, and Exploration: An Encyclopaedia*, to be published by Garland, and my article 'Il paradiso terrestre di Fra Mauro', *Storia dell'Arte*, 73–4 (January–June 1999), pp. 219–27.

57 The text of the rubric was transcribed by Gasparrini Leporace: *Il Mappamondo di Fra Mauro*, Table XXXVII C, p. 22: 'molton remoto de la habitation e cognition humana'.

58 See P. D. Harvey, *Medieval Maps*, p. 21; C. Delano-Smith, 'The Shape of England: English *Mappaemundi* and Maps of England before c. 1540', in *La cartografia anglesa/English Cartography*, cycle of lectures on the history of cartography (Barcelona, 1997), pp. 57–9.

59 See C. Jacob, 'Il faut qu'une carte soit ouverte ou fermée: le tracé conjectural', *Revue de la Bibliothèque Nationale*, xlv (1992), pp. 35–40.

60 See D. Woodward, 'The Image of the Spherical Earth', *Yale Architectural Journal*, xxv (1991), pp. 4–15.

61 See T. J. Reiss, *Knowledge, Discovery, and Imagination in Early Modern Europe: The Rise of Aesthetic Rationalism* (Cambridge and New York, 1997), and A. W. Crosby, *The Measure of Reality: Quantification and Western Society, 1250–1600* (Cambridge, 1997).

62 M. Luther, *Lectures on Genesis Chapters 1–5 Luther's Works*, vol. i, ed. J. Pelikan (St Louis, MO, 1958), pp. 87–91, 97–101.

63 C. Jane, ed., *Select Documents Illustrating the Four Voyages of Columbus*, vol. ii (London, 1933), p. 38.

64 C. Delano-Smith and E. M. Ingram, *Maps in Bibles: 1500–1600* (Geneva, 1991); E. Ingram, 'Maps as Readers' Aids: Maps and Plans in Geneva Bibles', *Imago Mundi*, xlvi (1993), pp. 29–44.

65 Delano-Smith and Ingram, *Maps in Bibles*, pp. 2–11, 19.

66 Ingram, 'Maps as Readers' Aids', pp. 32–3.

67 J. Hopkinson, *Synopsis paradisi, sive paradisi descriptio, ex variis . . . scriptoribus desumpta, cum chorographica ... tabula* (Leiden, 1593).

68 P. D. Huet, *Traité de la situation du paradis terrestre* (Paris, 1691); *A Treatise of the Situation of Paradise . . . Translated from the French Original* [by T. Gale] (London, 1694).

3 *Jerry Brotton: Terrestrial Globalism: Mapping the Globe in Early Modern Europe*

1 Benedict Anderson, *Imagined Communities: Reflections on the Origin and Spread of Nationalism* (London, 1983; 2nd edn 1991), p. xiv. See also pp. 170–78.

2 David Harvey, *The Condition of Postmodernity: An Enquiry into the Origins of Cultural Change* (Oxford, 1990), p. 240.

3 *Ibid.*, p. 241.

4 Arjun Appadurai, 'Disjuncture and Difference in the Global Cultural Economy', *Public Culture*, 2 (1990), pp. 1–24.

5 Michael J. Shapiro, 'Moral Geographies and the Ethics of Post-sovereignty', *Public Culture*, 6 (1994), pp. 479–502 (479).

6 Paul Virilio, *The Lost Dimension*, trans. Daniel Moshenberg (New York, 1991), p. 30. Virilio's text was first published in French in 1984 under the title *L'espace critique*.

7 *Ibid.*, p. 30.

8 Appadurai, 'Disjuncture and Difference', p. 20.

9 See Fredric Jameson, 'Postmodernism, or the Cultural Logic of Late Capitalism', *New Left Review*, 146 (1984), pp. 53–92.

10 On T-O and mappaemundi, see Jonathan Lanman, 'The Religious Symbolism of the T in T-O Maps', *Cartographica*, XVIII/4 (1991), pp. 18–22, and David Woodward, 'Medieval Mappaemundi', in J. B. Harley and D. Woodward, eds, *Cartography in Prehistoric, Ancient, and Medieval Europe and the Mediterranean*, vol. I of *History of Cartography* (Chicago, 1987), pp. 286–370.

11 See David Woodward, 'Maps and the Rationalization of Geographic Space', in Jay Levenson, ed., *Circa 1492: Art in the Age of Exploration* (New Haven, 1991), pp. 83–8.

12 On the transmission of Ptolemy's text, see O.A.W. Dilke, 'Cartography in the Byzantine Empire', in J. B. Harley and D. Woodward, eds, *Cartography in Prehistoric, Ancient, and Medieval Europe and the Mediterranean*, vol. I of *History of Cartography* (Chicago, 1987), pp. 258–75.

13 Woodward, 'Maps and Rationalization', pp. 84–5.

14 *Ibid.*, p. 84.

15 On Ptolemy's third projection, See Woodward, 'Maps and Rationalization', p. 84. Ptolemy was not alone in offering mathematical speculation on the calculations required to create terrestrial globes. Strabo's *Geographia* also contained references to the creation of giant terrestrial globes. See Peter van der Krogt, *Globi Neerlandici: The Production of Globes in the Low Countries* (Utrecht, 1993), p. 19. The best study of Behaim's globe remains E. G. Ravenstein, *Martin Behaim: His Life and his Globe* (London, 1908).

16 Regiomontanus' work on spherical trigonometry significantly influenced Copernicus. See Lisa Jardine, *Worldly Goods: A New History of the Renaissance* (London, 1996), pp. 350–52.

17 Mary Helms, 'Essay on Objects: Interpretations of Distance Made Tangible', in Stuart B. Schwartz, ed., *Implicit Understandings: Observing, Reporting, and Reflecting on the Encounters Between Europeans and Other Peoples in the Early Modern Era* (Cambridge, 1994), pp. 355–77 (356).

18 On the adoption of the armillary sphere as a royal heraldic device and its intimate relation to Manuel's title, see Levenson, ed., *Circa 1492*, pp. 145–6.

19 Mary Helms, *Ulysses' Sail: An Ethnographic Odyssey of Power, Knowledge, and Geographical Distance* (Princeton, 1988), p. 5.

20 On Portuguese comparisons of their own seaborne empire with that of the Roman empire, see Patricia Seed's excellent *Ceremonies of Possession: Europe's Conquest of the New World 1492–1640* (Cambridge, 1995), pp. 180–83.

21 In 1525 the Portuguese king João III commissioned a set of three tapestries from the

workshop of Bernard van Orley. The tapestries, entitled *The Spheres*, depicted the celestial, armillary and terrestrial spheres, with the final tapestry depicting João with his new wife presiding over a terrestrial globe studded with flags defining the purported extent of Portuguese maritime expansion throughout Africa and Asia. For an analysis of the significance of the tapestries see my *Trading Territories: Mapping the Early Modern World* (London, 1997), ch. 1.

22 Cited in E. H. Blair and J. A. Robertson, eds, *The Philippine Islands, 1493–1803*, vol. 1 (Cleveland, 1903), p. 134. Subsequent maps of the period such as the anonymous 'Cantino Planisphere' (c. 1502) clearly depict the line of division agreed between the two crowns.

23 Cited in E. P. Goldschmidt, 'Not in Harrisse', in *Essays Honoring Lawrence C. Wroth* (Maine, 1951), pp. 129–41 (135–6).

24 Cited in van der Krogt, *Globi Neerlandici*, p. 28.

25 *Ibid.*

26 On these printed gores, see Hans Wolf, ed., *America: Early Maps of the New World* (Munich, 1992), pp. 111–26; Rodney Shirley, *The Mapping of the World: Early Printed Maps, 1472–1700* (London, 1983), p. 29; and van der Krogt, *Globi Neerlandici*, pp. 27–9.

27 See Wolf, ed., *America*, p. 116.

28 See van der Krogt, *Globi Neerlandici*, p. 28; Edward Luther Stevenson, *Celestial and Terrestrial Globes*, vol. 1 (New Haven, 1921), pp. 72–3.

29 See Henry Harrisse, *The Discovery of North America* (London, 1892), pp. 470–71; Stevenson, *Globes*, pp. 31–2.

30 See Stevenson, *Globes*, p. 74, figs 36–7.

31 See van der Krogt, *Globi Neerlandici*, pp. 30–31; Shirley, *The Mapping of the World*, p. 45. The manual was entitled *A very clear description of the whole world, with many useful cosmographic elements and a new and more accurate form of our Europe than earlier*. Like Behaim, Schöner drew heavily on Regiomontanus' work on trigonometry (van der Krogt, *Globi Neerlandici*, p. 31).

32 Cited in Stevenson, *Globes*, p. 85. Schöner's 1515 globe was granted an imperial charter by the Habsburg emperor Maximilian I (van der Krogt, *Globi Neerlandici*, p. 31).

33 For a more detailed account of the dispute over the Moluccas, see Brotton, *Trading Territories*, ch. 4.

34 Maximilianus Transylvanus, *De Moluccis insulis* (1523), cited in *First Voyage Around the World by Antonio Pigafetta and 'De Moluccis Insulis' by Maximilianus Transylvanus*, ed. and trans. Carlos Quirino (Manila, 1969), pp. 112–13.

35 Cited in Samuel Eliot Morison, *The European Discovery of America: The Southern Voyages, 1492–1616* (Oxford, 1974), p. 324. Marcel Destombes has also noted that many of the supposed charts used by Magellan are referred to as 'poma e carta' and 'Plano esferico'. Whilst both appear to suggest charts in the traditional sense, the spherical description indicates that these references may have been to terrestrial globes, as well as charts drawn on a circular projection. See Marcel Destombes, 'The Chart of Magellan', *Imago Mundi*, 12 (1955), pp. 65–79.

36 For further details of the voyage see R. A. Skelton, ed., *Magellan's Voyage: A Narrative Account of the First Circumnavigation* (New York, 1969).

37 Although the Venetian cartographer Battista Agnese also produced a series of planispheres on an oval projection which traced the route of Magellan's voyage in the 1530s.

38 Cited in van der Krogt, *Globi Neerlandici*, p. 32.

39 Cited in Blair and Robertson, eds, *The Philippine Islands*, p. 177.

40 *Ibid.*, p. 177.

41 *Ibid.*, p. 185.

42 Robert Thorne, 'A Declaration of the Indies', in Richard Hakluyt, *Divers Voyages Touching America* (London, 1582), sig. c3.

43 *Ibid.*, sig. cɪ.

44 On Monachus' text see van der Krogt, *Globi Neerlandici*, pp. 42–4 and Shirley, *The Mapping of the World*, p. 61. Like Thorne, Monachus places the Moluccas within the western Castilian sphere, another piece of imaginative geography, as possession of the islands was not firmly established until the terms of the Treaty of Saragossa in 1529, under which the Portuguese, and not the Castilian crown, took possession of the islands. On the resolution of the dispute over the islands, see Brotton, *Trading Territories*, pp. 135–8.

45 Cited in van der Krogt, *Globi Neerlandici*, p. 76.

46 On Frisius and his terrestrial globe of 1535, see van der Krogt, *Globi Neerlandici*, pp. 48–54, and Robert Haardt, 'The Globe of Gemma Frisius', *Imago Mundi*, 11 (1952), pp. 109–10.

47 For what still remains one of the most comprehensive studies of the terrestrial globe in Holbein's painting, see Mary F. S. Hervey, *Holbein's Ambassadors: The Picture and the Men. An Historical Study* (London, 1900), pp. 210–18.

48 See Anthony Grafton and Lisa Jardine, '"Studied for Action": How Gabriel Harvey Read his Livy', *Past and Present*, 129 (1990), pp. 30–78.

49 Clearly such geographical speculation was ultimately translated into the subsequent exercise of European colonial power in both the Old World and the New World, but the exercise of such colonial authority was historically contingent upon the prior ability to rehearse such authority via earlier more speculative forms of political discourse, exemplified by the investments made in geography throughout the sixteenth century. For an analogous argument concerning the rehearsal of power in later Elizabethan theatre and culture, see Stephen Mullaney, 'Strange Things, Gross Terms, Curious Customs: The Rehearsal of Cultures in the Late Renaissance', in Stephen Greenblatt, ed., *Representing the English Renaissance* (Berkeley, 1988), pp. 65–92.

50 On this perception of the space of the modern nation-state see the highly influential discussion in Anderson, *Imagined Communities*, pp. 170–78.

51 A particularly significant example of the struggle over old and new perceptions of terrestrial space can be seen in the complex and painstaking mapping of France under the reign of Louis XIV from the 1660s onwards. See Lloyd Brown, *The Story of Maps* (New York, 1949), pp. 241–55, and David Turnbull, 'Cartography and Science in Early Modern Europe: Mapping the Construction of Knowledge Spaces', *Imago Mundi*, 48 (1996), pp. 5–24.

52 Virilio, *The Lost Dimension*, p. 34.

4 Lucia Nuti: Mapping Places: Chorography and Vision in the Renaissance

1 Peter Apian, *Cosmographicus liber* (Antwerp, 1533).

2 Claudius Ptolemaeus, *Geographia*, ed. and transl. by W. Pirckeimer (Basel, 1552).

3 *De incertitudine et vanitate scientiarum* (London, 1569), as quoted by John B. Harley, 'Meaning and Ambiguity in Tudor Cartography', in S. Tyacke, ed., *English Map Making* (London, 1980), p. 27.

4 Georg Braun referred to his townbook as a work of chorography in Georg Braun and Franz Hogenberg, *Civitates orbis terrarum*, preface to lib. ɪɪɪ (Cologne, 1581). Gierolamo Ruscelli, referring possibly to the same townbook, argued: 'As for chorography, that is concerned with giving lifelike drawings and paintings of towns in their true figure and form . . .' See Claudius Ptolemaeus, *Geographia*, ed. G. Ruscelli (Venice, 1574), p. 9. William Cuningham, in *The Cosmographical Glasse* (London, 1559), provides a perspective plan of the town of Norwich as a figurative example of his explanation of chorography. On the use of the term chorography in the sixteenth century, see also Denis Cosgrove, 'Mapping New Worlds: Culture and Cartography in

Sixteenth-Century Venice', *Imago Mundi*, XLIV (1992), pp. 65–89; Thomas Frangenberg, 'Chorographies of Florence: The Use of City Views and City Plans in the Sixteenth Century', *Imago Mundi*, XLVI (1994), pp. 41, 52–6; David Woodward, *Maps as Prints in the Italian Renaissance: Makers, Distributors and Consumers* (London, 1996), pp. 5–13.

5 Cristoforo Sorte thus describes his chorography 'of the town of Verona and its district'. See 'Osservazioni sulla pittura', in P. Barocchi, ed., *Trattati d'arte del cinquecento* (Bari, 1960), I, p. 277. In the same way Egnazio Danti refers to his father's chorography of Perugia and its district, a plan of the whole, and a detailed depiction of the sites. According to Danti, it differs from topography, that is a written description of particular sites. See Egnazio Danti, *Le scienze matematiche ridotte in tavole* (Bologna, 1577), tab. XXXIII, pp. 44–5.

6 Leon Battista Alberti, *The Architecture in Ten Books*, translated by J. Leoni (London, 1726), II, ch. 1, p. 11.

7 Filarete, *Trattato di architettura*, ed. A. M. Finoli and L. Grassi (Milan, 1972), pp. 434–5.

8 Renato Bonelli, 'Lettera a Leone X', in A. Bruschi, ed., *Scritti rinascimentali di architettura*, (Milan, 1978), pp. 480–81. The subject of this famous letter is the project for 'putting into drawing' ancient Rome. See also Howard Burns and Arnold Nesselrath, 'La costruzione di Roma antica', in C. L. Frommel, S. Ray and M. Tafuri, eds, *Raffaello architetto* (Milan, 1984), p. 437.

9 Alberti, *Architecture*, I, ch. 9, p.20.

10 Leon Battista Alberti, 'Descriptio urbis Romae', in G. Mancini, ed., *Opera inedita et pauca separatim impressa* (Florence, 1890). The most complete discussion is in Luigi Vagnetti, 'La "Descriptio urbis Romae", uno scritto poco noto di L. B. Alberti (contributo alla storia del rilevamento architettonico e topografico)', *Quaderni dell'Istituto di Elementi di Architettura e Rilievo dei Monumenti*, University of Genoa, Faculty of Architecture, 1, October 1968, pp. 23–59. See also Joan Gadol, *Leon Battista Alberti: Universal Man of the Early Renaissance* (Chicago and London, 1969).

11 See note 8.

12 The plan is in Windsor, RL n. 12284. Much has been written about the plan: the connection with Raphael was first described in Carlo Pedretti, *A Chronology of Leonardo da Vinci's Architectural Studies after 1500* (Geneva, 1962), pp. 157–71; the most thorough analysis of the mode of representation is in John Pinto, 'Origins and Development of the Ichnographic City Plan', *Journal of the Society of Architectural Historians*, XXXV (1976), pp. 35–50; an accurate discussion of the plan's history and related attribution problems is in Pietro C. Marani, 'La mappa di Imola di Leonardo', in *Il Codice Hammer e la mappa di Imola presentati da Carlo Pedretti: arte e scienza a Bologna in Emilia e Romagna nel primo Cinquecento* (Florence, 1985), pp. 140–41.

13 A 'circle that circumscribes the picture', as Alberti wrote (*Descriptio*, p. 37).

14 'Finally, to draw the whole properly, you need a paper shaped like a compass and divided according to the same degrees of the winds': Raphael on the projected drawing of Rome. See Bonelli, 'Lettera', p. 479.

15 On the choice of an abstract language in cartography see Franco Farinelli, 'Dallo spazio bianco allo spazio astratto: la logica cartografica', in *Paesaggio immagine e realtà* (Milan, 1981), pp. 199–207; Catherine Bousquet-Bressolier, 'De la "peinture géométrale" à la carte topographique: évolution de l'héritage classique au cours du XVIIIe siècle', in C. Bousquet-Bressolier, ed., *L'oeil du cartographe et la représentation géographique du moyen âge à nos jours* (Paris, 1995), pp. 93–105.

16 On the development of architectural drawing in the Renaissance see Christoph L. Frommel, 'Sulla nascita del disegno architettonico', in Henry Millon and Vittorio

Magnago Lampugnani, eds, *Rinascimento: da Brunelleschi a Michelangelo: la rapp-resentazione dell'architettura* (Milan, 1994), pp. 101–21.

17 William Leybourn, *The Compleat Surveyor* (London, 1653); see also William Folkingham, *Feudigraphia* (London, 1610), ch. 5, p. 54; Raleigh A. Skelton, *Decorative Printed Maps* (London, 1952), pp. 10–11, comments on the use of pictorial language in Renaissance maps.

18 Sorte, 'Osservazioni', p. 277 (my translation).

19 The anonymous text in the cartouche of the view of Genoa by Anton van den Wyngaerde is one of many examples. See Lucia Nuti, 'The Perspective Plan in the Sixteenth Century: The Invention of a Representational Language', *Art Bulletin*, LXXVI (1994), p. 119.

20 In 1574 Edoardus Bredin put these words beside the signature in his *Vray portrait de la ville de Dijon*. See Jean Boutier, *Du plan cavalier au plan geometrique: les muta-tions de la cartographie urbaine en l'Europe occidentale du XVI–XVIIIe siècle*, paper read at the Colloque du groupe de travail international en histoire urbaine, Paris, Maison des Science de l'Homme, November 1984, p. 7.

21 Georg Braun and Franz Hogenberg, *Civitates orbis terrarum* (Cologne, 1572), preface to Lib. I.

22 The most stimulating discussion about observational concerns in the visual arts and the sciences in Renaissance Europe is in Martin Kemp, *The Science of Art* (New Haven and London, 1990).

23 Francesco Negri Arnoldi, 'Tecnica e scienza', in *Storia dell'arte italiana, IV: Ricerche spaziali e tecnologie* (Turin, 1980), pp. 103–224, esp. the whole of paragraph 8.

24 Giorgio Vasari, *Le vite de' più eccellenti pittori scultori e architettori*, in G. Milanesi, ed., Le opere (Florence, 1906), VIII, pp. 173–4.

25 Jorgen Wadum, 'Vermeer and Spatial Illusion', in *The Scholarly World of Vermeer* (The Hague and Zwolle, 1996), p. 38.

26 Robert Ruurs, 'Pieter Saenredam: zijn boekenbezit en zijn relatie met der landmeter Pieter Wils', *Oud Holland*, XCVII (1983), pp. 59–68.

27 Danti, *Le scienze matematiche*, tab. XXXIII, pp. 44–5. The translation is by Frangenberg, in 'Chorographies of Florence', pp. 55–6.

28 A list of the most important books is given in Nuti, 'The Perspective Plan', p. 121.

29 Leybourn, *Compleat Surveyer*, ch. 47.

30 Rich imagery is displayed and commented on in Marica Milanesi, ed., *L'Europa delle carte: dal XV al XIX secolo, autoritratti di un continente* (Milan, 1990).

31 Skelton, *Decorative Printed Maps*, p. 12.

32 Sorte, 'Osservazioni', pp. 275–6.

33 Folkingham, *Feudigraphia*, p. 57.

34 Christian Jacob, *L'empire des cartes: approche théorique de la cartographie à travers l'histoire* (Paris, 1992), p. 390.

35 A wide discussion on oblique views and other modes of representation is in Lucia Nuti, *Ritratti di città: visione e memoria tra Medioevo e Settecento* (Venice, 1997).

36 Profile views are also discussed by Svetlana Alpers, *The Art of Describing: Dutch Art in the Seventeenth Century* (Chicago and London, 1983), ch. 4, and Margarita Russel, *Visions of the Sea: Hendrick C. Vroom and the Origins of Dutch Marine Painting* (Leiden, 1983), ch. 2.

37 Willem Barentz, *Caertbook vande Midlandssche Zee* (Amsterdam, 1596) and in the French edition, *Description de la mer Méditerranée au quel sont delinéé et descriptes au vif toutes le costes de la mer Méditerranée par Guillam Bernard Pilote*, only copy known in Paris, Bibliothèque Nationale (Amsterdam, 1608).

38 N. Muratore and P. Munafò eds, *Immagini di città, raccolte da un frate agostiniano alla fine del sec. XVI* (Rome, 1991), p. 102.

39 Leandro Alberti, *Descrittione di tutta Italia* (Bologna, 1550), p. 328.

40 A fascinating discussion about viewpoints and their cultural and political implication is in Jacob, *L'empire des cartes*, pp. 404–14.

41 All the following images are described and commented on by Stéphane Yerasimos, 'Istanbul au XVIe siècle: images d'une capitale', in *Soliman le Magnifique* (Paris, 1990), pp. 284–321.

42 The drawing remained in that location up to 1653. It is described by Johannes van Meurs in 1625: 'tum in tabula, passus decem ac septem longa, urbs ingens, Costantinopolis, calamo picta, admirando artificio'. See Johannes van Meurs, *Athenae Batavae, sive, de urbe Leidensi, & academia, virisque claris; qui utram ingenio suo, atque scriptis, illustrarunt: libri duo* (Leiden, 1625), p. 37.

43 The panel is now preserved in National Azulejo Museum, Lisbon.

44 On the subject see Kemp, The Science of Art, pp. 213–15; Silvia Bordini, *Storia del panorama: la visione totale nella pittura del XIX secolo* (Rome, 1984).

45 Boudewijn Bakker, 'Maps, Books and Prints', in *The Dutch Cityscape in the 17th Century and its Sources* (Amsterdam and Toronto, 1977), pp. 72–3.

46 Lucia Nuti, 'The Mapped Views by Georg Hoefnagel: The Merchant's Eye, the Humanist's Eye', *Word and Image*, II (1988), pp. 545–70.

5 *Michael Charlesworth: Mapping, the Body and Desire: Christopher Packe's Chorography of Kent*

1 See the short notice in *Huntington Library Quarterly* (1988) pp. 241–2. The chart's engraver was J. Mynde. Packe and his chart have received very little scholarly attention. He is mentioned in passing in an essay by Norman Thrower in Norman Thrower, ed., *The Complete Plattmaker: Essays on Chart, Map and Globe Making in England in the Seventeenth and Eighteenth Century* (Berkeley and Los Angeles, 1978), p. 182, but only in order to refer the reader to Eila M. J. Campbell's essay on the work of Packe, 'An English Philosophico-Chorographical Chart', *Imago Mundi*, 6 (1949), pp. 79–84, which goes some way beyond the entry on Packe in the *Dictionary of National Biography* to stand as the most substantial modern essay on the chart. Packe is barely mentioned (in the 'Informative Index' and 'References' only) in R. Chorley, A. Dunn and R. Beckinsale, *The History of the Study of Landforms or the Development of Geomorphology* (London, 1964), I, pp. 93, 668. Packe's earlier essay, 'A Dissertation upon the Surface of the Earth, as Delineated in a Specimen of a Philosophico-chorographical Chart of East Kent' (London, 1737) is discussed by Yi-Fu Tuan, *The Hydrologic Cycle and the Wisdom of God: A Theme in Geoteleology* (Toronto, 1968), pp. 29–31, 120–22.

2 Some of their correspondence survives in the British Library, Add. (Sloane) Mss. 4055, 4057, 4076, 4078.

3 Christopher Packe, *Ancographia, sive convallium descriptio. Or, an Explanation of the Plan of a New Philosophico-Chorographical Chart of East-Kent* (London, 1743), p. 1.

4 Packe, *Ancographia*, p. 9. Further references to this book will be shown as page numbers in the main text. All italics and capitalizations are in the original.

5 Svetlana Alpers, *The Art of Describing: Dutch Art in the Seventeenth Century* (Chicago, 1983) p. 147.

6 In naming his work a 'chart' Packe is presumably thinking of maritime charts which marked depths of soundings of the sea bed. This would also tend to provide a distinction, in his mind at any rate, between his chart and ordinary maps of dry land.

7 The Ptolemaic distinction between 'geography' and 'chorography' might seem to be suggested by this passage; however, one remarkable feature of *Ancographia* is that it

makes no overt and systematic use of this distinction, despite Packe's use of the word 'chorographical' in the title. Works in England that relied heavily on the Ptolemaic categories and that Packe might have reasonably been expected to know include William Allingham, *A Short Account of the Nature and Uses of Maps* (London, 1698), Thomas Blundeville, *A Brief Description of Universal Maps and Cardes and their Use* (London, 1589) and William Cunningham, *The Cosmographical Glass* (London, 1559).

8 He begins with a moment of genuine picturesque sensitivity: 'its Lights and Shades are splendidly, yet softly blended into one another by the exceeding-sweet mixture of White Roads and Yellow Arable Lands with the lovely Green Wolds, that steal down into their bottoms from the summits of their hills' (p. 57). However, this gives place to 'There at one season whistles the industrious Husbandman to his list'ning Team, while with his steady hand he directs the crooked Plough to turn up the willing Tilth.' At harvest time, we are told, workers carry home 'the golden labours of the year'. Given his interests, Packe had probably read James Thomson's lengthy poem *The Seasons* (1730–44) which contains many such moments. Praise of farming activities was rooted in Virgil's *Georgics* and *Eclogues*. Packe concludes this derivative passage with the thought that 'simplicity, plenty, and pleasure conspire to make this a Very Picture of Arcadia' (pp.57–8).

9 A striking example is the quotation from Lucretius inscribed over the sea: 'retroq remanat/ Materies humoris, et ad caput/ Amnibus omnis/ Confluit unde super terras/ redit agmine dulci/ Qua via Secta semel liquido pede/ detulit undas/ Lucret. lib.6 v.635': 'The wet matter moves back and everything flows together to the mouth of the spring, and from there it returns and carries along its water in a sweet column over the earth in the path once cut for its liquid foot' (Thanks to my colleague Dr Penelope Davies for help with the translation).

10 I borrow these terms from Roland Barthes, who expounded them most famously in *Le plaisir du texte* (1973), trans. Richard Miller as *The Pleasure of the Text* (New York, 1975). They are related to the celebrated split subject that features in psychoanalytic theory from Freud to Lacan. In this theory, to put it very crudely, the subject spends its time oscillating between two states – a situation itself related to the split between the conscious and unconscious minds. The states are a calm taking of pleasure in culture, on one hand, and, on the other, induced by the very fullness of sensory stimuli, a bereft sense of the subject's own splitness. These states Barthes discussed in part by using the terms 'pleasure' and 'bliss'. The latter state is more closely related to desire, which, of course, is evoked by or oriented towards a fundamentally unattainable object.

11 According to the same psychoanalytic authorities, the scopic drive – the compulsion to look – is related to the subject's desire in the form of being 'propped upon' it. 'What is the subject trying to see? What he is trying to see, make no mistake, is the object as absence . . . What one looks at is what cannot be seen': Jacques Lacan, *The Four Fundamental Concepts of Pscho-Analysis* (1973), trans. Alan Sheridan (New York, 1981), p. 182. See also p. 243: 'the object of desire is the cause of the desire, and this object that is the cause of desire is the object of the drive', and pp. 165–70. Since, in this view, desire is directed towards something essentially unattainable (a lack that is itself the cause of desire), it can never be fulfilled.

12 Similes drawn from the human or animal body had been used before to explain the movement of water through the earth, especially in the reversed hydrological cycle, in a tradition going back to Pliny the Elder. See Yi-Fu Tuan, *The Hydrologic Cycle* , esp. pp. 24–42. Tuan prints an image, vaguely explained as 'from a manuscript map in the *Ankographia* by Christopher Packe', of the rivers of Kent fitted into the outline of a giant male human form. The difference between this and the chart, where Kent looks like Kent, not a human body, is profound. If Tuan's image is by Packe, it is evident that

by 1743 his identification of Kent with a bodily form has reached a new level. A fairly recent example of the use of the simile before Packe is Thomas Robinson, *New Observations on the Natural History of the World of Matter* (London, 1696). Such similes were also used to discuss the movement of water over the earth and through the air. However, I contend that Packe raised what had been a simile and explanatory illustration to a different level of urgency, completeness and organization. The simile became metaphorical.

13 James Lovelock, *Healing Gaia: Practical Medicine for the Planet* (New York, 1991), p. 38.

14 *Dictionary of National Biography*, ed. L. Stephen and S. Lee (Oxford, 1921, 2nd edn), x, pp. 354–6 (355).

15 James Hutton, *Theory of the Earth, with Proofs and Illustrations* (Edinburgh, 1795), II, pp. 560–62.

16 Michel Foucault, *The Archaeology of Knowledge* (1969), trans. A. M. Sheridan Smith (London, 1972). Since I have invoked Foucault I had better make it clear that I am not interested, so far as this present essay is concerned, with his theorization of Jeremy Bentham's Panopticon, in *Discipline and Punish: The Birth of the Prison* (London, 1977), despite the fact that Packe uses a central viewing tower to make his map in what is apparently a formally similar way to the way Bentham uses a central viewing tower in his model prison. Packe's is an example of panoramic viewing, and the difference between panoramic seeing and panopticism can best be grasped by attention to the effect of each upon the people being looked at. In the Panopticon, prisoners quailed in subjection before the all-seeing eye and were therefore induced to internalize a power-relation operating through the gaze. In panoramic seeing there is no such effect; people are very rarely looked at so intensively and are usually not at all aware that they are being looked at. See Michael Charlesworth, 'Thomas Sandby Climbs the Hoober Stand: The Politics of Panoramic Drawing in Eighteenth-century Britain', *Art History*, XIX/2 (June 1996), pp. 247–66, esp. p. 253.

17 Lovelock cites other scientists – Yevgraf Korolenko, Vladimir Vernadsky and Lynn Margulis – as geophysiologists, in *The Ages of Gaia: A Biography of our Living Earth* (Oxford, 1989), pp. 9–10.

18 Hutton, *Theory of the Earth*, ii, p. 546.

19 James Hutton, 'Theory of the Earth', *Royal Society of Edinburgh Transactions*, I (1788), pp. 209–304 (304).

20 Lovelock, *The Ages of Gaia*, p. 86.

21 John Playfair, *Illustrations of the Huttonian Theory of the Earth* (Edinburgh, 1802), p. 138.

22 *Ibid.*, pp. 138, 140.

23 *Ibid.*, p. 139.

24 See, for example, Playfair, *Illustrations*, p. 114. Playfair's book was written largely in response to the counter-arguments of Richard Kirwan. The alternative theory was that the valleys had been provided by God for water to flow down, a provision that was often linked to the retreat of the water of Noah's flood (the 'catastrophist' theory). Cf. Chorley, Dunn and Beckinsale, *The History of the Study of Landforms*, I, pp. 3–99. Given the wording of the quotation from Lucretius that Packe used (see note 9) it could be inferred that Packe tended towards the 'catastrophist' view ('the path once cut for its liquid foot'). Again, the contrast with Packe's 1737 essay is instructive. Yi-Fu Tuan quotes a 'catastrophist' explanation of dry valleys from the earlier essay. The passage has no equivalent in *Ancographia*. In the six years of working on his chart, Packe has passed from catastrophist certainty to doubt.

25 Foucault asserts that the determination of theoretical choices is partly based on 'the *possible positions of desire in relation to discourse*' (emphasis in original), *The Archaeology of Knowledge*, p. 68.

6 *Paul Carter: Dark with Excess of Bright: Mapping the Coastlines of Knowledge*

1 Charles Harpur, *Selected Poetry and Prose*, ed. M. Ackland (Melbourne, 1986), p. 123.
2 J. G. Dalyell, *Shipwrecks and Disasters at Sea* (Manchester, 1837), p. iv.
3 Matthew Flinders, *A Voyage to Terra Australis*, 2 vols (Adelaide, 1974; orig. pub. 1814), vol. II, p. 145.
4 Geoffrey C. Ingleton, *Matthew Flinders: Navigator and Chartmaker* (Guildford, Surrey, 1986), p. 388.
5 Matthew Flinders, Private Journal, 14 September 1811, cited by Ingleton, *Matthew Flinders*, p. 403.
6 Ingleton, *Matthew Flinders*, p. 130.
7 A. H. Robinson, *Elements of Cartography* (New York, 1960), p. 129.
8 See 'The Book of Francisco Rodrigues' in *The Suma Oriental of Tome Pires*, 2 vols (London, 1944).
9 For this passage and discussion see Andrew David, 'From Cook to Vancouver: The British Contribution to the Cartography of Alaska', in S. Haycox, J. K. Barnett and C. A. Liburd, eds, *Enlightenment and Exploration in the North Pacific, 1741–1805* (Seattle, 1997), pp. 221–7.
10 These last from D'Arcy Wentworth Thompson, *On Growth and Form*, 2 vols (Cambridge, 1942), respectively vol. I, p. 356 and vol. II, p. 807. Wentworth Thompson's master work is among other things a brilliant history, and critique, of the application of linear mathematics to the modelling of organic systems.
11 Denis Wood, *The Power of Maps* (New York, 1992), pp. 146–7.
12 Leibniz: *Philosophical Writings*, translated by M. Morris (London, 1961), p. 236. The conventional hand-drawn bay resembles nothing so much as the class of curve known as the catenary, in which two points at different heights are imagined joined by a rope or chain which finds its own centre of gravity off-centre; the mathematical properties of catenaries were first identified by Leibniz.
13 Against Descartes, whose reasoning 'moves forward by a constant and gradual series of small steps' (and implicitly against Leibniz, who denied gaps in nature and hence the necessity of any *saltus*), *ingegno*, Vico explains, 'is the faculty that connects disparate and diverse things'. See James Robert Goetsch, Vico's *Axioms: The Geometry of the Human World* (New Haven, 1995), pp. 96–7 for an interesting elaboration of this distinction.
14 E. C. Frome, *Outline of the Method of Conducting a Trigonometrical Survey, for the formation of Topographical Plans* (London, 1840), p. 59.
15 See my *The Road to Botany Bay* (London, 1987), pp. 19ff. for the implications of this ambition in the Australian context.
16 As discussed below. Quotation is from John Playfair, 'Life of Dr Hutton', in G. H. White, ed., *James Hutton*, vol. V: *Contributions to the History of Geology* (New York, 1973), p. 193.
17 Matthew H. Edney, *Mapping an Empire: The Geographical Construction of British India, 1765–1843* (Chicago, 1997), p. 19.
18 *Ibid.*, p. 21.
19 Vancouver's problem near Port Chalmers in May 1794 was but a recurrent issue, as Alun C. Davies points out in 'Testing a New Technology: Captain George Vancouver's Survey and Navigation in Alaskan Waters, 1794', in Haycox et al., eds, *Enlightenment and Exploration*, pp. 106–8.
20 Frome, *Outline*, p. 2.
21 Davies, 'Testing a New Technology', p. 106.
22 Phillip P. King, *Narrative of a Survey of the Intertropical and Western Coasts of Australia*, 2 vols (Adelaide, 1969; orig. pub. 1827). See vol. I, pp. 191 and 363 respectively.

23 *Ibid.*, vol. I, p. 152.

24 Edward J. Eyre, *Journals of Expeditions of Discovery into Central Australia*, 2 vols (Adelaide, 1964; orig. pub. 1845). Along the Great Australian Bight Eyre frequently uses such phrases as 'sand-drifts of the coast' (vol. I, p. 236), 'hummocks of the coast' (vol. I, p. 276) and the like.

25 A. H. Robinson, *Elements of Cartography*, p. 128.

26 The calculation of latitude using Mercator's orthomorphic projection was also approximate. Different surveyors working in the same vessel might use tables for calculating the size of the intervals between different meridians at different latitudes that differed slightly from one another. See J. Ballard, *Mercator's Projection and Marine Cartography in H.M.S. Endeavour* (Duntroon, New South Wales: Royal Military College, Faculty of Geography, occasional paper No. 34, 1983), pp. 4–5.

27 J. J. Gibson, *The Ecological Approach to Visual Perception* (Boston, MA, 1979), p. 23.

28 King, *Narrative*, vol. I, p. xxxi.

29 Robin Fisher, 'George Vancouver and the Native Peoples of the Northwest Coast' in Haycox et al., eds, *Enlightenment and Exploration*, p. 200. As Fisher comments, 'Vancouver's own boundary lines were both physical and mental.'

30 Playfair, 'Life of Dr Hutton', pp. 176–7.

31 *Ibid.*, p. 186.

32 *Ibid.*, p. 193.

33 Gary Shapiro, *Alcyone: Nietzsche on Gifts, Noise, and Women* (Albany, NY, 1991), pp. 116–18 shows that Aristotle's acquaintance with the shoreline doesn't necessarily make him less superstitious about other kinds bi-elemental fauna.

34 For instance: 'At Batchian there are only two tolerable collecting-places, – the road to the coal-mines, and the new clearings made by the Tomoré people' (Alfred Russel Wallace, *The Malay Archipelago*, Kuala Lumpur, 1986, orig. pub. 1869, p. 346).

35 Wallace is explicit about his editorial intent. See *The Malay Archipelago*, pp. vi–vii.

36 Thucydides, *History of the Peloponnesian War*, translated by R. Crawley (London, 1876), pp. 3–4.

37 The sequel was dismal: revealing what had formerly lay hidden, Gosse brought about the destruction of what he most cared for. As his son reported, 'The fairy paradise has been violated, the exquisite product of centuries of natural selection has been crushed under the rough paw of well-meaning, idle-minded curiosity . . . my Father . . . had by the popularity of his books acquired direct responsibility for a calamity that he never anticipated' (Edmund Gosse, *Father and Son*, London, 1982, p. 97).

38 John Lort Stokes, *Discoveries in Australia, with an account of the coasts and rivers explored and surveyed*, etc., 2 vols (Adelaide, 1969; orig. pub. 1846), vol. I, p. 86.

39 *Ibid.*, vol. II, p. 319. See my *The Road to Botany Bay*, pp. 82ff. for a discussion of this passage.

40 Margaret Atherton, *Berkeley's Revolution in Vision* (Ithaca, 1990), p. 224.

41 *Ibid.*, p. 227.

42 David Appelbaum, *The Stop* (Albany, NY, 1995), pp. 24–5.

43 On faciality in nature and the art of colonization, see my 'Second Sight: Looking Back as Colonial Vision', *Australian Journal of Art*, XIII (1996), pp. 9–35.

44 Stokes, *Discoveries in Australia*, vol. I, p. 76.

45 King, *Narrative*, vol. I, p. 169.

46 Stokes, *Discoveries in Australia*, vol. I, p. 414.

47 Paul Carter, *Living in a New Country* (London, 1992), p. 163, discussing the military parade Flinders 'put on' for the Aborigines of King George Sound, Western Australia, in 1801.

48 Stokes, *Discoveries in Australia*, vol. i, p. 81.

49 See *The Road to Botany Bay*, p. xiii.

50 Stokes, *Discoveries in Australia*, vol. I, p. 81.

51 D. Cottom, *Abyss of Reason* (Oxford, 1991), p. 84.

52 Writing in 1875, quoted by Cottom, *Abyss of Reason*, p. 80.

53 Jean Houel, *Viaggio in Sicilia e a Malta* (Palermo–Napoli, 1977; orig. pub. 1782), p. 129.

54 Cottom, *Abyss of Reason*, p. 27.

55 C.E.A. Winslow, *The Conquest of Epidemic Disease* (Princeton, 1943), pp. 237–8. Winslow bases his remark on John Howard's report published in 1789, 'The Principal Lazarettos in Europe, with various papers relative to the Plague'.

56 Joseph Banks writing to Johan Alströmer, 16 November 1784, cited by Edward Duyker, *Nature's Argonaut: Daniel Solander, 1733–1782* (Melbourne, 1998), p. 110.

57 Edney, *Mapping an Empire*, p. 97.

58 See D. Cottom's discussion, *Abyss of Reason*, p. 134.

59 D. W. Waters, *Science and the Techniques of Navigation in the Renaissance* (London, Trustees of the National Maritime Museum, Maritime Monographs and Reports, No. 19, 1976), p. 2.

60 See note 49.

61 M. E. Hoare, ed., *The Resolution Journal of Johann Reinhold Forster, 1772–1775* (London, 1982), 4 vols, vol. II, p. 325.

62 King, *Narrative*, vol. I, p. 44.

63 See my *Living in a New Country*, pp. 51ff. for discussion of the persistence of this assumption of offshore provenance well into the twentieth century.

64 See the copiously documented entry 'Canoes' in R. Brough Smyth, *The Aborigines of Victoria and Other Parts of Australia and Tasmania*, 2 vols (Melbourne, 1972; orig. pub. 1876), vol. I, pp. 407–22.

65 Alain Corbin, *The Lure of the Sea: The Discovery of the Seaside in the Western World, 1750–1840*, translated by Jocelyn Phelps (Cambridge, *c.* 1994), p. 74.

66 John G. Paton, *Missionary to the New Hebrides* (London, 1919), p. 146.

67 *Ibid.*, pp. 147–8.

68 King, *Narrative*, vol. I, p. 445.

69 *Ibid.*, p. 196.

70 Immanuel Kant, *Anthropology from a Pragmatic Point of View*, translated by M. J. Gregor (The Hague, 1974), p. 88. This significance of Kant's nosology in a colonial context is touched on in my *The Lie of the Land* (London, 1996), pp. 257–8.

7 *Luciana de Lima Martins: Mapping Tropical Waters: British Views and Visions of Rio de Janeiro*

This is a revised and extended version of an article in *Imago Mundi*, 50 (1998), pp. 141ff. I am indebted to Denis Cosgrove, Catherine Delano Smith and Felix Driver for their comments. The research for this paper was supported by the Brazilian Post-Graduate Federal Agency (CAPES).

1 See John Bach, 'The Maintenance of Royal Navy Vessels in the Pacific Ocean, 1825–1875', *Mariner's Mirror*, 56 (1970), pp. 259–73.

2 George S. Ritchie, *The Admiralty Chart: British Naval Hydrography in the Nineteenth Century* (rev. ed., Edinburgh, Cambridge and Durham, 1995), p. 208.

3 G. S. Graham, *The Politics of Naval Supremacy* (Cambridge, 1965), p. 10 (my emphasis).

4 David Mackay, *In the Wake of Cook: Exploration, Science and Empire, 1780–1801* (London, 1985), p. 52.

5 Simon Schaffer, 'Visions of Empire: Afterword' in David Philip Miller and Peter Hanns Reill, eds, *Visions of Empire: Voyages, Botany, and Representations of Nature* (Cambridge, 1996), p. 336.

6　See Bernard Smith, *European Vision and the South Pacific* (New Haven and London, 1988); Michael Jacobs, *The Painted Voyage* (London, 1995); Ana Maria de Moraes Belluzzo, *The Voyager's Brazil: A Place in the Universe* (São Paulo, 1995), II, and I.S. MacLaren, 'From Exploration to Publication: The Evolution of a 19th-Century Arctic Narrative', *Arctic*, XLVII/I (1994), pp. 43–53.

7　On the European idea of tropicality, see David Arnold, *The Problem of Nature: Environment, Culture and European Expansion* (Oxford, 1996), pp. 141–68.

8　James Horsburgh, *Directions for Sailing to and from East Indies, China, New Holland, Cape of Good Hope, and the Interjacent Ports* (London, 1809–11), p. 38.

9　Rudy Bauss, 'Rio de Janeiro: Strategic Base for Global Designs of the British Royal Navy, 1777–1815', in Craig L. Symonds, ed., *New Aspects of Naval History* (Annapolis, MD, 1981), pp. 75–6.

10　Bauss, 'Rio de Janeiro', p. 76.

11　'Tedious' was the word used by the naturalist George Gardner, *Travels in the Interior of Brazil, Principally through the Northern Provinces, and the Gold and Diamond Districts, during the Years 1836–1841* (London, 1846), p. 3.

12　Bauss, 'Rio de Janeiro', p. 75.

13　*Ibid.*, p. 79.

14　For a detailed account of the South Atlantic Ocean circulation, see Charles H. Cotter, *The Physical Geography of the Oceans* (London, 1965), pp. 263–4. This route is similar to that still recommended in current navigational pilots for round-the-world cruises. See Jimmy Cornell, *World Cruising Routes* (London, 1995), p. 163.

15　See Rudy Bauss, 'The Critical Importance of Rio de Janeiro to British Interests, with Particular Attention to Australia in her Formative Years, 1787–1805', *Journal of the Royal Australian Historical Society*, 65 (1979), pp. 145–72.

16　See G. S. Graham and R. A. Humphreys, eds, *The Navy and South America, 1807–1823: Correspondence of the Commanders-in-Chief on the South American Station* (London, 1962), p. xxvi.

17　Barry M. Gough, 'Sea Power and South America: The "Brazils" or South American Station of the Royal Navy 1808–1837', *American Neptune*, 50 (1990), pp. 26–34.

18　Gough, 'Sea Power and South America', p. 26.

19　G. S. Graham, *Great Britain in the Indian Ocean 1810–1850* (Oxford, 1967), p. 26.

20　For a detailed account of the changing boundaries of the Cape and East Indies station, see Graham, 'Appendix', in *Great Britain in the Indian Ocean*, pp. 455–9.

21　As quoted in Gough, 'Sea Power and South America', p. 29.

22　R.J.B. Knight, *Guide to the Manuscripts in the National Maritime Museum: The Personal Collections* (London, 1977), p. xiv.

23　Barry M. Gough, *The Royal Navy and the Northwest Coast of North America 1810–1914: A Study of British Maritime Ascendancy* (Vancouver, 1971), p. 30.

24　Ritchie, *The Admiralty Chart*, p. 208.

25　Robert E. Gallagher, ed., *Byron's Journal of his Circumnavigation 1764–1766* (Cambridge, 1964), p. 25.

26　As quoted in John Hawkesworth, *An Account of the Voyages Undertaken by the Order of His Present Majesty for Making Discoveries in the Southern Hemisphere . . .* (London, 1773), I, p. 7.

27　As quoted in Archibald Day, *The Admiralty Hydrographic Service 1795–1919* (London, 1967), pp. 338–9.

28　Cook's Admiralty MS (PRO, Adm 55/40), quoted in Andrew David, ed., *The Charts and Coastal Views of Captain Cook's Voyages: The Voyage of the Endeavour 1768–1771* (London, 1988), I, p. 16. Bernard Smith suggests that a drawing of the bay of Funchal, Madeira, by William Hodges, from the *Resolution*, and Alexander Buchan's drawings of fortifications of Rio, from the *Endeavour*, were made in the ship's great cabin so the authorities would not see the sketching that was being done. See Bernard Smith, 'William Hodges and English *Plein-air* Painting', *Art History*, 6 (1983), pp. 143–52, esp. p. 146.

29 As quoted in R. A. Skelton, *Captain James Cook after Two Hundred Years* (London, 1969), p. 22.

30 Graham, *Great Britain in the Indian Ocean*, p. 132 (my emphasis).

31 *Ibid.*, p. 133.

32 See D. W. Waters, *The Rutters of the Sea: The Sailing Directions of Pierre Garcie, a Study of the First English and French Printed Sailing Directions* (New Haven and London, 1967), pp. 31–2 (32).

33 Norman Bryson, 'Semiology and Visual Interpretation', in Norman Bryson *et al.*, eds, *Visual Theory* (Oxford, 1996), p. 65.

34 Smith, *European Vision*, p. 9.

35 Military surveyors and draftsmen, such as the brothers Thomas and Paul Sandby, were trained in the Board of Ordnance Drawing Room, situated in the Tower of London. See Jessica Christian, 'Paul Sandby and the Military Survey of Scotland', in *Mapping the Landscape: Essays on Art and Cartography*, exhibition catalogue by Nicholas Alfrey and Stephen Daniels, Nottingham Castle Museum (Nottingham, 1990), pp. 18–22. The Royal Military College at Great Marlow, Buckinghamshire, opened in May 1802, with the artist William Alexander as the first Master of Landscape Drawing. See *William Alexander: An English Artist in Imperial China*, exhibition catalogue, the Royal Pavilion, Art Gallery and Museums, Brighton; Nottingham University Art Gallery, Nottingham (Brighton, 1981), p. 8.

36 Kim Sloan, *Alexander and John Robert Cozens: The Poetry of Landscape* (New Haven and London, 1986), pp. 22, 26.

37 *Ibid.*, p. 26.

38 The list comprises: I. A General, or Nautical Chart; II. Abbreviated Collections and Draughts; III. A Memorial Sketch; IV. An Eye-Sketch; V. An Ambulatory Draught; VI. A Disjunct Survey; VII. A Lineängular Survey; VIII. A Trigonocatenary Survey; IX. An Orometric Survey; X. A Stasimetric Survey. See Murdoch Mackenzie, corrected and republished with a supplement by James Horsburgh, *A Treatise of Marine Surveying* (London, 1819), pp. iii–xiii. The original edition by Murdoch Mackenzie, *Treatise on Maritim [sic] Surveying*, was printed in 1774.

39 Mackenzie, *A Treatise of Marine Surveying*, p. vi (my emphasis).

40 *Ibid.*, pp. vi–vii (my emphasis).

41 Alexander Dalrymple, *Essay on Nautical Surveying: Originally Published in 1771, now much Extended by Dalrymple* (London, 1806), p. 4.

42 As quoted in Howard Fry, 'Alexander Dalrymple and Captain Cook: The Creative Interplay of Two Careers', in Robin Fisher and Hugh Johnston, eds, *Captain Cook and his Times* (London, 1979), p. 57.

43 Paul Carter, *The Road to Botany Bay: An Essay in Spatial History* (London and Boston, 1988), p. 8. George Vancouver, in his surveying expedition of the north-west coast of America from 1792 to 1794, also 'bestowed names that signified the physical and technological aspects of surveying, and the particular circumstances of his voyage at different points in time'. See Daniel Clayton, 'Islands of Truth: Vancouver Island from Captain Cook to the Beginnings of Colonialism' (PhD dissertation, University of British Columbia, 1995), pp. 316–34 (328).

44 Carter, *The Road to Botany Bay*, p. 25.

45 Fry, 'Alexander Dalrymple', p. 239.

46 Mackenzie, *A Treatise of Marine Surveying*, p. 3.

47 The French Hydrographic Office was established in 1720; the Danish in 1784. The Spanish followed in 1800. See Day, *The Admiralty Hydrographic Service*, pp. 12–13.

The Ordnance Survey had been established by the British Army four years previously. See also A.H.W. Robinson, *Marine Cartography in Britain: A History of the Sea Chart to 1855* (Leicester, 1962), p. 97.

48	Admiralty instructions had been promulgated at least as early as October 1759 as 'Instructions to the Respective Maj^s Ships' (PRO, Adm 2/83, 516–18). I am grateful to Andrew David for drawing my attention to this document. In the 1804 version, a six-page enclosure 'Form of Remark Book' required details of the following: Situation; Directions for Sailing; Marks for Anchoring; Wooding and Watering; Provisions; Fortifications and Landing Places; Trade and Shipping; Inhabitants (from a final proof of a printed Admiralty circular letter sent to Dalrymple for agreement, 6 February 1804, PRO, Adm 1/3522). See also Day, *The Admiralty Hydrographic Service*, pp. 337–8.

49	I would like to thank Dr Andrew Cook for his expert advice on hydrographical issues.

50	Bernard Smith, 'The Artwork', in Bernard Smith and Alwyne Wheeler, eds, *The Art of the First Fleet* (New Haven and London, 1988), pp. 198–237 (198).

51	See T. M. Perry, 'Charts and Views', in Smith and Wheeler, eds, *The Art of the First Fleet*, pp. 70–107; Andrew David, 'Introduction', in David, ed., *Charts and Coastal Views*, I, pp. xxxviii–xli; and John E. Munday, ' "Hydrographic Views": Sea Officers as Topographical Artists', *Anais Hidrográficos*, 33 (1976), pp. 219–27.

52	The Hydrographic Office in Taunton keeps a number of albums with drawings of coastal views that were used in the first Admiralty charts. With the help of Andrew David, I was able to identify the 'View of the entrance into Rio de Janeiro, the Sugar Loaf, N W 1/4N, distant 12 miles' (View Album 8J) as probably the original drawing from which the view in the Admiralty chart 541 was printed.

53	*Alceste*'s muster-table (PRO Adm 37/5729).

54	John M'Leod highlighted the sailing qualities of the *Alceste*, remarking that the 'superior sailing of the frigate enabled us to touch at Rio Janeiro, without in any way delaying the general passage; as, not withstanding this, she nearly overtook her consorts at the Cape', John M'Leod, *Narrative of a Voyage, in His Majesty's late Ship Alceste, to the Yellow Sea, along the Coast of Corea . . .* (London, 1817), p. 18.

55	According to the *Eden*'s muster-table, however, Browne joined the ship on 25 April 1818, which renders the information on the cover doubtful (PRO Adm 37/6205).

56	M'Leod, *Narrative of a Voyage*, p. 6 (my emphasis).

57	See, for example, the illustration entitled Loo Choo Chief and his Two Sons, in Basil Hall, *Voyage of Discovery to the West Coast of Corea, and the Great Loo-Choo Island* (London, 1818), facing p. 97. In a manuscript version 'Nine Drawings for Captain Basil Hall's *Account of a Voyage to the West Coast of Corea 1817*', three pages in the book contain examples of printed fabrics. See *William Havell 1782–1857*, exhibition catalogue by Felicity Owen and Eric Stanford, Spink and Son Ltd; Reading Museum and Art Gallery; Abbot Hall Art Gallery, Kendal (Reading, 1981), p. 32.

58	'Narrative of the Proceedings of a Small Party, sent by Captain Owen, of HMS *Leven*, in July 1823, under the Command of Lieut. C. W. Browne RN, to Explore the Course of the River Zambezi, on the Eastern Coast of Africa', RGS Archives, LBR MS 407.

59	*Eden*'s muster-tables, 1818–1821 (PRO Adm 37/6205 to 6207).

60	W. J. Hamilton, 'Geography', in Robert Main, ed., *A Manual of Scientific Enquiry Prepared for the Use of Officers in Her Majesty's Navy and Travellers in General* (London, 1859, 1st edn 1849), pp. 190–218 (207).

61	As quoted in Hamilton, 'Geography', p. 192.

62	'Hints to Travellers', *Journal of the Royal Geographical Society*, 24 (1854), pp. 328–58 (355).

63	Clarke Abel, *Narrative of a Journey in the Interior of China . . .* (London, 1818), pp. 12–13.

64 M'Leod, *Narrative of a Voyage*, pp. 6–13.

65 The Reading Museum and Art Gallery holds the oil sketch, *The Braganza Shore, Rio de Janeiro*, by William Havell. In the Print Room of the British Museum, London, there are two watercolour sketches by the same artist, both entitled *Near Rio de Janeiro*.

66 Hall, *Voyage of Discovery to the West Coast of Corea*, p. ix.

67 *William Havell 1782–1857*, p. 15.

68 W.J.T. Mitchell, *Iconology: Image, Text, Ideology* (Chicago and London, 1987), p. 43.

69 Dominick Serres and John Thomas Serres, *Liber Nauticus, and Instructor in the Art of Marine Drawing* (London, 1805).

70 Resorting to human features to describe, or even to name, natural lineaments was a very common practice among navigators. As Reverend Walsh points out, describing the entrance of the harbour of Rio de Janeiro: 'The hills behind, which marked the horizon, presented a rough profile of a human countenance turned up, having a hooked nose and chin, and therefore called by the English, Lord Hood's face . . . As the attention of people is directed to craniology and physiognomy, they extract scientific subjects from rocks and mountains. Lord Hood's head is seen in Rio, Lord Nelson's at Edinburgh, and Dr. Johnson's on the granite rocks of Cornwall, at the Lands-end', R. Walsh, *Notices of Brazil in 1828 and 1829* (London, 1830), I, p. 129.

71 See J. B. Debret, *Voyage pittoresque et historique au Brésil, ou sejour d'un artiste français au Brésil* . . . (Paris, 1834), II, p. 2. The art historian Martin Warnke sees in the same image a horizontal figure 'reminiscent of a dead Christ', which 'reinforces the impression of paralysed power': Martin Warnke, *Political Landscape* (London, 1994), p. 89.

72 Anne Secord, 'Artisan Botany', in Nicholas Jardine, James Secord and Emma Spary, eds, *Cultures of Natural History* (Cambridge, 1996), pp. 392–3.

73 *Oxford Dictionary*, vol. II, part II (Oxford, 1893), p. 678.

8 *Armand Mattelart: Mapping Modernity: Utopia and Communications Networks*

1 A. Mattelart, *L'invention de la communication* (Paris, 1994), English edition: *The Invention of Communication*, trans. S. Emmanuel (Minneapolis, 1996).

2 M. Parent, *Vauban: un encyclopédiste avant la lettre* (Paris, 1982), p. 128.

3 Vauban, 'Mémoire sur la navigation des rivières' (1699), in *Oisivetés de M. de Vauban* (Paris, 1843).

4 P. A. Allent, *Histoire du Corps Impérial du Génie, des sièges et des travaux qu'il a dirigés depuis l'origine de la fortification jusqu'à nos jours* (Paris, 1805), vol. I; A. Guillerme, *Genèse du concept de réseau, territoire et génie en Europe de l'ouest (1760–1815)* (Paris, 1988).

5 P. Musso, 'Métaphores du réseau et de l'organisme: la transition saint-simonienne', in L. Sfez et al., eds, *Technologie et symboliques de la communication* (Grenoble, 1990).

6 Y. Chicoteau and A. Picon, 'Forme, technique et idéologie: les ingénieurs des Ponts et Chaussées à la fin du XVIIIe siècle', *Culture technique*, Paris, 7 (March 1982).

7 F. Braudel, *Civilisation and Capitalism: 15th–18th Century*, trans. and revised by Sian Reynolds (London, 1981–4), vol. III, *The Perspective of the World*, p. 322.

8 M. Chevalier, *Lettres sur l'Amérique du Nord* (Paris, 1837), vol. I, p. 1.

9 E. Cabet, *Voyage en Icarie* (Paris, 1842, 2nd edition), p. 20 (my emphasis).

10 Y. Stourdzé, 'Généalogie des télécommunications françaises', in A. Giraud et al., eds, *Les réseaux pensants: télécommunications et société* (Paris, 1978).

11 See Mattelart, *The Invention of Communication*, p. 103.

12 M. Chevalier, 'Système de la Méditerranée', *Le Globe*, 12 February 1832, p. 3.

13 Chevalier, *Lettres*, p. 4.

14 J. London, 'The Message of the Motion Pictures', *Paramount Magazine*, February 1915.

15 M. Fallex and A. Mairey, *Les principales puissances du monde* (Paris, 1906), pp. 1–2.

16 P. Kropotkin, *Fields, Factories and Workshops, or Industry Combined with Agriculture and Brain Work with Manual Work* (London, 1912).

17 J. Verne, *Robur-le-Conquérant* (Paris, 1886; facsimile reproduction Geneva, 1991).

18 S. Butler, *Erewhon* (1872, repr. London, 1979).

19 M. De Clercq, ed., *Recueils des traités de la France* (Paris, 1868), vol. 9, p. 252.

20 See J. Carey, *Communication as Culture: Essays on Media and Society* (Boston, 1989).

21 E. Zamyatin, *Islanders, and the Fisher of Men*, trans. S. Fuller and J. Sacchi (Edinburgh, 1984).

22 E. Zamyatin, *We*, trans. M. Ginsburg (New York, 1972).

23 N. Wiener, *Cybernetics: Control and Communication in the Animal and the Machine* (Cambridge, MA, 1948), p. 11.

24 *Ibid.*, pp. 161–2.

25 M. McLuhan and Q. Fiore, *War and Peace in the Global Village* (New York, 1968).

26 S. Nora and A. Minc, *L'informatisation de la société* (Paris, 1978), p. 72 (my emphasis). (English edn: *The Computerization of Society* [Cambridge, MA, 1980]).

27 J.-J. Servan-Schreiber, *Le défi mondial* (Paris, 1980).

28 A. Toffler, *The Third Wave* (New York, 1980), p. 436.

29 E. Le Boucher, 'Le média froid de la modernité', *Le Monde*, 7 January 1986.

30 G. Deleuze and F. Guattari, *Qu'est-ce que la philosophie?* (Paris), pp. 15–17.

31 Document circulated in March 1994 by USIA (United States Information Agency).

32 N. Negroponte, *Being Digital* (New York, 1995).

33 B. Gates, *The Road Ahead* (New York, 1995).

34 See A. Mattelart, *Advertising International*, trans. M. Chanan (London, 1991), p. 53.

35 A. Quételet, *Sur l'homme et le développement de ses facultés, ou essai de physique sociale*, 2 vols (Paris, 1835).

9 *David Matless: The Uses of Cartographic Literacy: Mapping, Survey and Citizenship in Twentieth-Century Britain*

1 On maps and power see J. B. Harley, 'Maps, Knowledge and Power', in D. Cosgrove and S. Daniels, eds, *The Iconography of Landscape* (Cambridge, 1988), pp. 277–312; J. B. Harley, 'Deconstructing the Map', *Cartographica*, 26 (1989), pp. 1–20; J. B. Harley, 'Historical Geography and the Cartographic Illusion', *Journal of Historical Geography*, 15 (1989), pp. 80–91; H. Speier, 'Magic Geography', *Social Research*, 8 (1941), pp. 310–30; D. Turnbull, *Maps Are Territories, Science is an Atlas* (Chicago, 1993). On subversive or alternative cartographies see D. Pinder, 'Subverting Cartography: The Situationists and Maps of the City', *Environment and Planning A*, 28 (1996), pp. 405–27. Pinder criticizes Harley's operation of a binary model of either power or protest. Harley also begins to break down this opposition in 'Rereading the Maps of the Columbian Encounter', *Annals of the Association of American Geographers*, 82 (1992), pp. 522–42. On maps see also D. Crouch and D. Matless, 'Refiguring Geography: Parish Maps of Common Ground', *Transactions of the Institute of British Geographers*, 21 (1996), pp. 236–55.

2 M. Foucault, *Discipline and Punish* (Harmondsworth, 1979), p. 28.

3 J. B. Harley, 'Cartography, Ethics and Social Theory', *Cartographica*, 27 (1990), pp. 1–23 (17, 1).

4 D. Matless, 'Moral Geographies of English Landscape', *Landscape Research*, 22 (1997), pp. 141–55; D. Matless, 'Visual Culture and Geographical Citizenship', *Journal of Historical Geography*, 22 (1996), pp. 424–39; D. Matless, '"The Art of

Right Living": Landscape and Citizenship 1918–39', in S. Pile and N. Thrift, eds, *Mapping the Subject* (London, 1995), pp. 93–122; see also S. Rycroft and D. Cosgrove, 'Mapping the Modern Nation: Dudley Stamp and the Land Utilisation Survey', *History Workshop Journal*, 40 (1995), pp. 91–105.

5 R. Hoggart, *The Uses of Literacy* (London, 1957).

6 For a critical account of the effects of the 'popular' and the 'people' in the formation of collective and individual identities see P. Joyce, *Visions of the People* (Cambridge, 1991); P. Joyce, *Democratic Subjects: The Self and the Social in Nineteenth-century England* (Cambridge, 1994).

7 The terms are regularly used by Frederic Jameson, including at the conclusion of his 'Postmodernism, or The Cultural Logic of Late Capitalism', *New Left Review*, 146 (1984), pp. 53–92.

8 N. Rose, 'Identity, Genealogy, History', in S. Hall and P. Du Gay, eds, *Questions of Cultural Identity* (London, 1996), pp. 128–50.

9 C. C. Fagg and G. E. Hutchings, *An Introduction to Regional Surveying* (Cambridge, 1930), p. 1.

10 P. Geddes, *Cities in Evolution* (London, 1915), p. 399.

11 D. Matless, 'Regional Survey and Local Knowledges: The Geographical Imagination in Britain, 1918–39', *Transactions of the Institute of British Geographers*, 17 (1992), pp. 464–80. On the international deployment of survey in connection with business interests see S. Naylor and G. Jones, 'Writing Orderly Geographies of Distant Places: The Regional Survey Movement and Latin America', *Ecumene*, 4 (1997), pp. 273–99. On Geddes and survey see also H. Meller, *Patrick Geddes: Social Evolutionist and City Planner* (London, 1990), chapter 9; P. Boardman, *The Worlds of Patrick Geddes* (London, 1978). For survey within the history of social science, see E. J. Yeo, *The Contest for Social Science: Relations and Representations of Gender and Class* (London, 1996).

12 G. E. Hutchings, 'Rochester and its Region', *Observation*, 4 (1925), pp. 200–203 (200).

13 V. Branford, *Interpretations and Forecasts* (London, 1914), p. 63.

14 C. C. Fagg, 'The Surface Utilisation Survey', *South-Eastern Naturalist*, 25 (1920), pp. 31–40 (40).

15 Branford, *Interpretations*, p. 64.

16 *Ibid.*, p. 66; Branford here demonstrates a general tendency in survey work to seek to rechannel supposedly 'negative' impulses for 'positive' ends. Branford and Geddes often refer in this context to William James's idea of 'moral equivalents for war', with the Scouts often upheld as exemplary.

17 *Ibid.*, chapter 2. Geddes distinguished the 'no-place' of Utopia from the 'good-place' of Eutopia, to be made out of present surroundings.

18 Fagg and Hutchings, *Introduction*, p. 48.

19 V. Branford and P. Geddes, *The Coming Polity* (London, 1917), p. 246, and see Matless, 'Regional Surveys'. On models see T. Ploszajska, 'Constructing the Subject: Geographical Models in English Schools, 1870–1914', *Journal of Historical Geography*, 22 (1996), pp. 388–98. For a suggestive essay on the geography of postcards see M. Crang, 'Envisioning Urban Histories: Bristol as Palimpsest, Postcards, and Snapshots', *Environment and Planning A*, 28 (1996), pp. 429–52.

20 Fagg and Hutchings, *Introduction*, p. 93.

21 *Ibid.*, p. 55; in their essay on Stamp and the Land Utilisation Survey, Rycroft and Cosgrove, 'Mapping the Modern Nation', discuss the use of colour in LUS maps in terms of its similar palette to landscape painting and book illustration of the time. I have not been able to trace the detail of the Winsor and Newton colour scheme.

22 Fagg and Hutchings, *Introduction*, p. 49.

23 C. C. Fagg, 'The Regional Survey and Local Natural History Societies', *South-Eastern Naturalist*, 1915, pp. 21–31 (25).

24 Branford and Geddes, *The Coming Polity*, p. 184. Geddes took his 'place-work-folk' formula from Le Play's 'lieu-travail-famille'. On Geddes and Le Play, and the influence of Comte's positivism on Geddes in terms of both observation and the unity of the sciences, see Meller, *Patrick Geddes*, pp. 34–45; the activities of the Geddes-inspired Le Play Society are noted below.

25 Geddes, *Cities*, pp. 13–14.

26 Branford and Geddes, *The Coming Polity*, pp. 184–5.

27 Matless, 'Moral Geographies'; Matless, 'Art of Right Living'. On the role of the map shown on the OS map covers designed by Ellis Martin and others see J. P. Browne, *Map Cover Art* (London, 1991); T. R. Nicholson, *Wheels on the Road: Maps of Britain for the Cyclist and Motorist 1870–1940* (Norwich, 1983).

28 Branford and Geddes, *The Coming Polity*, p. 69, citing Belloc's *The Old Road* (London, 1904) and *The Path to Rome* (London, 1902).

29 Belloc, *Path*; also cited in the scouting handbook by 'Gilcraft', *Exploring* (London, 1930), pp. 72–3. On earlier walking literature see A. Wallace, *Walking, Literature and English Culture: The Origins and Uses of the Peripatetic* (Oxford, 1993). For Belloc's life, his Catholicism and linked conservative social and political ideas see R. Speaight, *The Life of Hilaire Belloc* (London, 1957); A. N. Wilson, *Hilaire Belloc* (London, 1984). I am not suggesting here that regional survey followed his broader philosophy, though there are certainly parallels in Geddes and Branford's work regarding the social purposes of religion and a preoccupation with non-socialist forms of collective life.

30 Belloc, *Path*, p. 70; Belloc then lists his successive viewpoints on the road to Rome. On one, Weissenstein, looking from the Jura over to the Alps, he has a vision of his religion in terms of height, distance, fear, potential etc. (pp. 159–60).

31 *Ibid.*, p. 71; Belloc is defeated by the weather at a high Alpine pass and has to take a road route into Italy (pp. 215–17); he later succumbs to the temptation of a train into Milan (p. 250).

32 *Ibid.*, pp. 84–5.

33 M. L. Pratt, *Imperial Eyes: Travel Writing and Transculturation* (London, 1992), p. 7.

34 *Ibid.*, pp. 202–5.

35 See also Matless, 'Moral Geographies'.

36 *Discovery* (Ledbury, 1948), p. 1 (first published London, c. 1923).

37 V. Branford, 'A View of Hastings', *Observation*, 1 (1924), pp. 31–4 (34).

38 Fagg and Hutchings, *Introduction*, p. 33.

39 Sir A. Evans, *Jarn Mound* (Oxford, 1933), p. 17.

40 Matless, 'Regional Surveys'; Boardman, *Patrick Geddes*, pp. 137–45; Meller, *Patrick Geddes*, chapter 4; Geddes, *Cities*, pp. 321–6.

41 Branford, *Interpretations*, p. 85.

42 Fagg, 'Regional Survey', p. 30. Fagg had worked with Croydon Natural History Society and the Surrey Photographic Survey from 1912; on photographic surveys see J. Taylor, *A Dream of England: Landscape, Photography and the Tourist's Imagination* (Manchester, 1995), pp. 55–63.

43 C. C. Fagg and G. E. Hutchings, 'Report for the year 1925–26' *South-Eastern Naturalist*, 31 (1926), pp. xxxii–xlviii. Fagg and Hutchings met through this network on Fagg's visit to the Rochester Natural History Society in 1920. Hutchings served on the Section Committee from 1923, and much of their *Introduction to Regional Surveying* would draw on talks given at the Annual Congress.

44 Meller, *Patrick Geddes*, p. 307 terms this 'a roll-call of the most trusty warriors of the cause'.

45 C. C. Fagg, 'The History of the Regional Survey Movement', *South-Eastern Naturalist*, 33 (1928), pp. 71–94.

46 *South-Eastern Naturalist*, 36 (1931), p. xxv.

47 C. Pugh and G. E. Hutchings, *Stockbury: A Regional Study in North-East Kent* (Stockbury, 1928), p. 72; the frontispiece photograph showed 'The Old Road', the downland pilgrimage route from Winchester to Canterbury passing through the parish, described by Belloc in his earlier book.

48 Fagg and Hutchings, *Introduction*, p. 1.

49 Branford and Geddes, *The Coming Polity*, p. 188.

50 On the Turk as a moral Other in late nineteenth-century Britain see Joyce, *Democratic Subjects*, pp. 209–12.

51 C. C. Fagg, 'The Significance of the Freudian Psychology for the Evolution Theory', *Proceedings and Transactions of the Croydon Natural History and Scientific Society*, 9 (1923), pp. 137–64 (164); C. C. Fagg, 'Psychosynthesis, or Evolution in the Light of Freudian Psychology', *British Journal of Medical Psychology*, 13 (1933), pp. 119–42; see also Fagg's review article, 'Psycho-analysis and Sociology', *Sociological Review*, 25 (1933), pp. 294–304. Fagg also drafted a projected book entitled 'Sublimation or Perversion' under the pseudonym Christopher Kent, two chapters of which are held in the Freud Collection in the Library of Congress in Washington. I am grateful to Laura Cameron for this information.

52 Fagg, 'Psychosynthesis', p. 140.

53 *Ibid.*

54 *Ibid.*, p. 127.

55 *Ibid.*, p. 141. Fagg seems to take the anabolic/katabolic distinction from Geddes's work with J. A. Thomson, *The Evolution of Sex* (London, 1889), where the categories denoted essential properties of the female and male respectively. Fagg also argued for a relaxation of taboos on incest in relation to the fostering of the superman, p. 132, and set the superman against the 'mechanistic utopia' of democracy, p. 120. I am not aware as to whether Fagg pursued such ideas in a more directly political sphere in this period, though there are obvious authoritarian avenues opening up for such a philosophy in 1933.

56 Fagg, 'Psychosynthesis', p. 128.

57 Matless, 'Moral Geographies'. The citizen/anti-citizen distinction echoes the social and anti-social geographies of the Valley Section.

58 H. Roberts, *The Practical Way to Keep Fit* (London, 1942), pp. 184–6.

59 C. E. Montague, *The Right Place: A Book of Pleasures* (London, 1924), p. 41.

60 *Ibid.*, p. 43.

61 Fagg, 'Regional Survey', p. 23.

62 H. J. Fleure, 'Regional Surveys and Welfare', *South-Eastern Naturalist*, 34 (1929), pp. 73–82 (81); Fleure also suggested that: 'By demographic mapping we might demonstrate with intense reality the psychological isolation of the miners and the evil of absentee-capitalism, twin causes of the difficulties of the coalfield', p. 76. On Fleure see P. Gruffudd, 'The Countryside as Educator: Schools, Rurality and Citizenship in Inter-war Wales', *Journal of Historical Geography*, 22 (1996), pp. 412–23; J. A. Campbell, 'Some Sources of the Humanism of H. J. Fleure', *Oxford School of Geography Research Papers*, no. 2 (1972).

63 Fagg and Hutchings, *Introduction*, p. 51.

64 C. V. Butler and C. A. Simpson, *Village Survey Making: An Oxfordshire Experiment* (London, 1928), p. 26; also Matless, 'Regional Surveys', pp. 472–5.

65 Sir F. Ogilvie, 'The Educational Value of Regional Survey', *South-Eastern Naturalist*, 29 (1924), pp. 33–42 (40).

66 *Ibid.*, pp. 40–41.

67 *Exploration* (London, 1939); *Discovery*, op. cit.; for parallels between an imperial sense of the world-as-exhibition and survey's direction of its gaze towards the home region, see Matless, 'Regional Surveys', pp. 476–8.

68 For a general discussion of such educational methods see H. C. Barnard, *Principles and Practice of Geography Teaching* (London, 1933). For an account of field study in geographical education which stresses its late nineteenth-century development, see T. Ploszajska, 'Down to Earth? Geography Fieldwork in English Schools, 1870–1944', *Environment and Planning D: Society and Space* (forthcoming); also Gruffudd, 'The Countryside as Educator'. For an example of mapping at higher educational level under the influence of Halford Mackinder at Oxford and the London School of Economics, where students were required to describe a sheet of OS map in, as Mackinder put it, 'a geographical composition relating to a limited and accessible district', see Ellen Smith, *The Reigate Sheet of the One-Inch Ordnance Survey* (London, 1910, quotation from Mackinder's introduction, pp. xvii–xviii). Memories of such work are also given in D. Cosgrove, 'Models, Description and Imagination in Geography', in B. MacMillan, ed., *Remodelling Geography* (Oxford, 1989), pp. 230–44.

69 Butler and Simpson, *Village Survey Making*, pp. 12–13; Charlotte Simpson authored a series of texts on local survey and went on to run courses on field study for teachers at Cranham in Gloucestershire.

70 *Ibid.*, pp. v–vi; the popularity of imaginary maps in children's books of the time, for example by Arthur Ransome, A. A. Milne, C. S. Lewis and J.R.R. Tolkien, warrants further research. For a general discussion of mapping, adventure stories and masculinity see R. Phillips, *Mapping Men and Empire* (London, 1997).

71 Butler and Simpson, *Village Survey Making*, pp. 4–5; for an example see the illustration in Matless, 'Regional Surveys'.

72 Butler and Simpson, *Village Survey Making*, p. 14.

73 E. C. Mathews, 'Field Work in the Valley of the Brent', *The Geographical Teacher*, 5 (1910), pp. 314–18.

74 See also Keiller's 1997 film *Robinson in Space*, which takes the same approach around England.

75 S. H. Beaver, 'The Le Play Society and Fieldwork', *Geography*, 47 (1962), pp. 225–40. The work of the Society and its forerunners is currently being researched by Paul Merchant at the University of Nottingham.

76 Lord Meston, 'Foreword', in H. J. Fleure and R. A. Pelham, *Eastern Carpathian Studies: Roumania* (London, 1936), p. 6.

77 Fagg and Hutchings, *Introduction*, p. 63.

78 V. Branford and P. Geddes, *Our Social Inheritance* (London, 1919), p. xxi.

79 Branford and Geddes, *The Coming Polity*, p. 67.

80 *Ibid.*, pp. 75–6.

81 *Ibid.*, p. 78.

82 *Ibid.*, p. 89.

83 Branford and Geddes, *Our Social Inheritance*, p. 132. Branford and Geddes set up civic survey as a restorative practice for personalities fractured by war; city as well as country can be a convalescent space.

84 Ibid., p. 135; Branford and Geddes provide a composed and orderly antecedent to Iain Sinclair's recent London narratives in *Lights out for the Territory* (London, 1997).

85 Branford and Geddes, *Our Social Inheritance*, p. 204.

86 *Ibid.*, pp. 165–6.

87 *Ibid.*, p. 155.

88 *Ibid.*, p. 138.

89 Branford and Geddes, *The Coming Polity*, pp. 90–91.

90 For a later development of such arguments see E. A. Gutkind, 'Our World from the Air: Conflict and Adaptation', the opening essay in the influential geographical collection edited by W. L. Thomas, *Man's Role in Changing the Face of the Earth* (Chicago, 1956), pp. 1–44.

91 D. Haraway, 'Situated Knowledges', in *Simians, Cyborgs and Women* (London, 1991), pp. 183–201 (191, 188).

10 *James Corner: The Agency of Mapping: Speculation, Critique and Invention*

1 On the coercive aspects of mapping see Denis Wood, *The Power of Maps* (New York, 1992); Mark Monmonier, *How to Lie with Maps* (Chicago, 1991); and John Pickles, 'Texts, Hermeneutics and Propaganda Maps', in Trevor J. Barnes and James S. Duncan, eds, *Writing Worlds* (London, 1992), pp. 193–230. On the technocratic and reductive force of mapping see James C. Scott, *Seeing Like a State: Why Certain Schemes to Improve the Human Condition Have Failed* (New Haven, 1998), pp. 1–83. On the more revelatory attributes of maps see Stephen Hall, *Mapping the Next Millennium* (New York, 1992); and *Cartes et figures de la terre*, exhibition catalogue, Centre Georges Pompidou, Paris (Paris, 1980), cat. no. 206.

2 Gilles Deleuze and Félix Guattari, *A Thousand Plateaus: Capitalism and Schizophrenia*, trans. and foreword by Brian Massumi (Minneapolis, 1987), p. 12.

3 See J. B. Harley, 'Maps, Knowledge, and Power', in Denis Cosgrove and Stephen Daniels, eds, The *Iconography of Landscape* (Cambridge, 1988), pp. 277–312; J. B. Harley, 'Deconstructing the Map', in Barnes and Duncan, eds, *Writing Worlds*, pp. 231–47; and Scott, *Seeing Like a State*, pp. 38–76.

4 See David Buisseret, *Envisioning the City: Six Studies in Urban Cartography* (Chicago, 1998); and Ola Söderström, 'Paper Cities: Visual Thinking in Urban Planning', *Ecumene* III/3 (1996), pp. 249–81.

5 See Anthony Giddens, 'Living in a Post-Traditional Society', in Ulrich Beck, Anthony Giddens and Scott Lasch, *Reflexive Modernization: Politics, Tradition and Aesthetics in the Modern Social Order* (Cambridge, 1994). Giddens likens 'expert systems' to 'abstract systems', wherein credibility and 'truth' are accorded to certain abstract systems of representation precisely and only because they are constructed by experts. Similarly, much of mapping and planning goes unquestioned because of the apparent sophistication of their respective abstract systems, a sophistication that in itself is taken to be true and correct. See also Theodore M. Porter, *Trust in Numbers: The Pursuit of Objectivity in Science and Public Life* (Princeton, 1995). Porter demonstrates how 'mechanical objectivity' shown in various abstract forms of representation is more effective in democratic bureaucracies than expert 'judgement' or expert 'opinion' because the latter are always still suspected of holding self-serving interests.

6 See Scott, *Seeing Like a State*, pp. 44–63; Peter Hall, *Cities of Tomorrow: An Intellectual History of Urban Planning and Design in the Twentieth Century* (Oxford, 1988); Söderström, 'Paper Cities'.

7 See Söderström, 'Paper Cities', pp. 272–5. Söderström argues this point from the perspective of the institutionalized scientization of planning methods that has occurred throughout the twentieth century, where objective, empirical procedures have become so ingrained in state bureaucracy and decision-making processes that fresh approaches towards urban issues remain intellectually repressed.

8 See Rudolph Arnheim, *Visual Thinking* (London, 1970), p. 278. See also Arthur H. Robinson and Barbara Bartz Petchenik, *The Nature of Maps* (Chicago, 1976), pp. 1–22.

9 See James Corner, 'Operational Eidetics in Forging New Landscapes', in *Recovering Landscape: Essays in Contemporary Landscape Architecture* (New York, 1999) and 'Representation and Landscape', *Word & Image*, VIII/3 (1992), pp. 243–75.

10 See Robert Marks and R. Buckminster Fuller, *The Dymaxion World of Buckminster Fuller* (New York, 1973), pp. 50–55, 148–63.

11 See Robert Storr, ed., *Mapping* (New York, 1994).

12 *Ibid.*, p. 26.

13 There have been a few exceptions, but none has exerted a particularly strong influence upon design practice. Some of the more interesting explorations are summarized in Jane Harrison and David Turnbull, eds, *Games of Architecture: Architectural Design Profile 121* (London, 1996).

14 See Hall, *Cities of Tomorrow*; Söderström, 'Paper Cities'.

15 Harley, 'Deconstructing the Map', p. 231.

16 Jorge Luis Borges, 'Of Exactitude in Science' (1933), reprinted in *A Universal History of Infamy* (London, 1975).

17 Jean Baudrillard, *Simulations* (New York, 1983), p. 2.

18 *Ibid.*, p.2.

19 D. W. Winnicott, *Playing and Reality* (London, 1971).

20 Jacob Bronowski, *Science and Human Values* (New York, 1965).

21 Ernst Cassirer, *The Philosophy of Symbolic Forms*, vol. 2 (New Haven, 1955), p. 30; quoted in Robinson and Petchenik, *The Nature of Maps*, p. 7.

22 See Reyner Banham, *Los Angeles: The Architecture of Four Ecologies* (London, 1973).

23 Rem Koolhaas and Bruce Man, *S,M,L,XL* (New York, 1995), p. 1248.

24 David Harvey, *Justice, Nature, and the Geography of Difference* (Cambridge, 1996), p. 419.

25 *Ibid.*

26 *Ibid.*, p. 420.

27 Michel de Certeau, *The Practice of Everyday Life* (London, 1984), p. 94.

28 Jean Piaget and Barbel Inhelder, *The Child's Conception of Space* (New York, 1967), p. 452; quoted in Robinson and Petchenik, *The Nature of Maps*, p. 101.

29 *Ibid.*, p. 454.

30 Robinson and Petchenik, *The Nature of Maps*, p. 74.

31 Brand Blanshard, *The Nature of Thought* (London, 1948), p. 525; quoted in Robinson and Petchenik, *The Nature of Maps*, p. 103.

32 See Ken Knabb, ed., *Situationist International Anthology* (Berkeley, 1981); Cristel Hollevoet, Karen Jones and Tim Nye, eds, *The Power of the City: The City of Power* (New York, 1992).

33 De Certeau, *The Practice of Everyday Life*, p. 95; see also Cristel Hollevoet, 'Wandering in the City', in Hollevoet *et al.*, eds, *The Power of the City*, pp. 25–55.

34 Fredric Jameson, *Postmodernism, or the Cultural Logic of Late Capitalism* (Durham, NC, 1991), p. 51.

35 See Hollevoet *et al.*, eds, *The Power of the City*.

36 See Richard Long, *Richard Long* (Düsseldorf, 1994); R. H. Fuchs, *Richard Long* (London, 1986).

37 See de Certeau, *The Practice of Everyday Life*. This book is about how everyday 'users' 'operate', arguing for various modes of situated and tactical actions. Things such as 'making do', 'walking in the city', 'reading as poaching', 'diversionary practices' and '*détournement*' are cited as techniques by which dominant structures are resisted.

38 See Bernard Tschumi, *Cinegramme folie: le Parc de la Villette* (Princeton, 1987); Bernard Tschumi, Architecture and Disjunction (Cambridge, MA, 1994), pp. 171–259; Koolhaas, *S,M,L,XL*, pp. 894–935;

39 See Jean-Francois Bedard, ed., *Cities of Artificial Excavation: The Work of Peter Eisenman*, 1978–1988 (Montreal, 1994), pp. 130–85; Peter Eisenman, *Eisenman-amnesie: Architecture and Urbanism* (Tokyo, 1988), pp. 96–111.

40 See Jonathan Jova Marvel, ed., *Investigations in Architecture: Eisenman Studios at the GSD, 1983–1985* (Cambridge, MA, 1986).

41 Bedard, *Cities of Artificial Excavation*, p. 132.

42 *Ibid.*, p. 132.

43 See Raoul Bunschoten, *Urban Flotsam* (Rotterdam, 1998); Raoul Bunschoten, 'Proto-Urban Conditions and Urban Change', in Maggie Toy, ed., *Beyond the Revolution: The Architecture of Eastern Europe: Architectural Design Profile 119* (London, 1996), pp. 17–21; Raoul Bunschoten, 'Black Sea: Bucharest Stepping Stones', in Peter Davidson and Donald Bates, eds, *Architecture After Geometry: Architectural Design Profile 127* (London, 1997), pp. 82–91.

44 Bunschoten, 'Proto-Urban Conditions', p. 17.

45 Bunschoten, 'Black Sea', p. 82.

46 *Ibid.*, p. 83.

47 See de Certeau, 'Walking in the City', and 'Spatial Stories', in *The Practice of Everyday Life*, pp. 91–130; Scott, 'Thin Simplifications and Practical Knowledge: Metis', in *Seeing Like a State*, pp. 309–41.

48 Deleuze, *A Thousand Plateaus*, p. 6.

49 *Ibid.*

50 *Ibid.*, p. 12.

51 *Ibid.*, p. 4.

52 See Charles Joseph Minard, *Tableaux graphiques et cartes figuratives de M. Minard, 1845–1869*, Portfolio (Paris, 1869); E. J. Marey, *La methode graphique* (Paris, 1885); Arthur H. Robinson, 'The Thematic Maps of Charles Joseph Minard', *Imago Mundi*, 21 (1967), pp. 95–108; Tufte, *The Visual Display of Quantitative Information*, pp. 40–41, 176–7.

53 See Greg Lynn, ed., *Folding in Architecture: Architectural Design Profile 102* (London, 1983); Sanford Kwinter, 'The Reinvention of Geometry', *Assemblage*, 18 (1993), pp. 83–5; Davidson and Bates, *Architecture After Geometry*.

54 See Winy Maas and Jacob van Rijs, *FARMAX: Excursions on Density* (Rotterdam, 1998); 'Maas, van Rijs, de Vries, 1991–1997', *El Croquis*, 86 (1998).

55 See James Corner and Alex MacLean, *Taking Measures Across the American Landscape* (New Haven, 1996).

56 Paul Virilio, *The Art of the Motor*, trans. Julie Rose (Minneapolis, 1995), p. 139.

57 Rudolf Arnheim, *Art and Visual Perception* (Berkeley, 1964), p. viii.

58 This 'extension' of pervasive conditions towards new, more critical ends underlies in part some of the arguments made in Corner and MacLean, *Taking Measures*. Here, there is an attempt to view the mostly technocratic, utilitarian approaches that are assumed in shaping the larger American landscape as things that are *potentially* positive. Measure, in both its numerical and instrumental sense, is less criticized or replaced by some other concept than it is expanded and enriched. In design and planning terms, the suggestion here is to see logistical, technical, economic and environmental constraints not as limits but as vehicles of creativity and efficacy. See also Stan Allen, 'Artificial Ecologies', *El Croquis*, 86 (1998), pp. 26–33 and note 5.

59 Much of the profession of architecture and planning today is concerned more and more with complex tasks of management and organization, especially of information. The forms of creativity suggested in this essay suggest a shift from a traditional emphasis in design upon forms of *space* to new, emergent emphases upon creative forms of *practice*. The difficulty today lies less at the level of formal innovation and design talent but more at the level of operational innovation: how to set new and exciting things in motion given the general inertia that currently surrounds planning and design projects. See Beck, *Reflexive Modernization*; Allen, 'Artificial Ecologies'; and

Koolhaas, 'Whatever Happened to Urbanism?', in *S,M,L,XL*, pp. 961–71, and Corner, 'Operational Eidetics'.

60 See Jeffrey Kipnis, 'Towards a New Architecture', in *Folding in Architecture*, pp. 46–54; see also James Corner, 'Landscape and Ecology as Agents of Creativity', in George F. Thompson and Frederick R. Steiner, eds, *Ecological Design and Planning* (New York, 1997), pp. 80–108.

11 *Wystan Curnow: Mapping and the Expanded Field of Contemporary Art*

1 Svetlana Alpers, *The Art of Describing: Dutch Art in The Seventeenth Century* (Chicago, 1983).

2 Peter Fend, 'Building a Bridge from Art to Architecture', in P. Fend, ed., *Mapping: A Response to MoMA* (New York, 1994), p. 11. It is worth noting that only one of the exhibitions mentioned here, *Under Capricorn/The World Over*, treated its own site as an act of mapping, despite the fact that some of them went on tour. This exhibition offered mapping opportunities for artists making new work for both its sites in Amsterdam and Wellington; I discuss below the works Ruth Watson made for them.

3 Robert Hobbs, *Robert Smithson: Sculpture* (Ithaca and London, 1981), p. 105.

4 J. B. Harley, 'Deconstructing the Map', in Trevor J. Barnes and James S. Duncan, eds, *Writing Worlds: Discourse* (London and New York, 1992), p. 246.

5 R. H. Fuchs, *Richard Long* (New York), p. 99.

6 *Ibid.*

7 *Ibid.*, p. 206.

8 See Hamish Fulton, *One Hundred Walks* (Netherlands, 1991), pp. 80–81.

9 See David Reason, 'Echo and Reflections', in Stephen Bann and William Allen, eds, *Interpreting Contemporary Art* (London, 1991), for an extended reading of a Fulton text.

10 Michael Auping, 'Tracking Fulton', in *Hamish Fulton: Selected Walks, 1969–1989* (Buffalo, 1990), p. 7.

11 See Georges Bataille, *The Accursed Shade* (Cambridge and London, 1988), pp. 19–41.

12 Robert Storr, *Mappings* (New York, 1994), p. 19.

13 Denis Wood and John Fels, 'Designs on Signs: Myth and Meaning in Maps', *Cartographica*, XXIII (1986).

14 Germano Celant, 'Luciano Fabro: The Image that Isn't There', *Artforum International* (October 1988), p. 108.

15 Herbert Muschamp, *Man about Town: Frank Lloyd Wright and New York City* (Cambridge, MA, 1983), p. 117.

Bibliography

Alpers, Svetlana, *The Art of Describing* (Chicago, 1983)

Andrew, David, ed., *The Charts and Coastal Views of Captain Cook's Voyages: The Voyage of the Endeavour 1768–1771* (London, 1988)

Bagrow, L., *History of Cartography*, rev. R. A. Skelton (Chicago, 1951)

Barnes, Trevor J., and James S. Duncan, *Writing Worlds: Discourse, Text & Metaphor in the Representation of Landscape* (London, 1992)

Black, Jeremy, *Maps and History: Constructing Images of the Past* (New Haven, 1997)

Bousquet-Bressolier, C., ed., *L'Oeil du cartographe et la représentation géographique du Moyen Age à nos jours* (Paris, 1995)

Brotton, Jerry, *Trading Territories* (London, 1997)

Brown, Lloyd A., *The Story of Maps* (Boston, 1949)

Browne, John P., *Map Cover Art: A Pictorial History of Ordnance Survey Cover Illustration* (London, 1991)

Bryson, Norman, Ann Holly Michael, and Keith Moxey, eds, *Visual Theory: Painting and Interpretation* (Oxford, 1991)

Buisseret, David, ed., *Envisioning the City: Six Studies in Urban Cartography* (Chicago, 1998)

——, *From Sea Charts to Satellite Images: Interpreting North American History Through Maps* (Chicago, 1990)

——, *Monarchs, Ministers and Maps* (Chicago, 1992)

Campbell, James B., *Introduction to Remote Sensing* (London, 1996)

Carter, Paul, *Living in a New Country: History, Traveling and Language* (London, 1992)

——, *The Road to Botany Bay: An Exploration of Landscape and History* (London, 1987)

Cartographical Curiosities, exh. cat. by Gillian Hill, British Library (London, 1978)

Chinese and Japanese Maps, exh. cat., British Library (London, 1974)

The City in Maps: Urban Mapping 1900, exh. cat. by James Elliot, British Library (London, 1987)

Conley, Tom, *The Self-Made Map: Cartographic Writing in Early Modern France* (Minneapolis, 1996)

Cormack, Lesley B., *Charting an Empire: Geography at the English Universities, 1580–1620* (Chicago, 1997)

Cosgrove, Denis, and Stephen Daniels, eds, *The Iconography of Landscape* (Cambridge, 1988)

Delano-Smith, Catherine, and Elizabeth M. Ingram, *Maps in Bibles 1500–1600* (Geneva, 1991)

Dilke, O. A. W, *Greek and Roman Maps* (London, 1985)

Dorling, Daniel, and David Fairbairn, *Mapping – Way of Representing the World* (1997)

Downs, Roger M., and David Stea, *Image and Environment: Cognitive Mapping and Spatial Behaviour* (Chicago, 1973)
——, *Maps in Minds* (New York, 1977)
Edney, M. H., *Mapping an Empire: The Geographical Construction of British India 1765–1843* (Chicago, 1997)
Edson, Evelyn, *Mapping Time and Space* (London, 1997)
Fagg, C. C., and G. E. Hutchings, *An Introduction to Regional Survey* (Cambridge, 1930)
Goss, John, *The Mapmaker's Art* (London, 1993)
Gould, Peter, and Rodney White, *Mental Maps* (London, 1974)
Harley, J. B., and David Woodward, eds, *The History of Cartography*, 2 vols (Chicago, 1987)
Harvey, David, *The Condition of Postmodernity* (London, 1989)
Harvey, P. D. A, *The History of Topographic Maps: Symbols, Pictures and Surveys* (New York, 1980)
——, *Mappa Mundi: The Hereford World Map* (London, 1996)
——, *Medieval Maps* (London, 1991)
Jackson, Peter, *Maps of Meaning: An Introduction to Cultural Geography* (London, 1988)
Jacob, Christian, *La Description de la terre habitée de Denys d'Alexandrie ou la leçon de géographie* (Paris, 1989)
——, *L'Empire des cartes: Approche théorique de la cartographie à travers l'histoire* (Paris, 1992)
——, *Géographie et ethnographie en Grèce ancienne* (Paris, 1990)
——, and M. Baratin, *Le Pouvoir des bibliothèques: La Mémoire des livres en Occident* (Paris, 1996)
Keats, J. S., *Understanding Maps* (1996)
Kemp, Martin, *The Science of Art: Optical Themes in Western Art from Brunelleschi to Seurat* (New Haven, 1990)
King, Geoff, *Mapping Reality: An Exploration of Cultural Cartographies* (New York, 1996)
Lefebvre, Henri, *The Production of Space* (London, 1991)
Lestringant, Frank, *Mapping the Renaissance World: The Geographical Imagination in the Age of Discovery* (Oxford, 1994)
Levenson, Jay A., ed., *Circa 1492: Art in the Age of Exploration* (New Haven, 1991)
Lewis, Martin, and Karen E. Wigam, *The Myth of the Continent: A Critique of Metageography* (Los Angeles, 1997)
Livingstone, David, *The Geographical Tradition* (Oxford, 1993)
Lynam, Edward, *The Mapmaker's Art: Essays on the History of Maps* (London, 1953)
Lynch, Kevin, *The Image of the City* (Cambridge, MA, 1977)
MacEachern, Alan M., *How Maps Work: Representation, Visualisation and Design* (New York, 1995)
Mackay, David, *In the Wake of Cook: Exploration, Science & Empire, 1780–1801* (Wellington, NZ, 1985)
Mapping, exh. cat. by Robert Storr, Museum of Modern Art (New York, 1994)
Mapping the Landscape: Essays on Art and Cartography, exh. cat. by Nicolas Alfrey and Stephen Daniels (Nottingham Castle Museum, 1990)
Mattelart, Armand, *The Invention of Communication* (Minneapolis, 1996)
——, *Mapping World Communication* (Minneapolis, 1994)
Milanesi, Marica, ed., *L'Europa delle carte: Dal XV al XIX secolo, autoritratti di un Continente* (Milan, 1990)
The Mirror of the World I: Antiquarian Maps, exh. cat., British Library (London, 1983)
Mitchell, W. J. T, *Iconology: Image Text, Ideology* (Chicago, 1986)

Monmonier, M., *Drawing the Line* (New York, 1995)
——, *How to Lie with Maps* (Chicago, 1996)
Muehrcke, Phillip C., *Map Use: Reading, Analysis and Interpretation* (1986)
Nora, S., and A. Minc, *L'Information de la société* (Paris, 1978)
Nuti, Lucia, *Ritratti di città, visione e memoria tra medioevo e settecento* (Venice, 1997)
Pile, Steve, and Nigel Thrift, eds, *Mapping the Subject* (London, 1995)
Portugali, Juval, ed., *The Construction of Cognitive Maps* (Dordrecht, 1996)
Ritchie, George S., *The Admiralty Chart: British Naval Hydrography in the Nineteenth Century* (Durham, 1995)
Robinson, Arthur H., *Elements of Cartography* (New York, 1960)
——, and Barbara Bartz, *The Nature of Maps: Essays Towards Understanding Maps and Mapping* (Chicago, 1976)
Rodney, S., *The Mapping of the World: Early Printed Maps, 1472–1700* (London, 1983)
Rotberg, Robert I., and Theodore K. Rabb, *Art and History: Images and Their Meaning* (Cambridge, 1988)
Russel, Margarita, *Visions of the Sea: Hendrick C. Veroom and the Origins of Dutch Marine Painting* (Leiden, 1983)
Schwartz, Seymour I., and Ralph E. Ehrenberg, *The Mapping of North America* (New York, 1980)
Seymour, W. A., ed., *A History of the Ordnance Survey* (Dawson, England, 1980)
Shirley, R. W., *The Mapping of the World: Early Printed World Maps 1472–1700* (London, 1993)
Skelton, R. A., *Explorer's Maps: Chapters in the Cartographic Record of Geographical Discovery* (London, 1958)
Smith, Bernard, *European Vision and the South Pacific* (New Haven and London, 1988)
Thrower, Norman J. W., *The Complete Mapmaker: Essays on Chart, Map and Globe Making in England* (Los Angeles, 1978)
——, *Maps and Civilization* (Chicago, 1996)
——, *Maps & Man: An Examination of Cartography in Relation to Culture and Civilization* (New Jersey, 1972)
Turnbull, D., *Maps Are Territories, Science Is an Atlas* (Chicago, 1993)
Van der Krogt, P., *Globi Neerlandici: The Production of Globes in the Low Countries* (Utrecht, 1993)
Virilio, P., *The Lost Dimension* (New York, 1991)
Voir, Carey J., *Communication as Culture: Essays on Media and Society* (Boston, 1989)
Whitfield, Peter, *The Charting of the Oceans: Ten Centuries of Maritime Maps* (London, 1996)
——, *New Found Lands: Maps in the History of Exploration* (London, 1998)
Wilford, John N., *The Mapmakers* (London, 1981)
Winearls, Joan, *Editing Early and Historical Atlases* (Toronto, 1995)
Wolter, John A., and Ronald E. Grim, *Images of the World* (New York, 1997)
Wood, Denis, *The Power of Maps* (New York, 1992)
Woodward, David, ed., *Art and Cartography: Six Historical Essays* (Chicago, 1987)
Zrubavel, Eviatar, *Terra Cognita: The Mental Discovery of America* (1992)

Relevant journals include *Cartographica, Cartographica Helvetica, The Globe, Imago Mundi, Terra Incognitea* and *Word & Image*.

Photographic Acknowledgements

The editor and publisher wish to express their thanks to the following individuals, institutions or other sources of illustrative material and/or permission to reproduce it:

Bayerische Staatsbibliothek, Munich: p. 79; Biblioteca d'Arte Beato Angelico, Rome: p. 100; Biblioteca Civica di Verona/Umberto Tomba: p. 54; Biblioteca Nazionale Marciana, Venice: p. 63 (bottom); British Library/BL Reproductions: pp. 61, 62 (top), 69, 86, 96, 97, 152, 160; Raoul Bunschoten/CHORA, London: pp. 242, 243; © James Corner, from James Corner and Alex MacLean, *Taking Measures Across the American Landscape* (New Haven, CT, 1996): p. 248; Wystan Curnow: pp. 263, 266; Peter Eisenman Architects, New York: p. 238; The Buckminster Fuller Institute/Estate of Buckminster Fuller: pp. 218, 219; Collection of the Fundación Torres-García, Montevideo: p. 220; Galleria delle Mappe Geografiche, Vatican City: cover; Germanisches National Museum, Nuremberg: p. 75; The Huntington Library, San Marino, CA: pp. 110, 111, 112; Ithaca Historic City Plans: p. 107 (bottom); Koninklijke Bibliotheek, The Hague: p. 95; Richard Long: p. 234; Metro Pictures: p. 262; Ministero per i Beni Culturali e Ambientali, Florence: pp. 104–5; Musée de la Révolution Française, Vizille: p. 137; National Maritime Museum, London: pp. 161, 162; OMA, Rotterdam: pp. 236, 237; Reading Museum: p. 165 (bottom); Rijksmuseum-Stichting, Amsterdam: pp. 106, 107 (top); The Royal Geographical Society, London: pp. 159, 163, 165 (top); Edward Tufte, *The Visual Display of Quantitative Information* (Cheshire, CT, 1983): p. 245; and Universiteite Bibliotheek, Leiden: pp. 101, 103.

Index

Aerial
  photography 5
  view 5, 212
Aerial navigators survey the terrestrial scene (Jules Verne) *182*
aesthetic 2, 10, 11, 13, 113, 115, 116, 117, 127, 194
  picturesque 138
Akoé 32–3
Alberti, Leon Battista 15, 91
  De re aedificatoria 91, 92, 93
  Descripto urbis Romea 92
Alexandria 26, 29, 30, 32, 40, 41, 47
Alexandrian library 32, 33, 34, 41, 44
  map 30–1, 46
al–Idrisi 37
Alpers, Svetlana 114, 254
Anaximander 26–7, 28, 30
anthropomorphism 126–7
Apian, Peter 90
Appadurai, Arjun 72, 73
architecture *see* planning
Aristotle 28, 135
  'Natural History' 135
armchair cartographers 45
art (*see also under individual artists*) 253–68
  Dutch painting 15
  Holbein, Hans 86–7
  installation 6, 264–8
  and mapping 6, 218–20, 231, 232–3, 253–68
  performance 231, 264, 265
  portraying paradise 59–60
  Renaissance 94
  Situationist 231–3, 243
astronomy 8, 28, 46, 129

Balboa, Vasco Núñez de 82

Banham, Reyner 226
Baudrillard, Jean 222, 223
Baumgarten, Lothar 265–7
  America. Invention 266
Bede 58–9, 66
Behaim, Martin 75–7, 78, 81, 87
  terrestrial globe 75
Belloc, Hilaire 15, 198–9
  route map from his Path to Rome *199*
Bematists 33
Blake, William 19
body, human 15, 74, 113, 120, 170
  anthropomorphism 126–7, 166–7
  as metaphor 120, 122, 170
boundary 57–8
  Portuguese and Castilian crowns 81–2
  Treaty of Tordesillas 77–8
Branford, Victor 195–6, 198, 202, 203, 210–11, 212
British Royal Navy *see* Royal Navy
Brown, Charles William 160–6
  Aqueduct – Rio de Janeiro 161
  Corcovado and Gloria Church 165
  Rio de Janeiro 162
  View from Lake to Mountain 163
Bunschoten, Raoul 240–1
  Four planning fields for Bucharest, Romania 242
  Toponymy, Alexandrov, Russia 243

camera 104
  movie 5
  obscura 104, 201
cartography *see also* mapping 3, 7, 18, 38, 46, 193, 211
  ancient Greek 24, 26–9
  armchair cartographers 45
  cartographic paradigm 38–9
  cartographic shift 67–8, 70, 75

and citizenship 194
critique 3, 211, 214–17, 218, 219, 221, 223–4, 231
Enlightenment 35
Eratosthenes' model of 42
history of 3, 7, 24
imagination 5
medieval 63
military 170–1
model of Alexandrian 43
modern 66
non–European 8
of paradise 52
Ptolemy's model 78
small–scale 23
Cassirer, Ernst 223
Castilian crown 81–3, 88
dispute with the Portuguese crown 77, 81–4
Treaty of Tordesillas 77, 82, 83–4
Chart making *see* map making
chorography 18, 31, 90–108, 121
all–embracing view 98
Bosse, Abraham *Allegory of painting* 95
Leybourn, William *illustration from The complete surveyor* 97
painting in 94, 96–8
profile approach 98–9, 101, 105–6
chronometer 9, 21, 130
coast 125, 131–3, 134, 136–8, 141, 142, 146
Forrest, Thomas *The view of the island of Ouby...* 133
Houel, Jean *Plan de la barriére du Bureau de la Santé, à Malte* 142
Taurel, Jean–Jacques *A view of the temple of Paestum* 137
coastline 125–47, 153, 238
coastal cut 135
drawings 126, 153, 155, 157–8, 166–7
Forrest, Thomas *The view of the island of Ouby...* 133
representation of 136
Cochlaeus, Johannes 78
colonialism 3, 125, 135
Columbus, Christopher 68, 81
communication technology 185, 186
conventional cartographic signs 12
Cook, James 127, 131–2, 152–3
and place names 155–6
Corner, James
Pivot irrigation 248
Windmill topography 248

cosmography 18, 56, 78–80
cosmology 9, 26–7

D'Anville, Jean–Baptiste 35–7
Carte d'Italie 36
Papiers géographiques 36, 38, 44
da Gama, Vasco 150
da Vinci, Leonardo 15, 95
plan of Imula 92
Dalzel, Archibald *The African Pilot* 159
Danti, Egnazio 94
de Barbari, Jacopo *Plan of Venice* 100
de Certeau, Michel 228, 232
Debord, Guy *Discours sur le Passions de l'amour* 232
Deleuze, Gilles 5, 22, 188, 213–14, 244–5
rhizome 244–50
Desargues, Gerard 94
Dionysius Periegetes 47–8
discoveries 76, 81, 155
Balboa, Vasco Núñez de 82
Columbus, Christopher 68, 81
da Gama, Vasco 150
Magellan, Ferdinand 82–3
Vespucci, Amerigo 79, 81
Donne, John 15

Earthly Paradise *see* Paradise
Ebstorf map *see* mappaemundi
Edney, Matthew 129, 143
Edson, Evelyn 63
Eisenman, Peter 237
with Laurie Olin, *Sketch Site Plan ... at the University of California* 238
Enlightenment 8, 16, 18, 19, 21, 130, 132, 146, 174, 220
epistemology 128, 129, 136
and space 88
Eratosthenes 30, 33, 34, 37, 38, 41, 43–6, 48
model of cartographic work 42
world map 39–41
experience 4, 12, 53, 104, 137
contemporary 22
place 210
spatial 227, 232, 249
urban 15, 233
Euclidean geometry 40, 70, 72–3, 74, 88
space 65, 67

Fagg, C. C. *see also* Regional Survey 15, 194, 197–8, 201, 202, 203, 210

and Hutchings, *The 'Valley Section'*
 with rustic types 203
 and psychological types 203–5
Filarete 92
Flanders 98, 99
Fra Mauro map *see mappaemundi*
frame 10, 63, 92–3, 103, 105, 215, 220,
 229–30, 240, 252
Freud (Freudian theory) 22, 203
Frisius, Gemma 85–6, 87
Fuller, Buckminster
 Air Ocean World Map 219
 Dymaxion Air Ocean World Map
 217–18, *218*

'game board' maps (*see also* maps) 239–44
Garden of Eden *see* Paradise
Geddes, Patrick *see also* Regional Survey
 5, 12, 15, 195, 198, 201, 202, 203,
 210–11, 212
'genital erotism' 204
geographical imagination 74, 149, 160,
 167, 168
geographical knowledge 25, 44–5
 and Homer 45
'global village' 186, 189
globalism 72–3
globe 14, 180
 in art 261–3, 262
 Behaim's terrestrial 75–7
 and the dispute between the Castilian
 and Portuguese crowns 81–4
 Frisius, Gemma 85–6, 87
 and Holbein's *The Ambassadors* 86–7
 as imperial symbol 77, 81
 Monachus, Franciscus *De Orbis Situ ac*
 Descriptione 85, 86
 and the Portuguese crown 77
 Schöner, Johannes 80, 81
 Simmons, Lauri *Bending globe* 262
 sixteenth–century terrestrial 80, 87, 89
 terrestrial 82, 85, 88, 89
 voyages 81, 83, 85
 Waldseemüller, Martin *woodcut show-*
 ing terrestrial globe gores 79
 Waldseemüller's gores 79–81
Greek mapping *see also* cartography 10,
 17, 26–9
Guattari, Félix 5, 22, 188, 213–14, 244–5
 rhizome 244–50

Harley, Brian 3, 184, 221
Harvey, David 71, 227–8
Harvey, Paul 63
Havell, William 161–2, 164
 On the Coromandel Coast, South India
 165
Hecataeus of Miletus *Periegesis* 27
Helms, Mary 76, 77
Hereford map *see mappaemundi*
Herodotus 28
Holbein, Hans *The Ambassadors* 86–7
Homer 27, 48
 Iliad 42, 46
 Odyssey 27, 42, 45
Hutchings, G. E. (Geoffrey) *see also*
 Regional Survey 15, 194, 197–8, 201,
 202, 203, 210
Hutton, James 121–3, 129, 133–4
hydrography
 charts 131
 office 156
 survey 157

image 59, 96, 125, 149, 166
 of the body 170
 communication 178, 180
 computer generated 6
 of the globe 71, 72, 73, 80–1, 85, 89, 261
 graphic 12, 149, 157
 of landscape 149
 of paradise 55, 60, 104
 of Rio de Janeiro 157–67
 spatial 6
 town 94, 98, 102, 104
imagination 15, 118, 222
information society 184–6, 189–90
information technology 6, 72, 185
installation art 264–8
Istanbul 101–2
 Lorichs, Melchior *Istanbul 101*
Italy 98, 99

Jarn Mound 200–1, *201*

Koolhaas, Rem 'The generic city' 227, 235
 Layer diagram for the parc de la villet
 236
 Program map 237

landscape 99, 117–19, 154, 199–200, 201,
 253
 hybrid landscape 149, 167, 168

of Paradise 51
planning (architecture) 220, 221, 224,
    225, 235, 237–8, 251
tropical 166
Latour, Bruno 32
Le Play, Frederic 12, 198
Le Play Society 208, 209–10
Leardo, Giovanni *'Earthly Paradise' from a
    world map* 54
Leibniz, Gottfried 128
Leonardo da Vinci *see under* Da Vinci
Leybourn, William 96
    The complete surveyor 93, 97
line *see also* coastline 39, 127–9, 130, 132
Long, Richard 230, 233–4, 247, 256,
    258–9, 265
    *A seven day circle of ground/seven days
    walking...* 234
longitude 4, 9, 21
Lorichs, Melchior *Istanbul 101*
Lovelock, James 121–2
    'Gaia Hypothesis' 122

macrospace 55, 63
Magellan, Ferdinand 82–3
mappaemundi 14, 18, 35, 51, 63–8, 74
    Ebstorf map 64, 67
    Fra Mauro map 66–7
    detail showing the Earthly Paradise 62
    Hereford map 60, 67
    detail showing the Earthly Paradise 61
    and Paradise 63
    Psalter map 60, 61, 64–5, 67
    and space–time 64, 67, 68
    Thorne, Robert world map 84–5
mapping 1–23, 57, 146, 225, 228–52,
    253–5, 268
    and art 6, 218–20, 230, 231, 232–5,
    253–68
    chorographic 20
    cognitive 7
    computerized 88
    as a creative activity 217, 230
    and drawing 126, 127, 157
    early eighteenth century 115
    Enlightenment 16
    European colonial 11
    field survey 114
    'game board' 239–44
    geographical 20
    GIS (Geographical Information
        Systems) 221

Greek 10, 17, 26–9
layering 235–9
medieval 50
modernist 22
Packe's scientific 115, 116, 120
panoramic 12, 104–5, 113, 114
Paradise 56, 61–3
and planning 215–16, 224, 235–9, 250
practices of 113–14
Ptolemy's model 78
and regional survey 198
rhizomatic 244–6
scientific 19, 21
seventeenth century town 105
shift 67–8, 70, 75
sixteenth century 67
sixteenth century town 105
sketching by eye 126–7
techniques 220–1, 252
Treatise on surveying 129
trigonometry 129
urban 12, 15, 20, 240–4
and vision 108
walking as 258–60
maps 2, 12, 23–4, 25, 28, 37, 41, 42, 50, 85,
    193–4, 198, 206, 214–16, 221, 225, 254
    and aesthetic 115, 116, 193, 194, 206
    Alexandrian 30
    in architecture 224–5
    Carte d'Italie 36
    and citizenship 205
    Dutch seventeenth–century 13
    and education 196
    and Enlightenment 129, 130, 146
    French seventeenth–century 13
    Fuller's Dymaxion 217–18, 218, 219
    as 'game board' 239–244
    geographical 10
    and geometry 37, 40, 41
    Italian sixteenth–century 13
    material object 14
    Mercator 217
    metaphor 4, 26
    Ordnance Survey 6, 197, 247
    Paradise 60–3, 68, 69
    and power 29–31
    regional 35, 39
    relief 172
    Roman 24
    route map 3
    semiotics 261
    small–scale 35, 37

and survey 5, 197
'T–O' 74
as text 47–8
thematic 11
topographic 5, 10, 131, 143, 171, 194,
257, 259
USGS (US Geological Survey) 6, 247
world *see also mappaemundi* 8, 37, 39,
217–18
map makers *see also under individual
names* 34–5, 43, 48
readers as 48
map–making 25, 26, 28–31, 32, 35–6, 38,
41, 48, 125–6, 129
maritime survey 13, 154
and drawing 154–5, 157
McLuhan, Marshal 186
memory 11, 154
and drawing 161, 163–6
mental maps 47, 232, 234
metaphors 15, 28, 47, 73, 120, 135, 170,
174
geometrical 28
microspace 55, 63
'milieu' 223, 224–5, 228, 233, 239, 250, 251
Minard, Charles Joseph *Carte
figurative…* 245
modernity 18
Moluccas islands 82–4
Monachus, Franciscus 85
De Orbis Situ ac Descriptione 86

NASA 6, 185, 186
navigation 21, 131, 156, 173–4, 218
and drawing 152, 153, 154–5, 159
network 21, 169–70, 174, 179, 191
ARPANET 185
imaginary 181
information 184
*network plan of attack on
… Maastricht* 173
performance 249
railway 175, 178–9
SAGE 185
and Saint–Simon 174
and Saint–Simonianism 175, 178, 179,
181
telegraph 176–8, 180, 183

Ordnance Survey 6, 197, 247

Packe, Christopher 18, 20–21, 109–24

Ancographia, sive convallium descriptio
111, 114, 115, 116, 119
*A New Philosophico Chorographical
Chart of East Kent 110, 111, 112*
field survey 114
panoramic viewing 113, 114
and the picturesque 117–18
and place names 116
panorama 103–4, 108, 113, 114, 116, 254
Garibbo, Luigi *Panorama of Florence
104*
Woudanus, Jan Cornelisz *engraving
from* Bibliothecæ cum pulpitis *103*
Paradise (garden of Eden) 10, 14, 15,
51–70
in art 59–60
boundaries of 56–8
and Columbus 68
Fra Mauro *detail showing Earthly
Paradise from a world map 62*
as geographical space 59
*Grandes chroniques de saint–Denis
(detail showing Earthly Paradise) 62*
Leardo, Giovanni *Earthly Paradise from
a world map 54*
location of 65–6, 69
as macrospace 55
maps of 12, 51, 60–3, 69
medieval manifestation 54
Rüst, Hanns *detail showing Earthly
Paradise from a world map 62*
in regional maps 68–9
Syrus, Ephrem *Hymns on Paradise 59*
Tymme, T. *map of Eden 68*
visual imagery of 53
performance art 231, 264, 265
perspective 15, 94, 101, 105, 196, 224
all–embracing view 98
bird's eye perspective view 105
de Gheyn, Jacob *Plan and perspective
plan of Schiedam 106*
orthographic 12
plan 100, 104, 105
profile approach 98
sailors' 105
Stalpaert, Daniël *Amsterdam 107*
Piaget, Jean 222, 229
Pimentel, Manoel *Coast of Brazil 158*
'piss pride' 204
place names 116, 155–6
planning (architecture) 220, 221, 224, 225,
235, 237–8, 251

Polybius 41, 42, 43, 44, 46
Portuguese crown 77–8, 81–3, 85, 88,
    150–1; dispute with Castilean crown
    81–4
post–structuralism 7
Pratt, Mary Louise 199
projection 10
    imaginative 15
Psalter map *see mappaemundi*
Ptolemaic dynasty 29, 34
ptolemaic world map 10
Ptolemy, Claudius 8, 18, 37, 40, 46, 47,
    75–6, 90–1, 96
    and chorography 96
    Geography 17, 38–9, 46, 66, 74, 91
'purse pride' 204

Raphael 92
regional survey 12, 15, 21, 195, 197, 198,
    200–3, 205
    A specimen transect diagram, from
        Introduction to Regional Surveying
        197
    Branford, Victor 195–6, 198, 202, 203,
        210–11, 212
    and citizenship 207
    Fagg, C. C. 15, 194, 197–8, 200, 201,
        203–5, 210
    and Hutchings, *The 'Valley Section'*
        with rustic types 203
    Geddes, Patrick 5, 12, 195, 198, 201,
        210–11
    Girls with map, from Roberts *The*
        Practical Way to Keep Fit 205
    Hutchings, Geoffrey 15, 194, 197–8,
        200, 203, 210
    the Outlook Tower 201
    and psychology 202–6
    Regional survey conspectus diagram
        196
    'Valley Section' 203
Relief plan of Neuf Brissach 173
remote sensing 5, 220
Renaissance 8, 94
    architects 16
    and town portraits 20, 98
    town view maker 99–100
representation 3, 10, 102–3, 153, 222, 233
    cartographic 12
    coastline 136
    graphic 9
    modes of 98

of Rio de Janeiro 150
spatial 6, 18
textual 9
Rio de Janeiro 150–3, 157–67
    Laurie and Whittle, *Plan of the Bay and*
        Harbour of Rio–Janeiro... 160
Royal Navy 148, 151–2, 155, 156
Rüst, Hanns *detail showing the Earthly*
        Paradise from a world map 62

Saint Simon, Claude–Henri de 174
Saint–Simonianism 20, 175, 178, 179, 181
satellite photography 5, 220
scale 9–10, 18, 76, 95, 96, 129, 156, 198,
    215, 230, 247, 258, 264
Schöner, Johannes 80, 81
sight (seeing) 5, 137–8
Simmons, Lauri *Bending globe* 262
'site' 224–5
    'nonsite' installation by Smithson
        257–8, 265
Situationists 231–3, 232, 243
Smithson, Robert 257–8, 265
    'nonsite' installation 257–8, 265
Sorte, Cristoforo 93, 97
space (in urban planning) 227
    perception of 88
spatial representation 4, 6, 7, 18
Stalpaert, Daniël *Amsterdam 107*
Stokes, John Lort 132, 136, 138–140, 141
    Discoveries in Australia 140
Strabo 41, 42, 43, 44, 46
    Geography 25–6, 31–3
survey 93, 197 (*see also* Regional Survey)
    Aerial navigators survey the terrestrial
        scene (Jules Verne) *182*
    coastal surveyor 126, 129–30, 152–3
    hydrographic survey 157
    and maps 197
    maritime survey 130, 138, 154
    and memory 163–4
    Treatises on surveying 129, 156
Syrus Ephrem *Hymns on Paradise* 59

Tabula Peutingeriana 24
Taurel, Jean–Jacques *A view of the temple*
        of Paestum 137
telegraph 176–8, 180
    inauguration of the optical telegraph
        177
Thorne, Robert world map 84–5

Torres–García, Joaquín *Inverted Map of South America* 220
town plans 106
town portraits 98, 99–101
  de Barbari, Jacopo *Plan of Venice* 100
  Honje, Gaspar *Bari* 100
  Rocca, Agostino *The fading profile of Bari* 99
  Tanesse, I. *Plan of New Orleans* 107
Treaty of Tordesillas 77, 82–4
triangulation 8, 10, 129, 131, 142, 220

urban planning 214, 215, 217, 227, 240–1, 251–2
'urethral libido' 204
utopia 21, 228
  techno– 188, 190
  social 174, 175–6, 180–1
  and urban design 16, 181

Van Diemen's Land (map of) 10

Vasari, Giorgio 94
Vauban, Sébastian le Prestre de 170–3
  Relief plan of city and fortifications at Besançon 171
  Traité de l'attaque des places 172
Vespucci, Amerigo 79, 81
Virilio, Paul 72, 88, 249
vision 5, 48, 50, 64, 67, 84, 90, 96, 98–102, 105–8, 124, 134, 195

Waldseemüller, Martin 78–81
  '*Cosmographiae introductio*' 78–80, 81
  gores 79–81
  woodcut showing terrestrial globe gores 79
Watson, Ruth *Lingua geographica* 263
Winnicott, Donald 222–3
Woodward, David 3, 63, 74

Zubler, Leonhard *illustration from* novum instrumentum geometricum 96